Public Relations

PUBLIC RELATIONS

Averill Gordon

OXFORD
UNIVERSITY PRESS

OXFORD
UNIVERSITY PRESS

Great Clarendon Street, Oxford OX2 6DP

Oxford University Press is a department of the University of Oxford.
It furthers the University's objective of excellence in research, scholarship,
and education by publishing worldwide in

Oxford New York

Auckland Cape Town Dar es Salaam Hong Kong Karachi
Kuala Lumpur Madrid Melbourne Mexico City Nairobi
New Delhi Shanghai Taipei Toronto

With offices in

Argentina Austria Brazil Chile Czech Republic France Greece
Guatemala Hungary Italy Japan Poland Portugal Singapore
South Korea Switzerland Thailand Turkey Ukraine Vietnam

Oxford is a registered trade mark of Oxford University Press
in the UK and in certain other countries

Published in the United States
by Oxford University Press Inc., New York

British Library Cataloguing in Publication Data

Data available

Library of Congress Cataloguing in Publication Data

Data available

Typeset by TechType, Abingdon
Printed in Great Britain by Ashford Colour Press Ltd,
Gosport, Hampshire

ISBN 978-0-19-956574-0

3 5 7 9 10 8 6 4 2

To my daughter Irena and in memory of my father.

Preface

This textbook applies public relations theory to current practice and is illuminated by case studies. It draws on my academic career as a senior lecturer and director of studies of communication degrees at the University of Gloucestershire, where I developed a new public relations degree and also continued my own postgraduate studies in communications, media and higher education.

Central to the textbook is its professional focus which is based on my experience as a director at Weber Shandwick, the largest public relations consultancy in the world, where I set up the healthcare division in London and worked internationally.

This textbook aims to stimulate students to develop their own creativity and link theoretical concepts to good practice in consultancies and organizations, nationally and globally.

Current practice is presented through award-winning case studies which include publicity stunts, consumer campaigns, reputation management, corporate responsibility programmes, issues, crises and of course social media activities. These examples are analysed theoretically and practically in order to identify key aspects which can be applied to new programmes.

Overall the book is divided into three Parts which explore the thinking behind a public relations programme. In Part A ('The PR framework'), chapter 1 starts with the evolution of public relations and draws on the development of communications sciences, communications technology, and historical case studies to show how public relations has been influenced over time. This is followed in chapter 2 by an outline of communications models which explore how and why people communicate, make decisions, and change their behaviour in different situations. Chapter 3 on media communication focuses on the role of the media in public relations (and links to chapter 12 on online media).

In Part B ('Developing a PR campaign'), chapter 4 on intelligence gathering provides guidelines on how to research for a public relations programme and leads into chapter 5 on identifying the behaviour and influence of individuals, different groups, and organizations which are either impacting the campaign or affected by it.

All public relations proposals must link to the business objectives of an organization and this is clarified in chapter 6 which covers objectives and strategy, and clarifies these two often confusing terms. Chapter 7 on implementation presents ways to create tactics, action plans, and budgets and to harness creativity. This is followed by chapter 8 on evaluation and its increasingly high profile in the industry, although the importance of monitoring and evaluating a programme for formative reasons is also emphasized throughout the book. This section ends with a chapter on communications for business which focuses on the diverse styles and formats of persuasive writing and interpersonal communications required for different purposes and publics.

In Part C ('The broader context'), issues and crises are illustrated and differentiated in chapter 10 through powerful and diverse examples examining the role public relations plays in ensuring these are identified as well as managed and even averted. Chapter 11 defines and analyses the role of corporate responsibility, and how it has become embedded in organizations. The integration of ethical and legal principles in public relations practice is emphasised as are the legislative and regulatory elements within a corporate framework. Chapter 12 explains the content of online media and social media capabilities leading to how it has replaced mass communications and led to a new type of openness which can change an organization's value and its publics.

Finally, chapter 13 on public relations trends alerts students to the growing influences upon public relations, and the different directions it is taking in both industry and academia. It explores how it is not only online technology transforming public relations but also rapid changes in the economy, globalization, and progress in research areas ranging from sociology to neurology.

The chapters follow the same format which makes them easy to follow and dip into. The subject of every chapter is defined in detail and its theoretical and historical roots discussed, followed by what is influencing its development and how it is applied to the industry. Each chapter also includes a relevant public relations tool which outlines how to carry out a related and valuable skill with confidence. The exercises at the end of each chapter help to embed the chapter's content.

I thank all my clients from my consultancy days in London whose exacting standards helped to refine my approach and stimulated me to seek more challenges. Also I wish to thank the many colleagues at Weber Shandwick who inspired me professionally, particularly Lord Chadlington, the founder of Shandwick (who agreed to chair the professional advisory panel for the public relations degree at the University of Gloucestershire); Colin Byrne and Chris Genasi (who both feature in this textbook), Alison Clarke, Mike Murphy and Paula McNulty. In addition, I am grateful to the ongoing enthusiasm and support from my international GlobCom colleagues, especially Dr Volker Stoltz and Enric Ordereix, and the many global students participating in our annual virtual team projects around the world. I am of course indebted to the scholars in public relations who have researched concepts and developed theories which I have used liberally.

The ideas used in this book were consolidated while I lectured and researched at the University of Gloucestershire. I would like to thank all my students who were my compass for this book's direction.

Developing a book on public relations draws on published research but also needs input from numerous people. I also thank colleagues and friends from the University of Gloucestershire, particularly Dr Michael Pinfold for his intellectual rigour and humour, and Jim Beaman and Dan Lee for their advice on chapter 3. I am also very grateful to Dr Nigel Jackson for his support and David Phillips whose generous contribution to the chapter on online PR was invaluable.

In addition, I am very grateful to all the practitioners who were interviewed as well as those who so willingly provided the case studies. I am especially indebted to Guy

Woodcock, the CEO of Montpellier PR, for his enthusiastic commitment to public relations practice and education which was evident in his ongoing supply of case studies and ideas.

When I moved back to New Zealand my colleagues at AUT University, especially Joseph Peart and Dr Alan Cocker, were very supportive. Also I am very grateful to friends who, in their many different ways, helped me to get this textbook to the finishing line, in particular, Clive Ashby, David Backinsell, Sr Carol Buirds, Neri McGinley, Dale Morrison, Helen Shale, my sister Briar Mogan, and of course, my daughter Irena.

Outline contents

Detailed contents

How to use this book

Gordon's *Public Relations* is enriched with a range of features designed to help support and reinforce your learning. This guided tour shows you how best to utilise your textbook and get the most out of your study.

Learning outcomes

Each chapter begins with a bulleted outline of the main concepts and ideas you will encounter in the unit. These serve as helpful signposts for learning and revision.

Practitioner insights

Based on interviews with public relations practitioners, these real-world experiences help you to understand the issues faced by today's PR specialists.

End-of-chapter case studies

Each chapter is supplemented by a short case study designed to contextualize the information in the chapter and encourage you to apply your learning to real-life situations.

Chapter summary

The key points of each chapter are summarized in a form that helps to fix them in your mind and provide a useful tool for revision.

Discussion points

A series of discussion points at the end of every chapter provides a basis for group analysis and debate, and helps you to develop your understanding of key concepts as part of a team.

> **Discussion points**
>
> A. Making summaries
>
> Access Twitter and identify research reports summarized in brief and the web link to them. How effective is the short Twitter summary in making you want to read the report?
> Go to websites of environmental organizations such as National Heritage and the Royal Society for Protection of Birds and check the summaries of their research reports. How effective are these in making you want to access the report? Could they be shortened further to use on Twitter?
>
> B. Personal space
>
> Select three people in your seminar, one who you know well, another who you know rea-

Examples of industry tools

Each chapter contains examples of public relations techniques in action, to help increase your awareness of effective PR tools and methods.

> **PR Tool**
>
> A model for online evaluation
>
> A representation of what the world is thinking about an organization can be found through carrying out a semantic analysis of all the web pages—which reach an organization's publics—on the same day
> Then identify the organization's own web pages and record the difference between what is on that site and what people are talking about and doing on the other pages. However, to measure social media, a large sample is needed in order to review many different conversations. A public relations practitioner must then plan to reduce this communications gap by engaging in the social media world through blogs, wikis, news sites, etc
>
> **Online evaluation can be analysed as follows.**
>
> 1. Outputs

Referral to Online Resource Centre

References to the book's Online Resource Centre appear throughout the text, to direct you to additional information and web-based resources for completion of exercises relevant to the chapter.

> communicating the possible hazards associated with a particular process safeguards and benefits which it offers.'
> However, the impact of an issue varies with different people therefore a analysis needs to be carried out to see how each public is affected and interpret the issue (see chapter 5). People have their own attitudes formed and cultural factors which influence their behaviour and are difficult to example, in November 2009 the UK government launched a campaign to issue of the high number of teenage pregnancies. According to experts, the UK teenage pregnancy is twice that of Europe is because British teenagers about contraception or sex in the same open way as do their European (Dade 2009).
>
> **Go to the Online Resource Centre to access a link to the government campaign to reduce teenage pregnancies**
>
> Identifying how much an issue affects an organization decides how prioritized, that is how urgent it is and how much should be spent on it. Th provides some guidelines and models for identifying the impact of an is process to go through in analysing it.

Glossary

Key terms are compiled and defined in a glossary at the end of the book.

> **Above the line** Payment is made for the actual costs of the activities, which is the space in the print media or the time on television.
> **Active publics** Group of people communicating and doing something about an issue.
> **Activism** Vigorous and sometimes aggressive action in pursuing a political or social end.
> **Activists** Those who are carrying out activism.
> **Advertising** Where media space or time is paid for in order for an organization to send its messages.
> **Advertising Standards Authority (ASA)** The UK's independent regulator of advertising across all media, including TV, internet, sales promotions, and direct marketing which, in addition to consumer protection law, help to keep UK
>
> **Audit Bureau of Circulation (ABC)** Ow the media industry and provides det detailed circulation, distribution, att traffic, and related data across a broa media.
> **Avatars** An icon or representation of a us shared virtual reality.
> **Aware publics** Group of people who rec an issue affects them.
> **B-roll** Quality footage which present a n angle and works as a type of broadca and can help to encourage media int
> **B2B (business to business)** Where a bus services or products to another busin than an individual.

About the Online Resource Centre

The Online Resource Centre that accompanies this book provides students and lecturers with ready-to-use teaching and learning resources. These are free of charge and are designed to maximize the learning experience.

http://www.oxfordtextbooks.co.uk/orc/gordon/

For Students

Progress tests

A suite of multiple-choice and true/false questions, with automatic feedback, is provided for each chapter in the book, to allow you to test your knowledge of key themes and concepts.

Full versions of the case studies appearing in the book

Read extended case studies to help further apply your learning to real business situations.

Web links

A selection of regularly updated web links makes it easy to research those topics that are of particular interest to you.

Online glossary

Key terms from the book are compiled and defined online.

Links to PR company profiles

A diverse selection of links to company profiles and PR departments helps to keep you informed and connected to developments in the world of PR.

Learning skills portfolio

An outline and definition of key skills required in the PR industry with advice on how to develop them and exercises to enable you to apply them.

For Registered Adopters of the Book

Instructor's manual

Lesson plans for each chapter are included in a helpful guide for instructors. This also incorporates the answers to all of the questions set in the textbook.

PowerPoint slides

A suite of fully adaptable PowerPoint slides has been included for use in lecture presentations. Arranged by unit theme, the slides may also be used as hand-outs in class.

Test bank

A bank of multiple-choice and true/false questions and indicative answers can be used as progress tests in class.

Interactive exercises

A variety of student activities designed to encourage interactive study and peer marking. The exercises include briefs and marking criteria for presentations, advice on press release writing, event planning, and proposals with marking criteria.

Active learning games

Suggestions for role-playing activities are provided, with a list of instructions to the format of the game.

Discussion points

For use in seminars to help stimulate interest and encourage students to link PR theory to industry.

Practice examination questions

A bank of practice questions for each part of the book with indicative answers.

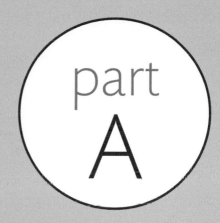

part
A

The PR framework

The evolution of public relations

(1)

Learning Outcomes

1. Demonstrate an understanding of the concept of PR by being able to discuss a broad range of PR campaigns and identify public relations in the news.

2. Assess the industry's interpretation of PR by evaluating case studies according to definitions by professional organizations.

3. Identify the historical events and personalities throughout history which have influenced PR by discussing how PR has evolved and what has had an impact on that.

4. Describe how different disciplines and experiences have contributed to make PR a valid discipline, especially in how it connects public opinion and an organization's objectives.

5. Differentiate marketing disciplines and identify PR sectors by being able to define each of these areas and identify them in a campaign showing their integration.

6. Be able to contribute to a PR campaign by demonstrating an understanding of the process and logistics involved in a photocall.

Practitioner Insight

Colin Byrne
UK & European CEO
Weber Shandwick

Colin Byrne is one of the UK's leading PR practitioners with over twenty years' experience spanning domestic and international media relations, politics, global campaigns, and issues management.

He joined Weber Shandwick in 1995, rising to lead the public affairs practice in London in 1997 and is now CEO of the global agency's European network and a member of the global management team.

After several years in private and not-for-profit sector PR, Colin joined the British Labour Party's communications team in 1987 and was quickly promoted to Head of Press & Broadcasting. He served as deputy to then communications director Peter Mandelson (Tony Blair's most important strategist who also served as a European Commissioner and as Secretary of State for Business, Enterprise and Regulatory Reform) and press aide to Tony Blair, Gordon Brown, Jack Straw, and other Labour leaders.

In 1992 he became the first communications director of the Prince of Wales Business Leaders Forum, the international NGO founded and still today presided over by Prince Charles and supported by many leading international firms. He managed CR communications for the Forum globally and worked with leading global firms on the communication of their own CR activities. Clients at Weber Shandwick have included IKEA, Oracle, the Marine Stewardship Council, the Sutton Trust, Coca-Cola, and the British Government.

How did you start in public relations?

I wanted to be a music journalist, then got interested in communications when I ran campaigns at college. I got a buzz out of seeing the campaigns, and myself quoted, in the local paper. After I left college I persuaded my first employer, the AA, that my thin experience but keen enthusiasm would make me an ideal junior PR. They believed me and gave me a break.

What is your interpretation of public relations and where is it going as a profession?

I still like the textbook definition—the interaction between an organization and its publics or stakeholders. As to where it is going, digital is changing everything and is certainly levelling the playing field with advertising. But off or online, PR has to be about two-way relationships.

What is the most exciting project you have ever worked on?

Labour's 1997 general election campaign when Tony Blair became Prime Minister. I was a consultant to Peter Mandelson.

What are your thoughts on public relations being a strategic field?

Public relations is emerging as a key strategic—and creative—discipline. The changes over recent decades, started by television and more recently driven by the internet, means communication and dialogue have to be at the heart of every company or organization's strategy. At the same time trust in other forms of communication, like advertising, is falling, making real dialogue and engagement even more essential. This is the most exciting time for PR professionals and those looking to join the profession.

Do you think public relations is really about influencing public opinion?

It is more complex than that. And it depends what you mean by 'public opinion'. Public opinion is ever more complex and layered and subsected. Your 'public' could be your employees, or a handful of political decision makers, or a group of tech bloggers, or the whole voting age public of a country. Real audience insights—the strategic planning discipline common in advertising—and research are more important than ever in modern PR.

What are the biggest influences in PR now?

Again it depends on your target audience. For any audience, campaign, or issue it will vary from friends and family, to celebrities, to traditional media, to bloggers, to the commentariat. The common thread though is third party advocates. People who tell your story for you, rather than you just telling it yourself.

What advice would you give to students entering PR?

Think about what sort of PR you want to specialize in. PR is now a very specialized business. My own agency includes everything from medical education, to lifestyle PR, to lobbying, to multi-cultural communications, to crisis management, digital and social media, strategic planning, financial PR, and mainstream consumer PR. Secondly, be prepared to demonstrate a real interest in the media and the world around you. Thirdly, live the digital lifestyle. Fourthly, be prepared to work hard.

1.1 Definition of PR

Studying public relations (PR) means embarking on an exciting career where every day promises to be different. It could be organizing top-level celebrities to promote an exotic resort, working with an international health organization to communicate disease prevention in a developing country, briefing business leaders on an international company merger, or lobbying the government to change regulations on behalf of an organization.

Public relations is a popular profession, consistently ranked among graduates' top three career choices (Hilpern 2008), and more public relations professionals are sitting on the boards of companies, making a real difference to the way organizations are run and how their reputations are managed.

Everyone has a different definition of PR because it is always changing and adapting to the world and this is especially evident with the growing power of the media. PR is developing relationships to help communicate about an organization, an issue, a person, or a product. It means identifying the anticipated outcomes in order to know how to communicate in the most effective way with different groups of people, at variable times, often through the media but also through events, individuals, and groups.

In public relations people are divided into groups depending on how they affect or are affected by an organization, and called 'publics'. Some public relations may refer to these groups as target audiences but this term suggests that people are passive rather than interacting with messages and responding to them. By identifying particular publics, specific messages and activities can be developed to reach them most effectively. Therefore, the expression 'general public' is seldom used in public relations practice.

Each year, on a global scale, the World Health Organization (WHO) launches a PR campaign called 'World No Tobacco Day' with different annual themes to reach selected groups. The campaign is announced on a specific day but can run during the year; the official day simply provides a focal point to launch the campaign with facts on the dangers of smoking, statistics on its prevalence, and research results on its negative impact. This information is used to help to stop smoking and lobby governments to control its use through banning advertising and sponsorship.

In 2009, the World No Tobacco Day focused on 'Tobacco Health Warnings' (WHO 2010). It profiled tobacco product packaging as critical to any effective tobacco control strategy (see Figure 1.1). The theme in 2010 was 'Gender and Tobacco' and presented how the tobacco industry was trying to glamorize smoking and make it attractive to women and girls. It also highlighted the need for governments to ban all tobacco advertising, promotion, and sponsorship and to eliminate tobacco smoke in all public and work places. The campaign was launched with a symposium on the theme in the National Cancer Centre, Tokyo, which is a WHO collaborative centre (WHO 2010).

⊕ Go to the Online Resource Centre to access a link to the PR resources used in this campaign

31MAY:WORLD**NO**TOBACCO**DAY**

World Health Organization

Chic?
No, throat
cancer.

Protect women from
tobacco marketing and smoke.

SMOKING
IS UGLY

WWW.WHO.INT/TOBACCO

Fig 1.1
**World Health
Organization—World No
Tobacco Day**
Source: © World Health
Organization (WHO)
2010. All Rights Reserved.

Influencing thinking and behaviour

In order to get people to adopt an idea or behave in a certain way organizations, people, or products have presented themselves and their argument in a manner that would persuade or convince people. Organizations have realized that in order to get their point of view across, their policies accepted, or their products sold, more was needed than just clever inventions or ideas. They needed to make people receptive to them as well as position themselves in the best way, depending on what they wanted to achieve.

Reputation is recognized as an organization's greatest asset. Coca-Cola is the world's most valuable brand, worth £38.2 billion, and most of this is based on reputation alone (PriceWaterhouseCoopers 2010). By understanding the diverse publics that affect an organization and developing relationships with them, PR can protect and manage an organization's reputation. From international organizations such as Greenpeace and the WHO, to county councils and private enterprises, PR is a powerful tool.

For example, Greenpeace frequently uses global PR to gain the world's attention for its campaigns. *The Times* described Greenpeace's tactics against whalers at sea as constant 'harrying' and 'blocking' resulting in the Japanese whaling fleet returning home 'in despair' (Lewis 2008). Greenpeace also carried out a highly visible protest against the Deepwater Horizon, an offshore drilling rig operated by BP which blew up and sank in April 2010 causing one of the worst oil spills in history at that time. The following month, Greenpeace protesters climbed BP's head office in London and raised a flag reading 'British Polluters'. This stunt attracted media photographers and the image appeared around the world drawing more attention to the crisis and Greenpeace's actions (Greenpeace 2010).

When Oxfam wanted to engage world leaders on the dangers of climate change, it linked the message to the Copenhagen global climate change conference on 5 December 2009 at which all global leaders would be present. Beatwax, Oxfam's public relations consultancy, aimed to engage broadcast media audiences with a compelling message to start an ongoing programme 100 days before the conference:

> **We have not got long to reverse the effects of climate change, the clock is ticking, the global summit in Copenhagen represents a real chance for world leaders to commit to massive resolutions to combat climate change.**

As part of the campaign, television companies were invited to film a family living at the 'bottom of the sea' to highlight the rise in sea levels. A scene was created of a stereotypical family of mum, dad, and child enjoying a TV dinner with a difference ... in a living room especially installed at the bottom of the shark tank, containing turtles, at the London Aquarium (see Figure 1.2). This showed the outside world looking in at an average front room in which were seated the average family in their average clothes, with scuba masks and breathing gear.

The scene was intended to illustrate the adaptations that ordinary people would need to make to daily life in the event of rising sea levels brought about by climate change. Although this depiction was both humorous and exaggerated, the message was obvious and the scenario was the top story on BBC Breakfast News programmes between 6 am and 9 am that day (BBC News 2009). Coverage ran for 100 days from the global climate change conference in Copenhagen. Sky News featured the activity as its top story as did Al Jazeera on a global level. Extensive chatter was created around the internet in relation to the stunt, and print coverage with images featured in New York, Ireland, China, and Australia among other countries.

ⓦ **Go to the Online Resource Centre to access the link to some of the most recent complaints about newspaper reporting**

Fig 1.2
Living through climate change
Source: Courtesy of Beatwax

Definitions of PR by professional organizations

Public relations has professional and industry bodies which provide guidance and assistance for those who work in the industry. The following describes a selected few of these organizations and, in some instances, includes their definition of public relations.

Go to the Online Resource Centre to access links to these organizations

Chartered Institute of Public Relations

The Chartered Institute of Public Relations (CIPR), founded in 1948, is the UK's leading public relations industry professional body and serves the professional interests of around 10,000 members. It aims to raise standards within the profession through supporting the professional interests of its members, promoting education and skills in public relations, as well as in public understanding of the industry. It also acts as the authoritative body of the industry (CIPR 2010).

The CIPR defines public relations as:

Public relations is about reputation—the result of what you do, what you say and what others say about you.

Public relations is the discipline which looks after reputation, with the aim of earning understanding and support and influencing opinion and behaviour. It is the planned and sustained effort to establish and maintain goodwill and mutual understanding between an organization and its publics.

(CIPR 2010)

Public Relations Consultants Association

The Public Relations Consultants Association (PRCA) is a trade association which was set up in 1969 and represents a large proportion of PR consultancies. It offers members networking opportunites and professional tools to make them more profitable as well as representing their interests with clients, government, and and the media (PRCA 2010).

The PRCA uses the CIPR definition of public relations but also identifies publics:

> **Public relations is all about reputation. It's the result of what you do, what you say, and what others say about you. It is used to gain trust and understanding between an organization and its various publics—whether that's employees, customers, investors, local community—or all of those stakeholder groups.**

Confederation Européenne des Relations Publiques

The Confederation Européenne des Relations Publiques (CERP)—the European Public Relations Confederation, represents approximately 22,000 PR practitioners, consultants, in-house specialists, teachers, researchers, and students in Europe.

Its main objective is to represent the European PR profession and to establish contacts, exchanges, and cooperative links between PR associations and their members worldwide. In 2006 CERP became closely linked to the Global Alliance for Public Relations and Communication Management (GA), positioning itself as its 'European wing' (CERP 2010).

The Global Alliance for Public Relations and Communication Management

The Global Alliance (GA) is the umbrella organization linking PR and communication professionals around the globe to create a unified voice on public relations.

The Global Alliance builds on the cooperative efforts of PR professional bodies (which build on the cooperative efforts of PR professionals) to tackle common problems with a global perspective. By partnering with national bodies to increase professionalism in PR, the Alliance works to enhance the influence of the public relations industry among its constituents around the world (Global Alliance 2010).

International Public Relations Association

A Board of elected directors runs the International Public Relations Association (IPRA). The IPRA aims to be the world's most relevant, resourceful, and influential professional association for senior international public relations executives (IPRA, 2010).

The IPRA aims to provide intellectual leadership in the practice of international public relations as well as to provide a service to help practitioners professionally. It has developed Codes and Charters seeking to provide an ethical and professional climate for all members (IPRA 2010). The codes include the Code of Venice which outlines professional conduct, the Code of Athens which outlines ethical behaviour, and the

Code of Brussels which outlines ethical conduct regarding public affairs (see chapter 11 for more on ethics and these codes).

Public Relations Society of America

The Public Relations Society of America (PRSA) provides professional development, sets standards of excellence, upholds principles of ethics for its members, and advocates for greater understanding and adoption of public relations services (PRSA 2010). The PRSA 1982 National Assembly formally adopted a definition of public relations, which remains widely accepted and used today:

> **Public relations helps an organization and its publics adapt mutually to each other.**
>
> (PRSA 2010)

The PRSA uses the term 'organization' to emphasize the wide remit of public relations in many different areas such as business, schools, communities, governments, institutions, and voluntary associations.

It uses the term 'publics' to mean many diverse groups, such as employees, members, customers, local communities, shareholders and other institutions, and society at large.

Features of public relations

Third parties

A key feature of PR is its use of third parties, that is, credible people who support the organization's views but are more influential as they are seen as independent and not part of the organization. An example of this is when, to demonstrate their support, a celebrity attends the launch of a product and may even be involved in other personal appearances associated with the campaign.

PR has grown through exploring how to communicate with people in a way that would motivate them towards an organization's particular objectives. PR is increasingly focusing on building relationships. Heath (2001: 6) states that instead of trying to control people, public relations has progressed to where it fosters trust and builds community.

> **Public relations is a relationship-building professional activity that adds value to organizations because it increases the willingness of markets, audiences, and publics to support them rather than to oppose their efforts.**
>
> (Heath 2001: 8)

Academic disciplines

PR has developed from many different disciplines, such as psychology which identifies what motivates people; sociology which assesses the influences to which people are subject; media communications which observes audience's behaviour and how they relate to the media, and business studies which assesses how to reach publics in the legal, political, and economic climate of an organization. These are constantly developing in a world with more organizations and technological developments making communications faster, more global, and more competitive with more diverse publics.

PR skills

In addition, PR practitioners must have strong and creative communication skills, such as writing and presenting, to ensure clear and persuasive expression to appeal to diverse groups. Practitioners must also be able to initiate and manage events which create an opportunity for organizations to talk to their publics and develop a dialogue. All these abilities must use creativity in order to appeal to diverse and specific groups.

Free expression

Consequently, PR is concerned with managing an organization's interaction with its ever-broadening range of publics. It has roots in activism which means that over the years PR has raised issues that may never otherwise have been heard. Duncan Green (2008), the author of Oxfam International's report, *From Poverty to Power*, says that it is only by giving people in poor communities a voice that we will end a global tragedy that leaves one in six people lost in poverty, hunger, and disease.

Examples of public campaigns that give people a voice include those which have helped people in rural India get access to work, given indigenous people in Bolivia the right to own land, and allowed HIV-positive people in South Africa better access to antiretroviral drugs (Mylrea 2008).

PR has a great role in democracy where people need to hear dissenting voices and allow for free expression. Increasingly, it is offering strategic advice to help a company communicate, whether to launch a product, develop relationships with its consumers, community, or employees or other publics, or to navigate its way through a crisis.

1.2 Historical context

Historically, PR has been used to influence public opinion as well as to act as a communication mediator between publics, leaders, and organizations in an effort to change attitudes and, frequently, behaviour.

It is generally considered that PR started as propaganda whereby the communicator of the message manipulates its publics for its own ends, and disregards any other viewpoints. Propaganda did not always mean this and comes from *Congregatio de propaganda fide* (Congregation for propagating the faith) a religious organization founded by Pope Gregory XV in 1622 to educate missionaries to spread Catholicism (Encylopaedia Britannica 2010). Any religion could be defined as a quintessential PR story with its events, persuasion, spokespeople, and publications which are all able

Go to the Online Resource Centre to find more on this publication to reach out and communicate with different publics. This does not undermine the veracity of the message but demonstrates the effectiveness of the communication.

PR has drawn on many different disciplines and is seen to be evolving into a role of ensuring mutual understanding where both sides (the public and the organization) interact and have equal involvement in the message development and the way they can affect an organization and its reputation (Motscahll 2001).

PR for farmers and kings

Cutlip et al (2006: 88) argue that 'communicating to influence viewpoints and actions' can be traced from the earliest civilizations. They report how farm bulletins in Iraq in 1800 BC instructed farmers on how to farm crops, they also describe how the kings of ancient India used PR when they employed information gatherers to keep them informed of public opinion and then put out positive news to the public about the government. In addition, they note that English kings appointed a Lord Chancellor to facilitate communication between governments and the people.

Public Relations in the US

The form of PR recognized today arose in the nineteenth century. For example, in the US the 1830s anti-slavery society in New York ran massive PR campaigns where it linked high-profile people and held meetings which provided an opportunity to run petitions and distribute information. The book *Uncle Tom's Cabin*, by Harriet Beecher Stowe in 1852, acted as a public relations activity. The novel attacked the cruelty of slavery and communicated the anti-slavery message to educated people (Coombs and Holladay 2007).

The promoters

American PR is generally traced to the highly creative business entrepreneur and showman P.T. Barnum, who during the 1840s to 1860s promoted circuses, concerts, and the theatre, which he transformed into respectable middle-class entertainment. He believed in attracting people to his circuses and his museums through exaggerated claims such as 'the greatest show on earth' and profiling freak characters including midgets and Siamese twins. His approach is often brought up as an example of 'one-way communication' which does not value the importance of truth and relies on 'hype'.

The activists

In the 1880s, the US movement against excessive drinking led to large campaigns where speeches, events, and publications created public awareness and support. This temperance movement held large public meetings and parades which were designed to attract attention and generate publicity in order to abolish the sale of alcohol. Coombs and Holladay (2007: 64) report on an activist called Carry Nation who left her alcoholic husband in the early 1880s and began a crusade against alcohol by travelling to various towns lecturing on the dangers of alcohol. Before giving a public speech she would first enter the local saloons and smash the bars with a hatchet. To link this activity to her campaign she published a regular newsletter called the 'Smashers Mail' and sold little pewter hatchets as mementoes of her campaign. The campaign gained momentum and created an awareness which resulted in pressure for social change and eventually to outlawing the sale of alcohol (Coombs and Holladay 2007).

In the US at the turn of the twentieth century, industrialization, urbanization, and immigration were affecting social standards leading to poverty, crime, and corruption. Corporate leaders were called 'robber barons' as they were profit-driven at the expense of their employees who had poor working conditions and practices. The rising awareness of the workers' plight created great industrial turmoil especially when workers started using the growing media to publicize their appalling industry practices and appealed to the public to drive social reform (Edwards 2009). For example, one journalist infiltrated the meat packaging industry and published a book on its insanitary conditions and abuse of the workforce. This eventually led to a government investigation and finally to new regulations including, in 1906, the Pure Food Act and the Meat Inspection Act (Coombs and Holladay 2007).

However, despite publicizing issues which resulted in government reform and consequently societal change, such as child labour laws, the journalists were labelled 'muckrakers' by President Theodore Roosevelt which undermined their activities. On the other hand, growing literacy, along with an evolving media such as the telegraph, radio, and more newspaper outlets meant that companies could also use the media to sway public opinion. This led to public relations consultancies being created to defend companies against negative media coverage.

The truth-tellers

In the 1900s, Ivy Lee, a former US news reporter began working for large companies and through the media he improved their image to the public. Lee explained to the company management that they needed to work with newspapers just as the activists did, in order to win over public opinion. His key strategy was to insist that businesses be more open and tell the journalists the truth. This led to his Declaration of Principles in 1906, in which he promised to deliver information to the media—on behalf of his clients—that adhered to accuracy, authority, and fact. When one of his clients, Pennsylvania Rail, had a train crash, Lee advised the company to explain what had happened and brought reporters to the scene to cover the story. These actions showed open communications and resulted in public cooperation (Edwards 2009: 9).

Today, using the media, especially the internet, to report poor company practice also has a great impact on public opinion, and a global effect. For example, in 1996 the CBS News programme detailed the abuse of Nike workers in Vietnamese factories. The Vietnam Labour Watch (VLW) investigated these working conditions and released a report which has created an ongoing worldwide campaign against sweatshops and the companies which use them (BBC 2000).

The social psychologists

In the early twentieth century, public relations drew on the study of social psychology which found that people were prone to social influence and could be persuaded by the power of argument and ideas. Public relations was used to organize effective support for the First World War, arranging thousands of speakers in communities across the US to give short speeches. President Wilson created the Committee on Public Information, headed by George Creel, which aimed to unite public opinion behind the war (Cutlip et al 2006: 2).

After the First World War, the US made a shift to a consumer culture and a fascination with the notion of public opinion and attempts to influence it. There was a newfound prosperity and mass culture and capitalism evolved together as corporations began to encourage people to buy brand name products. (Penning 2008: 346). Legislation was then passed to ensure that any paid-for media content had to be labelled as advertising to protect people from deceptive practices.

Penning (2008: 348) notes that it was at this time of growing consumerism, concern for public opinion, and journalistic introspection that 'public relations' emerged as a concept and became a formal occupation.

Edward Bernays—the US 'Father of Public Relations'

Edward Bernays was a press agent for the Committee on Public Information (http://pr-museum.com) where he helped to present the First World War as a force for democracy. After the war he realized that he could apply the theories of mass psychology and persuasion to the needs of corporate and political organizations and in 1919 he launched his own consultancy (http://prmuseum.com). He also realized that there was a growing awareness for interpreting the public interest and advised businesses on policies and programmes to maintain public support and, in turn, interpreted business to the public. The attempts to influence public opinion became greater as more PR consultancies were set up.

Bernays was influenced by the growing research on the unconscious mind. Most of this was research carried out by Bernays' uncle, Sigmund Freud, the German psychoanalyst. Bernays applied this social psychology to his PR practice and showed American organizations how to make people want things they didn't need by linking mass-produced goods to their unconscious desires (http://prmuseum.com). He explained how public relations could mould public opinion by publishing his own reports and case studies in books such as *Crystallising Public Opinion* (1923). Furthermore, he used this information to create a scientific argument which helped substantiate public relations as a valid discipline.

In 1920, on behalf of American Tobacco, Bernays was able to encourage more women to smoke at a time when it was a social taboo for women to be seen smoking in public. He did this through an event which linked research on smoking to a social cause; the women's liberation movement. He announced the results of the research, which suggested cigarettes empowered women, through a media event which photographed

Go to the Online Resource Centre to access a full case study a parade of glamorous women in Central New York, in view of the Statue of Liberty, lighting up their cigarettes as symbols of freedom. The campaign was consequently named the 'Torches of Freedom'.

Social psychology and social research

In the 1930s, social psychology research developed further and revealed that people could be divided into groups with predictable characteristics, allowing communications to be developed and targeted to selected groups. For example, people could be divided into age, sex, geographical location, and income. This is now called **demographics**. Advertising used this research very effectively by developing advertisements that appealed to different groups. Today more and more subgroups are being identified and thereby targeted more accurately with messages appropriate for them.

Surveys were created to gauge public opinion and offer greater insight to perceived attitudes. It was found that by surveying a relatively small number of the population the results were the same as if a much larger group had been surveyed. As social psychology showed that people could be influenced by each other's opinions, President Franklin Roosevelt's administration used opinion polls to inform the population what most people thought or felt and thereby mobilized public opinion in favour of the welfare state. **Opinion polls** today are a common market research tool which identify public opinion in order to segment people so that marketers can promote products and messages which appeal to these different groups.

The persuaders

The Depression in the 1930s meant that public relations suffered a setback as many questioned the social value of business. However, President Roosevelt promoted recovery strategies and ensured that he was always on the front page of the newspaper thereby developing his charismatic leadership style and subsequent ability to persuade the public.

During the Second World War a PR movement supported the war and 3,000 PR staff were hired to sell 'air power' to generals who were used to fighting on the ground. These PR efforts used publicity and censorship, and also assisted war correspondents (Cutlip et al 2006).

Post-Second World War

Post-war, the US moved towards a consumer-oriented economy and this was fuelled by the emergence of television. Cutlip et al (2006) suggest the controversy and distrust of the government over the Vietnam War made the government realize that it needed to engage more with public opinion. Additionally, public demonstrations about companies that were damaging the environment, such as large pesticide companies, meant that the public's concerns about private enterprise had to be addressed. Additionally, the civil rights movement, such as the one led by Dr Martin Luther King, showed that public opinion was powerful and the government realized it must take notice of its concerns.

Public relations in the UK

Miller and Dinan (2000: 7) claim that it is 'generally agreed' that PR originated in the US at the end of the nineteenth and twentieth centuries. However, it might be more accurate to say that it was only the term 'public relations' that was coined in the US by Edward Bernays. In the UK it is estimated that 48,000 people now work in the public relations profession which is estimated to contribute almost £3.4 billion to the country's economy (Centre for Economics and Business Research). This makes the industry second in size to the US which has the largest PR industry in the world.

Evolution from local government

Leading UK PR theorist, Jacqui L'Etang (2004: 223) argues that the development of public relations in the UK was largely driven by local government. The first wide-scale publicity campaign was carried out for the government-owned Post Office in 1876, in which a million handbills were issued to alert the public to the virtues of government savings schemes, life insurance, and annuities (Miller and Dinan 2000). In 1918, the first Ministry of Information was formed from the Home Office Information Bureau and various other Whitehall units.

During the Depression, local governments set up orchestrated PR campaigns to combat negative attitudes towards their tax and rates collections and also to gain support from local communities when threatened with reduced budgets from central government (L'Etang 2004).

The influence of central government on PR

Central government departments were also instrumental in developing public relations. The UK Ministry of Health was created in 1919 and used many PR techniques in its public health campaigns which focused on preventative medicine. After the First World War, the Empire Marketing Board (EMB) was created as a public relations channel to promote UK trade with the Commonwealth. Stephen Tallents, a former civil servant who was later knighted for his contribution to PR, led these promotional initiatives. He went on to head the Institute of Public Relations, the professional organization for PR professionals which is now the Chartered Institute of Public Relations.

Tallents' PR strategy was to raise awareness of the UK through identifying its unique culture and heritage—for example its monarchy and navy—largely via the media. The EMB organized press and poster campaigns, exhibitions, shopping weeks, Empire shops, lectures, and radio talks. Most famous was the EMB film unit led by John Grierson, considered the creator of the documentary film (COI 2010).

Tallents then moved to the General Post Office, where the first full-scale government public relations division was created where he brought in Grierson to make a documentary film as a communications tool.

During the Second World War, PR was used to recruit soldiers, explain government issues, and unite the population. Local authorities, especially in London, carried out press relations as a form of mass communication to inform the public of evacuations, ration books, and the effects of bombing. In 1944 the Beveridge Act laid out the vision of a welfare state where the schooling, council housing, new towns, and replanning of London had to be explained. As a result of this communication, local government achieved much closer relations with its communities.

Influence of the Central Office of Information

In 1946 the Central Office of Information (COI) was formed—mainly from the Ministry of Information, including its regional organization and film unit—to provide communication services for all government departments at home and overseas. It aimed to use its communications expertise to help government achieve policy objectives. After the war and the resulting food shortages, the COI worked with the Ministry of Food on public communications to raise awareness of the need for children to have a balanced diet (COI 2010).

The labour shortage also led the government to run campaigns with the COI which encouraged immigration from the colonies and mobilized the labour force to rebuild priority industries. The COI also promoted the new National Health Service, and launched preventative healthcare films with titles such as 'Coughs and sneezes spread diseases' (COI 2010). In addition, it promoted the feeling of national pride for the London Olympic Games in 1948 and the Festival of Britain in 1951.

In 1948, the PR practitioners in the local government trade union, the National Association of Local Government Officers (NALGO), developed the professional status of PR through setting up the Institute for Public Relations (IPR), which was developed along the lines of the civil service. It had a code of conduct, educational initiatives, and a tiered membership structure with PR practitioners who were called 'officers', a term sometimes still used today.

Go to the Online Resource Centre to find a link to find a link to coughs and sneezes

Post-war changes

Post-war technological developments stimulated new industries, products, and markets and in the 1950s, with the explosion of broadcast media and communications technology, PR consultancies emerged representing many organizations. Their work would be considered a very simplified form of PR today as it mainly comprised editorial services; that is, writing copy that would interest the media. In 1960, the PR consultancies set up their own professional group called the Society of Public Relations Consultants which is now the Public Relations Consultancy Association where members are PR consultancies not individuals (see page 9).

Britain joined the European Economic Community in 1973 and the COI worked with the Department of Trade and Industry on the integrated campaign for the 'Single European market', which involved publications, radio, and presentations for business and regional government services.

High unemployment in the 1980s—resulting from a shift in employment in the old industrial manufacturing sectors changing to newer service industries—meant there was a need for new jobs, skills, and the restoration of many industrial cities. Large government public relations campaigns launched 'Action for jobs' and 'Action for cities', Training and Enterprise Councils, the Enterprise Initiative, and the largest ever adult training programme (COI).

Privatization of national utilities

In the 1980s and 1990s the PR industry expanded significantly, largely because national utilities, such as British Telecom, British Gas, Rolls Royce, BAA, and the water industries were privatized and sold on the stock market. PR campaigns, led by the COI, educated the public about these companies and encouraged them to buy shares. These newly privatized companies continued working with PR consultancies to grow their investment (Miller and Dinan 2000).

Going global

The expansion of PR was further developed with the UK's global campaigns such as the COI's preventative health campaign for AIDS, which helped the Government to host the first world AIDS summit, with delegates from 149 countries and hundreds of journalists.

Communications technology, such as an electronic news distribution services, also encouraged expansion of public relations as it meant press releases could be sent instantly to every national newspaper and broadcaster. The RAF and the Navy were the first to use new and sophisticated databases and telephone response systems in their recruitment campaigns (COI 2010).

The Twin Towers' terrorist attack in the USA in 2001 and the 2005 terrorist attacks on the London Underground and bus systems meant that terrorism dominated communications and became a global issue. The UK Government realized that people had to be persuaded in a certain way to ensure they were in agreement with government. Large PR campaigns were used to reach the increasingly diverse publics with different cultures, religions, and education to highlight the threat of terror and support the government in going to war in Iraq and Afghanistan.

However, an independent review of government communications, published as the 2004 Phillis Report, found that the UK Government had to work harder than ever to reach and convince its publics and needed a sustained and radical change in its communications (Government Communications online). It reported that the public's mistrust of authority, social diversity, fragmented audiences, and a vast array of communication channels made the task increasingly complex.

PR in Europe

Most European public relations practitioners believe that European PR is broader, public-oriented rather than business-orientated, more long term and less profit-oriented than that in the US or UK (Ruler et al 2001). PR in Europe is expanding rapidly, largely influenced by the growing international ownership of companies and agencies, and global focus of markets and publics, education and research (Rapp and Ruler 2006).

PR in Germany

Alongside the US and the UK, Germany was very active in its social psychology research which has influenced the development of public relations. Germany created a press department in its Foreign Ministry in 1871 and the Navy had press officers in 1894 (Edwards 2009). It was in the development of the Third Reich during the Second World War that Hitler used PR to unite Germany through his rousing speeches, use of pioneering documentary film, and the hosting of the Berlin Olympics which profiled Germans as a heroic race. The *Triumph of the Will*, by the filmmaker Leni Riefenstahl, was an early political documentary and covers the events of the Sixth Nuremburg Party Congress. Its innovative techniques included images of Hitler in an aeroplane descending towards the people which encouraged them to believe he had command over an entire nation.

China–a leading economy

Although China is a leading global economy, advertising and promotion were considered unnecessary during the early years of Communist rule and banned during the Cultural Revolution of 1966–76. It was not until the 1976 economic reforms that advertising was approved as a legitimate business. Market research is considered by the West to offer valuable insights into consumer behaviour but applying Western research methods in China is not always relevant. This is because in the West publics are segmented into groups by age, income, etc but this does not fit with the Chinese family and regional and language differences. In addition, results of research are affected by the many-layered processing that Chinese data must undergo for bureaucratic reasons (Amber and Witzel 2004). However, internet usage is high despite government restriction and regulations.

The key aspect of PR in China is that the Chinese are more visually focused than Westerners and they respond more to pictures and diagrams. Additionally, where PR sees relationship-building skills as crucial, these skills are already highly developed having been based on the importance of business first arising from Chinese family connections and relationships (Amber and Witzel 2004).

Global media

Today's 24-hour global and fragmented media demands instant information for many publics which, in turn, requires practitioners to be informed about their organization and publics and whatever is affecting them in order to respond proactively and quickly at any time. Furthermore, it is now a government requirement that organizations are more open about their activities, and this is called corporate transparency. PR is now becoming invaluable in advising companies about their publics and how they need to be kept informed.

> **PR is the management function that establishes and maintains mutually beneficial relationships between an organization and the public on whom its success or failure depends.**

(Cutlip et al 2006: 22)

With communications becoming more global, an organization is exposed to a broader range of different publics. These publics have differing interest and expectations, different consumer behaviour, different economic circumstances, cultures, and ethnic backgrounds, laws, and regulations.

1.3 Influences

Table 1.1 shows key communications developments and world events which have had an impact on the evolution of PR or mark a key date in PR development.

Table 1.1 Key dates influencing the evolution of public relations

1446	Johannes Gutenberg invents a printing press with metal movable type which allows handbills and broadsides to promote various causes
1450	Newspapers appear in Europe
1623	Pope Gregory XV creates the College for Propagating the Faith, the origin of the term 'propaganda'
1773	Boston tea party carries out large PR stunt of dumping tea into the water to demonstrate against UK taxation
1830–40	US social reform such as anti-slavery and alcohol abuse
1835	Morse code invented by Samuel Morse
1861	Telegraph wires linked east and west coasts of the US delivering Morse code signals
1865	Slavery abolished in the US
1867	First typewriter
1868	P.T. Barnum (US), introduces the concept of promotion to his circus, theatres, and museums
1876	First telephone by Alexander Graham Bell
1882	Public relations term used first by Dorman Eaton, a lawyer addressing New York Law School
1887	Gramophone invented by Emile Berliner
1893	Women begin to get the vote—New Zealand the first country
1895	Comic strips begin in newspapers
1896	First motion picture Wireless telegraphy invented by Guglielmo Marconi
1898	First electrical sound, invented by Valdemar Poulsen
1900	First film with sound
1902	First radio signal (in Morse code) across the Atlantic Ocean by Gugliemo Marconi

1905	Formation of NALGO, National Association of Local Government Officers (U.K. government officials) for public administration. Lobby for their rights to pensions, salary scales promotions etc
1906	Radio transmits speech and music Ivy Lee (US) writes the Declaration of Principles for PR to have open relationships with the media Conditions of US workers written about by journalists ('muckrakers') leads to Pure Food Act and to Meat Inspection Act Lloyd George, Chancellor of the Exchequer (UK) organizes a team of lecturers to tour the country and explain the old age pension UK Government uses PR to ensure that the public understands health and housing schemes
1911	A.A. Brill (later consultant to Bernays in Torches of Freedom campaign) founds the Psychoanalytical Association of New York
1914	Outbreak of First World War
1915	First cross-continental telephone calls
1916	Creel Committee on Public Information (US Creel Committee) increases support for war First radios with tuners for different stations John Logie Baird (UK) transmits first television signal
1918	First World War ends in November with armistice
1919	Ministry of Health (UK) establishes and runs preventative health campaigns
1920	US voting rights to women
1922	Every NALGO office has a press correspondent and publicity committee
1923	Bernays (US) publishes Crystallizing Public Opinion, about how the mind can be controlled through persuasive techniques
1926	Documentary pioneered by John Grierson (UK) as education on social issues Stephen Tallents becomes secretary of Empire Marketing Board (UK) to raise awareness of imports from British Empire
1930	First television broadcasts in the US UK government employs 44 people in press/publicity offices
1932	NALGO PR campaign on public administration
1934	Joseph Begun invents first tape recorder for broadcasting
1939	Germany invades Poland starting Second World War Britain, France, Australia, and New Zealand declare war on Germany UK government departments use publicity and/or PR as a legitimate function
1940	Mussolini declares war on Britain and France
1944	First PR journal (US), written by Rex Harlow UK Beveridge Act for a welfare state
1945	End of Second World War
1946	Central Office of Information (COI) is born 32 PR posts formed in local government (UK)
1948	Birth of the NHS Transistor radio invented IPR (UK) starts
1949	'Public Relations and Publicity', by J.H. Brebner, the first British book bearing 'public relations' in its title Women in China and Costa Rica get the vote

1950	Colour television Women in Canada get the vote
1955	Bernays published his book 'The Engineering of Consent' which explains how PR could shape and mould public opinion
1959	Vietnam War starts (ends 1975)
1960	Shell has 200 people in PR. PR well established in U.K. government through officers' trade union.
1969	Internet developed ARPANET (Advanced Research Projects Agency Network)
1970	APPLE home computer
1971	Computer floppy disk invented
1971	Swiss women get vote
1973	First international connections made to ARPANET at the University College of London and Royal Radar Establishment in Norway Britain joins the European Economic Community
1976	J. Grunig publishes first of a large number of PR research studies
1977	First cellular phone communication network starts in Japan
1978	IBM PC first sold
1979	Mobile phones trialled
1980	Sony Walkman invented First laptops sold to public Mass production of compact disk which saves music digitally, as computer data, eliminating vinyl
1984	Grunig and Hunt identify four PR Communication Models as basis of the contemporary academic and operational paradigm about PR
1989	Berlin Wall falls
1991	World wide web developed by Time Berners-Lee to provide easy access to any form of information anywhere in the world
1993	Launch of Mosaic, first web browser
1997	Term 'weblogs' first used
1999	RSS (Really Simple Syndication) feeds introduced which allow for blogs and podcasts to be received Blogger software introduced—a simple system to create and upload blogs
2001	George W. Bush, 43rd US president September 11 terrorist attacks on Twin Towers (US) Launch of the online encyclopedia, Wikipedia, that could be edited by anyone
2003	Invasion of Iraq by US and UK troops MySpace founded and allows for building networks of friends and adding content
2004	Phillis review of UK Government communications Creation of Flicker—later sold to Yahoo Facebook launches for students at Harvard University Web 2.0 term introduced US hands over power to Iraqi interim government Tsunami devastates Asia; 200,000 killed
2005	Tony Blair becomes first Labour Party leader to win three successive terms London hit by Islamic terrorist bombings Nintendo releases Wii YouTube, video-sharing website where users can upload, view, and share video clips

2006	Twitter launches as a free social networking and microblogging site
2008	Worldwide recession owing to US 2007 subprime mortgage crisis
2009	US presidential elections use social media, especially Twitter, and Barack Obama, the first African American elected president Swine flu global epidemic
2010	Haiti earthquake causes highest recorded death toll BP oil spill in US Gulf of Mexico creates huge environmental disaster Icelandic volcanic ash disrupts European air traffic Greek economic crisis affects European economy

Differentiating PR

Because PR is an umbrella discipline that spans advertising and marketing, PR practitioners need to have an in-depth knowledge of business issues and all areas of communications, including advertising, marketing communications, market research, and sales promotion. This section explains some of their differences and how they can be integrated.

Marketing

The Chartered Institute of Marketing is the leading international body for marketing and business development. It defines marketing as follows:

> **Marketing is the management process responsible for identifying, anticipating and satisfying customer requirements profitably.**
>
> (Chartered Institute of Marketing)

Marketing originates from economics and focuses on a product or service, how it is priced, how it is to be the best in order to be sold, and how it is branded and positioned to ensure it meets consumers' needs and desires.

Marketing is called upon very early in a product's or service's life. Sales, advertising, and promotional activities are part of marketing and focus on having a good product which is available, at the right place, at the right price, and promoted to let people know it exists. These are called the four Ps: product, price, place, and promotion. Marketing relies on research to find out what people want and then develops and sells a product which fits what the research has shown. On the television programme *Dragons Den* the panel of judges assess the product or service against the 4Ps to see the potential of the innovation. There is some confusion and even rivalry between public relations and marketing with each trying to defend its own territory and frequently public relations for products is called marketing communications.

Advertising

The Institute of Practitioners in Advertising (IPA) is the industry body and professional institute for leading agencies in the UK advertising, media, and marketing communications industry. It defines advertising as follows:

Advertising presents the most persuasive possible selling message to the right prospects for the product or service at the lowest possible cost.

(IPA 2010)

The key strength of advertising is that it reaches large audiences and develops brand awareness, values, and associations. Because the advertisement can reach large audiences the cost per contact can be very low.

Advertising fits into the marketing department of an organization and relies on market research to know about its publics and then how to target them. Generally advertising uses paid-for media which means it buys time on television or the radio, space in a newspaper or magazine where it places copy or images to promote a product or service, banners on websites and social media sites, and in cinemas.

Advertising is generally a non-personal form of mass communication that is well controlled, that is, it is known exactly where the advertisement is going, what media is used to deliver the message, when it is available and for how long, and what the advertisement is.

Go to the Online Resource Centre to access a link to more on the advertising industry

Above the line

Advertising is called an above-the-line activity as payment is made for the actual costs of the activities, which is the space in the print media or the time on television.

Below-the-line expenditure includes all the other methods such as competitions, special offers, and media relations and consultancy advice that is charged on a time basis. Public relations is a below-the-line activity and is paid on how much time is put into a project, that is because PR works on a fee basis.

Direct marketing

Direct marketing is a move towards personalized communications, such as direct mail, telemarketing, and interactive communications online. It targets individuals to deliver personalized messages and builds a relationship with them based on their responses to direct communication. Direct communication can be through direct mail, and use of telephone numbers or emails from ads, or through telemarketing or online or text messaging

Sponsorship

If a company decides to sponsor an event it may pay for the whole event to ensure that the event is branded with its name. The company gets 'rights' which can be television rights where they control how the event is shown on television. This is common in sports sponsorship where the sponsor can obtain a great deal of television coverage. However, there are also other aspects of sponsorship that companies can buy, such as hospitality for their guests, special seats, banners, and advertisements at the site. They may sponsor a leaflet, book, research, or an activity, such as a sport.

Most sponsorship can be broken down into different aspects and public relations can often help an organization decide what would work best. A sponsorship should resonate with the client's own messages, in order to strengthen them. For example, a car manufacturer may sponsor the Grand Prix. However, some sponsorships are not so directly related and that is because the publics the sponsor is trying to reach may be the same as the ones who are attending an event or associated with an event. For example sponsoring a football match, which attracts a high young male audience, may also be an ideal way for a drinks company to reach that audience.

PR activates sponsorship by developing activities that link to the sponsorship and ensuring the messages that the organization wants to get across are communicated through its sponsorship.

There is always an overlap between marketing, advertising, and public relations and a fully integrated campaign ensures that communications are consistent for the organization. PR is an industry which has few boundaries and is constantly changing, shaped by the very people who are working in it and driven by communications technology and developments in the media. It works across a diverse range of industry sectors and comes under many titles; these include public information, investor relations, public affairs, corporate communication, marketing, or customer relations (CIPR 2010).

Consultancy and in-house

Currently PR is either in consultancies with specialist practitioners working as consultants to organizations, or in-house where employed practitioners provide PR services to their employer. A PR consultancy is often called an agency and employs PR practitioners who carry out PR for an organization.

Consultancy PR

The consultancy will usually give the client a budget at the beginning of the project which estimates how long the project will take and what other costs are expected. To ensure the client is kept informed of the PR activities, the consultancy will send the client regular written reports and hold regular meetings to review their progress and agree next actions.

The benefit to the client in hiring a consultancy is that the client can have temporary and expert help without having to hire anyone permanently. In consultancy, practitioners work in a team for different clients, sometimes up to six clients at one time. An in-house PR practitioner works within an organization but may bring in assistance from a PR consultancy.

In-house PR

An in-house capability can be a dedicated PR or corporate communications division or function as part of marketing. The consultancy reports to the client's own in-house PR team, if it has one, or its marketing team, or corporate communications, public affairs, or even directly to the CEO depending on the nature of the PR. If it is crisis management, the PR team will usually liaise with the CEO of the organization. As companies realize that reputation is their greatest asset and that they need PR, corporate communications is taking on a central role, and practitioners are becoming board directors involved in company decisions.

The functions across in-house and PR consultancy are similar, although in-house has more internal communications and public affairs whereas consultancy carries out more corporate PR and strategic planning.

1.4 Application to industry

PR is divided into different areas which require different talents, interests, and abilities. For example, in the consumer sector a practitioner may be hosting a media launch for a product and inviting a celebrity whereas in public affairs they are more likely to be attending meetings with government officials.

PR consultancies may specialize in particular industry sectors such as finance, technology, healthcare, internal communications, and public affairs. There are also generalist consultancies which offer services across a broad range of PR activities and have specialist divisions within them. Nevertheless, all these sectors overlap and a comprehensive campaign for an organization would draw on all these areas.

The following outlines some of these sectors.

Public sector

Public sector PR helps the government explain its policies, decisions, and actions and informs the public about their rights and responsibilities. It is largely led by the government's communication department, the COI, and includes national and local government initiatives such as education, health, and the police. It must reach diverse audiences from the entire population to very specific groups such as teenagers or the elderly.

Public affairs

Public affairs involves working with government regulations and legislation and often requires lobbying of government officials in order to change current rulings in order to help the organization progress. This could include changing regulations or gaining planning consent. For instance, an airport wishing to expand may want to speed up its local planning process. The public affairs campaign would try and get support from local residents and political stakeholders and may focus on communicating how the airport helps the UK economy.

Technology PR

Technology PR demands knowledge of the technological businesses so that practitioners can talk to publics and the media about a diverse range of technological products and services. For example, Gorillabox is an organization which streams video content to any mobile phone in Europe or the US using 3G networks. This PR requires digital specialist knowledge and is aimed at informing operators and content providers about the potential avenue of marketing to people on their handsets (PR Week 2007).

Not-for-profit PR

The not-for-profit sector includes charities, voluntary organizations, sports clubs, trade unions, and public arts organizations such as museums and art galleries, as well as government and non-governmental agencies, for instance the WHO and the Red Cross. They do not give profits or funds to owners or shareholders, but instead use them to reach their own goals.

A global not-for-profit example is the 2007 Red Cross HIV campaign which highlighted the effect of the HIV pandemic on young people wherever they are in the world through a micro site and a highly rated nano-soap which led into social networking sites.

Go to the Online Resource Centre to access a link to this nano-soap

Consumer PR

Consumer campaigns are highly creative and often build associations with an event or a third party to promote a brand. For example the hotel chain, Travelodge, communicated the advantages of its clean and comfortable low priced rooms where people could have a good night's sleep en route to the airport or a business meeting, by positioning itself as an expert on sleep. It appointed a director of sleep and launched innovations such as 'cuddle pillows' and put relaxing fish tanks in its rooms (Blythe 2010). Consumer campaigns are often centred on events such as the 2010 World Cup where brands ranging from clothes, food, and travel are promoted by tapping into the passion of fans and capitalize on football-related content.

Healthcare PR

Healthcare campaigns usually focus on pharmaceuticals or medical devices and range from lobbying for changing government regulations to dealing with medical opinion leaders and communicating with patients. This may include setting up patient groups as well as working for, and with, associated not-for-profit organizations such as the Meningitis Trust, to help raise awareness of a medical condition and its treatment.

Corporate PR

Corporate PR, also called corporate communications, includes programmes that affect the overall organization. It focuses on the organization as a whole rather than the different disciplines within public relations. Cornelissen (2008) argues that corporate communications is a management function that oversees and coordinates the work of practitioners in the different areas of the organization such as media relations, public affairs and internal communication. It demands an integrated approach which looks after the public relations of the whole organization. It takes responsibility for presenting the organization to its stakeholders, that is, the people whom the organization influences and who in turn influence the organization. Corporate PR is probably the most visible when it is dealing with company mergers where the company's brand is focused on and can impact its business. It is often linked to investor relations which ensures its investors are informed of activities that affect the financial value of the company. Corporate responsibility is a part of corporate communications and considers the economic, social, and environmental impacts of an organization's activities (see chapter 11 for more on corporate responsibility).

Issues management

Issues management identifies the threats around a business and develops relationships and communications in order to avert them. It also prepares for these eventualities, which if they occur may become a crisis. (See chapter 10 for more about issues and crises.)

Internal communications

Internal communications deals with PR within the organization ensuring that employees are aware of developments and are supported and motivated. PR involvement can include a newsletter, posters, email bulletins, and the intranet. Internal communications is particularly important in times of crisis and when an organization is going through change, where it becomes important that everyone works together to achieve the organization's goals.

The following corporate case study shows how an organization can build its reputation among many different publics by linking to an environmental cause.

Case Study

Coca-Cola Recycling
Source: Courtesy of Grayling and Coca-Cola GB

As part of its sustainable packaging and recycling strategy, Coca-Cola has reduced the weight of 500ml PET bottles to just 24 grams, down from 39 grams in 1994; it has also reduced the weight of its iconic glass bottles by 20 per cent. Glass bottles now contain approximately 30 per cent recycled glass, and aluminium cans contain around 50 per cent recycled content. Over 90 per cent of the waste produced at Coca-Cola manufacturing sites is recycled, with just 10 per cent going to landfill—a 68 per cent reduction since 2002.

Undertaking campaigns to educate and inspire positive consumer behaviour is an equally vital component of Coca-Cola's sustainability strategy. This is done by encouraging consumers to recycle by placing clear and consistent 'Recycle Now' logos on all products and by running innovative consumer recycling schemes such as 'Talent from Trash' (www.talent-fromtrash.co.uk) and 'Recycling Zone', which enables people to recycle 'on the go'.

Recycle Week is an annual awareness campaign organised by WRAP (Waste & Resources Action Programme) and forms part of the wider Recycle Now initiative. The campaign provided a great platform to educate UK consumers on the benefits and simplicity of recycling aluminium and plastic drink containers by demonstrating Coca-Cola's support of Recycle Week.

Objective

Inspire consumers to recycle more while highlighting Coca-Cola's packaging and recycling achievements and commitment to the environment.

The challenge

Instigating media interest and dialogue about recycling presented difficulties as the topic had received a lot of exposure and other environmental matters such as energy and technology were in the limelight. Sourcing artists and locations as well as regional and national recycling statistics and government spokespeople in a limited time frame presented further difficulties.

The strategy

By educating consumers on the tangible benefits and simplicity of recycling aluminium drink cans, through marking the beginning of Recycle Week 2008 (2–8 June) with Coke can sculptures modelled on four of Britain's most prominent landmarks:

- Big Ben, London
- Angel of the North, Gateshead
- Clifton Suspension Bridge, Bristol
- Bullring Bull, Birmingham.

The PR consultancy Grayling sourced and briefed regional artists who had a passion for recycling. Each Coke can sculpture had to be visually striking and strong enough to generate regional media coverage, with Big Ben appealing to both London and national audiences. To generate a national story, the use of all four images was necessary, timing was crucial, and all images had to be available before Recycle Week began on 2 June.

The Coke can creation programme fitted the wider Coca-Cola environmental strategy which focused on minimizing the impact of Coke products and operations in three key ways:

- reducing energy use
- reducing water use
- driving sustainable packaging and recycling.

Execution

Local authority support was key in securing photocall locations near the 'real' landmarks and in ensuring synergy with other local events running during Recycle Week. Risk assessments were conducted at each site to ensure maximum impact.

Nationally renowned sculptor Robert Bradford unveiled his six-metre high impression of Big Ben made entirely out of plastic and aluminium Coke drink containers on London's Southbank with Westminster's Big Ben dominating the background (see Figure 1.3).

For the second sculpture, local up-and-coming artist Samuel McGeever unveiled his monumental five-tonne impression of the Angel of the North—with an eight-metre wing span—in the hills just by Gormley's Angel, Newcastle, creating a surreal angel shadow.

The third sculpture, by local artist Stuart Murdoch, was unveiled as an eight-metre span impression of the Clifton Suspension Bridge, Bristol which was erected by the river basin below the bridge.

Finally, local artist Pamina Stewart unveiled her impression of the Bullring Bull, Birmingham, next to the original, producing striking photos (see Figure 1.4).

Extensive print and broadcast media coverage appeared regionally and nationally far exceeding the original targets and creating positive comment about Coca-Cola and its recycling efforts.

PR Tool

Photocall

A picture in the media can gain more interest for an organization than a written story—its effects are more immediate and often more powerful. It can also drive a newsworthy story out to the media which is followed by the media release. Photocalls are constructed to control the message and to get media attention. Many demonstrations start when the media arrives. The success of any photocall lies in the preparation:

Preparation

1. Select the location and prepare it with branded materials. Think about the weather and time of day to best reach relevant media.

2. Brief the celebrity/other personalities and arrange for them to arrive at the location on time. Be clear to them on how the photographs will be used (they may require a contract and a fee).

3. Commission and brief a photographer by first reviewing their portfolio to see if they are appropriate. They must be able to send photographs to the media and have their own success stories.

4. Identify the photo desks and contact them one week beforehand and again two days before and then once more on the day. Discuss the photocall with them, building in aspects which they want.

5. Develop a media statement to go with the photograph.

6. Arrange for coverage to be monitored.

The shoot

1. Contact photo desks the evening before the shoot, or that morning if it is an afternoon shoot.

2. Organize props and people in the shot; confirm with the commissioned photographer so photos are definitely taken.

3. Start activities when the photographers arrive. Make sure the people photographed are doing something active to gain photographic interest.

4. Direct the shoot—get the shots required, otherwise photojournalists can hijack the shoot and move props and celebrities to create their own agenda; therefore stay in charge.

5. Get contact details of all journalists attending to follow them up.

6. Provide information to go with the photographs to ensure the story gets across.

After the shoot

1. Send photographs to the media who did not attend.

2. Some of these will not have such tight deadlines as their publication dates are later, eg glossy magazines, but ensure that the photograph will still be relevant on their publication date.

3. Report to the organization.

4. Thank everyone for attending.

Ideas for photoshoots

For a photoshoot, the photograph should show something which the media's photo desk cannot normally get. It can be a very large product or an unusual point of view, eg a photocall to promote a book exhibition showing a photograph of a miniature book under a magnifying glass.

Branding should be evident but must be subtle, maybe on a chair, a bag, or a hat. Celebrities can create interest and encourage the media to attend a photocall but only if they are connected to the campaign. Just having a celebrity will not get the coverage wanted. Make the picture active and have props which people can hold or sit on.

Go to the Online Resource Centre to access examples of current photocalls in the media

Summary

Today public relations is complex and technical and precise, whereas in the early days the science of PR was relatively straightforward, where one had practitioners with general experience and knowledge. Now practitioners are needed who are very specialized in the field in which they work because the world is increasingly competitive and more and more products are competing in a market with less and less money.

However, PR is divided not only into different types of industries or interests but also into different public relations expertise which require specialized knowledge and skills.

Public relations has evolved from the need to communicate to different publics by a diverse range of organizations, governments, and individuals which all have their own reasons for wanting to reach people. It has been influenced by national and world events, communications technology, economics, and the development of different industries.

Today public relations is also driven by a rapidly developing media communications technology creating a fragmented media, with more diverse publics who have many different and overlapping interests. Identifying these publics and reaching them must also recognize their influence on organizations. Now public relations is evolving as it helps both publics and organizations to adapt to each other and reach mutually fulfilling relationships.

Public relations is a people industry, where identifying and understanding people's opinions and desires and developing them alongside an organization's objectives requires enormous creativity, knowledge, and ability to move with the times. This has been, and always will be, the key to PR excellence.

Discussion points

A. PR definition: these discussions explore the definitions of PR

1. In a group, brainstorm your own definitons of PR and then write them down.

    Then review the definitions from the CIPR, the PRCA, and the PRSA and develop a grid, which shows what they have in common and where they differ.

    Draw out commonalities between your brainstorm and the grid of the professional organizations.

2. Review the case study in this chapter and see if you can apply it to the CIPR definition.

    Where does it fit/not fit? Is there a better fit with one of the other definitions or with your group brainstorming?

    How has this changed your view of PR?

3. Go to the Online Resource Centre and download the PR interview template which provides draft questions.

    Interview a PR practitioner and ask their definition of PR.

    Use this to bring your interview to class and compare with the others as well as with the professional definitions and the brainstorming ones.

B. PR history: using history to formulate PR campaigns

1. Go to the Online Resource Centre to view the video *Century of the Self*.

    How does Bernays make you feel? Do you admire/dislike his style—why?

    Can you see yourself in his role?

2. Describe one of the PR campaigns mentioned in the video and why it was successful.

3. List the PR terminology as you listen to the video and discuss their meanings.

C. PR timeline: understanding PR history to build on ideas

1. Review the timeline and identify the key communications technology events.

    How do you think each of these has changed public relations?

    What opportunities have these opened up for PR?

    What do you think current communications technology is doing for PR?

    What events do you think have created an impetus for PR development?

4. Identify the use of opinion polls and the effect they had on PR. Can you see the use of opinion polls today?

References

Ambler, T. and Witzel, M. (2004) *Doing Business in China*. London: Routledge

BBC (2000) 'Gap and Nike: No Sweat', 15 October. Available at: http://news.bbc.co.uk/2/hi/programmes/panorama/970385.stm

BBC News Science (2009) 'Oxfam Pushes For Climate Deal', 28 August. Available at: http://news.bbc.co.uk/2/hi/science/nature/8225895.stm

Blythe, A. (2010) 'Priced to Sell', PR Week, 23 June: Available at: http://www.prweek.com/uk/news/search/1011915/Priced-sell/

Central Office of Information (2010) 'History of COI'. Available at: http://www.coi.gov.uk/aboutcoi.php?page=87

Chartered Institute of Marketing. Available at: http://www.cim.co.uk/home.aspx

Chartered Institute of Public Relations (2010). Available at: http://www.cipr.co.uk/content/about-us

Confederation Européenne des Relations Publiques. Available at: http://www.cerp.org/

Coombs, T. and Holladay, T. (2007) It's Not Just PR: Public Relations In Society. Oxford: Blackwell

Cornelissen, J. (2008) Corporate Communication: A Guide to Theory and Practice (2nd edn). London: Sage

Cutlip, S., Center, A., and Broom, G. (2006) Effective Public Relations (9th edn). Upper Saddle River, NJ: Pearson

Edwards, L. (2009) 'Public Relations Origins: Definitions and History' in R. Tench and L. Yeomans (eds) Exploring Public Relations. Harlow: Prentice Hall

Encyclopaedia Britannica (2010) 'History and Society: Propaganda'. Available at: http://www.britannica.com/EBchecked/topic/478875/propaganda/23822/Propaganda-and-related-concepts#ref=ref387465

Global Alliance of Public Relations. Available at http//www.globalliance.org

Green, D. (2008) 'From Poverty to Power' Available at: http://www.oxfam.org/en/policy/from_poverty_to_power/

Greenpeace (2010) 'Protest at BP's London headquarters'. Available at: http://www.greenpeace.org/international/en/multimedia/photos/Protest-at-BPs-London-headquarters/

Heath, R. (2001) 'Defining the Discipline' in R. Heath (ed) Handbook of Public Relations. London: Sage

Hilpern, K. (2008) 'Make an Impact; PR is a Popular Profession for Both Graduates and Career Changes', The Independent, 16 June. Available at: http://www.independent.co.uk/news/media/make-an-impact-r-is-a-popular-profession 16/06/2008

Institute of Practitioners in Advertising. Available at www.ipa.co.uk

International Public Relations Association. Available at http://www.ipra.org.

L'Etang, J. (2004) Public Relations in Britain: A History of Professional Practice in the Twentieth Century. London: Routledge

Lewis, L. (2008) 'Greenpeace Wages War at Sea Against Tuna Fishers in Pacific Ocean', The Sunday Times, 23 April. Available at: http://www.timesonline.co.uk/tol/news/world/asia/article3799365.ece

Miller, D. and Dinan, W. (2000) 'The Rise of the PR Industry in Britain 1979-98', European Journal of Communication 15/5: 4–35

Museum of Public Relations. Available at: http://www.prmuseum.com/bernays/bernays_1990.html

Mylrea, P. (2008) 'Reminder That PR is a Force for Good', PR Week UK, 26 June. Available at: http://www.prweek.com/uk/news/search/823292/Reminder-PR-force-good/

Penning, T. (2008) 'First Impressions: US Media Portrayals of Public Relations in the 1920s', Journal of Communication Management 12/4: 344–58

PR Week (2007) 'Red Lorry Yellow Lorry to Build Gorillabox Brand', 19 October. Available at: http://www.prweek.com/uk/news/search/747117/Red-Lorry-Yellow-Lorry-build-Gorillabox-brand/

PriceWaterhouseCoopers (2005–2010) 'Corporate Brand Reputation & Corporate Social Responsibility'. Available at: http://www.pwc.com/gx/en/retail-consumer/brand-reputation/corporate-brand-reputation-corporate-social-responsibility.jhtml

PRSA Public Relations Defined (2010). Available at: http://www.prsa.org/AboutPRSA/PublicRelationsDefined/

Public Relations Consultancy Association (2010). Available at: http://www.prca.org.uk/

Raupp, J. and van Ruler, B. (2006) 'Trends In Public Relations and Communication Management Research: A Comparison Between Germany and The Netherlands', Journal of Communication Management 10/1: 18–26

Review of Government Communications. Available at: http://archive.cabinetoffice.gov.uk/gcreview/

Van Ruler, B., Vercic, D., Flodi, B., and Buetschi, G. (2001) 'Public Relations in Europe. A Kaleidoscope Picture', Journal of Communication Management 6/2: 166 75

World Health Organization (2010) 'Tobacco Free Initiative World No Tobacco Day 2010'. Available at: http://www.who.int/tobacco/en/

2 Public opinion and communication models

Learning outcomes

1. Demonstrate an understanding of public opinion by describing its development and its link to public relations.

2. Identify the building blocks of the models which led to the current understanding of communications.

3. Be able to analyse the progression of public relations and discuss the validity of the two-way symmetrical model.

4. Explore how communication models and communications theory can be used to analyse how the organization is viewed in the media.

5. Explore how publics develop attitudes and opinions using reception theory uses and gratifications; semiotics; and also the psychology of communications.

6. Be able to develop a message content analysis for use in a public relations proposal.

Practitioner Insight

Michael Brown
Managing Director
Beatwax

How did you get into PR?

I took an unusual route into the industry. My background is in the music business both as a manager and artist. I came into that business at the tail end of the 1980s. The struggle with the effects of what was then termed new media on their business model was beginning to take hold and the future was not looking good for recorded music.

I had two multi-album contracts with first Arista and then MCA just before it became Universal. My ultimate failure in this business was actually a failure of marketing on the part of the record company rather than failure of talent and ambition on the side of the artist, and I needed to know the machinations of marketing to understand why such failure was possible. I came into PR and marketing because of this.

What is your thinking behind publicity stunts?

A stunt works most effectively if you are able to portray a narrative which has depth behind the image you are trying to create. Our stunt of Homer Simpson beside the chalk giant shows a narrative arc in the image which provided multiple layers of story and an irresistible reason for editors to run with it. The image depicts Homer practically naked cowering from a sexually aggressive advance by the chalk giant. We were able to use the fact that the giant sports an erection and is brandishing a giant club above his head as the set up to a joke. The punch-line is that Homer defends himself in the only way he knows—by protecting himself with his own giant donut. The resulting imagery is funny and therefore irresistible to picture editors.

To make the image more than just a picture caption a depth is needed. The juxtaposition of Homer, a classic American pop culture icon, against the world heritage icon could be seen as an act of cultural vandalism. We capitalized on the protests of various special interest groups and made them part of the story; the Pagans denounced it as an affront to the ancient fertility symbol—it is the sort of thing that could happen in an episode of *The Simpsons*.

How does your work influence target publics?

Beatwax deals in affecting consumer choice. That is, shall I go to see this film over that film? Should I buy this product over another product? Our best work provides an extra spike to the wider marketing campaign, a sit up and take notice moment close into the launch date that gives a launch a competitive media edge just before the consumer is poised to make a purchase option.

What is the value of celebrity in public relations?

Celebrity is now, and has probably always been, a blunt instrument. However, if your campaign can find a genuine reason for living without need for a celebrity association, because it resonates at a deeper level than the superficiality of celebrity, then you are on to a winner. At Beatwax we have strived to find PR solutions in which the work itself is the star of the campaign; to conceive ideas that are so spectacular, or of genuine human interest, that celebrity is not needed.

How important is social media in public relations?

Social media is a key part of the mix and in many cases it is the most important platform to consider as this is the place where most of your work, thanks to the speed of the medium, will now break whether you want it to or not. There is no such thing as an embargo in social media. This has advantages in that even the most regionalized campaigns can quickly achieve truly global reach and ramp up your results delivery. Used correctly, social media can give greater longevity to your work long after the initial news spike at traditional media as social media groups share, discuss, debate, and critique your work to create a deeper level of interaction with the story.

What has been your most exciting project?

Our promotion of *Up*. This was a logistical operation. Setting aside the actual process of building an airworthy prototype hot air balloon that looked like a house being airlifted by a huge bunch of fairground balloons, we had to engage with multiple levels of local authority, governmental, and private stakeholder organizations and gently move them all forward to a favourable decision: granting us permission to proceed. Convincing them that our vision could be done safely was no mean feat. That was a glorious feeling and relief at the end of a very drawn-out logistical operation.

2.1 Definition

Public relations shows that influencing public opinion can achieve objectives ranging from persuading people to become aware of healthy eating to promoting a politician so people will vote for them. Public relations must be able to identify the current public opinion and either consolidate it or move it to a new position.

Opinion, according to Price (1992: 46) is the 'expression of an attitude with words'.

McQuail (2010: 515) defines an **attitude** as an underlying predisposition or feeling towards something. When an attitude is communicated it becomes an opinion. When an opinion develops it is then expressed through behaviour such as buying something or deciding not to buy something, voting for someone or, as reported below, avoiding certain groups of people.

The *Guardian* (2009) reported research which found there had been 'overwhelmingly negative coverage' on teenage boys which 'focused disproportionately on crime' and referred to them as 'yobs, thugs, sick, feral, hoodie, louts, heartless, evil, frightening, scum, monsters, inhuman and threatening' (see Figure 2.1). Teenage boys interviewed about the media coverage said they now avoided teenage boys they did not know and almost half claimed it was because of the 'media stories'. The representation of this age group in the media created a public opinion about teenage boys that also influenced their own behaviour.

However, what does the expression 'public opinion' really mean? Is it what everyone expresses, or just what some people express? Could it be what the media are reporting or is it just the comments of a few influential people. Maybe it is just the opinion of those who shout the loudest.

Collective view

One definition of public opinion is called the **general will** or **consensus** or **collective view**. It assumes that people have come to an agreement on something. However, this could simply mean that a group, or some authoritative individuals, have put forward their own very strong opinion and have suppressed the opinion of others in the process. For example, one UK doctor's research published in 1998, but later retracted in 2010, led to many

Fig 2.1
Teenage boys received negative media coverage
Source: Copyright OUP

parents having the opinion that certain childhood vaccinations led to autism and for more than a decade many children were not vaccinated for many contagious illnesses.

Aggregate view

Another definition of public opinion is the majority or aggregate view, which means the opinion of more than half the public as measured by opinion polls, that is more than half agree. This is how reputation is built—it is formed through a drawing together of individual opinions. Phillips and Young (2009: 4) state that:

> Reputation can be seen as an aggregation of lots of individual opinions, some derived from personal experience, such as buying something that does not work any longer, but more often it is a synthesis of fragments of information derived from a wide range of sources, some more accurate than others such as not having taken a particular course but have heard others talk about it.

As L'Etang (2008) points out, public opinion changes all the time and public relations must work with those changes. This can be revealed through analysing opinion polls, media coverage, the internet, scientific research, etc. When developing a public relations programme the practitioner must first identify the prevailing public opinion on an issue, or an organization and its trends.

When drawing all these together to develop a picture of public opinion, Price (1992) argues for the need to consider the focus of the opinions, what has influenced the responses, how well considered are the responses, the context, whether there are strong opinions and whether other views are included.

Spiral of silence

Many people are guided by what they think is the public opinion. Research by the German scientist, Noelle-Neumans, from 1974 to 1991 on how people were influenced through the mass media, found that individuals fear being isolated and society threatens to isolate people who are different (McQuail 2010). Noelle-Neumans identified that people are more likely to conceal their views if they think they are in a minority. For example, today few people would admit that they did not agree with recycling as it would go against the majority view. The result is that the assumed dominant views become even more dominant and the minority views are seldom heard. Noelle-Neumans called this suppression of opinion the spiral of silence or the tyranny of the majority.

Public relations often uses this theory to shape public opinion. It will spearhead media stories by creating a public opinion survey to gain results which generate media headlines about people raising a particular issue. Through the spiral of silence theory more people are encouraged to support the issue. This can often have the effect of normalizing or promoting a particular point of view, thereby shaping public opinion. Advocacy often works like this where celebrities speak out about an issue and this gets more people to support it.

Public opinion is caused by events and so is usually reactive, rather than proactive. For instance, the BP oil spill in the Gulf of Mexico in 2010 led to outrage at the ecological disaster it caused. Environmental groups such as Greenpeace led the news issue, and it appeared in the media where the public formed an opinion, reacting to what they saw and read.

Public opinion and polls

In the early twentieth century, mass media, such as newspapers and radio, along with better education and growing literacy, meant that social classes were starting to form into crowds and publics with their own opinions and wills and were no longer simply turning to the state and taking on the view of the government (Price 1992). In turn, as social and psychological sciences emerged, researchers started analysing the influence of emotional and intellectual factors on public opinion and how it could be controlled or modified.

Researchers found that surveying a sample of a population was quite accurate in representing what the larger population thought. This meant that not everyone needed to be surveyed—just a small proportion of the defined group.

These social surveys put people into demographic groups such as age, income, and gender and then identified the opinions belonging to these groups. As more consumer goods became available and people had more disposable income to buy these products, surveys were used to find out what people wanted so that companies selling these products could form marketing plans that focused on addressing the desires of specific groups. In the same way, surveys were also very useful in monitoring the success of political campaigns.

In 1922, Walter Lippman wrote about the growing interest in the nature and power of public opinion (Cutlip et al 2006: 104). Social scientists explored public opinion and how it was affected by mass communications. In the 1930s, some communications researchers and public relations professionals, such as Edward Bernays, and Harold Lasswell (a leading American political scientist and communications theorist), argued that propaganda was needed for the 'efficient conduct of a modern society' (Glander 1996: 374). They believed that people needed to be controlled and influenced in line with what was appropriate for the nation's well-being. Sophisticated opinion surveys and measurements were introduced at this time and Bernays used these for his public relations. For example, for the Torches of Freedom campaign described in chapter 1, Bernays commissioned research by a psychoanalyst to find out why women smoked, and the results suggested that women felt empowered though smoking. Bernays then released this research to the media to encourage more women to buy cigarettes.

Modern public opinion polls deal with important current political, social, and economic issues and provide an opportunity for government officials, public and private institutions, and the public to know where people stand (Gallup 1981).

Influencing public opinion is challenging and a public relations practitioner must not only know what public opinion is, but also the processes involved in its development in order to know when information is exchanged among people and when to intervene to influence it.

2.2 Historical and theoretical context

The study of public relations links sociology, psychology, and communications theory as well as strategic business management. Over the years these disciplines have helped to create an understanding of how people communicate with each other and the influences on their communication.

The process of communication

How people communicate has been developed into diagrammatic models which have evolved over time reflecting the role of the latest communications technology and how people interact with it.

Shannon and Weaver model

An early and influential communications model was created in 1949 by two scientists, Claude Shannon and Warren Weaver, who carried out a communications research project for the Bell telephone company. Their model aimed to guide engineers to find the best way of transmitting signals from one location to another (Shannon 1949). As a result they developed the significant linear communication model showing a sender communicating a message to a receiver and the transmission interference that can distort the message and its meaning (Windahl et al 2009)).

Shannon and Weaver (cited in Windahl et al 2009) showed that certain information that was not intended by the sender is unavoidably added to the message. This additional input, called noise, affects the meaning of the message and can come from the receiver's own knowledge, attitudes, or beliefs as well as from transmission interference such as poor reception (see Figure 2.2). This model was developed further by two other communications researchers.

Osgood and Schramm model

Wilbur Schramm, a prominent US communications expert and educational director at the war office during the Second World War, advised the government on communica-

Fig 2.2
Adaption of the Shannon and Weaver model of communication

Source: S. Harrison (1995) *Public Relations— An Introduction:* Fig 3.1, p 30. Permission: Cengage Learning EMEA International Thompson Press

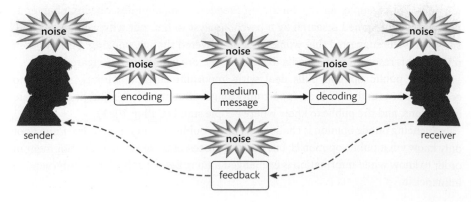

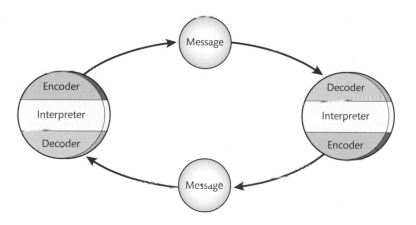

Fig 2.3
The Osgood and Schramm circular model

Source: London: Sage, McQuail and Windahl (1983) *Communication Models for the Study of Mass Communication:* Fig 2.2.3, p 19. Permission: Pearson EMA.

tion issues, which led to him creating communication research centres in US universities (Glander 1996). In 1956 he and a university colleague, Charles Osgood, a psychology professor, recognized that the sender and receiver encode and decode messages simultaneously, according to their own attitudes and the context of the message. They then respond to the decoded and encoded messages based on their own ongoing interpretations, creating immediate or delayed feedback which, in turn, is responded to by the other participant. The two colleagues used this information to transform the Shannon and Weaver model into a circle, called the Osgood and Schramm circular model (see Figure 2.3).

The model showed how both participants interpret the information and the feedback from each other, creating meaning and an endless circle of two-way communication, although it is still a linear process as there is no interactivity from other sources. For example, university tutors mark assessments to provide feedback to help students

Fig 2.4
Assessment marking is a form of encoded feedback

Source: Copyright OUP

improve on their next assessment. This is delayed feedback as students have to wait for their work to be marked. In addition, the tutor encodes the message in his or her own understanding of how it should be marked and in the context of other students' work.

The student then decodes the feedback based on what he or she was expecting, that is their own attitudes, and also what other marks they have which form their context. The student may then feed back their own comments to the tutor or change their standard of work to which the tutor will respond and this goes on. A circle of communication has been set up, yet it is still a linear process going from one participant to another and then back again (see Figure 2.4).

Westley and MacLean model

The Osgood and Schramm model did not focus on the role of the mass media. However, communication researchers, Westley and MacLean, developed a model in 1957 called the Westley and MacLean model (Windahl et al 2009) (see Figure 2.5), which showed the process of communication performed by the communicators involved in mass communications and their roles as follows:

1. The advocacy role which has the purpose of influencing people. In mass communications this role can be played by many sources of information such as the public relations consultant of an organization.

2. The channel's role that is, how the medium gives the information to the public. This model was the first to introduce the idea of the media as having a gatekeeper role where a journalist selects information it wants from a diverse range of sources. This is involved in setting the news agenda where the media decides the news topic and how it is constructed.

Fig 2.5
Westley MacLean model

Source: Permission: Sage S. Windahl and B. Signitzer with J. Olson (2009) *Using Communication Theory: An Introduction to Planned Communication* (2nd edn). London: Sage, p 154

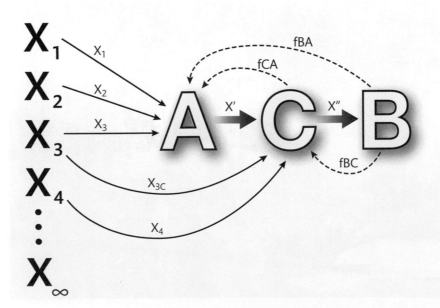

3. The behavioural role, that is how the publics take in the messages, which is usually from reading, viewing, or listening. The media can also get information from other sources such as events, publics, competing organizations, and other media, which now include chatrooms, blogs, and newsgroups and will filter that to the publics.

For example, information on the launch of a movie would be generated by the producer/director or on their behalf by the public relations practitioner. This would be delivered to the journalist in order to raise awareness about the movie and encourage ticket sales. The journalist has an important role as gatekeeper and may decide not to use this information or may just select some of it and take information from other sources. This may be about the actors, the movie's success in other countries, or even something quite different such as a fall in general movie ticket sales.

Consequently, the journalist acts as gatekeeper, filtering a variety of information from diverse sources to create at least one news story which may be quite unexpected from what the public relations practitioner anticipated.

Traditional media has limited feedback but publics can respond by writing letters to the media, phoning with comments, or completing research questionnaires. The public could also respond to the movie producers directly, as well as through their action of buying movie tickets. This model shows feedback from all the participants, from the media to the advocate and from the public to the media and to the advocate via the media and directly. With the internet there is the opportunity of interactivity and consequently greater feedback and therefore the media has less of a gatekeeper role (see Figure 2.6).

Fig 2.6
There is more interactivity over the internet
Source: Copyright OUP

Historically, public relations focused on developing strong relationships with journalists, taking on board their feedback, and building relationships with them in order to influence their opinion. Now with the internet, the public relations practitioner has more **unmediated** contact with publics and can receive direct feedback to which it needs to respond.

The Westley and MacLean model is not a closed loop but shows the connection between sender, the media, and the receiver as well as how they interacted with other information sources. This shows how a Journalist may change the information given to them in order to select what fits their **media agenda**, they may add other information, use a different spokesperson, and even take a different angle than intended which can be altered regularly and unexpectedly to address the feedback they receive from the public.

Practitioners need to ensure that there are numerous opportunities to reach people and that the messages are communicated through many different media to which the publics have access.

The Maletzke model

Psychology research continued looking at communication models and in 1963, Gerhard Maletzke, a German mass communications researcher, developed a model showing that communication is an overall interactive process affected by the motivations, environment, and personal influences of the sender, message, and channel as well as feedback from all these sources (Windahl et al 2009). This was called the **Maletzke model** and identified that the sender develops the message in a certain way specific to his or her own style, culture, and background, and additionally that their personality and motivation influences how they communicate (see Figure 2.7).

Public relations specializes in making messages appeal to a particular public and this also affects the way a message is developed.

Fig 2.7
The Maletzke model

Source: Courtesy of Permisson: Sage S. Windahl and B. Signitzer with J. Olson (2009) *Using Communication Theory: An Introduction to Planned Communication* (2nd edn). London: Sage, p 160

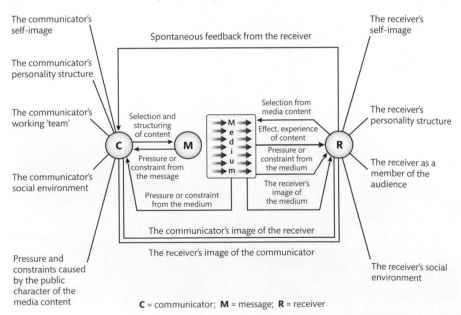

C = communicator; **M** = message; **R** = receiver

For example, a message transmitted in a press release follows an inverted pyramid style (see next chapter). This means the most important information is at the beginning, it must be interesting and immediately attention grabbing and the journalist will be inclined to read further and then use the story for their particular media outlet.

How a public receives a message depends on personal factors and their environment, as well as what media they use. Public relations practitioners must be aware of their publics and the influences on them in order to control how a message is developed and consequently interpreted. They need to ensure the words and images used fit the public's level of understanding as well as their cultural, educational, and social backgrounds. That is why assessing a public and their opinion is so vital at the beginning of a campaign and is often carried out through public opinion surveys.

Decision-making and psychology

Understanding how people are influenced and how they make decisions is a crucial aspect of public relations. Psychological research has helped understand how people are persuaded and affected by the media.

The hypodermic needle

The hypodermic needle model suggested that the mass media had a direct, immediate, and powerful effect on a mass audience (Rogers 1983: 272). In the 1930s, a group of German researchers, called the Frankfurt School, fled Nazi Germany for the UK as they feared state control of their country through the mass media. They saw the effects of advertising on radio and film and how the Nazi Party in Germany used the media for its propaganda and was able to influence people's behaviour. Through their research they suggested that the mass media message simply went inside people's minds and was unchanged and accepted (McQuail 2010). They believed that the new mass media had a very strong effect and that people were passive and could be easily persuaded. The advent of television suggested that the media would be used to influence behaviour. This theory, also known as the magic bullet, was represented as a hypodermic needle in the form of a diagram, and was one of the first communication models (see Figure 2.8).

The hypodermic needle model assumed people would act in a certain way to the content of the media message. It suggested that people were socially isolated and not influenced by anyone else when using the media and therefore completely persuaded by its messages. Eventually, more sophisticated communications research methods gave more precise research and doubt was cast on the model. The hypodermic needle model is now considered as showing an 'overconfidence' in the media (Windahl et al 2009).

However, McQuail argues (2010: 51) that the fall of communism, the Balkan wars, and the two Gulf wars have confirmed the media as having a powerful role in any international power struggle where public opinion is a factor.

Between the two world wars, mass communication was considered to have very strong effects. There was debate about the positive and negative role of the mass media with many arguing that it was really a tool for propaganda, which was considered to be a manipulation of the unconscious. With the onset of the Second World War, US

Fig 2.8
Hypodermic needle or magic bullet
Source: Permission Pearson EMA. McQuail and Windahl (1983) *Communication Models for the Study of Mass Communication:* Fig 3.2.1, p 62

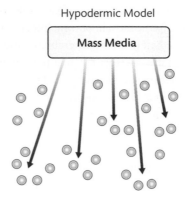

Hypodermic Model

Mass Media

Isolated individuals constituting a mass

government organizations funded social science research, especially propaganda, so that they could understand how to raise morale and influence public opinion to support the war. The US Office of War Information developed persuasive news stories from the War Department to support the war effort and encourage men to serve in the forces (Cutlip et al 2006: 112).

The two-step flow and the multi-step flow

In the early 1950s, television was making a big impact on American life, changing politics, leisure patterns, and social behaviour, reinforcing the view that it was too influential in changing public opinion. However, in the 1940s and 1950s two communications researchers, Katz and Lazarsfeld, built on research from the hypodermic needle model showing media information needed a personal influence to really persuade people (McQuail 2010). These influences were called opinion leaders, that is, people such as teachers, doctors, parents, and lawyers, who were considered by their peers to have specialized knowledge in a particular area. Opinion leaders took the information from the media to their own social groups. This process of opinion leaders mediating the messages in order to pass on the information was called a two-step flow model. Katz and Lazarsfeld (McQuail 2010) then developed a multi-step flow model which shows that opinion leaders get information from other opinion leaders and not just the media and communicate to others in a socially mediated process (see Figure 2.9).

Opinion leaders can be individuals or groups most likely to have the greatest impact on the opinions of their peers. They pass on their interpretations of information as well as content from the mass media. The two-step flow model and subsequent multi-step flow model directly replaced the hypodermic needle theory and showed that information travels spontaneously and indirectly. It connects mass and interpersonal communications and shows that people communicate among themselves and are not simply isolated (Windahl et al 2009) (see Figure 2.10).

Fig 2.9
A doctor is an opinion leader
Source: Copyright OUP

Public relations campaigns use opinion leaders who may be celebrities or people respected in different areas to influence people. When developing a campaign it is important to identify opinion leaders and prioritize them depending on their reputation, position, ability to reach people, and their impact. For instance, the International Motorcycle Show at the NEC in Birmingham wanted to reach beyond the show's traditional male attendees between 35 and 49 years old (see Figure 2.11). Two opinion leaders, motorcycle adventurer Charley Borman and racing legend James Toseland, agreed to participate in a photocall to promote the show and speak to the media about the show, thereby successfully attracting younger attendees (PR Week 2008).

Research by Insignia Communications and the University of Wolverhampton on how spokespeople communicated during the swine flu crisis in 2009, found that those who

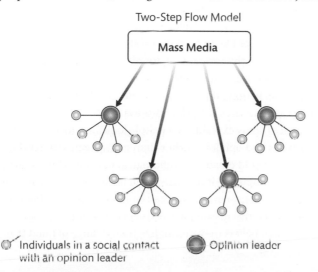

Two-Step Flow Model

Mass Media

Individuals in a social contact with an opinion leader

Opinion leader

Fig 2.10
Two-step flow model
Source: Two-step Permission: Pearson EMA. McQuail and Windahl (1983) *Communication Models for the Study of Mass Communication:* Fig 3.2.1, p 62

Fig 2.11
Motorbike manufacturers want to reach younger publics
Source: Copyright OUP

Fig 2.11
Motorbike manufacturers want to reach younger publics
Source: Copyright OUP

were serious yet personable and offered practical advice were the most effective in communicating on health issues. In contrast, spokespeople who appeared in a formal setting and did not give practical advice were less convincing (O'Reilly 2009).

Even in small social groups there are opinion leaders. When someone intends to travel to another country they may seek out an opinion leader in order to access additional information and it will be someone knowledgeable and experienced in this area. People can also be opinion leaders in one area and not in others.

The cognitive dissonance theory and binge drinking

Further research on how people were persuaded was carried out in 1957 by Leon Festinger, a US social psychologist, who developed the cognitive dissonance theory. His theory argued that people do not like to hold two views which are psychologically inconsistent. Perloff (2003) gives the example of cognitive dissonance occurring when someone knows that junk food is bad for them but still wants to eat it. These opposing views are not illogical but as Perloff points out, psychologically it does not make sense to engage in something that increases the risk of disease.

The cognitive dissonance theory explains that people look for information that agrees with their existing attitudes and opinions rather than going against what they believe or feel familiar with which would create a psychological tension. This means that it is generally easier to persuade someone if they are given information that supports their existing views; people prefer consonance—where the familiar is more important than the unfamiliar. However, cognitive dissonance also shows that when people find proof that contradicts their original beliefs they rationalize their change of mind to fit in with their new view.

Fig 2.12
Binge drinking campaign images have to be realistic
Source: Copyright OUP

When the UK government spent four million pounds on an anti-binge-drinking campaign in 2008 it showed 'TV images of young people injuring themselves, being violent and smearing vomit on themselves'. Research on the campaign found that young people saw this representation as 'laughably unrealistic' (BBC News 2009) and did not see their own drinking cultures reflected. This suggests that they experienced cognitive dissonance, as the messages went against their own existing views. The campaign only succeeded in alienating young people (see Figure 2.12).

Go to the Online Resource Centre to access the link to this campaign and a video of the advertisement

I Love Marrow

In contrast, a very creative and clever campaign encouraged young men, a notoriously difficult to reach target public, to join the bone marrow register, run by the Anthony Nolan Trust, an independent charity that provides life-saving bone marrow donors to patients with leukaemia. The Anthony Nolan Trust takes back lives from leukaemia by managing—and recruiting new donors to—the UK's most successful bone marrow register.

Men aged between 18 and 25 are the preferred choice as bone marrow donors because they can generally provide a greater volume of blood stem cells than female donors or men outside this age group. Despite this, they make up a small proportion of the register.

The campaign first identified the attitudes of young men, and then used a humorous and edgy viral video campaign to reach the target males. Further information was provided later about donating marrow, but only when the campaign had developed the men's attitudes and subsequent opinions.

The video campaign involved a fictional character, Brian Tyler, and his love of vegetable marrows. Brian encouraged viewers to 'love marrow' by signing up to the Anthony Nolan bone marrow donor register (see Figure 2.13). The film directed audiences to Brian's website http://www.ilovemarrow.com to find out more about the campaign and sign up to the register. The film was placed on YouTube and Brian had a page on social networking sites Facebook, Bebo, and MySpace and postcards promoting the campaign were distributed in bars, clubs, and cafes across the UK. The campaign also focused on building relationships with media targets, such as Touch, PopBitch, Stuff, and Men's Health, which had real cut through to young men.

This has resulted in an increased dialogue with the charity's prime target publics, the website's highest visitor rate in 18 months, and hundreds of potential new bone marrow donors. The website, http://www.anthonynolan.org, is continuing to receive hits.

🎬 **Go to the Online Resource Centre to access a link to this video**

Diffusion of innovations theory

Persuasion is key to public relations and psychology research has found that people are not all persuaded in the same way and some are not persuaded at all. However, in 1962, Rogers, a US communications researcher, presented research showing that most people go through the same process of accepting or rejecting new information but it happens over different time scales. He called this the diffusion of innovations theory. Innovation is the new idea or object and diffusion is how an innovation is communicated over time among members of a group and eventually adopted (Rogers 1983). It is important to understand the adoption process as a multi-step model, in order to develop the appropriate intervention techniques to encourage favourable decision making.

The diffusion of innovations process (Rogers 1983: 165) (see Figure 2.14):

1. Knowledge—this is the stage where people become aware of something and public campaigns are very active in raising awareness of a topic. A survey is often used in public relations as the starting point of a campaign in order to create news.

2. Persuasion—where individuals form an attitude and then an opinion. Interpersonal channels are an important influence at this stage.

3. Decision—where people begin to use or reject the innovation. A free sample would help to influence decision making.

4. Implementation— individuals begin using the innovation and must know where it is and how to use it.

5. Confirmation—people require reinforcement of information to make a decision, therefore the period after adoption is vital. In public relations it is important to reassure adopters that they have made the right decision. It is therefore essential for public relations to continue well after the implementation period and ensure that there are still positive messages at this time.

For example in 2008, the UK telephone directory enquiries service, 118118, wanted to encourage mobile phone texters to use their number. The PR consultancy, Resonate

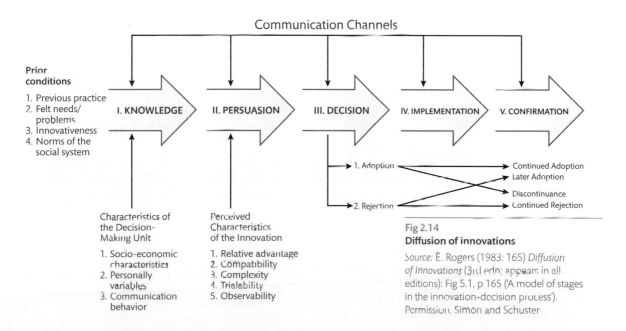

Fig 2.14
Diffusion of innovations

Source: E. Rogers (1983: 165) *Diffusion of Innovations* (3rd edn; appears in all editions): Fig 5.1, p 165 ('A model of stages in the innovation-decision process'). Permission. Simon and Schuster

Fig 2.15
Safe text pads attached to lampposts

Source: Image and Case Study courtesy of Alex Wood and Gavin Lewis, Resonate Communications, part of the Bell Pottinger Group

PR, created awareness by commissioning research that found in the previous 12 months, one in five Britons had suffered a walk-and-text injury. Publicizing these results in the media set the scene for 118 118 to launch a safe text campaign with the street safety body, Living Streets. Specialized 'Safe Text' pads were attached to lampposts in Brick Lane in London, a text accident blackspot, to protect pedestrians (see Figure 2.15). New safe texting guidelines, such as 'turn on predictive text', 'set up template messages', etc, were released and people could access these guidelines through texting 118 118. The campaign meant texters started to use the directory service. The subsequent media coverage, which also reported on the success of the campaign, reinforced the texters' actions. As a result, the campaign created an 11 per cent increase in text volume to the 118 118 service.

The elaboration likelihood model

In 1986 two US psychologists, Petty and Caciioppo, also looked at how people were persuaded. They showed that taking a peripheral or central route to making a decision depended upon their motivation. For example, when buying a washing machine a consumer may choose one based on rational and relevant issues such as its specifications according to its comparative price. That is, they give thoughtful consideration to their purchase and take a central route. However, if they are not motivated to analyse the price and how it relates to the machine's specifications, they may be persuaded through a campaign that uses a peripheral route with cues such as celebrity endorsement, where less relevant information is considered (Petty and Carcioppo 1986: 21).

The elaboration likelihood model found that when attitudes change owing to relevant arguments, ie the central route, they are longer lasting, more effective, and less likely to change than decisions made through a peripheral route where less relevant information is considered.

Propaganda

Propaganda overlaps with persuasion as both describe how people are influenced. Perloff (2003: 17) identifies three differences between propaganda and persuasion.

1. Propaganda has a mass influence through mass media whereas persuasion happens through mediated settings and in interpersonal and organizational contexts.

2. Propaganda is when a group totally controls the information, for example Nazi Germany, and although persuasion can be slanted and one-sided it allows for free flow of information and people can question the persuader.

3. Propaganda has negative connotations whereas persuasion—such as in a public health or education campaign—can produce positive outcomes.

The four public relations models

By 1984, in the midst of this growing understanding about communications processes, two key public relations researchers, James Grunig and Todd Hunt, had identified how public relations managed the communication between an organization and its publics. They drew on Katz and Kahn's earlier systems theory that compared communications in an organization to a new biology theory which showed that a system, such as an eco-system, is full of interacting elements that may or may not interact with the outside environment. This theory demonstrated that organizations which interact with the environment are open systems. Conversely, an organization that does not allow for any external interaction does not change and is a closed system.

Grunig and Hunt (1984) identified four communication models representing the different ways public relations is used, based on the systems theory.

Press agentry model (one-way communication)

This model originated in the nineteenth century and is when an idea, product, or person is being promoted and often uses publicity and stunts. The truth is not always considered important and is frequently exaggerated. Feedback from the environment is not considered relevant as the organization will not change. P.T. Barnum in the nineteenth century was recognized as using this model (see chapter 1) to create excitement around his circuses. Celebrities, such as Paris Hilton, reflect this model in the way they create attention and excitement through their highly publicized stunts.

A prime example of a publicity stunt is that mentioned by Michael Brown of Beatwax in the Practitioner Insight above, which was used to launch *The Simpsons* movie in 2007, and generated mass national and regional media coverage. Alongside the chalk giant of Cerne Abbas, Dorset, carved into the side of the rolling Dorset downs in the sixteenth century, Beatwax created a 70m x 50m giant Homer Simpson mirroring the actions of the giant and brandishing his very own magical symbol, a donut, which caused quite a stir. It took over two days to make and used more than 200 litres of biodegradable paint, creating a mockery of the national landmark in a cheeky and ironic manner epitomizing what has made *The Simpsons* so popular over the last 17 years (see Figure 2.16).

Fig 2.16
**Homer Simpson vs
Cerne Abbas Giant**

Source: Courtesy
of Beatwax

Public information model (one-way communication)

The second model called the public information model dates from the early twentieth century. The flow of information is one-way from the sender to the publics as feedback is not considered important, but the truth is. This model reflects situations in which the goal is to send vital information out to people and it is used for public service announcements concerning action during public disasters, and also describes drug and other health education campaigns. HM Revenue & Customs often run their public service campaigns using this model when it reminds taxpayers when to submit their tax returns.

⚉ **Go to the Online
Resource Centre to
access a link to more
footage on this
campaign**

Two-way asymmetric model

The two-way asymmetric model relies on persuasion and is used to influence behaviour such as buying or voting. It emerged after the Second World War when there were more consumer products available and people were encouraged to desire them. In addition, the government used this model to gain support in order to create political stability and generate national pride. Although this model shows that the organization considers the public's views in its communication, it then uses these to help to achieve its own goals. The communicator gathers information from publics to help it develop messages that are most likely to persuade publics to behave as the organization wants. As Dozier et al (1995: 13) argue, this information is not used to moderate the goals, objectives, policies, procedures, or other forms of the organization's behaviour.

The two-way symmetric model

The two-way symmetric model describes the public relations processes that arose in the 1960s and 1970s. The organization engages in a dialogue with its publics and both parties adjust their attitudes to achieve mutual understanding and consequently goals that benefit both sides. This model requires knowledge and understanding of publics to counsel senior management and execute communications programmes. It seeks to manage conflict and promote mutual understanding with key publics.

Communicators try to negotiate solutions to conflicts between their organizations and key publics and this model serves as a tool for compromise (Dozier et al 1995: 13). Working with activists to reach mutually agreeable solutions are typical of a two-way symmetrical model, where both parties have to make concessions and change their behaviour.

This is considered the ideal and most ethical communications model for public relations because power is evenly distributed (Windahl et al 2009). For example, the public relations model of universities is tending to be more transparent and invites a two-way symmetrical communication. University documents which highlight course development and any university issues and finances are usually accessible to the public. Availability of this information as well as access to lecturers and open discussions means the candidates are more likely to feel empowered in making their choice about the course they will take.

The US presidential campaign for Barack Obama allowed voters to contact the candidate's team through Twitter and find out where Barack was at any time of the day, as well as receive short campaign messages. It also allowed Obama's team to collect Twitter comments as public feedback and use them to develop more effective political messages that appealed to the voters. However, although many people may have thought this was two-way symmetrical communication where they were influencing the campaign, in reality it was asymmetrical as it was taking on the views of the public in order to develop more persuasive messages.

Grunig (2009) believes that social media shows great potential for two-way symmetrical communication and suggests that organizations should make more use of blogging in order to have a dialogue with people who want to communicate with them.

Grunig, in Heath (2009: 9) states that the two-way symmetrical model still requires persuasion and negotiation but also demands that both parties listen to each other and build understanding and relationships in an effort to resolve conflict rather than gain compliance.

Windahl et al (2009: 98) argue that participants in the communication process may arrive at mutual understanding but this may not lead to mutual agreement and collective action. They suggest that even mutual understanding is not always fully achieved as some people may understand or misunderstand more than others and this can trigger new solutions for a problem.

The two-way symmetrical model is increasingly important as publics are demanding to know more about an organization and expect it to consider the public's opinion. This is especially relevant when taxpayers' money is being used. Elliott and Koper (2002) believe that the two-way symmetrical model shows how people and communities make decisions about a company depending on how they relate to it. Persuasion is used in the two-way symmetrical model to negotiate with all parties and reach a mutual understanding. In addition, the public relations practitioner may first need to persuade the organization to develop more dialogue with its publics in order to reach a mutual understanding.

⊕ **Go to the Online Resource Centre to access Chelsea Football Club Twitter site and see if there is two-way communication**

Chelsea Football Club is making an effort to communicate to fans and has an official Twitter group (Markowicz 2009). Although other football clubs have their own Twitter groups, Chelsea expects its officials and players to 'tweet' and allows its fans to understand the 'inner workings of the club'. This open communication style is contrary to the usually tightly controlled communications of a football club and Twitter comments are likely to appear as news in other media as well as to stimulate two-way symmetrical communications.

2.3 Influences

The increasing diversity and amount of media and content make it harder to find out where information actually comes from and where it is going as it moves around the world at an ever-increasing speed as a result of the latest technology.

Instant news

News can be created immediately with ordinary people acting as journalists by sending their video or photographs of an event to the news channels (McQuail 2010: 139). People are creating content; they are no longer passively receiving information but are searching the media and interacting with it to create user-generated content such as blogs and social media sites. This means that the original linear model of a sender, messenger, channel, and receiver does not reflect what happens in this type of dynamic and complicated communication. The communication process has become a networked interactive system rather than information flowing from the sender to the receiver.

The new network model

Windahl et al (2009: 97) describe this new network media model as made up of individuals in groups, often referred to as nodes, and connected by communication flows. There is more equality in this new style of media communications as individuals can talk to people at all levels which changes their social and cultural boundaries, allowing everyone to feel as if they can talk to anyone. For example, in a Twitter group one can access the conversations of senior public figures and even 'follow' them.

Table 2.1 shows a list of these individuals and their roles (Windahl et al 2009: 101).

Identifying these groups is valuable as a public relations programme can use the different roles to influence public opinion. For example, as the 'stars' have wide networks, public relations could work with them to help to communicate the organization's messages. The microblogging site, Twitter, operates in this way as do single bloggers. These diverse relationships are bridging gaps between private and public worlds, that is, between organizations and people (Gregory 2008).

Public relations has moved on from merely being about press relations. Communications research shows that it is important to build and maintain relationships between an organization and its publics. An organization's sustained relationship with

Table 2.1 The roles of those in a network media model

Nodes	Roles
groups and clusters in a network	membership
individuals who link clusters together	liaison
individuals who are linked to many other individuals	star
individuals who have very few links	isolate
those who link the network to the environment	boundary spanning
those who link two or more groups together	bridge
those who do not communicate within a network	non-participatory

its publics will help to stave off the effects of a crisis. Elliott and Koper (2002) point out that today's public relations graduates must be able to develop and implement PR strategies and tactics that will help an organization to manage relationships.

The future

Appadurai (1990: 220), a US social-cultural anthropologist, explores how people deal with the massive amounts of information which can be accessed from the media. He believes people are becoming a matrix of activity influenced by powerful global flows of information which have no boundaries. These flows are changing and bringing together financial, ethnographic, and technological worlds. They are influencing each other and building a media world which is affecting how everyone lives and develops their ideas and culture.

2.4 Application to industry

The more that is known about how decisions are made, the more successful communication will be. For example, a university has a choice of how to persuade applicants to enrol on its courses. The elaboration likelihood theory suggests that if an applicant is not very well motivated in enrolling at university, they may take the peripheral route and make a choice based on irrelevant information such as the university's trendiness, the clothes other students wear, and even by a colourful brochure or an awe-inspiring website.

Alternatively, a more motivated applicant may have found out the best course on offer through taking a central route in their decision-making which means looking at relevant factors such as the graduation levels, calibre of the lecturers, the course's academic rigour, and subsequent vocational opportunities (see Figure 2.17).

Developing attitudes through a central route means the decisions will be much more certain. Students who take a peripheral route in decision making are much more likely to change their mind about the course.

Festinger's cognitive dissonance theory suggests that the university must lead applicants through arguments that they agree with—for example, that are 'consonant' with their beliefs—and argue against their objections. A student may be unsure about

Fig 2.17
Choosing a university takes a psychologically peripheral or central route

Source: Copyright OUP

enrolling because they are worried about their finances. A cognitive dissonance approach could emphasize the long-term financial gain of having a vocationally valued degree which provides potential for high earning power.

Transparent communications means that the boundaries of an organization are less obvious. When university applicants meet senior university personnel informally and can access social media networks set up by current students they gain an insiders' view which helps them to make choices. There are many different approaches and these just apply some theories. However, the first step in any communication is for it to reach its publics and attract their attention. This is outlined in the following award-winning case study.

Case Study

Promoting the Movie *Up*

Source: Courtesy of Beatwax

🌐 **Go to the Online Resource Centre to access a link to footage on this campaign**

Beatwax PR created a worldwide promotion for the release of the movie *Up*, a 2009 computer-animated comedy adventure film which opened the Cannes Film Festival that year. It centres on an elderly pensioner (Carl) who flies to South America in his house, suspended by helium balloons. On his journey he realizes that an eight-year-old boy (Russell) is a stowaway.

Beatwax created the theme of Up, Up and Away! Carl and Russell will be flying over a country near you!' The strategy mirrored the film's theme to superimpose Carl's journey onto the real world. It considered a 'what if' notion—what if people could look up and see

Carl on his journey in the skies? What if they could track that journey through the media and anticipate him flying over a town and wave him on his way? Imagine the excitement you would create on landing? Imagine the media partnerships you could tie in if you let some people fly in Carl's house? Imagine the photo opportunities as he flew by world-famous landmarks. The strategy was to go on a genuine PR adventure in true Disney style.

Beatwax materialized Carl's house and the thousands of balloons protruding out of his chimney in a specially designed envelope of more than 500 mini balloons singularly stitched to the 84,000 cubic foot basic shape, which when inflated looked like a cluster of helium balloons mimicking Carl's handiwork and wrapped around an inflatable Carl's house.

The balloon-powered house would perform a daring flight past a prominent landmark witnessed by local media in France, Germany, Italy, and the UK at the time of the movie's release.

This was supported by activity such as offering journalists balloon flights, enlisting the movie's voice talents for photo opportunities, and large cinemas featuring special days with a balloon visit, a screening of the film, and flights for guests which all built the balloon's apparent journey.

The balloon appeared in Disneyland Paris, at the French film premiere in Marseilles, the Chocolate Museum in Cologne, the Leipziger Platz in the centre of Berlin, and at Germany's two largest balloon festivals. In also appeared in Turin as part of a competition winners' day and a flyover of the Alps.

The UK saw a spectacular PR stunt as the balloon flew through the open drawbridge of London's Tower Bridge to global media acclaim, once the authorities had been persuaded that this could be done safely.

There was widespread global media coverage on all aspects of this campaign; the Tower Bridge stunt alone achieved broadcast news coverage at prime time on both NBC and ABC news in the USA and in news shows from China to Mexico (see Figure 2.18). A Google search reveals thousands of entries in multiple languages and the major television networks in each country featured their local activity. The widespread media coverage succeeded in ensuring audiences were aware of the movie and its storyline.

Fig 2.18
Going under Tower Bridge

Source: Courtesy of Beatwax

PR Tool

Media content analysis

Media content analysis explores what is said about an organization in the media and how it is said. It uncovers the reach of an organization's messages, changes in journalists and other opinion-formers' positions, and how different publics form opinions. Drawing these elements together gives valuable insights to shape a communications strategy.

According to Price (1998) media content analysis helps answer questions such as:

- How is an organization seen through the media?
- How effective is the public relations?
- What issues are important and what should be planned?
- Who are the new opinion leaders who can be involved?

Even the context of the media will affect how the message is interpreted. For example, if the news appears on an entertainment channel, the people watching it are more likely to be using the media for entertainment or as a diversion, not for information and therefore it will not have the same impact. This will also help to identify which media to target.

Table 2.2 can be used to help to analyse an organization in the media. It can help to understand the media opinion and identify opportunities for developing a campaign.

Table 2.2 Media analysis

Topic:				
Date				
Media and journalist: Who created the meaning?				
For whom is it intended?				
Demographic/psychographic				
Size/time				
Sources of information (organization, websites, publics)				
Message—significant phrases and words				
Opinion Leaders: Who are they? Are they formal/informal? What advice do they offer?				
Context				
Feedback				
Is it persuasive? How?				
Interaction with other topics				
Overall message				
Opportunities for campaign development				

This can be further analysed into the messages communicated in each type of media (social, traditional, or broadcast).

Summary

Public relations must identify the relevant public's opinion and then either consolidate it or develop it to achieve an organization's objectives. Public opinion is reactive and difficult to determine. It can be built in many ways such as through agenda setting, or through silencing other parties, through the communication of a group's view or alternatively the view of a powerful minority. It can be assessed through opinion polls which can segment the different types of people surveyed. Analysing media information can also identify how the public are being influenced. Practitioners need to understand communication processes in order to see how this can be done. Communication models give simple diagrammatic representations of communications processes and how they have changed over time.

The process of communication was influenced by technology and diagrammatic models have shown how this has progressed. The Shannon and Weaver model identified the sender and the receiver and how extraneous messages or noise could influence meaning. The Osgood and Schramm model looked at both parties encoding and decoding simultaneously and how feedback affects the interpretation of a message. The Westley and MacLean model incorporated how the media influenced communication and how it acted as a gatekeeper. Maletzkhe found that the development of messages is affected by the sender's own style, and who they are communicating with also influences the style of the information and how it is interpreted.

As mass media developed along with the advent of the Second World War, there was a fear that the media had the effect of a hypodermic needle and created and controlled public opinion. This led to examining the different ways people made decisions and what psychology influenced them. The two-step flow introduced the idea of opinion leaders and the multi-step flow showed that opinion leaders are also informed by other opinion leaders, showing that media information is mediated through social networks.

The study of persuasion revealed the concept of cognitive dissonance showing that people look for information that agrees with their own views. The diffusion of innovation theory shows that people go through a predictable decision-making process over different times to accept or reject an innovation. The elaboration likelihood model found that depending on their motivation, people base their decisions on relevant facts or are influenced by other relatively non-important factors but have less long-term conviction.

Key to public relations is systems theory that sees organizations as part of a system that interacts with itself and at different degrees with the outside world. Based on systems theory, Grunig and Hunt divided public relations practice into four models: press agentry, public information, asymmetric, and symmetric. The latter is considered the most favourable model for carrying out public relations as it invites dialogue and change from its internal and external publics in order to achieve mutual goals.

A more recent theory, the network theory model, where individuals form interconnected groups which guide the flow of information, can be applied to current public relations, especially those of online communities. In addition, convergence of the media means there is more information available than ever before and people may be dividing themselves into groups based on their knowledge area which public relations can target.

It is evident, when applying these theories to case studies, that communication is compli-cated and there are a diverse range of ways to manage communication between an organi-zation and its publics. Despite advanced technology and mass audiences, communication is increasingly through small networks or individuals who use emails, blogs, and discussion groups. At the same time, these connect to an ever-enlarging group of people and therefore an even greater share of information.

Within such a changing and fast-moving world with increasingly fragmented media, pub-lic relations cannot be guided by one communication model. It is the understanding of the different models and different influences which is needed in order to plan effective public relations programmes which influence public opinion.

Discussion points

A. Public opinion and public relations

In a group, discuss why public relations professionals should understand public opinion.

What campaigns can you identify that have understood public opinion before they started?

Identify some campaigns where public opinion has been changed dramatically—what persuasion techniques do you think were used?

B. Communication models

Review the case study in this chapter and the communication, psychology and PR models.

Discuss which ones fit. Can you see why more than one model can apply?

Discuss how this has changed your view of PR.

C. Communications technology

How do you think this is changing the communication models from a linear form? Discuss how the convergence of media is changing information flows.

What is your ideal media?

D. Decision-making process

Think about a decision you have made and the stages you have gone through. Did you need your decision to be reinforced afterwards? What happened to your decision-making pro-cess? Compare this to Rogers' adoption aspect of his diffusion of innovations theory.

References

Appadurai, A. (2001) 'Disjuncture and Difference in Global Cultural Economy' in S. During (ed) *A Cultural Studies Reader*. London: Routledge, pp 220–32

Bardoel, J. (1999) 'Beyond Journalism: A Profession between Information Society and Civil Society' in H. Tumber (ed) *News: A Reader*. New York: Oxford University Press, pp 379–91

Barthes, R. (1993) *Mythologies*. Vintage: London

Bowdon, F. (2009) 'Hoodie Winked', Guardian Online, 9 March. Available at: http://www.guardian.co.uk/media/2009/mar/09/media-news

BBC News (2008) 'Young "Ignore Alcohol Campaigns"', 28 December. Available at: http://news.bbc.co.uk/2/hi/uk_news/7801640.stm

Cutlip, S., Center, A., and Broom, G. (2006) *Effective Public Relations* (9th edn). Upper Saddle River, NJ: Pearson

Dozier, D. with Grunig, L. and Grunig, J. (1995) *Manager's Guide to Excellence in Public Relations and Communication Management*. Mahwah, NJ: Lawrence Erlbaum

Edwards, L. (2009) 'Public Relations Origins: Definitions and History' in R. Tench and L. Yeomans (eds) *Exploring Public Relations* (2nd edn). London: Prentice Hall

Elliott, G. and Koper, E. (2002) 'Public Relations Education from an Editor's Perspective', Journal of Communication Management 7/1: 21–33

Gallup, G. (1981) Gallup International Association. Available at http://www.gallup international.com/ home

Glander, T. (1996) 'Wilbur Schramm and the Founding of Communication Studies', Educational Theory (Summer), 46/3: 374–91

Gregory, A. (2008) 'Public Relations and Management' in A. Theaker (ed) *The Public Relations Handbook* (3rd edn). London: Routledge

Grunig, J. (2001) 'Two-way Symmetrical Public Relations: Past Present and Future' in R. Heath (ed) *Handbook of Public Relations*. Thousand Oaks, CA: Sage

Grunig, J. (2009) 'Paradigms of Global Public Relations in an Age of Digitalisation'. Available at: http://praxis.massey.ac.nz/prism on-line journ.html

Grunig, J. and Hunt, T. (1984) *Managing Public Relations*. New York: Holt, Rinehart and Winston

Harrison, S. (1995) *Public Relations—An Introduction*. London: Routledge

L'Etang, J. (2008) *Public Relations: Concepts, Practice and Critique*. London: Sage

McQuail, D. (2010) *McQuail's Mass Communication Theory*. London: Sage

Markowicz, C. (2009) 'Chelsea Goes All A-Twitter', PR Week, 1 April. Available at: http://www.prweek.com/uk/news/search/895816/Chelsea-goes-a-Twitter

O'Reilly, G. (2009) 'Study Outlines Traits of Best Spokespeople', PR Week, 4 December. London: Haymarket

Perloff, R. (2003) *The Dynamics of Persuasion: Communications and Attitudes in the 21st Century* (2nd edn). Mahwah, NJ: Lawrence Erlbaum

Petty, R. E. and Cacioppo, J. T. (1986) *Communication and Persuasion: Central and Peripheral Routes to Attitude Change*. New York: Springer-Verlag

Phillips, D. and Young, P. (2009) *Online Public Relations: A Practical Guide to Developing an Online Strategy in the World of Social Media* (2nd edn). London: Kogan Page

Philo, G. (1993) 'From Buerk to Band Aid: The Media and the 1984 Ethiopian Famine' in J. Eldridge (ed) *Getting the Message: News, Truth and Power*. London: Routledge

PR Week (2008) 'Event Campaign: Motorcycle show revs up fresh regional interest', PR Week online, 10 April. Available at: http://www.prweek.com/uk/news/search/801247/EVENT-CAMPAIGN-Motorcycle-show-revs-fresh-regional-interest/

Price, S. (1998) *Media Studies* (2nd edn). Harlow: Longman

Rogers, E. (1983) *Diffusion of Innovations* (3rd edn). New York: Macmillan

Shannon, C. (1948) 'A Mathematical Theory of Communication', reprinted with corrections from The Bell System Technical Journal (July/October) 27: 379–423, 623–56, July, October. Available at: http://hq.sk/~mandos/fmfiuk/Informatika/Uvod%20Do%20Umelej%20Inteligencie/clanky/shannon1.pdf

Windahl, S. and Signitzer, B. with Olson, J. (2009) *Using Communication Theory: An Introduction to Planned Communication* (2nd edn). London: Sage

Worcester, R. (2009) 'Public Opinion: Why it is Important and How to Measure It, Comment and Analysis', IpsosMori, 19 June. Available at http://www.ipsos-mori.com/newsevents/ca/ca.aspx?oItemId=33

Media theory and news

$$\boxed{3}$$

Learning outcomes

1. Assess the historical pathway of today's fragmented media by discussing how it has involved, including regulatory issues, and its impact on public relations.

2. Understand the needs of the journalist by being able to identify relevant media and news angles and the process of media liaison.

3. Be able to recognize the different and changing media, its format, and its target publics, including readership, viewing and listening audiences, and web users, in order to plan a public relations programme for an organization.

4. Demonstrate an ability to write a press release through an understanding of news and writing which includes using the inverted pyramid format and incorporating news values.

5. Be able to apply concepts such as uses and gratifications, semiotics, and reception theory to review how people make meaning from the media.

6. Be able to assess the role of the media as a tool to implement a PR programme through identifying different ways of working with all media.

Practitioner Insight

Tom Bowden-Green
Associate Director, Grayling

I am member of the senior management team in Grayling's Bristol office, and head up business to business and community relations accounts. I studied English at Exeter University, edited the student newspaper and was the South West college rep for Sony BMG. After work experience, I started at Grayling PR in Bristol in 2002. I serve on the CIPR West of England committee which I chaired in 2009, running the successful Communicator's Conference and launching the 'Traverse-Healy Forum' lecture series.

I am also a university guest lecturer and have run the CIPR Diploma in Bristol, and was an examiner for other regions. I have the CIPR Advanced Certificate (Merit), the CIPR Diploma (Merit), and latterly, an MSc in Corporate Communications.

How do you interpret PR?

To me, PR is about developing relationships with 'publics' or audiences. By 'publics', I don't mean a mass, but groups of people who share similar viewpoints on specific issues.

What has been your most exciting media coverage?

Media coverage that I am most proud of was at the start of my career and for a small pub company, based in Wiltshire. The company was keen to attract new tenants across the country, but wanted to distinguish itself from high-street bars and clubs. I created a campaign linking the company's name to the concept of 'community pubs'. This was based around research that many communities value pubs above churches. It was a highly successful campaign, achieving national coverage. I've run bigger campaigns since then, but this early success gave me a lot of confidence to think strategically.

What is the value of media coverage?

Unless you can track specific peaks in sales, it's very difficult to attribute a financial value to media coverage. What's more important is proving that media coverage has changed behaviour or perceptions. We can use readership figures to demonstrate that messages have potentially reached a specific number of people, but the real evidence of success is monitoring what people think or do after reading that message.

What are the influences of social media on current practice?

Social media has given a voice to many 'publics' and should be viewed as an opportunity. Whereas discussion in a pub or over a garden fence may have previously gone unnoticed, such discussion on social media is transparent, meaning that public feedback can be quickly identified and responded to if necessary. Organizations need to embrace this opportunity to engage and develop two-way relationships through social media.

What advice would you give to students entering PR?

Do work experience before applying for jobs. Although it may mean sacrificing some holiday, work experience is the best way to really understand PR. When you're then searching for a job, be realistic about what to expect. As a new entrant you'll be expected to support a team, often undertaking administrative tasks rather than directing strategy. Don't despair though—if you're good you will quickly progress.

Be flexible, you need to accommodate unusual demands and last-minute changes, perhaps even sometimes unsociable hours. If you persevere, it will be a very rewarding career.

3.1 Definition

Public relations aims to raise awareness of an organization, product, or idea among distinct publics. It then works to change the attitudes and subsequent behaviour of these publics to achieve predetermined goals. In the last chapter, various models showed how public opinion could be influenced. However in order for people to have an interest in the message and act on it, public relations must first attract the attention of its target publics. This chapter explores how public relations works with the media to attract and persuade publics.

The media

The media is generally print (newspapers and magazines), broadcast (television and radio), and the internet. The media is an outlet where daily issues are presented, debated, and explained in TV or radio discussions, speeches, documentaries, and political meetings. Davis (2007) states that the media provides a framework for social reality and tells us what is happening about culture and values. Davis (2007) believes that people therefore use the media as a point of reference for normality, that is, the media influences people in deciding whether or not something is socially acceptable.

How PR affects a brand

Research commissioned by the PR consultancy Text 100, showed that the media does influence how people think about a brand and this affects a brand's value (Text 100

2008). The research analysed how often certain key brands, such as Gap, Audi, Visa, Pizza Hut, Colgate, and Rolex appeared in news articles, documentaries, or features where the brand has been developed into a media story. That is, the research looked at media coverage of the brand and not the brand's advertising. The results of this large study showed that a very significant value of the brand, at least one quarter, is linked to its media coverage.

The Text 100 (2008) research suggested that there may be a relationship between media coverage and brand value in that the more important the brand the more likely the media will write about it. Likewise, the more the media write about the brand, the more important it becomes.

ⓦ Go to the Online Resource Centre to access a link to this research

Growing media

The world is increasingly dominated by media which has growing importance. Its massive reach and technology means that it can reach vast numbers of people at once. The growing fragmentation of the media, where the press, radio, television, and the internet offer many different channels and many different programmes in an array of formats targeted to particular interests and ages, can reach many small and diverse audience groups. At the same time, it is becoming increasingly difficult to reach the mass audiences with one programme.

The most popular programmes on UK terrestrial television in the late 1990s could expect to attract audiences of 16–17 million. Nowadays, 14 million is a much more likely number (http://ofcom.org.uk). This is because few programmes are able to attract widespread interest across all ages as there is so much diversity within the audience and much more choice.

Nevertheless, to ensure information gets onto the traditional media such as TV, radio, newspapers, or magazines, a story must be created which sufficiently interests individual journalists to ensure they put it on their media. However, once a story is released to the media, control over its content is lost as the journalist will take the angle they want. They may take information from other sources which support or negate the public relations' source. They may also give the story a different emphasis or only use a small part of the information. They may introduce opinion leaders that change the story's focus and even undermine it (Treadwell 2005).

Apart from not being able to control the content of a media story, a public relations practitioner must realize that there is also a risk in losing control over its timing. Once a public relations practitioner has offered the journalist a story it may be developed and then published immediately or later, depending on many factors including whether there are related topics in the media which may make the story more topical, as well as the requirements of the medium. When a journalist submits a story to television, coverage will be immediate, whereas a magazine story may come out weeks or even months later so it may be better to use the magazine to reinforce an earlier TV news story. In addition, the story may explode into an even bigger story which may or may not be positive, or there may be minimal coverage or none at all. Bearing all this in mind, organizations are often fearful of dealing with the media and hence the need for a public relations practitioner to really know the media, have good media relationships and understand the processes involved in obtaining media coverage.

The public relations practitioner will usually expect to have their story in many different media, often with many different angles to ensure they reach their target publics and also appeal to different media agenda.

Journalist thinking

Also a practitioner needs to know how the journalist thinks. A journalist wants a story just for that day, they write the story and that is the end of their job. A public relations campaign must be sustained therefore a practitioner should think strategically, that is they must be concerned with not only the story getting into the media and achieving the organization's objectives but also in gauging the ramifications of the story, its potential ongoing effects, and how these can be influenced.

The story may generate comment; it may require interviews and need more angles to ensure it is sustained. Key factors which influence coverage are timing, content, and media liaison. The internet, which includes social media, blogs and viral film, does not need a journalist to develop a story, and this is discussed later.

The challenge

The public relations role in using the media is a three-fold challenge. Practitioners must constantly analyse the media in order to select the best ways to reach their target publics accurately. Secondly, they must develop attention grabbing, persuasive, and memorable media information at the right level and in the correct format to persuade the media to develop the story. Thirdly, they must ensure they have messages that present the organization in the required way to achieve its objectives.

It is important to ask what agenda that medium takes, what is the readership, circulation, or viewers of that media. The number of readers of a printed publication is much higher than its circulation, that is, numbers sold. For example, the circulation of The Times is 611,000, but its estimated readership is approximately 1.9 million because the paper is shared among people. (Audit Bureau of Circulation 2009). How many would read the same copy in the library for example?

In the UK the Audit Bureau of Circulation, which is owned by the media industry, provides details of the detailed circulation, distribution, attendance, traffic, and related data across a broad range of media platforms including:

- national, regional, and free newspapers
- consumer and B2B (business to business) magazines
- consumer and trade exhibitions
- digital media such as web, email, video and audio, podcasts, databases, directories, ad serving, etc (Audit Bureau of Circulation, 2009).

Readership

The National Readership Survey (NRS) is a type of large opinion poll and estimates the number of readers and their social grading. The figures are used by advertisers to plan their advertising in newspapers and magazines. The NRS has established six social grade classifications which are determined by the occupation of the chief income earner (CIE) in the household. A brief description of the six grades is shown in Table 3.1.

Table 3.1 Lifestyle data

Social grades	All adults 15+ in Great Britain	% of population (NRS 2009)
A	Higher managerial, administrative and professional	4
B	Intermediate managerial, administrative and professional	22.6
C1	Supervisory, clerical and junior managerial, administrative and professional	29.1
C2	Skilled manual workers	21.1
D	Semi-skilled and unskilled manual workers	15.2
E	State pensioners, casual and lowest grade workers, unemployed with state benefits only	8

Source: Courtesy of National Readership Survey 2009

Print media collects all this information, mainly to inform their advertisers, but it is also useful for public relations and can be accessed from the publishers. The circulation figures and demographics of national magazines as well as more details about their readers are on the National Magazine's website. The Radio Joint Audience Research organization (RAJAR) collects the type and number of radio listeners.

The Broadcasters' Audience Research Board (BARB) measures television ratings in the UK and collects the television viewing figures and audience sizes. These can be accessed freely on the respective websites although a subscription fee is needed for greater detail.

Demographics define certain aspects about people such as age, income, and gender. For example, according to demographic research on media use by the Central Office of Information(COI 2009), the group of people who are classified as ABC1s use the internet much more than those who are classified as C2Ds. This latter group watches television more often. However, the COI research found that although people automatically drop to an E classification within six months of being unemployed, their media use may stay the same as it was when they were in a higher demographic classification. This is important to the government as in a recession it must ensure it communicates to all those out of work about education, training, jobs, and welfare.

It could be concluded, that based on the research, when the government wants to reach the unemployed it must consider the previous demographic that people were in as they would still use the media of that group. For example, the current unemployed who used to be in the ABC1 group would be more likely to be reached through the

Go to the Online Resource Centre to access a link to BARB, RAJAR, and NRS internet whereas those who were in the C2Ds group would be reached through the local newspaper and radio.

Knowing what publics the different media reaches helps to identify which media to approach in a campaign. However, Bland (1996) emphasizes that public relations practitioners need to enhance reputation and at times that may be by keeping the organization out of the media.

Analysing the media

- What agenda does it take?
- What is the circulation, the listeners, or viewer numbers?
- What sorts of people are using that media in terms of social grades?
- What are its deadlines? A deadline is when the journalist needs the information in order to be able to cover the story. A newspaper will have a much shorter deadline than a magazine, and television could be instant.

Media convergence

Practitioners need to be aware that information should be available to be used in ways that fit all the different ways that it is being delivered. This is crucial in the tendency towards convergence where different content formats such as audio, video, text, and images reach people through a range of digital networks, such as the internet, mobile infrastructure, satellite, cable, digital, and terrestrial as well as consumer devices such as PC, TV, mobile, etc (Ofcom 2009).

3.2 Historical and theoretical context

Media that was available to wide groups of people started with the printing revolution, which was a result of the invention of a technical device for reproducing a large range of texts. The first English newspaper was the *Oxford Gazette* in 1666, as the king was in residence in Oxford at the time, and this was followed by the publication of the *London Gazette*. Technological advancements allowed more newspapers to be printed at low cost and to grow their advertising revenue as they were reaching more people.

Nowadays, as people get their news from the internet, newspaper groups are hit by falling circulations and advertising revenues. More than 500 years after the printing revolution which gave people access to much more information than ever before, broadcast technology gave rise to mass communication where, for the first time, people all over the world could have access to images and news.

The BBC

In 1922, the British Broadcasting Company started broadcasting radio to the general public. The hours of broadcasting were restricted, unlike today where there is 24-hour radio. Radio was financed by radio licences obtained from the post office. This later became the radio and television licence although today people pay only a television licence (see Figure 3.1).

The first television transmission was in 1925 by Logie Baird in the UK and several years later there were television broadcasts by the British Broadcasting Commission which was established in 1927 from the British Broadcasting Company following a Royal Charter.

There is a growing range of television channels depending on cable, satellite or terrestrial delivery. Viewers vary in age, sex, ethnic origin, religion, and lifestyle. The number of viewers has grown over the years but viewers can flick between increasing numbers of channels meaning that the viewing is more fragmented. Therefore it is more and more difficult for one channel to reach a significant fraction of viewers at one time.

The growth of subscription television, pay-per-view, and interactivity suggests a move from passive viewing to active use of the media. People are demanding convenience and control. In addition, viewing has become more entertainment orientated with less current affairs and factual programming. Therefore the public relations practitioner must be aware of these factors when developing a story for the media.

The arrival of the internet

Brown (2009: 7) claims the internet is not really a medium as it is richer and more complex than the traditional media channels. It provides a platform that allows traditional

Fig 3.1
People pay a licence fee to watch television
Source: Copyright OUP

Fig 3.2
The internet has become part of our lives
Source: Copyright OUP

media to place its content and reach varied audiences. It also allows new media platforms that encourage user interaction and user generated content. Platforms can also mix with each other such as YouTube which provides content for Facebook and in turn Facebook can draw content from a wide range of sources (Brown 2009: 7).

The precursor to the internet was the ARPANET (Advanced Research Projects Agency Network) which began in 1969 as a way to communicate and exchange data between university computers. It developed to the stage where it not only stored information but connected people to each other. The World Wide Web which connected people to vast amounts of information started in 1991. In 1993 the arrival of the World Wide Web browser (called Mosaic) and improved storage meant more people wanted to connect to the internet. Although the internet works as an extension of a newspaper on the content side, it has increasingly new capabilities of interactivity and content and focuses on user-generated content such as corporate websites, blogs, encyclopedias, news sites, social media, and video games. It includes instant messaging, the world wide web, weblogs, videogames, mobile devices, interactive TV, and chatrooms (Phillips and Young 2009).

At the end of 2009 there were 1,802 million internet users which is a 26.6 per cent penetration rate. That is, just over a quarter of the world is online (Internet World Stats News 2010), with China having more internet users than the US. Everyone with internet access has an equal voice to put out their comments leading to consumer user-generated content online (see Figure 3.2).

The internet is distinctive from any other media with its technology, its different uses, range of content and services. It does not exist as a legal entity although users are accountable to laws and regulations of the country in which they are living.

The internet has changed the practice of public relations not just through information exchange but also through the growth of social media sites such as Facebook and MySpace, and file sharing sites such as Flickr and YouTube and virtual communities, information-sharing sites, and blogs is changing public relations.

Practitioners must explore and experiment with new technologies and new ways of thinking to get their message across and interact with publics—in an environment which has been made far more transparent, due to social media. For example, the number of Twitter users reached 75 million by the end of 2009 and is still growing, but the growth rate of new users is slowing and a lot of current Twitterers are inactive, according to research reported in Computerworld (Gaudin 2010). However, the number of people using Twitter in February 2009 increased by 700 per cent within a year compared to the same month in 2008. Go to chapter 12 for more on the internet.

Media regulation

The media's production, distribution, and consumption can be controlled by restricting its ownership and its outlets as well as its content. However, the degree of control is determined by the type of media and also the political and social climate.

For example, liberal pluralists, who believe in tolerating the many different groups within society, believe that media ownership is not important as long as there is diversity of content (Washbourne 2009: 71). That is, there must be many different and independent voices, political opinions, and representatives of different cultures in the media.

In contrast, the political economy view believes that covering all views can demonstrate a superficial diversity and therefore hides a lack of real diversity. However, many think that as corporations are the most powerful forces in our society, they control what views are presented in the media and therefore there is no real diversity presented. In other words, whatever is presented takes on the view of the current political and economic climate.

In the UK the press is self-regulated which means that the industry monitors itself. It does this through the Press Complaints Commission, an independent self-regulatory body which deals with complaints about the editorial content of newspapers and magazines (and their websites). It has its own code of conduct and claims that it aims to keep standards high by training journalists and editors.

Ofcom was created by the Office of Communications Act 2002 as the regulator for the UK communications industries, with responsibilities across television, radio, telecommunications, and wireless communications services (Ofcom 2010). It regularly reviews the Government's rules on cross-media ownership in the public interest. Ofcom regulates standards on television and radio, and has responsibilities for the regulation of the commercial public service broadcasters. The BBC, as a non-commercial public service broadcaster, exists by Government charter, and is primarily regulated by the BBC Trust, and partly by Ofcom.

In contrast, the internet allows open and free access to a diverse range of information and has the largest capacity of all media to provide content at a low cost. In traditional

Go to the Online Resource Centre to access the link to some of the most recent complaints about newspaper reporting

media, messages were transferred from the sender to the receiver but the internet has more options, and encourages a more active use of the media. This new technology increases freedom but there are institutional controls over its flow and its reception, such as broadband availability and cost.

Media convergence

Although the media is fragmented with more channels, more technology devices, and more sites, there is also media convergence, a coming together, of the different types of media. Mobile phones link to each other and to the internet and have more and more applications, integrating with interactive television and games also available on personal digital devices as well as on laptops. Social media networks are linked with more messaging and networking options and news can be transmitted immediately to an array of media outlets anywhere in the world.

There are huge changes in the speed and accessibility of the media, creating the potential for an enormous amount of information being exchanged immediately and from everywhere. How people exchange and share this information may be what defines them, and how they are grouped.

Media convergence is likely to mean that more and more information about an organization is made available and it will be less possible to hide anything. This is affecting how an organization relates to its publics as it will be less able to have private issues and plans or even conceal information. If an organization is to have successful communication its communication needs to be open and clear.

Making meaning

Public relations is very involved in putting an item on the news agenda and this is often called 'advocacy' as it attempts to influence public opinion. It is evident that public relations programmes need to be aware that cultural and social backgrounds affect the interpretation of words and images.

Maslow's hierarchy of needs

The growing understanding of communication and the US government's funding of communications research meant that social psychology became an increasingly important academic discipline (Glander 1996). In 1954 an American psychologist, Abraham Maslow, researched how people were motivated by different levels of needs and depending on these, took notice of certain messages and ignored others.

Maslow developed a model that introduced the idea of a hierarchy, a pyramid of needs, now called Maslow's hierarchy of needs, which showed how people must satisfy each need in turn. For example, he found that people needed to satisfy their thirst before their hunger, then they moved on to deal with their shelter needs followed by their safety needs and subsequently their emotional needs until they reached the level of self-actualization which focuses on the need for personal growth (see Figure 3.3).

Fig 3.3
Hierarchy of needs pyramid based on Maslow's hierarchy of needs

Source: http://Businessballs.com and http://www.Businessballs.com.maslow.htm

Maslow's hierarchy of needs

Self-actualization
personal growth and fulfilment

Esteem needs
achievement, status, responsibility, reputation

Belongings and love needs
family, affection, relationships, work group, etc.

Safety needs
protection, security, order, law, limits, stability, etc.

Biological and physiological needs
basic life needs–air, food, drink, shelter, warmth, sex, sleep, etc.

🌐 **Go to the Online Resource Centre to access link to an interactive self-test on Maslow's hierarchy of needs**

This is important to public relations so that practitioners can develop the correct messages aimed at the needs of the most relevant publics. Maslow's research suggests that if the needs on a lower level have not been met people would not take any notice of messages addressing higher level needs. This is why politicians always focus on how they will improve housing and schools and energy costs rather than focusing on nationwide financial issues or the international agenda when talking to ordinary voters.

Semiotics

Research found that people made meaning in different ways and over variable times.

It was semiotics, the study of signs that explained how words and images were given meanings. Semiotics was first researched by the Swiss linguist Ferdinand de Saussure. The French philosopher, Roland Barthes then applied semiotics to sociology (Barthes 1957). He identified that words have two meanings: a literal meaning, its standard meaning, called its denotation and another meaning implied or suggested by a word depending on its context and our cultural and social background, is called connotation.

Semiotics found that in particular contexts a different meaning is signified. Words or images are known as the signifier, and the meaning it has acquired through the context is called the signified. For instance, around any lecture room is a fire safety notice in red. The colour red is the signifier. Danger is the signified.

Semiotics shows that meanings are not straightforward. For example, the Nazi swastika is simply black two lines crossing but to us it is a powerful and disturbing symbol. The symbol is the signifier and Nazism is signified. However, a similar symbol in Hinduism and Buddhism stands for good luck (Hall 2007: 18). Numbers, too, can signify different meanings depending on the culture in which they appear.

Fig 3.4
Our interpretation of images to build meanings
Source: Copyright OUP

Public relations and advertising regularly use symbols, images, and words that signify a different meaning from their denoted meaning in order to be more persuasive (see Figure 3.4). For example, wearing a suit to an interview may command respect as a suit has come to have the connotation of formality, power, and even capability. Yet a suit is simply—according to its denoted meaning—a matching jacket and trousers or a skirt. This connotated meaning is absorbed into Western culture to become the definition of suit. For example, in advertising the executives who liaise with the client and deal with budgets and other business aspects are commonly called 'suits' to differentiate their role from that of the creative team.

The image of a seaside can be the signifier that signifies a holiday; the holiday becomes the signified. Many UK holiday brochures have a picture of a deck chair against a blue background to signify a summer holiday. Words and images mean different things to different people and their meanings amongst different groups can be used to build campaigns that reach target publics more effectively. Analysing messages and images also helps to understand what and how people are thinking and making decisions.

Number 13 is the signifier for bad luck (which becomes the signified) in the UK and US cultures; in Russia it is six and in Japan, four.

Preferred, dominant and oppositional readings

Reception theory introduced the idea of how people make meaning from the media. This approach suggested that the media text has many alternative meanings and people interpret it differently (McQuail 2010: 386). However, Stuart Hall, a UK cultural theorist and sociologist (cited Fiske 1982: 113) argued that the media aimed to control or direct the interpretation of meaning which could also be resisted by the reader. He found that people either took the preferred reading through agreeing with the messages and

Fig 3.5
The UK Parliament represents different things to different people
Source: Copyright OUP

their associated ideology, or rejected that and created their own meaning, which Hall called the oppositional reading, or they juggled to create a negotiated reading between the preferred and oppositional readings.

For example, in the UK, the annual State Opening of Parliament is an elaborate and traditional event in which the Queen formally opens Parliament. Viewers who watched this on television may take the preferred meaning that the Queen as Head of State was conferring her authority on Parliament (see Figure 3.5). Others may find it outdated, too opulent, and costly but agree with the system of monarchy so may form a compromise and create a negotiated meaning. Others may think it shows Britain as an undemocratic authoritarian society which was not the intended meaning and is an oppositional reading of the programme.

Public relations programmes need to ensure that their target publics take the preferred meaning. If more hits are wanted on a website it helps if people find the site and its information credible. Developing user-generated content is one way to increase its trust and credibility. Presenting information that is not coming from just one source increases the chance that the readers may identify with the other users and therefore the content.

🌐 **Go to the Online Resource Centre to access a slideshow of the opening of Parliament**

The uses and gratifications theory

McQuail (2010: 426) draws on further research that demonstrated that people are not passive media users but active users, motivated to use the media as they are rewarded by its psychological effects, that is, it provides gratification in certain areas. These could be for information, social companionship, entertainment, or for personal identification. Therefore public relations needs to know that each group needs to be reached differently. Two US communications researchers, Blumer and Katz, developed the uses and gratifications theory in 1974 and argued that audiences had psychological and social needs that led to different expectations and use of the mass media.

Instead of just receiving and accepting messages, audiences were active in seeking out content that answered their needs and this affected their interpretation of it. The researchers outlined ways in which people use the media and McQuail (2010: 427) developed it further into:

- information and education
- guidance and advice
- diversion and relation
- social contact
- value reinforcement
- cultural satisfaction
- emotional release
- identify formation and confirmation
- lifestyle expression
- security
- sexual arousal
- filling time
- personal identity—people want self-knowledge and to reinforce their own personal values
- social needs—people get companionship through the media as well as when watching or reading the media with others
- entertainment/diversion—people can use the media to escape from everyday problems and to fill time.

These needs must be taken into account during a public relations campaign as why people use the media, such as particular blogs. For example, many people search the internet for a diversion, a break in their work routine, and are not looking to be informed.

In order to attract attention viral videos need to be entertaining and have qualities that make them worth accessing when surfing the net.

Applying the uses and gratifications theory can help explain why applicants enter a university's website, look at the prospectus and associated information. The viewing may be social, that is to examine a range of university websites to identify similarities between students and themselves. Most universities therefore have pictures of a diverse range of students so there are plenty of opportunities for potential applicants to identify with some of them.

Website information can be geared to different stages of decision making. By making university websites interesting people may be attracted to them when just internet surfing, ie as a diversion activity. The site therefore needs to be interactive to draw people in as at this early stage, they may not be committed, they may be stalling, or not fully understand the courses available. By getting people to apply online for a prospectus determines how to reach them as well as what to send to them.

3.3 Influences

Public relations is influenced by the type of media available and how it is changing and expanding. Every public relations practitioner must know the media and the different aspects of it, what sort of format it has, the type of information it covers and how, its ownership, its distribution, its frequency, its readership, listeners, or viewers. Knowing the media helps to understand what influences its selection of stories and what is needed to build coverage about an organization. Careful selection of the media and developing stories specifically for a particular outlet will increase the media opportunities of any public relations campaign.

Newspaper formats

Each newspaper is made up of different sections. It is important to identify these in order to know where a story can be placed and also how to develop it. Generally, in a newspaper the first page is home news which covers events happening locally or nationally, followed by a column by the editor (leader page) which analyses and comments on the news and the newspaper's stance. This section tells the reader what sort of paper it is, its political stance, and its general view. The finance and business sections follow and they may contain information about the media or advertising, world business, the economy, the stock exchange, and details on companies. Sport comes at the end of the paper. There are also other sections or columns such as technology, health, education, and gardening.

This sequence can change in different newspapers. The *Guardian*, for instance, has home news, international news, finance news, the leader page, and then sport which could be a whole section in itself. In some papers, the editorial leader may be earlier in the paper and then comments related to it may be later. Traditionally, these were opposite the editor's comments and that is why they are called **op cits** (opposite editor). These op cit sections are pieces where journalists present their own opinion and are persuasive pieces of writing about specific issues.

Broadsheets

There are really two sorts of newspapers: broadsheets and **tabloids** and these terms refer to the style and size of the paper. The smaller sized newspaper, the tabloid, was the low cost newspaper introduced for everyone. As literacy spread it reached mass audiences and was a commercial enterprise with its large advertising revenues and was dubbed the popular press. A broadsheet may be the same size as a tabloid, such as *The Times*, but calls itself a 'compact' paper because the publisher wants to differentiate it from the news style of a tabloid.

Broadsheets have the general news sections of home news, international news, finance and business, educational and comment, sport and weather, obituaries, and features. The features are usually in another section of the newspaper or may even form their own section, such as the media section in the *Guardian* on Mondays, and are broken down into various subjects such as fashion, film, and media depending on the day of the week. Features are sometimes called 'soft news' as they intend to entertain, inform, or instruct readers. Their style is longer and therefore more in-depth and analytical than a news piece.

It is important for the practitioner to be aware that there are news stories and feature stories and to consider these two aspects when approaching the media about their stories. If it is a news story, the editor or reporter of that section must be contacted the day before as the story will run in the next edition. Features are regular topics completed several days before the paper is published and often written over one week. Usually there is at least one feature or feature section for each day of the week.

Unlike news, the PR practitioner can work with the specialist writer to develop a feature in a particular area. Features should really be exclusives, and should not be offered to another newspaper and should not be in a press release. To get a feature developed means liaising with the feature's reporter regularly throughout the week and often several weeks beforehand providing expensive and ongoing information as well as interviewees and even case studies. A business feature can profile a company giving details of its products or current activities. A practitioner needs to have good relationships with features editors in order to build the story with them over a week or even several weeks.

Tabloids

A tabloid newspaper such as the *Daily Mail* in the UK takes a popular stance, which means it writes about human interest stories with not as much analysis as a broadsheet. On a story about a new treatment for a disease, a tabloid will want to use the celebrity personality aspect, which is the human interest angle and likes to focus on personalities involved. A broadsheet will be more likely to discuss the statistics of the disease, whether treatment is funded, and what the government is doing. However, this is changing and broadsheets are moving to more human interest angles. Apart from sport, the tabloid may not have features but will have an editorial comment and other commentary alongside.

Tabloids have different styles within their own genre. The 'red tops' such as the *Daily Mirror* and the *Sun* have a more sensationalist approach. Other tabloids such as the *Daily Mail* and *Daily Express* still focus on human interest but take a much more serious tone and have a clearer political stance. For example, the *Daily Mail* takes a conservative stance and focuses on maintaining society as it is, with a few fear stories and moral issues.

Newspapers are also becoming more interactive. The *Financial Times* is a significant UK broadsheet which focuses on business news. In 2009 it announced that it would respond to readers' views posted on its blog in the day's leader and thereby readers' comments will develop part of the newspaper's editorial (Brook 2009).

Magazines

There is a plethora of consumer magazines, some for international audiences, some for national and some specialized for particular audiences. Magazines have an overall marketing strategy for attracting advertisers and therefore the list of features is developed in advance. The practitioner can access this list and offer the relevant journalist material which will help them to build their feature.

Magazines have less hard news, being mostly features and articles taking a more considered view as their timing is different. There is no immediacy as they are produced no more than weekly, fortnightly, monthly, or even quarterly and they are able to go into more details than newspapers as there is more space. They have an audience who is informed about the magazine's topics, particularly in a professional magazine.

Magazines can be broken down into consumer general interest and consumer special interest and business publications. Consumer general interest magazines have a high sales volume. Many women's magazines and celebrity magazine such as *Hello!* come under this heading. There is plenty of opportunity to get media coverage in magazines. In consumer magazines there are sections ranging from finance to housekeeping. These magazines also run competitions for their readers where organizations supply editorial and a prize. Competitions offer two opportunities for coverage, one to announce the competition and another to announce the winner. However, magazines usually stipulate a prize amount therefore it may be an expensive way to get editorial. Magazine editors often like reader offers, or quizzes based on a news item.

Consumer specialist interest and business publications usually have a controlled circulation list and are often not available to buy from shops, they are generally on subscription. Many business publications are for professions and trades in a particular area, such as journals about the food trade. For example, *The Grocer* is read by people marketing food and keeps them informed about different products as well as their marketing plans.

There are professional journals which are often produced by the professional bodies. For example, PR professional bodies produce a journal for their own members. A professional UK PR journal is *PR Week* which talks about industry client wins, campaigns, changes in regulations, salaries, and other topics of interest to public relations practitioners, keeping them informed of their own industry.

@ Go to the Online Resource Centre to access the links to the CIPR publication and *PR Week*

Regional media

This covers local media and is an important aspect of all public relations programmes. Practitioners need to find local aspects and spokespeople to gain coverage on local newspapers, radio, and television.

A key aspect of a public relations campaign is arranging local field trips so that journalists can visit an organization; see a new product in operation or a factory in action. Field trips to a new holiday destination are appropriate to travel journalists in order for them to write about the location. However, getting journalists to write about a museum opening or an art exhibition means arranging a trip to the venue which profiles the organization in an interesting way and must also provide people for them to interview.

Radio

Radio, like television, is influenced by the different channels or stations, the ownership, trends, whether it is commercial or a public service channel, and whether it is regional or national.

Beaman (2000) argues that the advantage of radio for public relations is that there is greater and more diverse public access to radio than television. In addition, radio has more channels than television and is cheaper to produce and also has more audience interaction. Coverage can be arranged immediately and interviews organized without too much planning. In the UK there are many different types of radio. The British Broadcasting Corporation (BBC) radio is funded by public funds paid via the UK licence fee. It is broken down into key stations which are broadly (Beaman 2000)

1. New music for a younger audience.
2. Popular music light entertainment for a mature audience.
3. Classic music and jazz.
4. Speech-based current affairs, drama, documentaries, and features.
5. 24 hours of news and sport.

The BBC world service is aimed at overseas audiences. There are also BBC digital audio broadcasting services of different types of music, comedy, and the Asian network.

The BBC also has regional and local services which include BBC Radio Scotland, Radio Wales, and Radio Ulster and about 30 BBC country-wide local stations with talk and music for local audiences, eg BBC Radio Kent and Radio Leeds.

Apart from the BBC, the UK has many commercial radio stations such as Classic FM, Talk Sport, Virgin Radio, and independent national radio. There is a wide range of digital audio broadcasting stations and more than 200 music and local news stations with usually smaller coverage areas than the BBC and new contracts are awarded annually by Ofcom. Local community stations also cover local news and events and are run by volunteers.

To get a radio reporter to cover a subject it is essential to know the station and then the relevant programme. To get regional coverage it is necessary to find a local angle of interest. Many public relations campaigns can involve tours around the country so that the same event is held in different towns and therefore this creates potential to gain national and regional news interest. If it is news, it could be developed into a feature with a talk-back element. It is important to think of sounds to use for radio which can be recorded to add texture and colour to a programme. Media information sent to a radio reporter should explain how it can be used on the radio. For example, a food product could have a chef describe a recipe against a backdrop of chopping and cooking sounds.

Television

Television is the main source of news and information for most people and is the single largest channel of advertising. Although it is rarely live there is a great sense of intimacy and personal involvement. It is primarily a medium of entertainment but it also plays a vital role in politics as it is the main channel of communication between politicians and people, especially during elections. However, despite its mass communication and side coverage it is not autonomous. Television has less freedom than the press to express views and act with political independence (McQuail 2010).

Key television channels

On UK television there are numerous channels. The five most watched ones are:

1. BBC 1: the BBC's national flagship general entertainment channel.
2. BBC 2: the national alternative entertainment and informative channel.
3. ITV: a network of regional and national commercial TV franchises and a popular commercial channel.
4. Channel 4: the state-owned national channel funded by commercial activities including advertising.
5. Five: funded by subscription providers and owned by RTL group and United Business media.

Other broadcasters

Other broadcasters include:

- BSkyB: a satellite TV service with numerous Sky TV channels
- UKTV: owned by both BBC worldwide and Virgin Media and includes a number of channels broadcast nationally and internationally
- Other broadcasters such as Virgin Media and Disney.

When planning where a story can get coverage it is essential to identify the programming format. Although this is variable from channel to channel there is a regular format in the main terrestrial channels. Depending on the channel, the day starts at around 6 am with either breakfast news with regional updates or with children's programmes. These are followed by lifestyle programmes such as gardening, property shows, and human interest chat shows or children's programmes. Lunchtime brings the news, and drama shows follow. Children's shows start again at around 3 pm and game shows and lifestyle programmes continue to the early afternoon. News bulletins are on at 6–7 pm with regional news. Dramas follow, along with games shows, reality shows, documentaries, and news chat shows. Primetime television is around 7–9 pm and sports programmes are on in the evening, such as on channel five. The news has a regular format which usually includes an item for each of the following areas: regional, international, political, health, financial, crime, and human interest. Therefore, a public relations practitioner should ensure their story fits one of these areas by developing this particular angle as well as other news values. Morning and noon news shows on regional television are looking for interesting people, businesses, and topics that relate to people's interest in the universal topics of health, wealth, and love with a local tie-in. To get national media coverage, it is vital to keep abreast of breaking news, and to constantly ask what can be added to this.

When trying to get coverage on television it is best to call the producer or the researcher of a programme and tell them about the story and listen for their feedback. A good interviewee should be offered, especially someone who is an expert in their area, has had media experience, and is interesting and lively.

There are also channels which have special interests and it is valuable to keep updating this information as it can change frequently.

Television needs images and is constantly looking for good visuals and a story that can be told succinctly in sound bites. It is also looking for people who are articulate and comfortable on camera and fit its short, fast-paced segments. It is a good idea to have a 'B' roll of footage and offer that to television in order to give them an idea of the story and to use. A 'B' roll is video footage along with a script that explains the images and the story and can be used to fit the channel's purposes. In other words, it works like a visual press release and can be incorporated into a news story. The images should be ones that the channel cannot easily obtain and will therefore want to use—it is expensive to go out and shoot footage therefore any quality images that are rare or unusual or distinctive are more likely to be used on television.

A practitioner must find out what is important to television producers and what they are interested in. Timing is also important on television and producers prefer a day's notice on breaking news, but are set up to respond within minutes or hours to true breaking news. However, it is best to give them as long as four weeks on non-breaking news.

Go to the Online Resource Centre to access a link to the a Sky newsroom in action and participate in creating the news

News agencies

Most of the media gets some of it news from news agencies, that is, a service which employs its own researchers and journalists to collect news as it is happening in order to develop news reports and sell them to the media. The world's largest international multimedia news organization is Reuters which has almost 200 news bureaux around the world and provides 'Global information and news services to the world's newspapers, websites, television networks, radio stations, as well as direct to business professionals' (Thomson Reuters 2010).

There are also agencies which can distribute an organization's press releases to specific media outlets for a fee.

Go to the Online Resource Centre to click a link to access the link to a picture wire to see the best news images in the last 24 hours

Go to the Online Resource Centre to access the link to the latest press releases and for full information on PR newswire

Internet

The internet is becoming known for releasing the news before any other media. In 2008 it was the internet that first announced the ten coordinated shooting and bombing attacks across Mumbai, India by an alleged terrorist organization. Social networking tools, including Twitter and Flickr, provided live coverage about the attacks and the experiences and perceptions of the individuals present. Most organizations have their own websites which provide online information about the company and where regular news updates can be posted. An interesting and well-designed website can add value to an organization by attracting publics and then influencing them through its information.

Blogging gives a voice to anyone with an opinion and an internet connection. Solis (2009: 10) states that bloggers have high readership and participation and have the ability not only to influence people, but also to drive traditional media reporters to cover the same topics. Getting to bloggers is not unlike talking to reporters, it is still about cultivating and building relationships which require respect and communication.

According to Solis (2009), providing bloggers with early access to information allows news to bubble up, gaining credibility and momentum to the point where it attracts attention from traditional journalists with influential pundits defining and stimulating activity in every demographic possible. Solis believes that the interconnectivity between bloggers has formed an incredibly powerful network of authority that changes how people find information and make decisions in every facet of life. Bloggers are ranked based on the links back to them, the traffic to their site, the amount of subscribers to their feed, as well as how well they grasp the industry they represent.

When thinking about using online media for public relations, consider its key aspect—its immediacy.

Online conversations are immediate, making the internet valuable for events. Social microblogging sites such as Twitter, identify relevant groups and then put out comments. These people will pick up information because they are already interested in it. Therefore it gives them the words to use in their discussions, gives them enough information and links to images and to the event itself so they can generate discussion. Although their conversations may be happening outside what a public relations programme has planned, these people are interested therefore their existence should be acknowledged by giving them information which they can pick up, make their own conversations about, and pass on.

3.4 Application to industry

The media want news and this is news in its broadest sense—interesting information which makes the media want to use it in its news, in its documentaries, in chat shows, in features, on radio interviews, and as entertainment. It is vital the public relations practitioner knows how to prepare newsworthy information and how to communicate with the media to ensure it is covered in the way that achieves the organization's objectives.

What is newsworthy?

With its pressure to attract audiences, news must offer immediacy, endless interest, constant availability, and a global agenda. But what makes newsworthy information? The idea of a list of news values was first developed by two Norwegian researchers in 1965, Gaultung and Ruge, who described news as events that are reported according to eight criteria. Brighton and Foy (2007) note that Gaultung and Ruge developed their news criteria from their country's newspapers when there was no internet or user-generated content and they did not look at broadcast media.

New news values

However, the list provided a starting point for what makes news and Brighton and Foy (2007: 79) identified seven criteria of relevance, topicality, composition, expectation, unusualness, worth, and external influences.

1. Relevance: Make it significant to the viewer listener or reader. This means the story may need a local connection, even when preparing a global plan, public relations must be relevant to each country targeted. The swine flu epidemic would not have had as much interest in the UK if there had been no risk of it affecting people there. Often case studies work really well, showing the reality of story. A new medicine is more effective with a human angle about someone suffering from a disease and taking this treatment but this person has to be relevant to the readership of the media chosen. Therefore, it is important to have a selection of different people.

2. Topicality: Make it new, current, and immediately relevant. A treatment for influenza is launched at the beginning of winter. Novels and coffee table books are often promoted just before Christmas. Treadwell (2005) claims that trendiness is a new category of news determinant and it is what is current, cool, or happening. Therefore, a key skill of a public relations practitioner is to be aware of what is going on in the world.

3. Composition: Ensure it fits with items around it—so consider, for example, the running schedule of broadcast news.

4. Expectation: Present it as something that the public should know about.

5. Unusualness: Position it as different or unusual. Using rarity is a great way of getting media coverage—it could be the smallest, the largest, the most intelligent, or the strangest.

6. Worth: Justify its appearance in the news. Important people attract attention and comments from opinion leaders and celebrities may give more weight to a story.

7. External influences: Use other aspects that affect the development of news, for example, the swine flu identified in 2008 had external influences such

as the previous bird flu and Sars which had already created an agenda for a forthcoming epidemic.

News values for PR

The challenge for public relations is to create newsworthy stories. An award-winning campaign in 2008 promoted the ethos 'shopping is good for you' to both a national and local audience. A national survey was carried out and revealed that on average women burn more than 12,000 calories per year just by shopping. The campaign 'Drop a Dress Size', was a month-long challenge to help shoppers to slim down and feel good, with the incentive of winning a £1,000 make over. A shopping centre teamed up with local slimming groups and organized activities including mall walks, exercise demonstrations, and local media published weekly slimming tips. It achieved massive local involvement which is vital for a shopping centre and also created headlines in the *Daily Mail*, the *Sun* and GMTV (http://fidopr.co.uk, accessed 25 May 2010).

The media run 24 hours and being constantly available could suggest that more and more information is needed for the media. Brighton and Foy (2007) claim that this is not really the case. Stories are actually being stretched more thinly; they are repeated more often in rolling formats and subjected to different treatments. This helps public relations as it means the life of a story can be extended by offering another angle and different spokespeople, thereby creating a more sustained campaign.

There are also other factors that affect media attention. Brighton and Foy's (2009) analysis of the newspapers found that hard news contents reduce on Sundays because newspapers have all Friday's events to work with. This may mean only pitching a story on Friday if it is strong otherwise it could get lost. Therefore calling them earlier in the week would be preferable. Political coverage is more evident in September to October when the UK Parliament is in session, and the same happens again in spring owing to party conferences. The opening of the parliamentary session means a story at this time could be made newsworthy if a political angle is created.

There is little value in getting a huge amount of coverage if it is not relevant to the organization's goals. That is why full proposal development with long and short-term objectives is essential in public relations. See the following chapters for proposal development. Satisfactory media coverage which is sustained, targeted, and valuable cannot be achieved on an ad hoc basic. It must be in line with the organization's overall public relations plan.

Media liaison

Media liaison is contacting the media about a story. This means contacting the correct reporter and media. Journalists can be sent a press release to develop a news article or a backgrounder to develop a feature. If it is television, the newsroom needs to be contacted or if the story is more appropriate for a chat show it is necessary to speak to the researcher or producer of that programme.

It is vital to be enthusiastic and lively and listen to the reporter's feedback. They may be interested but want to take a different angle. A spokesperson should be immediately available to be interviewed and should have some media experience.

Blogospheres take reporting a step further as they mine down to experiences and perception of individual citizens. Bloggers have direct relations with people and thrive on their participation.

The following case study is an excellent example of how news was created to bubble up through social media, creating ongoing promotional efforts for Queensland tourism.

Case Study

The best job in the world
Source: Queensland Tourism Board

The 'Best Job in the World' was an innovative campaign to encourage travellers from around the world to visit the islands of the Great Barrier Reef in Queensland, Australia (see Figure 3.6).

The Queensland Tourism Board generated massive coverage on all media through part of a tourism campaign to publicize northeastern Queensland. They advertised for a candidate for the 'best job in the world'. Print advertisements were placed in international newspapers and on employment websites.

Fig 3.6
Tropical Queensland
Source: Courtesy of Tourism Queensland

The position included accommodation in a beautiful oceanfront villa on Hamilton Island for six months, time to explore the Islands of the Great Barrier Reef, and a salary of $Aus150,000. Applicants needed to post a 60 second video of themselves on the internet and users were invited to vote for their favourite applicant. This became a viral campaign through YouTube and social networking sites such as Facebook. A reality TV campaign followed, with the finalists arriving in northeastern Queensland and going through the final aspects of their interview.

The campaign relied largely on public relations and social networking activity and captured the imagination of the world. It generated TV, radio, and newspaper coverage, as well as special online discussion groups, bulletin boards, blogs, and websites with applicants critiquing their competition, having detailed discussions and swapping ideas and tips.

The 'Best Job in the World' was the lead story everywhere from the BBC to the *Daily Telegraph*; it was reported on CNN, Sky News, and Reuters and was talked about on major morning television and radio (BBC News 2009). The campaign created an ongoing narrative that worked globally; it used very good spokespeople and images.

@ Go to the Online Resource Centre to access the link to get an update on what is happening in this campaign

PR Tool

Media release

A media release is a most effective and, powerful public relations tool. It is written in a news style with a strong news angle based on news values which gain the media's attention and also communicate the organization's objectives. A media release should gain well-targeted coverage and persuasively communicates the organization's messages to its relevant publics.

@ Go to the Online Resource Centre to access link to a list of the latest most successful stunts

Before writing a press release it is vital that there is a public relations programme which identifies the news stories that can be developed. For example, a PR programme may include stunts to attract attention to a product or person, or it may commission a survey and then use the results of this in the release. In 2009, a leading UK bed company, Silentnight, promoted its mattresses by identifying one of its directors as a very effective mattress tester (BBC 2009). They developed this through insuring his posterior for £1 million, which they claimed was valuable for its sensitivity, and then announced it to the media. Television filmed the director at the factory and the story went worldwide reaching target publics and promoting the company's beds.

A press release is in a news style and different from other forms of writing. The headline should focus on the present, short paragraphs of two to three sentences are used and these sentences contain no more than 20 words. Long words should be avoided.

There is a particular format in which to write a press release. It is the opposite of most other forms of writing because it is important to catch the media interest at the beginning, otherwise they will not read any further. Therefore the most important information is at the beginning and then the body of the release explains why the story is so important. This is called an inverted pyramid style (see Figure 3.7).

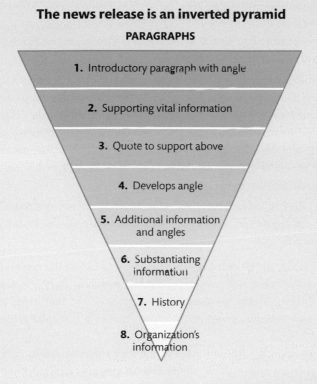

The news release is an inverted pyramid

PARAGRAPHS

1. Introductory paragraph with angle
2. Supporting vital information
3. Quote to support above
4. Develops angle
5. Additional information and angles
6. Substantiating information
7. History
8. Organization's information

Fig 3.7
The news release is an inverted pyramid

Key tips

- Date at the top of the page and on the organization or consultancy's letterhead.
- Heading which tells the journalist what the story is about in a few words, eg 'Leading doctor announces improved treatment for heart disease'.
- The first or lead paragraph must tell the whole story in fewer than 25 words and gain the interest of the media and must be short. It is important to create a strong lead paragraph which must include the who, what, when, where, why, and how of the story.
- The second paragraph adds more information and or a quote.
- The third paragraph includes a quote and or more information
- The fourth paragraph substantiates this quote and adds more detail.
- The fifth paragraph gives another quote and this can be from someone in the organization.
- More supporting comments and substantiation can follow
- A boilerplate, which is a short paragraph about the organization, must be at the end.
- 'Ends'—this word must always be at the end of a release; if the copy goes over a page then this must be noted.

- Contact information (landline, mobile, and email) should follow so the media can contact the writer at any time.

- There can also be a section at the end of the release called 'Notes to editors' which provides more detailed information.

- Any additional material forms a press pack and can include from the front going back: the release, a 'backgrounder' which provides more comprehensive information, a fact sheet of key points relevant to the release, biographies of key people involved in the organization and relevant to the release. Photographs, a DVD, and any other company literature that helps to explain the media story. These can be sent to the media and should also be accessible in the media section of the organization's website.

- Become familiar with the client's keywords and phrases—get these from their SEO (search engine optimization) agency if they have one—and ensure relevant ones are in each release.

The release should be sent out before an event or before the news is announced as the media want 'new news' not 'old news' and public relations can help to create this.

Media liaison: identify the media well in advance and then email the release to the correct person. Follow up with more information or a particular angle that affects their readers.

Record to whom the release has been sent, their response, and the follow up activity.

Embargoes are when an issue is not to be covered until a certain time. Brighton and Foy (2007: 38) argue that these should simply be considered as requests largely because an embargo on a really strong news story would be unrealistic and unenforceable. An embargo may be possible if its release is relevant to other events.

Go to Online Resource Centre to access a link to more tips on press release writing

Summary

Public relations uses the media as a tool to implement a public relations programme. Through creativity and media knowledge the practitioner can ensure information is seen as more credible if it is delivered to the publics via the media, and especially if it is through a third party, rather than by an organization's spokesperson speaking directly. Media liaison is crucial to be able to continue to develop a news story. This is even more important in social media, as the story can take on a life of its own.

Public relations programmes need to realize the diversity and growing fragmentation of today's media. The press, radio, television, and the internet offer many different channels and many different programmes in an array of formats targeted to particular interests and ages; it can reach many small and diverse audience groups. Practitioners need to create a variety of ways to appeal to different media as it is becoming increasingly difficult to reach mass audiences.

The public relations practitioner can ensure they work with the journalist to achieve their aim by offering a story with strong and relevant news angles. Apart from not being able to control the content of a media story, a public relations practitioner realizes there is also a risk in losing control over its timing. A public relations campaign must be sustained therefore a practitioner should think strategically, that is, they must be concerned with not only the story getting into the media and achieving the organization's objectives but also concerned with gauging the ramifications of the story, its potential ongoing effects, and how these can be influenced.

By knowing the media and identifying its format and its target publics, including readership, viewing, and listening audiences and web users, the practitioner can find out what influences its selection of stories and work with it to build coverage. Careful selection of the media and developing stories specifically for a particular outlet will increase the media opportunities of any public relations campaign. Media relations is all about building, investing in, and cultivating relationships which are, like any relationship, built on respect, understanding, communication, and information. This also applies when talking to bloggers.

It is vital the public relations practitioner knows how to prepare newsworthy information and how to communicate with the media to ensure it is covered in the way that achieves the organization's objectives.

The media is changing with its 24-hour supply of information and immediacy. Publics are influencing this change by demanding even more information and more immediacy. The internet has totally revolutionized the practice of public relations not just through information exchange but also the growth of social media sites such as Facebook, MySpace, Bebo, Flickr, etc, and of virtual environments, virtual communities, information sharing sites and blogs. PR practitioners must now explore and experiment with new technologies and new ways of thinking to get their message across—and in an environment which has been made far more transparent, due to social media (Phillips and Young 2009).

Discussion points

A. News stories: these discussions explore the origin of news stories

1. In a group identify some news stories in various newspapers.

    See if you think there was a media release behind any of the articles.

    What makes you think there was a press release?

    Discuss how much they represent the organization's point of view—do they bring in opposing angles which the organization is able to refute, suggesting it is prepared.

    Compare the same PR story. How is it different? What do you think has made them different from each other? Why do you think the newspapers covered this story?

B. Media liaison: this explores the media liaison role of the practitioner

1. Form pairs and identify a news release from an online service or a corporate website.

    Appoint one of you in the journalist role in a publication which is relevant to the release and the other public relations practitioner who tries to persuade the journalist to use the release in a two minute conversation. Record your impressions of each other.

2. Identify what worked and what did not work, what would have made it more successful?

    Did the journalist find the practitioner to be persuasive? Why or why not? What approach would have been better? What did the practitioner learn about dealing with a journalist? Think about things such as news values and relevance to the publication.

C. Media releases

1. Go to a PR newswire and download a news release.

    Identify its news values and format and discuss its newsworthiness.

2. Where do you think it is likely to get coverage?

    How could you change this release to improve its coverage?

    Explore the web to find relevant bloggers and then assess their value. What makes them credible?

    How much participation do they have on their blog sites?

3. What is it about the format of press release that makes it persuasive?

    How does it compare to news articles?

4. How is social media changing the format of traditional press releases?

    Think about what will happen in the future. Do you think press releases will cease to exist? What will take their place?

D. Semiotics

As a group think of some symbols and their deeper meaning. Do you think that it is easy to work out connotation and denotation? What influences the way you decode these?

E. Hierarchy of needs

Go to the Online Resource Centre to access the self-test to see where you are on Maslow's hierarchy of needs. Do you think this is a good way for public relations to know how to reach people?

F. Interpretation

Observe how you interpret an event and see if you can identify what cultural and social experiences are influencing your interpretation.

References

Audit Bureau of Circulation (2010). Available at http://www.abc.org.uk/Corporate/AboutABC/ABCrole.aspx

Beaman, J. (2000) *Interviewing for Radio*. London. Routledge

Brighton, P. and Foy, D. (2007) *News Values*. London: Sage

Brook, S. (2009) 'Financial Times Readers Asked For Input on Leader Columns', Guardian online, April 28. Available at: http://www.guardian.co.uk/media/2009/apr/28/financial-times-arena-blog#history-byline#history-byline

COI (2009) 'ABC1 Unemployed vs C2DE unemployed. In the Mix: Communications to Governments and the Public Sector', COI, Spring: 11. Available at: http://www.coi.co.uk

Davis, A. (2007) *Mastering Public Relations* (2nd edn). London: Palgrave

Fido Public Relations (nd) 'Drop a Dress Size at Golden Square'. Available at: http://www.fidopr.co.uk/3-26 Drop-a-Dress-Size-at-Golden-Square

Gaudin, S. (2010) 'Twitter Now Has 75M users; Most Asleep at the Mouse', Computerworld, 6 January, Available at: http://www.computerworld.com/s/article/

Glander, T. (1996) 'Wilbur Schramm and the Founding of Communication Studies', Educational Theory 46/3: 373–91

Hall, S. (2007) *This Means This This Means That: A Users Guide to Semiotics*. London: Laurence King

Internet World Stats (2010) 'Internet Ends 2009 with 1,802 Million', News, 4 April. Available at: http://www.internetworldstats.com/stats.htm

National Readership Survey (2010) 'Lifestyle data, Information about the Wealth of Profile Data'. Available at: http://www.nrs.co.uk/lifestyle.html

Mcquail, D. (2010) *Mass Communication Theory* (6th edn). London: Sage

Ofcom (2004) 'What People Watch, Television Viewing Behaviour', Ofcom review of Public Service Television Broadcasting (PSB) Phase 1. Available at: http://www.ofcom.org.uk/consult/condocs/psb/psb/sup_vol_1/tvb/section2/

—— (2010) 'Ofcom Licensing'. Available at: http://www.ofcom.org.uk/licensing/

—— (2010) 'The Communications Market'. Available at: http://www.ofcom.org.uk/research/cm/cmr09/

Phillips, D. and Young, P. (2009) *Online Public Relations: A Practical Guide to Developing an Online Strategy in the World of Social Media (PR in Practice)* (2nd edn). London: Kogan Page

Solis, B. (nd) 'The Art and Science of Blogger Relations', E-book online. Available at: http://www.docstoc.com/docs/3677236/eBook-Blogger-Relations-by-Brian-Solis

Text 100 (2008) 'Media Prominence; A Leading Indicator of Brand Value: How Effective Public Relations Contributes to Brand'. Available at: http://www.text100.com/files/marketing/Media_Prominence.pdf

Treadwell, D. and Treadwell, J. (2005) *Public Relations Writing: Principles in Practice*. Thousand Oaks, CA: Sage

Washbourne, N. (2009) 'Media Context of Contemporary Public Relations and Journalism' in R. Tench and L. Yeomans (eds) *Exploring Public Relations* (2nd edn). Harlow: Prentice Hall

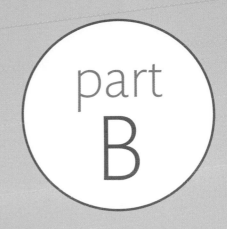

part
B

Developing a PR campaign

Intelligence gathering ④

Learning outcomes

1. Identify a planning model and be able to explore why it is necessary in order to develop a public relations programme.

2. Understand the organization's internal and external environment and the information arising from these areas and how to access it to develop a situation analysis.

3. Be conversant with research terms such as primary and secondary research, quantitative and qualitative methods, and the different types of research and how they can be used in forming a situation analysis.

4. Be able to identify and know what information is required and how to access it in order to develop a situation analysis which informs a public relations programme.

5. Recognize how analysis and synthesis can be used to develop a PEST and SWOT analysis in order to assess the current situation, issues, and a way forward.

6. Demonstrate an ability to assist with a focus group through developing such groups applied to a case study.

Our job is partly to anticipate consequences, planning around a range of outcomes of which we are not always in control.

(Hobsbawm 2004)

Practitioner Insight

**Guy Woodcock
Founder and CEO, Montpellier
Marketing Communications, Board
Director, Public Relations Consultancies
Association, Chair of PRCA South West
and Wales regions**

I fell into public relations through the unconventional route of first becoming a captain in the army. I trained at Sandhurst and became an army officer in the infantry, where my portfolio included a remit to engage with local communities and the media to encourage recruitment.

I left the army as Captain after five years of experience in media relations and set up Montpellier Marketing Communications in 1991 which is a stand alone public relations consultancy and comprises Montpellier PR, Montpellier Creative with Branding and Design, and Montpellier Interactive which includes software development. We represent a wide remit of communications activity which is indicative of how public relations can be unusual and exciting. It can lead to the integration of many different manifestations of communications in many different areas of an organization.

How do you approach a PR brief?

Even though the client may have provided a brief this usually only skims the surface. Seldom do we have a brief from the client which allows us to put a communications plan together. We have run communications programmes for a diverse range of industries including legal firms, healthcare organizations, security businesses, schools, and quangos so our approach is often based on experience as well as from the research we do.

However, it is always a process of in-depth investigation. I start by finding out the big idea that the client wants to achieve. I grill the client and go through the brief with them to tease out an understanding of their position and the objectives. I get the client to tell me what success looks like in a corporate or product sense and work back from that, influenced by the timescales and resources available.

Then it's a question of desk research to validate the client's assumptions and also challenge them on some of their other statements. I also want to know where the organization is on its corporate journey and where it wants to be. I need to know whether it's a marathon or a 100 metre sprint as the speed and energy needed affects the resources required.

How do you use the internet in the planning process?

The internet has become a powerful source of information to help us evaluate the marketplace, competitive products, trends and macroeconomics. We use the web as a way of gaining more background and armed with that we use our experience to put together a strategy.

W̶h̶a̶t̶ ̶t̶e̶a̶m̶ members are involved?

It is crucial that everyone in the account team joins a brainstorming session and contributes to generating ideas which help put together an innovative PR strategy. Before a brainstorming everyone is given detailed information on the client and the marketplace, as well as the client's aspirations and goals and then when everyone is at the same level of understanding we go through the communication channels.

What advice do you give to anyone starting in public relations?

Although it is important to remember that media relations is not the only constituent, the media are still a critical part of public relations. There are so many different media and a new raft of platforms, even in traditional media. I advise going out and meeting as many journalists as possible, befriend them and take the trouble to understand how they differ in their approach from each other, depending on their medium.

4.1 Definition

> **Public relations is a management function; it involves planning and problem solving.**
>
> (Grunig 1992)

A public relations plan, known as a communications plan or proposal, is a document that answers an organization's brief, that is, the organization outlines a problem or issue that requires a communications solution. The brief may concern communication issues for the whole organization or just a small part of it such as one of its products. The plan identifies the communications issues and how they will be addressed along with a budget, timescales, and evaluation.

By ensuring that plans are targeted at the right people, uses the right channels of communication and says the appropriate things at the right time, all within agreed timescales and budget, the foundations for success are laid. (Gregory 2009: 175)

People plan their own lives all the time, often without really thinking about it, and to varying degrees, using their own processes. Planning is also needed in public relations; it meets an organization's needs, manages teamwork, and evaluates progress.

Cutlip (2006: 283) outlines a four-stage public relations plan.

1. The first is called a situational analysis that identifies what is happening now and defines the public relations problems. This looks at the organization, its size, its competitors, its history, its marketing, and what communications it wants to achieve. It summarizes the research and draws out insights to make recommendations.

2. Strategy is the second stage and identifies what should be said and why and involves 'planning and programming'.

3. Implementation is the third stage and outlines when and how the project will be carried out.

4. The fourth stage is called evaluation, which involves assessing all aspects of the programme.

As noted by Lee and Smarr (2009) a number of researchers have also developed public relations planning models and include Hendrix (2002) who used ROPE (research, objective, programming, evaluation), Kendall (1999) who used RAISE (research, adaptation, implementation strategy, evaluation), and Marston (1963) who presented RACE (research, action, communication, and evaluation). Parkinson and Ekachai (2006) mention ROSTE (research, objectives, strategy, tactics, and evaluation). These models are also equally helpful in guiding public relations planning although Gregory (2006) claims that they do not provide enough information on which to base the plan.

It is up to the practitioner what research is incorporated into the general strategy and Lee and Smarr (2009) want practitioners to use a planning model that focuses more on campaign strategy with a rational analysis rather than the operational planning of a campaign.

Research is essential in public relations in order to set communication objectives, identify publics, and develop implementation plans. Research is also ongoing as it is needed to evaluate plans and improve the programme as it progresses. Chapter 8 discusses evaluation but uses the same research methodology.

Applying the planning model to a betting campaign

An example of using Cutlip et al's planning model (2006) from the briefing stage to evaluation is the week-long highly successful and creative Betfair campaign. Betfair, a betting company, briefed the public relations consultancy Mischief PR to increase the number of people placing bets during the 2008 London mayoral election.

Situation analysis

The research revealed that it was difficult for Betfair to get a media profile to attract betting people as there was considerable reluctance from the media to feature any gambling messages. In addition, other betting companies were already advertising heavily for people to place bets through them. Although high betting among Londoners was expected during election week it was likely that there would be intense competition from other companies.

Strategy

To bypass competitors, Mischief PR recognized that Betfair had to reach Londoners directly during election week when their betting would be highest. The research found that owing to the competition from other betting companies at that time, any communications had to be highly stimulating, creative, and memorable and the strategy to create a campaign was based on that research to differentiate Betfair from other betting companies and encourage media attention.

Implementation

A week-long stunt was created. Two large inflatable heads portraying each mayoral candidate were flown in London streets at different heights acting as swing-o-meters show-

Fig 4.1
The Betfair campaign
Source: Courtesy of Ken Lennox and Mischief PR

Go to the Online Resource Centre to access a link to find out more about Mischief PR

ing how Londoners were voting (see Figure 4.1). A press release supported the launch of a 'bet-o-meter' revealing how much carbon dioxide the two mayoral candidates were likely to emit speaking 'hot air' during the campaign. The hot air angle highlighted a key electoral green issue and provided a strong news hook for the bet-o-meter. Mobile bet-o-meter street teams approached Londoners directly and gave out free betting vouchers and Betfair teams served as a direct media resource. A short viral film was developed in the planning stage along with a microsite and both were released online.

Assessment

The campaign exceeded objectives in creating high betting figures, more than one million website hits, and very favourable media coverage resulting in a memorable campaign.

4.2 Historical and theoretical context

A public relations programme links to an organization's business objectives. This came about after organizations started managing their own business using the 'management by objectives' model devised by the business management guru Drucker in 1954. This meant an organization develops overarching goals and then its management teams develop objectives for their own areas that are linked to these goals. As the plans roll out the teams are guided and given feedback on how their goals work towards the organization's success.

Public relations tends to use this management style. It considers the organization's goals, and develops a programme to help achieve these. For example, if the organization's goal is to increase sales then public relations must provide the communications to facilitate this, which may be through internal communications to motivate employees and through external communications to raise awareness of a product to its publics.

Ferguson (2008) suggests the last 50 years have brought three key changes to public relations. Research is expected to be used in most stages of the programme; a public relations programme must now link to business plans and the organization's overall business strategy; and organizations are demanding measurable evaluation of public relations programmes. This requires the use of increasingly sophisticated research methods and technology that not only monitor outcomes but provide information that guides changes to the programme as it rolls out.

Research in the music industry

The research must examine the organization as well as its environment, the world in which it operates. According to systems theory (see chapter 2), an organization is affected by its environment and affects its environment. In other words, there is interconnectivity. For example, the music industry relies on these links from everyone involved in music. The British record industry's trade association, the British Phonographic Industry (BPI), represents the interests of music companies including the big record companies: Warner Music Group, EMI, Sony Music Entertainment, and Universal Music Group. In a speech to the music industry, its chief executive emphasized the interconnectivity between those involved in making and selling music and the music companies.

> I'm not trying to argue that record companies are more important in the music community than anyone else. My point is that the world of music is an ecosystem in which we are all co-dependent. As labels, we depend on the support of publishers, talented artists and songwriters, session musicians and producers of the highest quality and the excitement generated by live performances.
>
> (Taylor 2007)

Environmental monitoring

Lerbinger (1977) stated that the key elements of public relations research, or environmental monitoring as he called it, were:

- The organization's environment—that is the world in which it operates, the industry sector.
- The organization's structure—its own world, its own corporate internal world.
- The organization's publics—both internal, such as employees and external, such as consumers.
- The message—what the communication says.
- The effects—how the programme influences the publics.

Once acquired all the information can be analysed to develop a public relations programme. The situation analysis is created by sifting through the information and pulling out the main points that show a definite direction of what is best for the organization.

According to Cutlip et al (2006), a situation analysis is the process of defining the problem or the opportunity. It involves probing and monitoring knowledge, opinions, attitudes, and behaviours of those concerned with, and affected by, the acts and policies of an organization. Cutlip et al (2006) see this stage as the foundation for all the other steps in the problem-solving process as it answers the question 'what is happening now'. This step is used to make decisions about the communications plan.

A situation analysis requires research and includes:

- what is known about the situation
- the history of the situation
- what is influencing the situation
- those involved and affected within the organization and outside the organization; publics—who they are and what they want, the media, marketing objectives, and resources available and the environment.

The following is an example of how a situation analysis, which included the above factors, provided ideas for an ongoing public relations campaign

The Cheltenham Festival

The four-day Cheltenham Festival is a key racing event in the National Hunt calendar and the second largest sporting event in the UK after Wimbledon. Each March it attracts thousands of visitors to the town and is a high point for the hospitality, tourism, and catering industries. However, it was not popular for retailers and Montpellier Marketing Communications was asked to reverse this perception.

Their research found that shoppers believed that the town centre was packed and difficult to get into during the week and, as a result, retailers experienced a dip in trade. Local racegoers themselves are at the racecourse during the day so are not in the stores.

Montpellier PR also carried out research into how other iconic sporting venues improved community relations. The Galway Races in Ireland excelled in this area so Montpellier PR arranged a fact-finding mission to Ireland and held meetings with representatives from Tourism Ireland, Galway Racecourse, local media outlets, and town centre management. This revealed that retailers thrived in the weeks leading up to their festival because local racegoers were spending significant money on buying outfits and on hair and beauty, which was not the case in Cheltenham.

Montpellier PR developed a strategy focusing on communicating an added focus to the Cheltenham Festival, which would benefit retailers. Thus, the Cheltenham Festival 'Ladies Day' concept was conceived. It was first launched to the retailers at a private event where they enthusiastically agreed to participate in that as well as in the 'Best Dressed Lady' competition.

Cheltenham Ladies Day was a great success. Wide-ranging media coverage resulted in great awareness with higher attendance figures, the Ladies Day event itself attracted great interest and retailer relationships flourished (see Figure 4.2).

Fig 4.2
Winners of Ladies Day at the Cheltenham Festival

Source: Courtesy of Montpellier PR

Primary and secondary research

A public relations proposal is more likely to be valid if it is backed by substantial research which informs its implementation and allows the programme to be monitored.

There are two main approaches to research: primary research and secondary research. Primary research is new, original research that is collected through observing people or conducting a survey. This may involve asking questions or developing new information. It requires knowledge of survey design, questionnaire construction, sampling, or basic statistics. Primary research usually requires a research company that can handle large data. The role of the public relations practitioner is therefore to identify the research required and brief the research company on the research objectives and the type of report required. Other primary research is a content analysis, that is analysing information for what it means and how it is presented and who the audience is.

Secondary research refers to information gained from sources other than primary or new research. It is often called desk research and examines and applies someone else's data. Information is taken from journals, surveys, public records and policies, media coverage, databases including market research, and an organization's own information such as its marketing plan and annual report.

Quantitative and qualitative research

There are two key research methods—quantitative and qualitative. A situation analysis should comprise both methods. Quantitative is research that can be measured statistically. For example, the Broadcasting Authority Research Board's (BARB) reports on television viewing audiences are quantitative as they tell how many people watch a certain programme; the results are unambiguous and give a pattern of viewing. Opinion polls carried out during voting are often quantitative as they are trying to assess the number of people who will vote for a particular political party.

Qualitative research measures what people think about something. It gives insight and understanding but not numerical data. It provides more meaning than quantitative research. For example, it explains why people watch something which may offer greater insights than the figures on how many people watch it. Content analysis is qualitative research as it analyses how people interpret information and make meanings. For instance, the UK Central Office of Information (COI) carried out qualitative research when it ran a series of focus groups, workshops, and small group interviews when it wanted to understand how to communicate with ethnic minority communities more effectively. The COI needed to find out what affected how the ethnic minorities interpreted campaigns and what could be done to improve communication with them.

The COI identified the following objectives for its research (COI 2006):

- to explore the social, cultural, and attitudinal factors which impact on the communications needs of ethnic minority communities

- to provide strategic and creative guidance on communicating with ethnic minority communities.

The sample covered a range of socio-economic groups and included members of the Asian and Chinese communities who spoke little or no English and the fieldwork was conducted over three months in a range of locations in England. The sample focused on ethnic minority communities (specific groups were selected to fill in gaps in existing research) and comprised:

- Indian men and women aged 18–80

- Pakistani men and women aged 25–65

- Bangladeshi men and women aged 25–65

- Chinese men and women aged 18–65

- Black Caribbean men and women aged 18–80

- Black African men and women aged 18–60

- Mixed race men and women aged 18–24.

This research programme comprised two key research elements:

1. Desk research, which reviewed recent studies conducted by the COI.

2. Primary research which used qualitative methods, designed to provide insight and understanding, but not statistical or numerical data. The following range of qualitative research methods was used by the COI to maximize the value of the data, comprising various forms of interviews, that is focus groups, group interviews, individual interviews, and analysis of their media habits:

   - 24 workshops, involving conventional group discussion techniques and also a range of tasks lasting two hours

   - 14 individual interviews lasting one and a half hours

   - four paired interviews lasting one and a half hours

⊕ **Go to the Online Resource Centre to see sample questionnaires and access a link to developing an online survey**

- ten family visits, involving two researchers visiting a family in their home and spending the evening observing and videoing their media consumption, lasting 3–4 hours
- four group discussions lasting one and a half hours
- six site visits to community centres, involving the researcher visiting a centre, interviewing key workers, meeting any centre users where possible, and observing the use of publicity materials, lasting around two hours.

The results were submitted into a situation analysis which is presented later in this chapter and used to develop a public relations proposal.

Gathering intelligence

Gathering intelligence starts as soon as the public relations brief is received. For example, a Japanese camera brand, Nikon, appointed a public relations agency to provide support for it across its 26 European markets (Sudhaman 2009). To review the organization, the industry sector, the product, and the market thoroughly to find out how public relations can help to answer the brief, the consultancy would need to review the following:

1. The organization—its history, eg the beginning of Nikon—why it is successful and what it does, what are its products, and how are they selling?

2. The sector—how successful the camera industry is, what makes it successful, the marketplace, and the economic and political factors affecting the sector, eg the camera sector. Who are the customers, what do they expect?

3. The competitors—who are they, in what countries are they successful? Do they have the same type of products?

4. The product—what sort of cameras do they have? A detailed knowledge of the products is important.

Center and Jackson (2002: 3) stress that the first step in any project is to gather intelligence in order to understand the variables in the campaign. This can include identifying the key publics' opinions and attitudes and the opinion leaders and the groups who are concerned enough to act. Using that data helps to develop the situation analysis which can be used to form a public relations strategy.

Apart from the surveys mentioned for the COI, there are many other ways of obtaining information to develop a situation analysis and much of this is readily available. However, the practitioner needs to review it from a public relations perspective, looking at the business goals, the organization's values and existing communication, and how public relations can achieve its communication objectives.

A. Examples of primary research

Surveys

These provide primary data and an overview of patterns and trends. There are different formats for survey questions:

1. Open-ended: use why, how or what. They allow a complete answer and do not encourage a yes or no answer. For example, what do you believe is the best research for a public relations programme? Why do you think research is important in public relations?

2. Yes/no: expect a yes or no answer. For example, have you studied public relations before?

3. Multiple choice: there are three different types.

   - one answer only is selected such as yes always, sometimes, and never

   - more than one answer can be selected from a selection of preferences

   - preferences can be ranked.

4. Leading: the answer is in the question. Such as, why do you think public relations research is so important in planning a proposal?

5. Likert scale: asks for the level of agreement or disagreement with a statement such as:

Table 4.1 **Likert scale**

Public relations practitioners do not do enough research when planning a communications proposal	Strongly agree	Agree	Disagree	Strongly disagree

6. A semantic differential scale: ranks the attitudes towards different statements such as:

Table 4.2 **Semantic differential scale**

Is research necessary?	1	2	3	4	5	A waste of time
Is research expensive?						Inexpensive

Interviews are better than questionnaires for collecting qualitative information. Focus groups are small group discussions where a facilitator ensures participants discuss approximately six questions on a topic and this provides qualitative information. How to run a focus group is described in the PR tool section.

Surveys can include face-to-face interviews which means that interviewees can clarify questions and use scales and visual materials to help to ask the questions but there is no anonymity and it is expensive. In contrast, online surveys are inexpensive and anonymous but there is no control over who is contacted and there are low response rates. Telephone surveys are quick, questions can be explained and completed but there is limited use of scales and visual materials. Postal surveys are anonymous and time saving but have a low response rate and are therefore not representative (Szondi and Theilmann 2009: 207).

Once the results are collected, the data must be reviewed, measured, comparisons made, relationships between the findings examined, predictions made, and ideas tested. See the PR tool in chapter 5 on how to develop an opinion survey.

Content analysis

A content analysis reviews texts, often in the media, and analyses its meanings and their value, as well as who read or viewed them. It can help to assess public opinion about the organization and identify trends which can be addressed through public relations. It can be a powerful tool not only for reviewing what has happened, but also for planning ahead.

There are many online tools which help to identify online content and how it is viewed. An online newsreader which sits on the desktop is an effective way of receiving news on topics, as are RSS feeds which can drive news on selected areas to the desktop. Google Alert can provide regular email updates on the organization or product, particular issue, or a competitor and Google Trends monitors how often topics have been searched on Google over a period of time. It also connects to Google News and shows the number of times the search topic appeared in news stories.

Websites must be included in this analysis. It is vital to do online searches and to investigate the organization's website as well as that of its competitors. There will also be valuable information on blog sites and social media networks about the opinion people have on an organization. Google Analytics generates statistics about visitors to websites and tracks a website or blog by identifying location of visitors, whether hits are generated by search engines or referrals from other sites which means it identifies what is driving visits to a site and can therefore help analyse communications.

Alexa is another online tool that tracks the hits to a website, as well as information about it and its related links pages over time. Quantcast reports on the website's audience demographics and lifestyle by comparing information received from a variety of website publishers (Brown 2009).

A report by the media monitoring and analysis organization, Vocus (2009), states that engaging with social media always presents a risk as there are no guarantees. Therefore researching this area is valuable in order to develop a plan that understands any risks involved. For example, Vocus recommends identifying spokespeople, emerging topics, and fan groups which can be harnessed in a communications plan. Not only should discussions on the organization be monitored but also those about the competition. Analysing the different online discussions is necessary to know how to reach the different publics.

Public relations research needs to track where the organization is mentioned and stay informed of the conversations and their priority, assigning a value to it such as positive, negative, or neutral.

Communications audit

This looks at how well the organization's communications are reaching its publics both within and outside the organization and is usually developed by the public relations practitioner. Gregory (2006) points out that a communications audit reviews current attitudes and how these have formed. It analyses the nature and quality of communications between an organization and its publics.

This is carried out through reviewing existing communications plans and communications materials such as the organization's publications, website, blogs, and other literature about an organization with the objective of analysing how the organization communicates with the media, how the information was sent, whom it reached, and its effects and its relationships with its publics, including their feedback.

The communications audit will help to determine whether an organization has sufficient communications resources, examines whether it is making adequate use of what already exists, reviews whether what is done is properly planned and organized, and explores whether there is untapped potential to be exploited and gaps in resources that need to be filled.

B. Secondary research

Media audit

A full media audit needs to be carried out in order to assess and recommend the best channels that should be used for the organization's communications which includes social media, websites, broadcast, print, and radio. This means assessing each channel for its type of content, its agenda, deadlines, and its relevance to the organization, as well as the individual journalists to contact. See chapter 3 for more on identifying media and media audiences. An audit needs to include a list of media, media schedules, and feature schedules that are relevant to the organization and can be used to identify media opportunities for the organization.

Identifying media audiences can be done through the National Readership Survey (NRS) which estimates the number of readers and their social grading, the Audit Bureau of Circulation (ABC), which provides detailed circulation, distribution, attendance, traffic, and related data across a broad range of media, BARB which measures television ratings and collects the television viewing figures and audience sizes, and the Radio Joint Audience Research organization (RAJAR) which collects the type and number of radio's listeners. See chapter 3.

It is important to find the bloggers who are relevant to the organization. The Text 100 2009 Blogger Survey, which polled more than 400 technology, news, and lifestyle bloggers across 21 countries, found that 87 per cent of European bloggers welcomed contact from PR people (Sudhaman 2009). However, only 65 per cent of the region's bloggers are contacted once a week or more by PR people, compared to 96 per cent in the US.

Online monitoring tools, such as Technorati, track blogs and identify the number of links they have which measures their value. BlogPulse monitors blogs by showing the level of blog coverage about specific issues and its Conversation Tracker views conversations arising from blogs (Brown 2009: 139).

Monitoring trends in social media is essential to be able to build crediblity and influence the organization's online reputation. It is also important to know how to use different social media platforms. For example, Linkedin will require a more formal approach whereas others like Twitter are more about informal conversations and thoughts that can also have a great effect.

Research should also review what social media platforms have the greatest impact and how and whether they have affected sales numbers, attendees at events, and other media coverage. In addition, some platforms are more appropriate than others for different purposes. For instance, music is best promoted on Facebook but sold on MySpace.

Research should identify any social media platforms that have their own methods to promote valuable contributers. For example, Twitter has #followFriday, a designated day to recommend influential or interesting people to follow on Twitter and is a great way to get quality followers and establish a network.

Twitter search means all current feeds on Twitter can be followed by using a key word such as a brand name. This can identify who is twittering about it and what they are saying. It also means the practitioner can identify them and send information to them on the topic or involve them in discussions. There are many online monitoring tools and applications and these are discussed in later chapters.

Case studies

A case study is an in-depth study on people, organizations, events, or even processes (Stacks 2002: 71) and is valuable in providing information for a situation analysis. Case studies are used in business, medicine, and other applied disciplines and can offer valuable insights into public relations practice. They help to identify what worked and what didn't in a particular situation. Although Stacks (2002) admits that case studies cannot be reliably generalized to other situations, he argues that this limitation is overcome when they are used as examples of the effectiveness of public relations practice. Practitioners can develop case studies from historical research, interviews, and existing qualitative data although existing case studies can also be analysed further.

Market research

The organization's market research plays a vital role in providing information for developing a public relations campaign. The organization will have results of their own primary market research that provides data on the product, such as sales, buyer profiles and buying trends, and the organization, such as how its publics view it, what services they prefer, and how they use them. Frequently, organizations have carried out opinion polls that show a public's awareness, knowledge, opinions, and behaviours related to the organization and its issues. Much of the market research may be available in the organization's marketing plan.

Secondary market research can be derived from research organizations such as Mintel, a global market analyst, which shows market opportunities and trends in the UK, Europe, and the US and may also help to identify what competitors are doing. For example, if developing a proposal for Nikon as mentioned above, the 2008 Mintel report on 'Digital Cameras—UK' would be useful as it presents 'a review of the UK digital camera market and analyses the two key types of camera that can be found in the market, compact and SLR, as well as other digital camera units' (Mintel 2008).

Euromonitor International (2009) is another market research organization and is a leading provider of business intelligence. Similarly, GfK NOP provides quantitative and qualitative research surveys in the UK on international markets. Ipsos MORI is one of the leading political, social, and business research companies in the UK and Ireland. It produces numerous polls, reports, and thought pieces which review the research and opinion on a broad range of topics.

Although reports from these organizations can be commissioned they have executive summaries of their research that can be freely downloaded, providing insights into a market and its growth. In addition, there are archived media reports providing further information into the industry sectors. The research reports review the demographic, economic, social, political, and lifestyle trends and prospects to identify macro factors influencing their business environment.

Publics

Identifying publics is an important aspect of any public relations programme in order to engage with them so that the messages can be developed and delivered appropriately. Information about publics includes their demographics, that is, the age, gender and income of the publics; geographic, where they live, as there may be different ways of communicating with different communities, and psychographics, that is, their attitudes and lifestyles. What is their behaviour? What is their media use? This will also help to identify any professional organizations to which they belong and with whom it may help to form alliances during the campaign in order to reach the publics. It will also help to identify what they would want to know and the media they use. Much about publics can be identified from media research, marketing research, the annual report, and the corporate responsibility report.

Other sources of information about publics can be the media, public opinion polls, or published information as well as talking to customers, activist groups, journalists, government officials, work supervisors, and employees (Grunig 2006). See chapter 5 for more on identifying publics.

Third parties

The organization will have associations with external individuals, groups and other organizations and it is important to identify these in order to partner with them and ensure greater credibility of the messages. These third parties may be from:

- relevant interest and pressure groups
- organizations or people with similar interests, researchers, opinion leaders, politicians, and their communications
- government agencies, legislators, and officials with regulatory or legislative power affecting the organization and the problem situation.

For example, the makers of Hedrin, a treatment for head lice, developed a public relations campaign through presenting clinical research as interesting facts. This was compared it to research which uncovered a knowledge gap amongst parents about managing and treating lice infestations. Using this information, Hedrin developed a campaign that championed the role of parents, educating them on how to check for head lice and how to treat it. This built brand credibility and trust by raising awareness of the research drawn from clinical trials and case histories. See chapter **8** for more on this case study.

Corporate documents

The practitioner needs to review the organization's documentation in order to analyse its history and direction and identify any issues. This sort of research will provide understanding of the organization's history and its direction. As Cutlip et al (2006) note, finding out about the history of an organization can provide opportunities to think about creating a small museum, an anniversary event, or a biography of the CEO. By knowing the organization's direction the public relations plan can help to identify where it wants to be more visible or more active and how this can be achieved.

1. Annual report

Among the organization's documents is the annual report. This outlines how the organization is doing financially and how it will develop over the coming year. It includes financial information and identifies key employees, particularly the board members. Investors in the company rely on annual reports to let them know about the company; this can be used to see the strengths of an organization and identify its direction and the goals which the communications plan must support. It provides a context for the public relations activity.

Most annual reports can be accessed through the organization's corporate website. For example, the BBC's annual report (BBC 2010) is quick to download and easy to follow. The first section is an overall summary of the organization's progress by the chairman, and then what the organization has achieved based on the objectives which were stated the previous year, its financial situation, what is influencing the BBC and helping or deterring it from progress, and its overall role and services. Box 4.1 shows a list of its contents which review the corporation's performance, its plans for the future, and its management.

Go to the Online Resource Centre to access a link to the BBC annual report

---

Box 4.1 Contents page for BBC Annual Report 2009

Overview

- Chairman's foreword
- Performance versus strategy with objectives
- Financial performance
- Supporting and challenging the executive
- BBC services at a glance
- The trust's role.

Performance

- 2008/09 Plan
- Audience Councils
- Purposes
- Service performance
- Stewardship of the licensees
- Upholding Licence fee payers interests.

Looking Ahead

- Trust's Plans for 2009/10
- BBC Trustees
- Delivering value for money
- The BBC and wider economy
- Securing editorial standards.

Governance

- Serving all audiences.

Inside the trust

- Inside the trust
- Contacts.

Source:
BBC 2010

2. Mission statement

Most organizations have a **mission statement** which defines why the organization exists and what it hopes to achieve. A public relations programme needs to support the mission statement. For example, Virgin Atlantic's mission statement is

> **To grow a profitable airline ... Where people love to fly ... And where people love to work.**

(Virgin Atlantic 2010)

3. Organizational chart

Knowledge about the different roles within the organization and their reporting structure will help to form an idea about the company, its people, and how it communicates internally. This information is usually in a diagram presented vertically or horizontally and is called an **organizational chart**, which shows the reporting structure of employees, their titles, the relationships between the people leading different parts of the organization, their lines of responsibility or authority, and therefore clarifies how each part is linked. The CEO, Manager Director, or General Manager is at the top of the chart, the directors below with their teams, and lines connect the various positions (see Figure 4.3).

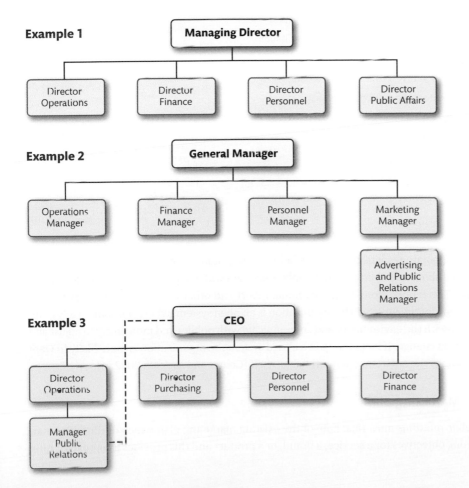

Fig 4.3
Examples of simple organizational charts

Looking at the job titles will help to identify the different functions within the organization and where different information lies as well as who is involved in dealing with it. This helps the practitioner to know who to contact for different expertise, who they can consider as spokespeople, and the existing communication channels.

4. Corporate responsibility report

The annual corporate responsibility report provides information about the organization's values and its engagement with its stakeholders. It presents its sustainability actions and what it is doing for the community. Reviewing the corporate responsibility report helps to understand if communications are in line with existing values, or may identify issues that need to be addressed. The corporate responsibility report for the international healthcare organization, GlaxoSmithKline (GSK 2010) has the list of contents shown in Box 4.2.

Box 4.2 **Contents page of GlaxoSmithKline's Corporate Responsibility Report**

- Message from the CEO
- Our Corporate Responsibility Principles
- Business case for corporate responsibility
- Our key issues
- Corporate responsibility governance
- Audit and assurance
- Risk management
- Stakeholder engagement
- Benchmarking
- About our reporting
- Corporate responsibility data summary

Source: GSK 2010

A corporate responsibility report helps to understand whether an organization is concerned about its publics' future or only concerned with its own immediate profit and success. This report, along with the annual report and other organizational literature, can help to identify whether the organization is an open system, where it is more likely to interact with the environment and communicate with publics and more likely to adjust and adapt to change. If it operating in a closed system the organization is more likely to want to change the environment than change itself (Center and Jackson 2002: 4).

5. Marketing plan

Public relations must take note of the existing marketing plan which outlines the marketing objectives for a service, a brand, or a product and this provides a context for public relations. The marketing plan will have used market research to identify who is buy-ing the product or services. The plan will be led by the business goals and marketing goals, such as how many products should be sold, the timescales, and the competitors.

Knowing the competitors and what they are doing can help practitioners to think about how they will communicate the differences between their organization, or product, from another.

In addition, it is important to identify the performance of the product or the organization—that is, its sales, market share, profitability—and compare it with previous years, looking at trends and identifying any problems that can be addressed through communications.

The following may also be found in the marketing plan or may need to be accessed from the marketing team:

- advertising plans—public relations needs to ensure it is cognisant of the advertising messages and works with them if appropriate
- salesforce plans and promotions—public relations can support these and raise awareness of them if appropriate
- information about the product/organization can inform the situation analysis.

If the PR programme concerns a product, it is important to know the stage of the prod-uct's lifecycle, that is, its development, introduction, growth, maturity, and decline, as this affects sales and profits. The maturity phase is a profitable time as it no longer has any product development costs, it is already established in the market, and it is at a profitable stage therefore organizations may involve public relations to try and extend this stage of a product. An organization may want to delay the decline stage of the prod-uct lifecycle and try to regenerate the product through public relations.

Go to the Online Resource Centre to access a link to GlaxoSmithKline's CR report

6. Other corporate documentation

Other documentation that should be reviewed includes key policies, existing corporate communications plans and product specifications, relevant EU and government regula-tions and legislation.

Organization's schedules

Planned events for the organization's product or services such as anniversaries, awards, events, and related community events provide communications opportunities. For ex-ample, in December 2009 *Viz*, the adult comic magazine, used the opportunity to cel-ebrate its 30th anniversary as a way to profile itself. External events that affect the or-ganization's plans, from seasons to actual days, are an opportunity to create some news or add more to a programme. Other dates such as launch times and competitor launch dates offer opportunities to think about using them in a campaign.

Organization's resources

Resources are an important part of any situation analysis and these include money, ex-pertise and teams. Time and availability of resources will affect what can be planned. These elements need to be identified and included in the situation analysis as they can hinder or help its development. Also it is important to assess the involvement of senior management, the more they are involved the more successful the programme will be as decisions will be made faster and actions supported.

4.3 Influences

A research structure ensures key factors are identified. PEST and SWOT formats. are recommended as ideal frameworks in which to present information. The PEST format identifies political, economic, social, and technological factors and can be used to give an overarching view of what is influencing the organization. The SWOT format identifies strengths, weaknesses, opportunities, and threats. It offers a closer view of the organization as well as identifying issues within the organization itself. They are done sequentially and provide a great way of structuring research findings.

Structuring intelligence with PEST

PEST stands for the four main forces affecting an organization: political, economic, social, and technological.

Using each PEST element in the research will ensure a full overview of the external environment of the company.

Political

Political covers the regulations and laws that affect the organization. It can be used to review how political bodies, such as the EU, national or local government control the legal and regulatory environment in which the organization operates. It can also show the influence of ethical codes and any issues arising from self-regulation of the industry sector.

Fig 4.4
There are many aspects to research in the music industry
Source: Copyright OUP

Economic

This analyses how the economy is affecting the organization such as interest rates, costs and suppliers that may influence pricing or competitors.

Social or cultural

These are aspects such as how the culture of people, age groups, religions, attitudes and social dynamics are affecting an organization. In the music industry for example, there are complex relationships between management and the record companies.

Technological

This reviews how technology is affecting an organization and its communications. There may be new research or new investment into technology. For example, changes in technology such as online music and downloads have affected the music industry as illustrated by Figure 4.4 (Allen 2007).

PEST analysis of the music industry

Record companies make a profit from identifying, developing, and promoting musical talent (Taylor 2008). Table 4.3 shows a PEST and SWOT analysis of the music industry for a music recording company. It gives a broad overview of the music industry and what affects it. There are many different sources of information and developing a PEST and SWOT analysis helps to identify what additional information is needed and what sources can be used.

Table 4.3 **Pest analysis of the music industry for a recording company**

Political	Economic
• Regulations cover the property rights affecting who owns the music. A DVD is divided into different ownership of the images, the music, and the lyrics as well as what the agent and the actual musicians get • Any communication has to consider the interests of these stakeholders • Proliferation of online copyright infringement damaged business but provided opportunities • Legislation in new markets such as licence rights in movies and advertisements, video games, and other digital outlets	• Sales of digital music have grown but much of it is illegal and tougher legislation is being called for • Money can come from concerts • Touring is expensive owing to rising transport costs and concert costs are expensive • Internet radio stations fail to pay royalties • Sales opportunities as demand for recorded music has exploded • With CD sales in a downward spiral, record labels and musicians rely on other revenue streams such as concert tickets, advertising deals, and licensing • Deluxe album additions are becoming a strong market • Singles growing but album market also growing • Record labels invest heavily in the music industry creating many of the opportunities that now exist for young artists, session musicians, songwriters, and publishers, and live music • Must pay royalties to artists • High costs of producing the music • High costs of selling the music • Must attract fans through promotions • Must ensure media play the music • Need to develop new markets such as selling licence rights in movies and adverts and now video games and other digital outlets

Social/cultural	Technological
• The music industry consists of artists, songwriters, musicians, managers, tour managers, venues, agents, publishers, record labels • More and more online social networks are emerging that use music as one of the key factors in establishing communities. Record labels are licensing services like Bebo, and MySpaceMusic, bringing new revenues into the business and helping to add value to such services with previews and exclusives • Music fans desire quality and diversity • Certain age groups have different preferences which affect the communications • In addition, people who buy DVDs are frequently also consumers of digital games	• Huge range of other entertainment services such as games • Distribution is easy because of social networking • There may be a trend towards music subscriptions being 'hidden' in mobile devices • Video games are boosting music sales CD business in decline with switch to digital

⊚ Go to the Online Resource Centre to access a link to a PEST template

This overview allows an understanding of what is happening and links the different issues to form the situational analysis. For example, the situation analysis would examine the potential of creating and sustaining online communities; it could discuss reaching buyers of DVDs through communicating with buyers of games.

Structuring intelligence with a SWOT

Following the broad sweep of a PEST analysis, a close up view can then be formed to identify how effective the organization is in influencing its publics.

A SWOT analysis stands for strength weaknesses, opportunities, and threats of its communication.

This looks at its reputation, customer loyalty, positive perceptions, its corporate responsibility programmes, its strong brands, media and internet presence.

Strengths and weaknesses usually arise from within an organization and are considered to be within its control. Strength is a capacity or a resource that can be used to achieve PR objectives. Weaknesses are usually limitations or faults and a PR plan must have a response to them.

For example, a recording company's strengths may be its high profile, its good reputation, strong financial position, positive media coverage, and its integrated approach to communications. Its weaknesses could be poor resources, poor product, slow production, staff changes, lack of customer loyalty, poor online presence.

⊚ Go to the Online Resource Centre to access a link to a SWOT template

Opportunities and threats are usually external matters factors over which the organization has little if any control, such as its competitors' actions. An opportunity could be new online opportunities or a new group of consumers. A threat could be a new competitor. When developing a SWOT the four elements usually link to each other.

4.4 Application to industry

A situation analysis allows for strategic thinking that involves considering how the organization can move forward. It refers to the research and identifies the issues, the publics, any problems, and provides enough information to develop solutions and likely outcomes. It looks at the consequences of the programme and various scenarios.

> Greater use of market research will promote a more sophisticated understanding of audiences, and this can only be a good thing for PROs, who can use this knowledge to devise campaigns that are more effective.
>
> (Jardine 2009)

A situation analysis can be structured in various ways depending on how much information is needed and how much time and budget has been allowed for its development. Cutlip et al (2006) believes we need to ask:

1. What is the source of the concern?
2. Where is the problem?
3. When is it a problem?
4. Who is involved?
5. How are they involved?
6. Why is this a concern?

Structure

A situation analysis should present the research findings in a logical and easily understood written order which forms the initial part of the public relations proposal. The following outlines a recommended three-part structure to form a situation analysis.

1. What has happened (or is expected to happen)

- The issue and its context: this defines the issue, which could be a product launch, and how it fits into the organization.
- The cause of the issue: this illuminates the historical aspects that have led to the situation and that will have an impact. For example, the launch of a product will need to consider timings, previous launches, and current products which are similar.
- The attitudes of those involved, that is what they think or what behaviour they exhibit that needs to be changed.

2. What is required?

- Whether attitudes are to be reinforced, modified, or crystallized (Maymoto CIPR).
- Whether behaviour is to be changed.
- Desired outcomes and barriers preventing them as well as supporting factors.

3. An outline of the proposed activity

- Different scenarios and recommended actions.
- The way forward, highlighting key recommendations.
- What will happen if the recommendations are not pursued?
- Barriers that may limit the effectiveness of a public relations plan, these can include reduced resources or poor buy-in from senior management.

Example of a situation analysis

As described on page 108, the COI, in an effort to improve communication with specific ethnic communities, carried out research to identify how these groups interpreted information. They then used the research findings to compile the following situation analysis which presents the current situation within an historic and forward-thinking context along with a synopsis of recommended communications.

Situation analysis: COI Common Good Research: Ethnic Minority Communities (2009). Source: Courtesy of COI

Ethnic minority communities shared many interests and media habits with the general population and this was particularly true of the younger generation. Thus, campaigns targeting ethnic minority communities do not always need to use specialist media, as mainstream channels will reach large sections of the communities. Minority and white audiences alike enjoyed all soaps, police shows, talk shows, home decoration, 'reality TV', science fiction, action movies and thrillers, and this should be remembered when planning media and advertising.

Specialist media are, however, essential to access key subgroups in these communities, such as women, older people, and those who speak little or no English. These people are often highly engaged in specialist media whilst they often appear uninterested in mainstream media and advertising. Specialist media also offer opportunities to communicate with the whole family in the Asian and Chinese communities, which is rarely achieved through mainstream channels. They can also communicate with an additional 'cultural closeness'.

In the mainstream media, there are ample opportunities to enhance the impact of advertising and marketing. People from ethnic minority communities want to see a wider range of realistic, credible characters playing 'normal', mainstream roles. They want to see appealing images that they and their families can relate to, and they do not want to be continually 'exploited' for their ethnic identity. Using characters in this way can help to cut through the media noise as black and Asian people do pay attention when they see interesting characters from their own ethnic backgrounds.

Among the Chinese and African communities, there are real opportunities to gain 'first mover advantage' by representing these communities in appealing mainstream roles from which currently they perceive themselves as absent. In targeted campaigns using specialist media, ethnic and religious identity can be used to enhance the relevance and closeness of the message to the communities. This might include using a credible spokesperson from the community, making reference to key religious festivals or cultural symbols, or including an identifiable and likeable portrait of family life.

There are also many opportunities for creative niche marketing through specialist media. Marketers could hook into the specific ethnic and cultural interests of particular groups or subgroups, and these can be tied into specific media channels. Government communicators could also develop relationships with local organizations and individuals to enhance the effectiveness of distribution and generate word-of-mouth publicity through existing community networks. Finally, community groups need to be seen as a target audience in their own right and not just as a channel for distribution. Materials need to be developed to meet their specific needs, and these should be properly publicized both externally and internally within the government department that produces them.

Go to the Online Resource Centre to access a link to this research

Applying research

Research that is carried out for a situation analysis is used to inform the development of a programme and can also be drawn on to provide news to the media during the campaign. The following case study shows how research identified fans around the world in order to develop activities which reached them more effectively as well as providing news for the fans.

Case Study

Barclays' sponsorship of the Premier League

Source: Courtesy of Lexis PR

Barclays sponsors the Premier League, the most watched domestic league competition in the world which is broadcast in 611 million homes in 211 countries. The London public relations consultancy Lexis PR was briefed to carry out research to identify the fans and understand their lifestyle and culture. This would help them know how to improve Barclays' interaction with them across the globe as well as plan the Barclays Premier League global public relations programme.

The research also needed to examine how developments in media and technology were helping supporters get closer to the league, while uncovering the characteristics that make it so popular for fans.

The research was commissioned and hosted on the official Barclays Premier League website, ensuring strong global visibility for the survey and reaching a worldwide online audience of 3.1 million unique users. A Mandarin version of the survey was produced to encourage more Chinese respondents.

More than 33,000 fans from 185 countries responded to the survey. The campaign also offered deeper insight into fans' passion for football and the Barclays Premier League. The survey questions elicited the most varied possible responses from fans, ranging from team support and viewing habits to football finance. Ex-Chelsea and French international legend Marcel Desailly was Barclays' ambassador and broadened the audience reach even further.

After identifying the key statistics, Lexis PR developed a report illustrating the findings in Europe, Africa, Asia, and the Middle East. This helped Barclays to understand its market and provided new information on how to communicate with the football fans. In addition, the research was released to the media in a powerful media campaign releasing in-depth insights into how the fans consume Barclays Premier League football. This project is developing into a regular and larger survey demonstrating sustained and successful outcomes (see Figure 4.5).

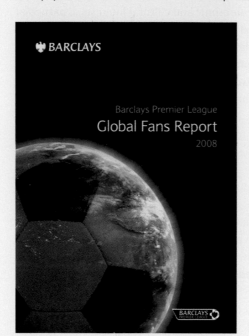

Fig 4.5
Report on findings of Barclays' campaign
Source: Courtesy of Lexis PR

🌐 **Go to the Online Research Centre to access a link to other research reports and their methodology**

PR Tool

Focus group

A focus group is a series of interviews in a group carried out in an informal setting where everyone participates. It is used as a preliminary research technique to explore people's ideas and attitudes. It is commonly used in marketing research to test out reactions and advertising concepts. In public relations it is often used to find out how to approach a campaign, and to discover opinions and attitudes of a representative group of people; therefore objectives need to be developed. For example, if a new bread is being launched the bakery may want to find out what people think of its taste and texture, rather than focus on its price or presentation.

A group of approximately six to ten people meet with a facilitator who leads the group's discussion and keeps the focus on the areas you want to explore that are in the objectives.

Preparing

Identify the objective of the focus group—what do you want to find out?
- Identify a facilitator.

- Invite six to ten members to the meeting with an agenda, session time, and list of questions that the group will discuss. Members are people who have some similarity, eg age, race, gender, or interest that is relevant to your research.
- Call members to invite them to attend.
- Develop approximately six questions that you can focus upon.

Implementation

The meeting should be approximately one and a half hours long.
- Meeting room: ensure a good room with refreshments.
- Seating: usually members sit in a circle or where they can see and converse with each other without any trouble.
- Make name tags for everyone.
- Recording: you will need to audio or video record the session so that you can act as facilitator and then have the recording transcribed.
- Agenda: greet and introduce everyone, announce the agenda, present the goal of the meeting, establish the ground rules, and start the questions and discussion.

Facilitating

The goal of the facilitator is to keep the focus group focused. That is, to ensure that the group understands the agenda and that there will be about six distinct questions that will be addressed and that everyone is expected to answer them.

Once the group is introduced the topic can be introduced, followed by the first question which must be delivered accurately. Each person should have a chance to answer and then the whole group can discuss it.

Group dynamics will show that some people sit back and are quiet while others dominate. As a facilitator it is important to encourage participation by drawing each person into the discussion and making it clear that everyone participates.

After the focus group

Make any notes abut the session—anything unusual, any special aspects, etc.

Ensure that the results are written up so that you can use this research as part of your intelligence gathering.

Send a note to thank all participants.

Summary

Planning is an essential aspect of public relations and this is based on research which identifies issues and recommends the way forward. A public relations plan or proposal is developed from various models and answers Cutlip's questions of what are we doing now; what should we say and why; how and when we say it and then how is it measured. This straightforward approach has led to practitioners developing plans which reflect on an organization's brief and then outlines a situation analysis, objectives, publics, strategy, recommendations, budgets, and evaluation. This means that public relations can be carried out which fits with an organization's objectives, is validated by research, and is based on a realistic budget and agreed evaluation benchmarks.

Research or environmental scanning is essential to define the communications issue, understand its context and know what affects it as well as the impact it has on its own environment. This may include primary research, otherwise called new research which usually involves commissioning market research or public opinion polls. Secondary research looks at existing research. Either of these methods can be quantitative, which is the collection of numerical data, or qualitative which interprets meaning.

There are different research tools such as a content analysis which looks at information presented in documents and other texts such as newspapers or broadcast media. Surveys are a valuable research tool and questionnaires can be in the form of interviews and focus groups. The findings must be examined and used to analyse a situation. Technology is allowing faster research and analysis and online surveys are increasingly popular.

Carrying out research means access to different sources of information is needed and these include corporate documents such as annual reports, mission statements, regulations and policies, as well as advertising campaigns and even information about the organization's employees. Online sources are also valuable, especially websites, bloggers, and social media groups. The marketing plans are needed to know what plans the organization has for itself and its products and how it intends to achieve these. Market research will also reveal valuable information on trends and publics. Third parties, whether they be organizations or individuals, need to be identified, whether they are supportive or otherwise, as they can be a source of assistance to a communications plan or may create opposition. A communication audit determines how an organization communicates and has the potential to communicate. It should include a full media content analysis of how an organization appears in the media as this view may be representative of the publics or may influence the public. Furthermore, a full schedule of the organization's own calendar of planned events will help to structure a plan as will awareness of the resources available.

Once the research is gathered it needs to be critically assessed and can be formatted into a PEST (political, economic, social, and technological areas) to analyse the overall external issues as well into a SWOT (strengths, weaknesses, opportunities, and threats) to analyse the issues which are affecting it directly. This leads into formulating a situation analysis which analyses the information and recommends the way forward. It can be structured in three parts starting with a breakdown of the issue, its context, and motivations; what is required in terms of how the public should be influenced whether it be opinions or behaviours; and then the actual activity or way forward proposed along with an outline of limitations, barriers, and expectations.

A situation analysis should outline how the proposal is to be structured and if possible highlight the validity of also using the research as a part of the programme's activities.

Discussion points

A. Focus groups

Set up several focus groups in the class to discuss how they feel about a controversial issue.

Identify a facilitator who will develop the questions around what you think of the product and if you would use it.

Carry out the focus group.

Discuss the findings—did you feel it was a good research tool? How would you use this to develop a PR programme? Do you think it helps you think of creative ideas?

B. Situation analysis

Form pairs and identify a client in which you are interested.

Outline the research you would do for a situation analysis.

What has influenced your approach?

C. Surveys

Go to the Online Resource Centre and download the survey. Answer the questions.

Which question formats do you think give the most accurate answers/provide the most information? Which questions do you think provide more research material than others?

Explore the web to find more surveys and how they are done. Develop your own survey using http://surveymonkey.com and distribute it among your group. What are the responses? How can you analyse the information?

D. Market research

Access a market research organization online and download a market research report. Scan the report.

What format does it follow? What do you think of the executive summary?

How can this report be used in a public relations plan? What other research would be needed?

References

Allen, K. (2007) 'Pubs and Puppeteers Are Unlikely Saviours of Struggling Music Industry', The Guardian, 19 May. Available at: http://www.guardian.co.uk

BBC (2010) 'About the BBC'. Available at: http://www.bbc.co.uk/aboutthebbc/purpose/

BBC (2010) 'Annual Report and Accounts' Available at: http://www.bbc.co.uk/annualreport/download_trust.shtml

BPI (2008) 'London Calling', 20 June. Available at: http://www.bpi.co.uk

Broom, G. and Dozier, D. (1990) Using Research in Public Relations: Applications to Program Management. Englewood Cliffs, NJ: Prentice Hall

Brown, R. (2009) *Public Relations and the Social Web: How to Use Social Media and Web 2.0 in Communications*. London: Kogan Page

Center, A. and Jackson, P. (2003) *Public Relations Practices: Managerial Case Studies and Problems* (6th edn). Upper Saddle River, NJ: Prentice Hall

COI (2009) 'COI Common Good Research: Ethnic Minority Communities'. Available at: http://coi.gov.uk/documents/common-good-bme-exec-summ.pdf

Cutlip , S., Center, A., and Broom, G (2006) *Effective Public Relations* (9th edn). Upper Saddle River, NJ: Pearson

Drucher, P. (1954) *The Practice of Management*. New York: Harper & Row

Fergusson, S. (2008) 'Public Relations Planning' in W. Donsbach (ed) *The International Encyclopedia of Communication*. Available at: http://www.blackwellreference.com

Grunig, J. (1992) 'Communication, Public Relations and Effective Organizations: An overview of the book' in J.E. Grunig (ed) *Excellence in Public Relations and Communications Management*. Hillsdale, NJ: Lawrence Erlbaum

Grunig, J. (2006) 'Furnishing the edifice: Ongoing research on public relations as a strategic management function', Journal of Public Relations Research 18/2: 151–76

Gregory, A. (2009) 'Management and Organization of Public Relations' in R. Tench and L. Yeomans (eds) *Exploring Public Relations* (2nd edn). Harlow: Prentice Hall

GSK (2010) 'Reports and Publications'. Available at: http://www.gsk.com/reportsandpublications.htm

Hobsbawm, J. (2004) 'Opinion: PROs have the power to shape the future', PR Week UK, 23 April. London: Haymarket

Jardine, A. (2006) 'Take The Best of Both Worlds', PR Week UK, 2 February. Available at: http://www.prweek.com/uk/news/search/539145/best-worlds/

Lee, Y. and Smarr, K. (2009) 'Examining Usefulness of Model of Resource Assessment as a Possible Tool for Gaining Public Relations' Influence'. Paper presented to the Annual International Public Relations Research Conference, March, Miami

Lerbinger, O. (1977) 'Corporate Uses of Research in Public Relations', Public Relations Review 3: 11–19

Mintel (2008) Digital Cameras, UK, International Reports (Academic USA) Technology. Available at: http://reports.mintel.com/sinatra/reports/search_results/show&&type=RCItem&page=0&noaccess_page=0/display/id=227704

Parkinson, M. and Ekachai, D. (2006) *International and Intercultural Public Relations*. Boston, MA: Pearson

Stacks, D.W. (2002) *Primer of Public Relations Research*. New York: Guildford Press

Sudhaman, A. (2009) 'Brands2Life Lands Pan-European Nikon Euro Account', 17 June. Available at: http://www.prweek.com/uk/news/913854/Brands2Life-lands-pan-European-Nikon-Euro-account/

Sudhaman, A. (2009) 'Text 100 Blogger Survey Finds European Corporates Overlook Bloggers', 26 June. Available at: http://prweek.com

Theilmann, R. and Szondi, G. (2009) 'Public Relations Research and Evaluation' in R. Tench and L. Yeomans (eds) *Exploring Public Relations*. Harlow: Prentice Hall

Taylor, G. (2009) 'Adapting to the Future in a Rapidly Changing Environment BPI', AGM Speech, 7 July

Treadwell, D. and Treadwell, J. (2005) *Public Relations Writing: Principles in Practice*. Thousand Oaks, CA: Sage

Virgin Atlantic (2010) 'Our Story'. Available at: http://www.virgin-atlantic.com/en/gb/allaboutus/missionstatement/index.jsp

Vocus (2009) 'The Dos and Don'ts of Creating An Effective Media Strategy', White Paper. Available at: http://www.vocus.com/wp/

Washbourne, N. (2009) 'Media Context of Contemporary Public Relations and Journalism in R. Tench and L. Yeomans (eds) *Exploring Public Relations* (2nd edn). Harlow: Prentice Hall

Publics

(5)

Learning outcomes

1. Identify the different and changing meanings of publics and public opinion and how these terms originated.

2. Understand how publics develop and how they can be identified through demographics, psychographics, adopters of innovations and how they affect and are affected by organizations.

3. Explore how publics develop and change through investigating different academic perspectives and online monitoring.

4. Understand the situational theory of publics by applying it to a public relations programme.

5. Review the purpose and development of an opinion poll through writing questions.

6. Value the need to identify and prioritize publics in order to carry out communication programmes which build relationships.

Practitioner Insight

Jim Hawker
Co-founder of Threepipe PR

Jim Hawker co-founded Threepipe (http://www.threepipe.co.uk) in 2004 as a consumer and sports PR agency. Since that time Threepipe has gone on to win over 20 industry awards including *PR Week*'s Best New PR Agency and the PRCA's Best Small Agency for its work with brands including Vodafone, Betfair, and Siemens.

What are the best ways to approach a consumer PR brief?

Ask lots of questions! Gain as much insight as possible from the client and spend a lot of time really trying to get under the skin of their business, their competitors, and get a sense of how they think, which will ultimately help you develop the right strategy and ideas.

How do you identify publics for a programme?

We look at their current customer base and what most influences them. There will be a wide range of stakeholders that ultimately affect purchasing decisions, so it's a case of ensuring that they are all exposed at varying degrees to the PR programme.

Can you describe the most successful campaign you have led?

A multi-award winning anti-bullying campaign for Vodafone which was targeted at teenage girls. We partnered with Joseph and his Amazing Technicolour Dreamcoat on London's West End stage. It was a fantastic partnership which led to a phenomenal response, which was underpinned by very strong case study placement into national media.

How do you use research to prepare a proposal?

A lot of it is primary desk-based research, talking to key media, and running focus groups. This is an area where there is huge room for improvement and you can see this by larger agencies hiring account planners. However, its is primarily ideas and creativity that wins pitches but they must be channelled commercially which is dependent on the availability of good information.

How can you draw out communications solutions from identifying publics?

By talking to them directly, reading the media they consume, and looking at discussion forums to see what they really think and identifying how brands can be part of those discussions.

What advice do you have for anyone starting in public relations?

This industry is full of bright people who are prepared to work hard—a strong work ethic is essential. It's a also a real team effort—anyone who doesn't enjoy working closely with colleagues and clients should look for a job elsewhere!

5.1 Definition

Public relations practitioners need to understand an organization's publics in order to find the best way to get their attention and stimulate their interest. There are many definitions of the word 'public' and its meaning depends on the context. It could mean people as a whole, the community, or the nation and in can also mean people in general. Originally, the word is from Latin, 'publicus' meaning people and developed into English through the French language which uses the word 'publique'.

The term public in public relations arose from the concept of mass communication and was first defined by Blumer (cited McQuail 2010: 59) in 1939 as a social formation distinct from a group or a crowd. He described a public as being large, widely dispersed, and enduring. A public tends to form around an issue or cause and moves an interest or opinion forward. Cutlip et al (2006: 323), argued that publics are defined by how groups of people are involved in a situation or affected by it.

Publics can mean potential or actual audiences connected to particular messages. It is also used to refer to communities, that is, groups drawn together by shared experiences, values, symbols, places and increasingly an online community. They may share a common interest as do university students, sportspeople, parents, IT users, consumers, doctors, and so on.

Grunig and Hunt (1984: 134) said that publics always have some common problem and are transient in how and when they exist. It all depends on what an organization does and how people react to that organization's behaviour. Grunig and Hunt (1984) saw publics arising out of a response to what an organization does, and believed that they were determined by how they are affected by an organization or how they affect an organization. They argued that if an organization did not affect a public then there was no need for a practitioner to consider that public in its public relations. Vasquez and Taylor (2001) build on this definition and suggest that publics are collectives that form in response to some issue or problematic situation.

Leitch and Neilson (2001: 128) recommend that public relations moves away from thinking about publics as simply consuming targeted messages from organizations or as a group involved with an organization. They argue that publics are more than this and

do not exist simply because an organization exists. They explain that publics are created and recreated as all the different types of people within a group interpret and act upon the messages (see Figure 5.1). According to research by Amaral and Phillips (2010), online publics form around a combination of personal beliefs and attitudes which they call values. People network with each other to share their own values through online conversations. See chapter 12 for more about online media and publics.

Stakeholders or publics

In addition to defining a public, there is ongoing debate over whether there is a difference between a 'stakeholder' and a 'public'. Mackey (2006) identifies the struggle there is in public relations literature to find a distinction between the two terms. Cutlip et al (2006) do not identify them as having different meanings. Coombs and Halliday (2007: 24) consider stakeholders to be any group that can affect or be affected by the actions of an organization and state that publics are a more identifiable group, whether inside or outside the organization, whose opinions on issues can affect the success of the organization.

Grunig (1984) uses the terms 'stakeholder' and 'public' in a different way. Grunig drew on Dewey's writings on public opinion to develop his definition of a public: that it is a group of people who face a similar problem, recognize the problem, and organize themselves to do something about it (Price 1992). Therefore, according to Grunig (1984), publics arise from stakeholders when they recognize an issue and decide to do something about it. Similarly, Gregory (2006: 46) states that stakeholders turn into a public when they become active about an issue, that is, when they communicate about it. In this book, the two terms are used interchangeably unless otherwise stated.

Knowing the publics

A key role for practitioners is to monitor the media and other sources of information and be alert to any matters which can influence the attitudes or behaviour of stakeholders and publics. For example, a practitioner involved in the launch of a new cancer treatment needs to be aware of the attitudes of researchers, doctors (particularly oncologists), pharmacists and other health carers, medicine regulatory authorities, competitors, as well as the patients themselves. In addition, the practitioner needs to monitor aspects that can influence the shareholders or investors of the organization as well as the employees.

Publics exist within, and are affected by, a constantly changing environment. The practitioner needs to know how the publics are being influenced in order to develop different communications strategies to engage them. Gregory (2006) emphasizes the need for collaborative practices with publics as they can quickly use the internet to communicate and galvanize people into action. In addition, there is increasing transparency of organizations, which means that outsiders can look in and view documents and gain knowledge on the organization and insiders can transmit messages outside the organization. Therefore having open and responsible communication between the organization and its publics is important.

Knowing the different publics, their characteristics, beliefs, attitudes, concerns, and lifestyles helps the practitioner tailor messages that are targeted to the correct public, and distributed through the most relevant media. Practitioners need to spend a lot of time dividing the public into smaller and smaller groups which have a common interest or common behaviour. The expression 'general public' is seldom used in public relations practice as in order for communication messages to be effective the PR practitioner must tailor them to a specific group.

Online activists

Previously unknown publics can arise unexpectedly and demand that the organization changes. For example, cyber activists or online protestors, can create DDOS (distributed denial of service) attacks where a website is bombarded by requests for pages, often taking it offline. Anonymous (http://www.whyweprotest.net/en) is a loose-knit group of individual protestors which began on internet message boards that require no registration. Its members have been linked to online protests against the Church of Scientology. The group has developed a wiki for use by 'anons' who can post end-content and recommend protest causes and activity to other members.

Organizations as a public

Organizations themselves can be a public. For example, Greenpeace is trying to influence organizations to improve their environmental policies and therefore it considers its publics to be the organizations themselves— these include chemical companies which may pollute the environment and food companies which use genetically engineered ingredients.

A typical organization interacts with many publics. Grunig and Hunt (1984) identified publics on how active or passive they are in relation to an issue. However, organizations can also identify their publics based on a list developed from Esman in 1972 (cited Grunig and Hunt 1984). Esman suggested four types of organizational links that can help to identify publics: enabling links, functional links, normative links, and diffused links. The following applies them to public relations today:

1. Enabling

These publics give the authority or assistance to help an organization exist, eg government bodies and regulators. For example, a financial organization reviewing its reputation would communicate with the Financial Services Authority which sets the standards for financial advisers to regulate the financial services industry. Public relations around these publics is usually called public affairs. A school would consider the education regulatory body, Ofsted, an important public and would probably ensure collaboration with Ofsted in its public relations campaigns.

2. Functional

These publics give something to a company such as raw materials, and others take or buy something from a company such as consumers. They are made up of suppliers; for example, foresters would be a supplier for a timber company. The public relations directed to suppliers is business-to-business public relations. Anyone who buys the products or uses the services is called a consumer.

3. Normative

These are peer organizations, that is, they share an industry interest and may belong to a joint association. For example, pharmaceutical companies in the UK belong to the professional organization called the Association of Pharmaceutical Manufacturers. This area is often called professional relations but there is a crossover with the enabling publics.

4. Diffused

These publics have no formalized relationship and may include people outside the organization where issues may arise but which are not immediately relevant. Grunig and Hunt (1984) suggest that these could be environmental groups or other diffused groups. These are increasingly important publics to reach as organizations develop their corporate responsibility programmes.

A list of publics

Finite resources mean that not all publics can be reached therefore a programme needs to identify which ones are the most important to the organization. Breaking down the publics further can help to reveal their agenda and how they affect the organization and how it affects them. The following is a list of publics based on Jefkins' (1998: 57) ten basic publics.

The community These are people around the organization who are affected by how it expands. Many employees will be from the community—or may be potential employees. The publics here are affected by what the organization does in relation to its immediate environment. Chapter 10 describes a crisis management case study where a chemical company spill affected the whole community. Public relations needed to focus on the local community to offer fast information and build trust to avoid any ongoing issues.

Potential employees These may be university students, people in competitive organizations, even clients (see Figure 5.2). Organizations may release surveys to these groups reporting on their employee satisfaction in order to boost their profile as a good employer and thereby increase their chances of attracting top employees.

Employees These can be from all parts of the organization and every wage level and type of employment from contracted to part time and full time, from sales staff to management. Many may work off site and communicate online only. These employees need to know what is going on in the organization and how it affects them; this is called internal communications.

Trade and suppliers These are a diverse range of organizations and individuals and are considered a business-to-business public and can be the people the organization deals with in buying or selling its products or services. Suppliers are not only organizations that provide the raw product but can be anyone who consults to the company, such as graphic artists, advertising and public relations consultancies. Apart from the organizations communicating with them directly, anything that affects this group can also have an impact, by association, on the organization.

Consumers and users These people buy the products or services and can be segmented into groups depending on their relevance and priority. This group can be

Fig 5.2
University students are potential employees

Source: Copyright OUP

subdivided and broken down into different groups depending on what they buy and how much they interact with the organization and how it affects them.

Third parties Third parties are opinion leaders or other organizations that support an organization, its brand or its products in some way. For example, a pharmaceutical organization will communicate its new treatment for heart disease to GPs through cardiologists. When an organization wants to launch a product it may first need to gain the approval and support of professional organizations, such as its associated regulatory bodies.

Shareholders and investors Shareholders and investors are people who have bought into the organization and own parts of it. Public relations for these publics is called investor relations or financial public relations and clear and regular information is important to these people as this can affect the share price. They are also informed of mergers and takeovers or anything else affecting the financial stability of the organization.

Jefkins (1998) lists the media as a public although they are really a channel to the publics. However, with the internet allowing user-generated content there is an increasing crossover of who the journalist is and who is the public. In addition, the internet can reveal publics that have been unknown, as in the case of the cyber activists.

Segmentation

People can also be identified through their demographics and psychographics which identify segments of the population that are similar to one another in one or more characteristics. A group of people who share particular demographic or psychographic characteristics are likely to behave or respond to messages in a similar way. Psychographics is about a psychological profile of a public, its attitudes and opinions, beliefs, and activities and tries to identify people's tastes and personalities. Demographics are easier to measure as these are observable statistics such as birth rate, age, gender, and income (Solomon et al 2006). They also include where someone lives, their education level, race, marital status, religion, employment, and number of children.

This type of market segmentation is particularly important to marketing communications programmes because it helps organizations target their publics more accurately as people with different ages and gender have different needs and wants and this affects their spending (Solomon et al 2006).

For example, a location may change owing to an increasing number of wealthy people buying into it, or an area may become more popular with a particular age group. Notting Hill in London is an example of a suburb that has become trendy and even famous after appearing in films and is now home to an increasing number of celebrities.

Health organizations may want to target families with young children, as they are more likely to be big buyers of health foods and fruit juices. Cafes and wine bars are often more interested in singles who are more likely to eat out. Social class and income is another variable and often determines with whom people socialize and the values they share. Race and ethnic group is also important as organizations can see opportunities to introduce products to areas with a specific ethnic mix.

However, online social media is usually defined by its demographics and it is important to monitor these rapidly changing statistics in order to ensure online conversations are made with the publics who are more likely to engage. For example, Facebook is no longer a site only for young people. Most users on the site belong to the 35–54 age group compared to the age group that used to be Facebook's main users, the 18–24 group who are now third in place just behind the 25–34 age group. In 2009 the number of users aged 55 and over grew from fewer than 100,000 to almost 6 million in six months (Schroeder 2009). Although the overall number of users of all ages is growing, they are growing at different speeds, and therefore the percentages have changed significantly. However, more recent research by Amaral and Phillips (2010) is showing that it is not simply demographics but also people's values, that is influencing online conversations.

5.2 Historical and theoretical context

Public relations practitioners always want to know more and more about publics in order to reach them, build relationships, and persuade them to change their opinion and subsequently their behaviour.

The philosopher Dewey in the early 1940s (cited Price 1992) studied crowds and saw how groups develop as they change their opinion through discussions, arguments, and reasoning. In 1946, Blumer, a sociologist, developed this further. He found that different groups formed depending on how they identified, discussed, and dealt with the same issues and he called these groups 'publics'.

A key aspect of public relations is to analyse and monitor how publics are formed in order to know how they are going to react to different aspects in the environment, as well as to identify what people have in common.

How publics form

There are different views on how publics form. One view is called the mass perspective (Vasquez and Taylor 2001). This defines publics as a mass of individuals who are constantly aware of what is going on in their country and community and this is what motivates them to act on most matters. However, people are not always active citizens and constantly involved in the day's issues.

Psychological and sociological thinking about crowds and behaviour in the early twentieth century suggested that publics can be formed into different groups by how they are affected by an issue or a problem. This led to a situational perspective on publics.

Grunig and Hunt (1984) related this to public relations by arguing that publics are created by how an organization affects them and how they affect an organization. This was called the situational theory of publics because it shows how publics respond to a situation. Grunig and Hunt (1984) identified three publics called:

1. Latent publics— those who are unaware of an issue. For example, a group of potential students may be unaware about impending higher student fees because perhaps they had not heard about it or not understood the information or were undecided about going to university and therefore had not looked into the costs.

2. Aware publics—those who recognize that an issue affects them. This would be those who are already at university, or enrolled in university the following year, and are concerned about the fees.

3. Active publics—those who are communicating and doing something about the issue, they could be active in the student union, be holding meetings to protest, and some may be taking on extra part-time work to fund themselves.

Non-publics was defined as a group that was not likely to be affected by an issue and Grunig and Hunt (1984) recommended that public relations did not need to reach them. They offered the example of a company that is causing air pollution through its manufacturing processes. The people who live nearby and who detect this and feel affected by it are the aware public. Those who then contact the organization to discuss it are the active public. Today, environmental issues have a wider reach and affect more people.

Moving from being a latent public to an active public

Grunig and Hunt (1984: 149) found that people moved from being latent publics to aware publics and then active publics as they were influenced by three independent variables.

Table 5.1 shows how the independent variables move latent publics to active publics using the example of the company causing air pollution:

Table 5.1 **Inferred variables moving publics from being latent to active**

Independent variable	Development of publics
1. Problem recognition—is it relevant?	Latent: communicate a lot to find out about the pollution and what to do
2. Constraint recognition—can I do anything about it?	Aware: determine what can be done about the pollution and seek information from the organization
3. Level of involvement—how much does it affect me?	Active: seek information and guidance on what to do

Source: Grunig and Hunt 1984; 149

Grunig and Hunt (1984) found that these variables influenced, and were influenced by, two other variables which observed how people receive information:

1. Processing information, such as just reading, viewing, or hearing information

   or

2. Searching for information, such as accessing websites and asking questions.

These two ways of getting information—passively or actively—were considered **dependent variables** as they are affected by the independent variables. Grunig and Hunt (1984) suggested that those with high problem recognition look for information to work out what to do about the issue. Once they feel they can do something about it their feeling of constraint around the issue lessens and their level of involvement rises.

For example, the 2008–9 swine flu epidemic showed that many people recognized it as a problem for them and felt they could do something about it. They became motivated to find out more information and to buy medical treatment.

Patient associations such as the Diabetes Association and Parkinson's UK offer information and support to people who have the respective illnesses, as they know people have a high level of involvement in the area owing to their condition and seek information on how to treat it. It is also a key reason for pharmaceutical companies to sponsor these associations in order to reach those publics.

> Go to the Online Resource Centre to access the link to patient associations

Publics, according to Dozier et al (1995), are identified by how they are affected by an organization's behaviour. As publics become more active, they may also be more active in accessing information. Active publics generate consequences for organizations and communications may ignore the latent or aware publics. However, proactive communicators seek to communicate with latent and aware publics while there is still room to negotiate.

Problem recognition, information seeking, and aware publics

An example of how publics form through these variables is a 2009 public relations programme by Mandate Communications for the large tissue brand, Kleenex. The organization wanted more people to buy tissues in the non-winter season and used the hay fever season to drive sales.

First, there needed to be a greater awareness of hay fever as an issue and Kleenex worked with a respiratory expert to produce a media report on hay fever designed to stimulate interest in the topic and get people to recognize that it was an upcoming issue.

Publics then started looking for more information and accessed the online video about hay fever. Kleenex created an interactive hay fever map, powered by Twitter, which allowed publics to rate their symptoms against their postcode. This appealed to these active publics as it offered an interactive and ongoing national geographic profile of hay fever symptoms.

Publics recognized hay fever as a problem that affected them; becoming aware of hay fever and its symptoms, such as a runny nose, as they searched for more information and participated in developing the interactive map.

Fig 5.3
Kleenex focused on hay fever

Source: Courtesy of Mandate Communications

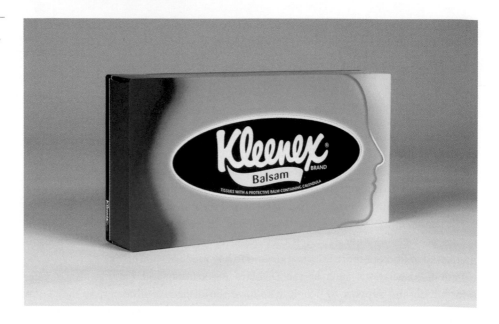

Go to the Online Resource Centre to access the interactive hay fever map

Constraint recognition, level of involvement, and active publics

Through seeking information people found out that they could do something about hay fever by identifying when it was likely to affect them, and this lowered their constraint recognition. The interactivity with the map and online video developed their feeling of involvement and they became active in buying tissues (see Figure 5.3).

In summary, Grunig and Hunt (1984) found that how people either simply processed or actively sought information depended on their problem recognition, constraint recognition, and level of involvement. If people do not recognize that a problem affects them, they stay as latent publics. Conversely, when a public recognizes a problem through processing information they look for more information and become an aware public; they may then do something about it and become an active public.

Grunig and Hunt (1984) urge practitioners to communicate with the latent public before it becomes active, as once active it will then seek information from other sources that have competing messages.

The power of publics

Coombs and Halliday (2007) believe that organizations should recognize the value of stakeholders because they can influence the organization's performance. Public relations can improve an organization's effectiveness by building relationships with its stakeholders (publics) and therefore facilitate what the organization needs. Both the organization and its publics have the same control over the relationship and power imbalances do occur. Public relations is about managing these mutually influential relationships.

Publics in turn, can suggest strategies to the organization and can push their own interests. If they have a high level of power or influence and interest, they are crucial to the organization. If they are powerful but have a low interest then the organization only needs to keep them informed. If they are powerful but unpredictable, they present the greatest opportunity and threat to the organization (Choo 2009).

Grunig (2006) argues that public relations can therefore add value when it helps the organization identify and segment its publics. It can then work with these publics to develop and reach goals in a symmetrical model of communication (see chapter 2). Grunig (2006) argues that if the wishes of the publics are not addressed they will pressure the organization to change. The following case study is an excellent example of how Land Rover developed its sustainability programme influenced by public demand.

Case Study

Stakeholders and Land Rover

Source: Courtesy of Grayling PR and Land Rover

Land Rover found that stakeholders could influence them to adopt a two-way symmetrical approach after Greenpeace invaded its manufacturing plant. Land Rover had already introduced a sustainable development policy with product improvements but these had not been communicated to its publics. Land Rover was further motivated to improve and communicate its sustainability by the increasing media focus on environmental issues and its negative phrases such as 'gas-guzzling 4x4s'.

When Greenpeace demonstrated on the Land Rover premises it galvanized the organization into working with stakeholders to address its image and gain support for its sustainable development policy. The consultancy Grayling PR's objective was to to protect and promote the Land Rover brand in order to tackle the stigma around 4x4s and their environmental impact.

It intended to do this through a strategy of focusing on the brand's sustainability, showcasing the company's product improvements, its conservation partnerships, and renewable energy investments as part of its CO_2 offset programme.

Implementation

Land Rover engaged with both positively and negatively affected stakeholders. These included its natural allies, for example the motoring organizations, and also its critics: the environmental charities and NGOs such as Greenpeace. Meetings with potential supporters focused on looking for opportunities to work together. Meetings with detractors centred on identifying some common ground and encouraging a more informed view of Land Rover's environmental impacts.

Fig 5.4
Land Rovers forming a red cross at Buckingham Palace

Source: Courtesy of Land Rover and James Wright, Managing Director, CSR and Not-for-profit, Grayling PR

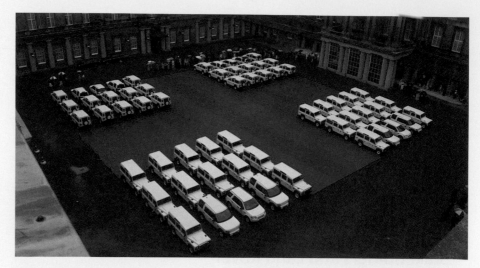

Partnerships

The vehicles play a big role in facilitation conservation work therefore partnerships were developed with five conservation charities—the Royal Geographical Society, Earthwatch, Biosphere, Born Free, and the Chinese Exploratory and Research Society (CERS) providing vehicle and financial support. Land Rover and the CERS also worked together on a CNN documentary in Tibet.

As part of the 60th anniversary of the Red Cross, Land Rover gave 60 vehicles to the British Red Cross which were officially donated by HRH the Prince of Wales at a Buckingham Palace garden party. The vehicles were arranged in the form of a Red Cross flag and generated photo opportunities and subsequent overage, including an online Red Cross video.

Fig 5.5
Land Rovers being put to use in Sierra Leone

Source: Courtesy of Land Rover and James Wright, Managing Director, CSR and Not-for-profit, Grayling PR

Half the donated vehicles will be used in countries such as in Sierra Leone, Lesotho, and Mongolia to transport vital supplies and emergency response personnel during natural disasters such as cyclones, floods, and earthquakes (see Figure 5.5). The remainder will help with UK operations such as flooding, off-road emergencies, and public events.

Go to the Online Resource Centre to access a link to a video on how Land Rover is working with the Red Cross in remote parts of Africa

Renewable energy investments

Land Rover conducts the world's largest consumer offset programme. It invests in renewable energy projects such as wind, solar, and technology change and energy efficiency.

Product improvements

New technologies—such as the hybrid engine—signposted a future direction and sustainability opinion leaders were consulted. The Chief Executive of Greenpeace met the managing director of Land Rover and visited Land Rover's HQ to review its sustainable technologies.

Land Rover now generates positive media coverage and is making inroads into the specialist environmental media and is in open dialogue with NGOs and pressure environmental groups.

Identifying strategic publics through their power and interest

Grunig (2006) recommends that public relations must identify strategic publics in order to hold long term relationships with them through symmetrical communication programmes. He recommends that public relations should be a 'bridging activity' in which organizations build links with stakeholders in their environment to transform and constitute the organization in new ways.

Prioritizing publics is very important in communication planning as it identifies who will be affected by the communications, any potential issues, and key people to partner to help the communications. The first step in assessing publics is to develop a list of them and then use a method to prioritize them. This is because it is unlikely that all publics can be reached and therefore it is best to categorize them based on how important they are and the influence they are likely to have.

Mapping a stakeholder's power and interest onto a grid based on the COI's methodology, shows the influence or power they have on an issue and compares this to how much interest they have in it (see Table 5.2). Drawing these together can help to determine the public relations activities needed to work with them. These can range from partnering with them in different activities, such as using them for spokespeople or as third parties, involving them in the programme, consulting them for their advice, or simply keeping them informed. The more interest and power stakeholders have, the more likely their actions will impact on the organization, therefore it is essential that the organization communicates with this group.

Table 5.2 Mapping stakeholders on their power and interest in the organization or issue according to COI methodology

Power/Interest	Action	Tactics
High Power and High Interest	Partner	Work together: use as opinion formers, plan campaigns, use as spokespeople, blog editors
High Power and Low Interest	Involve	Find common ground and work together: focus groups, team meetings, workshops, seminars, debates, consensus meetings
Low Power and High Interest	Consult	Listen to this group and respond to them through surveys, workshops, consultation, and social media sites
Low Power and Medium Interest	Inform	Require minimal effort but need to raise awareness through presentations, newsletters, and websites

Table 5.3 shows an example of an imaginary Department of Health campaign (2009), developed by the COI, aimed at reducing binge drinking in the UK. It also helps to identify and analyse publics in a programme.

Table 5.3 How to work with stakeholders in creating a campaign to reduce binge drinking

Stakeholder	How they will be affected, or how they will affect, the campaign	Influence/ Power	Interest	Relationship: how to work with the stakeholders when developing the campaign
Drink Aware	Part campaign team and part funding campaign	High	High	Partner: work together to reduce binge drinking
Home Office (Police)	Reduced costs dealing with alcohol-related disturbance and crime	High	Medium	Involve: work together where common ground exists
Alcohol retailers	May suffer from decreased revenue	Medium	High	Consult: listen and respond
Charity campaigning against violence against women	Knock-on effect of reduction in binge drinking could be less violence towards women	Low	Medium	Inform: tell them what you are doing

Source: COI 2009: 30

Problems with identifying publics

Grunig and Hunt (1984) identify publics as forming only when there is an issue or a problem; conversely, Hallahan (2000) points out that not all public relations activities revolve around issues, disputes, or conflicts. In fact, many public relations programmes run before any conflicts occur and there may be little difference between the organization's interests and the publics. Hallahan argues that public relations actually creates publics through attempting to build positive relationships with people connected to the organization before any issues start.

However, although it is true that public relations does not always revolve around issues, it is common public relations practice to create an issue within a programme in order to generate active publics. Publics can then be encouraged to recognize the problem. This gives public relations the opportunity to communicate and leaves publics feeling that can do something about it, encouraging their involvement and subsequent change in opinion and behaviour. For example, the Kleenex campaign discussed earlier in this chapter raised awareness about hay fever then led to behaviour change.

Another perspective on how publics form

The homo narran perspective is another way that publics are seen to form (Vasquez and Taylor 2001). They argue that individuals first communicate with each other, become aware of an issue, and then become a public. This recognizes that everyone's stories, narratives, or opinions are constantly overlapping with the opinions of others.

Publics are formed as a given number of people find common meaning or communicate in the same way. This view focuses on the individual's communications and looks at how, through communicating with each other, they raise and sustain a group consciousness around an issue and, as a public, try to resolve an issue. For example, students start talking about university fees and mix with each other. They may then take on different opinions and may eventually do something about the fees or arrange a group that will drive change.

5.3 Influences

Publics constantly change in how they act and in their relationship to an organization. However, by finding out how publics move from being latent to active in developing and acting on their opinion can help predict how publics will respond to messages and identify what communication will be most effective.

Grunig and Hunt's (1984) research showed that once publics have moved from latent to active they could then be divided into different levels of activity.

1. Publics who are active on all issues—these are highly involved in the issue, have high recognition of the problem, and challenge organizations on most issues.

2. Publics who are apathetic on all issues—these have low involvement, fatalistic behaviour.

3. Publics who are active only on hot issues—that is, what everyone else is interested in, whatever is current, eg educational standards, reacting to the latest health scare, climate change.

4. Single-issue publics—these are interested in one issue and ignore others, eg climate change.

Grunig and Hunt's research followed that of the sociology researcher, Rogers, who identified the diffusion of innovations theory in the early 1960s showing the process

Table 5.4 **Adopter categorization on the basis of innovativeness**

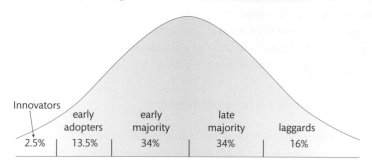

Source: E. Rogers (1983) Diffusion of Innovations (3rd edn; appears in
all editions) Fig 7.2, p. 247. Permission: Simon and Schuster

by which people accept or reject new information (see chapter 2). He found that they
went through the stages of acquiring knowledge, being persuaded, making a decision,
implementing the decision, and then confirming it. Drawing on this research Rogers
(1983: 246) also found that people fall into groups depending how long it takes them
to go through these stages and adopt an innovation (see Table 5.4). These groups are:

1. **Innovators:** These people are the first to do something or buy something and are
   a tiny percentage of the group; they are usually people who dare to take risks.

2. **Early adopters:** These people are usually opinion leaders and often a role model
   for others.

3. **Early majority:** These people adopt new ideas before the average person does but
   are not usually in a leadership position.

4. **Late majority:** These people are more sceptical and adopt ideas just after the
   average person. Adoption may be as a result of peer pressure or economics.

5. **Laggards:** These people are the last to adopt an innovation and are generally
   suspicious of new things.

Most people fall into the early and late majority groups. Identifying these groups is important in public relations in order to develop different approaches that will appeal to
the psychological make up of each group. More challenging and exciting messages are
needed at the start of a campaign to interest the early adopters, whereas more comfort-
ing and reassuring messages are needed at the end to persuade the laggards.

In addition, a campaign can plan for using the early adopters and early majority
to persuade others. The lifecycle for successful technology products also moves from
innovators to laggards. However, as soon as the buzz of innovation starts to fade,
the influential people at the start of the cycle move on very quickly and therefore the
recently adopted innovation can become almost old fashioned vey quickly.

Segmentation and communications technology

Segmenting populations is becoming more sophisticated with communications technology. This allows more people to be researched, more questions asked, and an earlier analysis of results along with a greater combination of results.

For example, the UK research organization, Caci, has developed a research technique called ACORN that stands for 'A Classification of Residential Neighbourhoods' (Caci 2009). It is used to identify and understand the UK population and helps to predict what products and services people want or need through analysing their location and demographics. Caci provides this information to businesses to help them to improve their understanding of customers and target markets so that they can make decisions on what sort of marketing would be effective, and which areas would be best suited to their type of service or product.

> Go to the Online Resource Centre to access a link to ACORN and find out about your street

5.4 Application to industry

The internet is bringing new ways of being able to identify publics. One way is by monitoring how users search the internet. This information can be used to obtain a profile of an individual and then group people into distinct publics to help predict what they are going to search for, and ultimately what they will buy. There are web research organizations specializing in how a web user can be defined based on their online activities, such as their search queries, the sites they search, what they are doing online, and the overall context of what they visit. These factors can also give an idea of their demographics such as their age and gender.

Web research tools analyse search queries, browsing history, and user interaction that can detect whether consumers simply want to process information or buy products. For example, if a customer searches for a specific product or brand this behaviour is classified as 'high buying-likelihood intent'. A full profile of the user is called a model of intent and predicts what the user is likely to do online and the product areas in which they are most interested. Phillips and Young (2009) recount how Goldstein coined the term 'MyWare'—where the sites people visit reveal their likes and dislikes, and allow publics to be segmented by their behaviours.

> Go to Online Resource Centre to access a link to these websites

Web tools that analyse user-generated content provide valuable information. This data can help to develop communications programmes which can provide what the users are looking for. Research by Phillips and Young (2009) on blogs about public relations found that press release topics were searched for first, followed by subjects relating to graduate advisers and internship experience.

The following case study demonstrates how publics formed as teenage girls became increasingly aware of bullying as a problem and subsequently increased their own involvement in an anti-bullying campaign.

Case Study

Mobile phone bullying

Source: Courtesy of Threepipe PR

One of Vodafone's key corporate responsibility targets is to help to reduce bullying by mobile phone, an increasing trend amongst young people who victimize others through text and video messaging. An estimated 450,000 young people are victims of bullying in the UK each year and the aim was to educate young people about the negative impact of bullying and advise those being bullied. This case study shows that moving people to recognize the problem and realize that something can be done about it, increased their level of involvement, and they then looked for more information which offered ways of dealing with bullying.

Vodafone had to move latent publics to become aware publics by getting them to recognize bullying as a problem that affected them and seek more information about dealing with it. Once they had high problem recognition, the next step was to ensure that they felt they could do something (low constraint recognition) about it and become engaged enough to want to act (high level of involvement). Teachers and parents were important as they could identify bullying behaviour, provide support, and reinforce awareness.

Anti Bullying Week

Vodafone launched a campaign coinciding with the government-backed Anti Bullying Week in November 2008; this meant that awareness of the issue was already on the media agenda.

Selecting the public

Key publics were girls (aged 10–16 years) as research found they are greater users of phones for bullying than boys who tend to resort to more physical intimidation. The campaign aimed to make teenage girls and parents aware of bullying and its consequences. A programme to encourage teacher participation was also used in developing active publics.

Creative partnerships

The public relations consultancy, Threepipe, arranged a partnership with the hit West End musical, *Joseph and His Amazing Technicolour Dreamcoat* that has a bullying storyline. The show was popular in UK schools and its leading star, Lee Mead, had a high media profile and a following of teenage girls and their mums. Mead had also acknowledged that he had been bullied while at school and was a keen anti-bullying ambassador.

Activity

Schoolchildren became involved through designing new 'technicolor dreamcoats' with imagery reflecting how they felt about bullying. This created a higher recognition of the problem as well as a high level of involvement and therefore encouraged more information seeking. Mead would wear the winning designs on stage during Anti Bullying Week.

Website

Threepipe, with leading anti bullying charity, Beathullying, created a campaign website with online resources about bullying, plus competition entry details and news updates throughout the campaign. The site also contained a teacher's pack to encourage entry into the Vodafone competition.

Campaign launch

The campaign launched in September 2008—the back to school period with media interviews with Mead about being bullied at school. An email newsletter was sent to Beatbullying's database of 3,000 schools with a link to the downloadable schools' resource pack. This activity was supported by a media relations campaign targeted to education areas.

Ticket competitions to the shows were placed in national and teenage girls' media to promote the campaign and links to the campaign website were promoted via http://Vodafone.co.uk and the mobile portal Vodafone Live!

Threepipe arranged a series of exclusive editorial opportunities in the *Mirror* and ITN News to coincide with the launch of Anti Bullying Week. The *Mirror* and ITN were given access, via the charity, to children being bullied as well as to parents whose children had committed suicide because of bullying. This was extremely sensitive as none of the parents had previously spoken to the media, but provided a powerful message about the seriousness of bullying.

The competition

Within four weeks, 2,000 coat design entries had been submitted. These were short-listed by a judging panel of Mead, Beatbullying, and Vodafone representatives. London College of Fashion students turned the chosen designs into real dreamcoats to be worn on stage, regional media covered the winning designers, and the teenage girls' magazine, *Bliss*, asked readers to vote for the winning coat design. Mead wore the winning coat on the first day of Anti Bullying Week (see Figure 5.6).

Anti Bullying Week (17–21 November)

Threepipe organized a VIP event for the first Joseph performance of the week, attended by government, charities, and key media, allowing Vodafone to launch its Anti Bullying Week

Fig 5.6
Lee Mead (Joseph) with the winning dreamcoat made during the anti bullying campaign

Source: Courtesy of Threepipe PR

campaign. Mead wore all seven winning coats on stage during the week, making a speech about the campaign at the end of each show.

Campaign results

In addition to the 2,000 competition entries, within one week 40,000 teenagers registered to vote for their favourite coats on the *Bliss* website. The *Mirror* ran a double-page spread for three consecutive days during the week, describing the campaign and featuring interviews with Mead, parents, and children who had suffered bullying. Mead also appeared live on GMTV to promote the campaign and reveal the winning coat. During the week, 91,000 theatregoers saw the show and were given Vodafone-branded information about the campaign. Charity collections were taken at the end of each performance and the seven winning coats were auctioned on eBay to raise funds for Beatbullying.

PR Tool

Opinion poll

An opinion poll is a survey that identifies the views of a representative sample of the population. It can be used to gauge the demographics and psychographics of a public as well as helping to identify whether publics recognize a problem, feel they can do something about it, and feel involved with it.

The objectives

The opinion poll should obtain information about the characteristics of a target population. Malhotra and Birks (2006: 357) see this population as a grouping together of all those who share some common set of characteristics and also represent the research issue such as a group of students, a group of mothers, or a group of doctors.

Define the sample

It is not necessary to talk to everyone and a sample of the population can be selected. A sample can be a random selection of this group in order to avoid bias or it can be quota of people selected according to specific aspects. The size of the sample is important and its size is a variable that should be noted in the research report along with whether it may affect the findings.

Malhotra and Birks (2008) state that the sample size depends on many factors, including the decision to be made from the survey results and the variables and the constraints on the survey, such as its cost. For important decisions more information is necessary but the larger the sample size the greater the cost. Although sample sizes are usually at least several hundred, an opinion poll can find very helpful information with a sample size of no fewer than 30 people.

The research needs to show reliability and validity therefore it is also important to consider the sample size when analysing the results. The questions should generate similar results from the same group each time they are used and there should be a consistency of answers that make it reliable (Treadwell 2005).

The survey

The survey needs to attract people to it and must be written to encourage people to answer the questions. Therefore, it must be clear and short asking for only the most important information. How to carry out the survey must also be decided: an opinion poll can be via the internet, or through telephone or face-to-face interviews, or through the post. Additionally, the survey must be explained with a short and interesting explanation which is either written or spoken. When written, it must stress the date of return and how to return it, such as by giving the email address. Offer a reward for its return and keep the survey short—increasing the length of questions and surveys decreases the chance of receiving a completed response.

Style of questions

Attract people to the survey by ensuring the early questions are interesting and not challenging or intrusive. These must be clear so that there is no confusion in the answers or your interpretation of the answers. Therefore, make questions specific.

Yes/no questions are quick to answer but they must be specific and clear to avoid any misinterpretation. Multiple choice questions are useful when the answer is known but not the ranking of their importance with different publics. Ensure each answer offers a clear choice to avoid confusion between choices. Keep the answers to a short list and use these with a mix of other questions as they can be too time consuming.

A scale can be used where a questions is asked, from strongly agree to strongly disagree. A semantic differential scale means the answer is ranked between two opposites. Make sure simple words are used with concise easy ways for anwering the questions.

What not to do

Avoid leading questions as these influence the answer. For example, 'You wouldn't want to have lectures on a Friday would you?' is a leading question. Also, some words such as 'could' or 'should' can change the results.

Open ended questions enable respondents to explain their answer but can be too time consuming and more difficult to analyse. Avoid two questions in one: 'What is your most interesting and intellectually challenging subject?' This should be made into two questions.

Format the survey

Order the questions and group them into a context. Start with broad questions then more specific questions and then easy questions which should include demographics (age and gender). Income questions may be considered too intrusive and are therefore optional.

Test the survey

Test the survey on a few people similar to the target market. Get their feedback on what they thought and whether they felt motivated to answer the questions. Carry out the survey and collate results which can then be analysed against the questions and draw conclusions.

Research report

A report presents the rationale for the survey, its background, and the objectives which clarify why the survey was conducted and therefore the importance of the findings. Then a summary of the key findings follows and the communications are recommendations based on them. The key findings should include facts that were important as well as unexpected ones. Explain the methodology used (opinion poll and how it was conducted; that is online, face-to-face, or by post, size of the sample and demographics). Next, outline the in-depth findings as well as recommendations from the research. For example, identify the aware publics to target this for key public relations activities, as well as a brief outline of suggested communications tactics that would be specific to this group.

Summary

Public relations needs to manage publics in order to develop public opinion and it is vital to understand how publics form and how to be involved in that process. Publics can be divided into their observable measurables such as demographics—age, gender, income, ethnicity, and lifestyle. These demographics show trends and can help to predict the size of markets for an organization.

In addition, a public relations plan needs to list publics that are involved in an organization. These should include internal and external publics and be subdivided into different groups, such as regulatory and professionals (third parties), internal (salesforce and employees), investors and shareholders, consumers (buyers and users), and business to business (other organizations who may buy from the organization or be influenced by it).

Academic fields have their own perspectives on how publics are formed. Public relations tends to focus on the situational perspective—this arose from the growing psycho-social research in the early twentieth century. Grunig and Hunt in 1984 developed it further into a situational theory of publics and identified publics in public relations as forming around a problem or situation and progressing from latent to aware to active. They found that there were variables that affected this process.

The independent variables were how much a public recognized a problem, how much it felt constrained or unable to deal with a problem, and lastly the level of involvement or engagement a public had to a situation. The dependent variables were to what degree they processed and looked for information. Analysing these variables allows practitioners to understand that many combinations are formed and help to identify what communication is needed during the different stages.

Overall, there are many ways of grouping publics. Web tools are used to identify how individuals search the internet, and the key words they use. This can create a model about the individual and what information they want and what sorts of products and services they are likely to buy. This individual can then be grouped with others into a specific public that public relations programmes can identify.

There are also other ways to identify publics and an opinion poll is a basic tool for finding out what public opinion is and the publics involved. This is a versatile tool and can be carried out face-to-face, online, or by post.

Knowing more about publics, their characteristics, beliefs, attitudes, concerns, and lifestyle means that practitioners can tailor their communications to increasingly specific groups. Identifying publics can be a complicated and drawn out process as it can involve analysing an enormous amount of data that investigates who publics are, how their opinions develop and change, and what influences this change. There are increasing debates and theories around this topic and it is also an expanding area owing to growing communications technology offering the promise of more research data and forms of analysis.

Discussion points

A. Demographics

Go to the Online Resource Centre and access 'upmystreet' and analyse your location at home and now at university.

Where do you think is the best place to live? What criteria do you base that on? Do you think the university affects the demographics?

B. Analysis

Form pairs and download the case study from the Online Resource Centre.

Identify the stages of the campaign in which the publics are likely to be latent, aware, and active. Map the inferred variables against these stages and apply the case study to the different combinations. For example, how would publics demonstrate a high problem recognition, low constraint and low involvement, and so on?

C. Surveys

Go to the Online Resource Centre and download the omnibus survey.

How would you use this survey to identify your publics? Identify which ones you think are latent, active, and aware.

D. Web search tools

Go to the Online Resource Centre and access the link to the website that develops a user's profile. Carry out the different online exercises and look at the profiles of yourself and how word searches identify profiles. Do you think it is an accurate measurement tool? How can you use this is in a public relations programme?

References

Amaral, B. and Phillips, D. (2010) 'Concepts of Values for Public Relations'. Available at: http://www.euprera.org/?p=69

Anon (2010) 'Why We Protest'. Available at: http://www.whyweprotest.net/en/

Article 19 (January 2003) *Comparative Study of Laws and Regulations Restricting the Publication of Election Opinion Polls*. London: Global Campaign for Free Expression. Available at: http://www.article19.org/search-results/index.html?freetext=opinion+polls

Caci (2009) http://www.caci.co.uk/acorn/acornmap.asp

Choo (2009) 'Audiences, Stakeholders and Publics' in R. Tench and L. Yeoman (eds) *Exploring Public Relations*. Harlow: Prentice Hall

COI (2009) 'Payback and Return on the Marketing Investment in the Public Sector', November. London: Government Comunication Network

Coombs, W. and Halliday, S. (2007) *It's Not Just PR: Public Relations in Society*. Malden, MA: Blackwell

Cutlip, S., Center, A., and Broom, G. (2006) *Effective Public Relations* (9th edn). Upper Saddle River, NJ: Pearson

Dozier, D. with Grunig, L. and Grunig, J.(1995) *Manager's Guide to Excellence in Public Relations and Communication Management*. Mahwah, NJ: Lawrence Erlbaum

Gregory, A. (2006) *PR in Practice: Planning and Managing Public Relations Campaigns* (2nd edn). London: Kogan Page

Grunig, J. (2006) 'Furnishing the Edifice, Ongoing Research on PR As a Strategic Management Function', Journal of Public Relations Research 18/20: 151–6

Grunig, J. and Hunt, T. (1984) *Managing Public Relations*. New York: Holt, Rinehart and Winston

Grunig, J. and Repper, F. (1992) *Strategic Management, Publics and Issues*. In Grunig, J. (ed) Excellence in Public Relations and Communication Management. N.J.: Lawrence Erlbaum pp 117–158

Hallahan, K. (2000) 'Inactive Publics: The Forgotten Publics in Public Relations', Public Relations Review 26/4: 499–515

Jefkins, F. revised by Yadin, D. (1998) *Public Relations* (5th edn). Harlow: Prentice Hall

L'Etang, J. (2008) *Public Relations: Concepts, Practice and Critique*. London: Sage

Leitch, S. and Neilson, D. (2001) 'Bringing Publics into Public Relations: New Theoretical Frameworks for Practice' in R. Heath (ed) *Handbook of Public Relations*. Thousand Oaks, CA: Sage

Mackey, S. (2006) 'Misuse of the Term "Stakeholder" in Public Relations', Prism 4/1. Available at: http://praxis.massey.ac.nz/prism_on-line_journ.html

Malhotra, N. and Birks, D. (2006) *Marketing Research* (3rd edn). Harlow. Prentice Hall

McQuail, D. (2010) *McQuail's Mass Communication Theory*. London: Sage

Phillips, D. and Young, P. (2009) *Online Public Relations: A Practical Guide to Developing an Online Strategy in the World of Social Media* (2nd edn). London: Kogan Page

Price, V. (1992) *Public Opinion (Communication Concepts)*. Newbury Park, CA: Sage

Rogers, E. (1983) *Diffusion of Innovations* (3rd edn). New York: Free Press

Schroeder, S. (2009) 'Facebook Users Are Getting Older. Much Older'. Available at: http://mashable.com/2009/07/07/facebook-users-older/

Solomon, M., Bamossy, G., Askegaard, S., and Hogg, M. (2006) *Consumer Behaviour: A European Perspective* (3rd edn). Harlow: Prentice Hall

Treadwell, D. and Treadwell, J. (2005) *Public Relations Writing: Principles in Practice*. Thousand Oaks, CA: Sage

Vallance, C. (16.03.10) 'Activists turn "hacktivists" on the web'. Available at :http://news.bbc.co.uk/1/hi/technology/8567934.stm

Vasquez, G. and Taylor, M. (2001) 'Research Perspectives on the "Public"' in R. Heath (ed) *Handbook of Public Relations*. Thousand Oaks, CA: Sage

Wallace, C. (2009) 'Healthcare: More to Kleenex Than Flu Season', 30 September. Available at http://www.prweek.com/uk/researchData/login/942143/

6 Goals, objectives, and strategy

Learning outcomes

1. Be able to understand the link between an organization's goals and the communications objectives.

2. Be able to understand how communications objectives will advance the organization's goals.

3. Be able to understand what makes up public relations strategic planning and the role of the practitioner.

4. Be able to link the four models of public relations to forming objectives.

5. Be able to develop objectives based on the hierarchy of effects model.

6. Be able to develop SMART objectives and strategies for public relations programmes.

Practitioner Insight

Rachel Jones
Public Relations Officer for the University of Gloucestershire

Rachel Jones is Public Relations Officer for the University of Gloucestershire. Rachel has worked in a number of public relations and communications roles over the past decade and has been a journalist and freelance writer. Rachel has taught public relations and professional writing for the BA in Public Relations at the University of Gloucestershire.

How do business goals influence a public relations proposal?

Working in-house in a large organization means there are huge demands upon the resource of a small public relations team. Much of our work is to respond quickly to media requests in a wide range of academic and other university topics as well as to maximize opportunities to be profiled in the media.

In order to align public relations messages with the organization's brand values, we need to understand the business strategy of the University and create public relations campaigns that reflect the needs and aspirations of the organization, with measurable outcomes.

How important is strategy to public relations?

As the higher education marketplace develops, we need to be clear about our place in that market and our explicit values, culture, and identity. Identifying our stakeholders is paramount, whether we are communicating to applicants and future students, current students, local communities, governing board, or our staff, we have to have strategies in place to ensure that messages about our organization are received and understood.

What are the most important aspects of communications?

Communications need to be targeted and choosing an appropriate communications medium is all important. Digital and electronic media are the best ways to communicate with our current students. Social media such as Facebook and Twitter allows us to be highly interactive with students.

Getting direct feedback from your communications by using social or digital media is much easier than with some forms of more traditional media. Our communications can be more dynamic and relevant as a result of this two-way interaction.

However, it's also important to understand the demographics of your publics and not make assumptions. Not all our students are confident with digital media, and therefore we always need to consider a range of communication strategies.

Are there any areas of public relations where strategy is more important?

A large and diverse organization like a university undertakes a wide range of core business activities that need a range of dedicated public relations strategies. For example to develop the reputation of a research unit or a faculty, or to develop an aspect of the University's strategic plan that focuses on a value, such as sustainability or enterprise.

As the higher education market develops and public sector funding diminishes, we are engaged in organizational change. Strategic communications is pivotal in securing stakeholder engagement and cooperation.

6.1 Definition

An enormous study of public relations organizations in Canada, the UK, and the US in the early 1990s, found that the ideal communications occurred when practitioners worked with senior management in the organization to develop its overall strategy and create a two-way flow of information between the organization and its publics (Dozier et al 1995). These practitioners had the expertise to know what publics would feel, know, and behave relevant to the organization's strategic decision making.

Most importantly, the study found that senior management valued this input and, along with the practitioners, understood that **excellent communication** was working towards symmetrical communications. This means creating dialogue and mutual understanding between a public and its organization, often resulting in behaviour change on both sides.

The study surveyed 321 organizations in the three countries in 1990–1 and followed up with exploring case studies from the research (Dozier 1995: ix). Conversely, in organizations where communication was not excellent, the study found that communication practitioners were only valued for their technical expertise and were not involved in any decisions about communications that contributed to the organization's strategy.

Goals

Business goals are the aims of the organization and can include increased sales, increased market share, increased profit, or reduced employee turnover (Parkinson and Ekachai 2006: 28). For example, some organizations may want more investors whereas a charitable organization will look at more successful fundraising or better use of its services.

The organization's goals are not always evident and a thorough situation analysis should have clarified them through drawing on the business plan, marketing plan, secondary research, and talking to management (see chapter 4). An organization operates on many different levels and also has many different functions such as research and development, marketing, finance, human resources, etc. Each of these areas has their own objectives and strategies that also link to the organization's overall business goal and objective.

When developing a public relations programme it is essential to know the organization's mission statement. Sometimes called the organization's vision, this statement communicates to the outside world what the organization does and encompasses its philosophies, goals, and ambitions (missionstatements.com 2009). Mission statements can be one sentence or longer and may be accompanied by a paragraph or more elaborating on the organization's values.

The following are examples of mission statements (missionstatements.com 2009):

Starbucks
To inspire and nurture the human spirit— one person, one cup, and one neighbourhood at a time.

The BBC
To enrich people's lives with programmes and services that inform, educate and entertain.

Oxfam International
Oxfam International is an international group of independent non-governmental organizations dedicated to fighting poverty and related injustice around the world. The Oxfams work together internationally to achieve greater impact by their collective efforts.

When developing a communications plan, it is important to go through a process that is recognized as being strategic which links public relations activities to the organization's goals and mission (Gregory 2010). If this is not done the communications will appear haphazard and will not work towards strengthening an organization's reputation.

For example, in 2010 the Pope and senior Vatican officials were accused of mismanaging or covering up the cases of child abuse by priests. There was no satisfactory media response from the Vatican and it was accused of not having a coordinated media strategy which defended the child abuse allegations. Their media spokespeople lacked a consistent message and many times different cardinals

Go to the Online Resource Centre to access the link to more mission statements

Fig 6.1
There is a call for a coordinated media plan in the Vatican

Source: Copyright OUP

made damaging statements or they were very defensive in denouncing any criticism as an attack against the Pope and the Catholic Church (BBC 2010).

These accusations were affecting the Catholic Church's credibility and image, as well as the moral authority of the Pope and the Holy See on the world stage. In other words, the Vatican appeared to lack a communications plan and as a result its worldwide reputation was being damaged.

In order to develop a communication's programme, Cutlip et al (2006) describes the following four-way plan:

1. Define the programme

Use research to find out about the situation and possible communications solutions. It is then crucial to understand the communication issue through a situational analysis (see chapter 4). It is only then that the publics can be analysed in order to identify who to target and what outcomes to expect.

2. Plan the programme

Make decisions about publics, public relations objectives, and actions. Publics are anyone that influences or can be influenced by the organization (see chapter 5). This could be customers, voters, opponents, consumer groups, employers, and shareholders. Grunig and Hunt (1984) recommend communicating with the most influential target public first because success with this public can influence others thereby creating a ripple effect of advocacy.

3. Taking action and implementing ideas

A strategy determines how an objective is going to be achieved and the tactics will explain how it is done.

4. Evaluation of the programme

The outcomes have to be measured to know if the objectives have been achieved, and ongoing monitoring will ensure the programme can be changed and is flexible and able to adapt to what is going on both within the organization and externally.

A communications plan analyses key publics reviewing their changing knowledge, opinions, and behaviours. Communications practitioners provide a channel between the organization and publics and coordinate activities that affect an organization's relationships with its publics.

Crucial to all public relations strategic planning is environmental scanning, otherwise called intelligence gathering (discussed in chapter 4) which is based on collecting and analysing research. Once all the information is available an overall communications approach can be developed through reviewing and questioning the direction of the business and deciding what is to receive the most emphasis.

Cutlip et al (2006: 312) explain that objectives should address the issues that have come out of the situation analysis, predicting and establishing the desired future and what the campaign is expected to achieve for each public. Objectives give a focus and direction to the programme and identify which publics are the most important and where to put resources such as time and money.

What is going on inside and outside the organization

Because communications programmes operate in what Cutlip et al (2006) call an open system of communication, that is, where organizations are interacting with the outside world (see chapter 2), communications objectives must take into account what is going on both inside and outside the organization.

For example, for the launch of a new sunscreen some of the research needs to investigate which other creams are available, what people are currently buying, what opinion people have towards the sun's effect on their skin, and the current opinion on sunscreens. This means that the practitioner needs to consider the changing environment of the organization which can be drawn together under the political, economic, social, and technological headings (PEST) presented in chapter 3. In addition, the changing organization itself may mean, among other things, new products, different staff, financial issues, and mergers. Strategic management is therefore the balancing of the internal processes of the organization with external factors and concerns in the outside world.

With all these factors in mind, communications objectives must be developed in order to facilitate and support the business objectives to reach an overall goal. There are four key aspects about public relations objectives noted by Gregory (2006) and developed further here:

1. PR Objectives must relate to organizational objectives

This means public relations must consider the overall business direction and connect to how the organization is competing in the marketplace, its progress and direction in research and development, how it markets its products and services, and the state of its finances. This is because the communication will be affected by what the company or organization is doing. For example, if a university is aiming to recruit more students its communication objectives will have to consider, among other factors, its league tables, competing universities, the state of its finances, the subjects that are the most successful, and the satisfaction level of current students.

2. PR Objectives must be about communications

Public relations objectives must advance the organization's goals through communications and are a brief statement about the publics it is addressing and the desired outcomes and timings conversely. Business objectives focus on producing something. For example, universities produce education and research; whereas other organizations may focus on share price (how much the organization is worth) or sales and market share (how much they can sell compared to other organizations). It is too easy for public relations practitioners to decide that the organization should produce a new product, invest in a new area or market in another country, and so on. However, the key to PR is to focus on communication objectives although organizational issues may be raised and considered in the situation analysis.

3. Objectives must be achievable and measurable

There is no point recommending an objective that cannot be achieved owing to the fact that it is too expensive, not linked to the business strategy, or is too ambitious. Therefore the objective needs to take into account the available resources. In addition, objectives can be used to monitor the campaign as the outcomes can be matched against the original objectives. If necessary, these measured outcomes can be used to change the objectives to ensure that the campaign is more realistic.

4. Objectives must have priorities

The programme should address specific publics and tight timing ensures that the objectives direct the programme.

Overall, well-written objectives ensure the campaign is focused and guided, that resources are anticipated, and that progress is being monitored. Parkinson and Ekachai (2006) state that communications objectives can guide strategic planning, serve as a tool for client persuasion, and are the foundation for campaign evaluation. They argue that objectives should follow six criteria:

1. Are realistic, short, and simple—that is, should be no more than one sentence long, be understood by everyone, and have an accurate time frame.

2. Support the organizational goals—these are aims or aspirations of the organization which may include increased market share, increased sales, increased profit, reduced employee turnover.

3. Specify a public—such as customers, voters, opponents, competitors, consumer groups, employees, and shareholders. Also latent publics who could be motivated to become active supporters of the organization as well as the active publics.

4. Specify the change in what publics do, think, or have. It can be changing their opinion so that they resist a new argument or attempt to change their behaviour that strengthens their existing opinion. In the case of a political campaign it could be to keep the ruling party in power.

5. Specify a time of accomplishment—this helps to measure the change and budget.

6. Ensure the plan is measurable. Often an opinion poll can be used to measure opinion change. Sometimes it is difficult to reach the target public therefore a secondary public can be used to influence them. One example of this is

grassroots lobbying which is done by individuals, for example those who write letters to their MP to influence change to legislation.

Objectives are a key part of planning and monitoring a public relations campaign. **Planning** decides the roles, mission, results, and effectiveness of a programme and how it can be measured. It is important to remember that public relations planning is a living process, that is, it must be able to change according to what is happening in the world and within the organization.

A recognized way of developing objectives is to focus on identifying a measurable change in a public's knowledge, attitudes, and behaviour over a specific time. Although this is a linear process it means that the campaign does not conclude with only a change in attitude but also follows through to behaviour change.

However, behaviour is much harder to change than attitudes or opinion and often public relations is used to create an environment of awareness in which advertising can then influence publics through its strong and direct messages.

For example, the UK government's 2008–9 swine flu campaign worked in this way, advised people about the illness to raise awareness and then it used advertisements to encourage people to use and dispose of their tissues.

Introducing strategy

The term **strategic thinking** is used frequently in organizations and refers to predicting or establishing a desired future goal state, determining what forces will help and hinder movement towards the goal, and formulating a plan for achieving the desired state (Cutlip et al 2006). However, there are many subtle variations is the meaning of strategy and its role in a public relations programme.

Strategic management is defined by Greene et al (cited Steyn 2003) as a continuous process of thinking through the current mission of the organization, the current environmental conditions, and then combining these elements to guide decisions and results.

Steyn (2003) claims strategy is the thinking and logic behind the actions. Gregory (2006) argues that strategy is the overall approach to a programme to achieve the objectives which have been set. She describes it as the rationale behind the programme often called the 'big idea'.

Cutlip et al (2006) describe strategy as the overall game plan, concept, and approach whereas Henry (2006) states that strategy is achieving a competitive advantage for an organization. As an organization is in a constantly changing environment, it needs to constantly consider who it should target, what it should offer, and how it can do this effectively.

The **corporate communications** strategy gives focus and direction for an organization's communication. It builds relationships with strategic stakeholders and decides what should be communicated rather than how it should be communicated. A practitioner would therefore be expected to understand the business and societal factors that the organization is facing to in order to formulate corporate communications strategy.

@ Go to the Online Resource Centre to access a virtual press conference about swine flu

This means focusing on assessing the external environment, identifying publics and then prioritizing issues.

Parkinson and Ekachai (2006: 33) claim PR strategy is conceptual or abstract:

Strategy describes messages, themes or guidelines for the overall public relations effort. One simple way to think of a strategy is as an expression of an idea or messages that will motivate the target public to change to meet the public relations objective.

Examples of strategy:

The following example looks at how to improve the health of babies in Pakistan (Parkinson and Ekachai 2006: 33).

The objective was to increase the number of pregnant women in Pakistan who eat high-calcium diets. The proposed PR strategy was to inform these women—the target public—that such a diet improves their children's health. This strategy assumed that the mothers valued the health of their children and will act on doing something about their diet because it affects their children. It provides a link between what the pregnant women eat and their children's health.

Another example is a failing school in England which was faced with closure owing to its poor quality control and student results. The school reviewed its policies and put in place many educational initiatives, but in people's minds it was still the same school. The communications objective was to relaunch the school with a new identity among the local people and encourage attendance to a specific level. It aimed to achieve this through a rebranding strategy positioning the school as a new educational establishment and breaking all connections to its old reputation. The tactics focused on a new school name and mission statement and a new head teacher. As a result, the school recruited well and is now successful.

A PR strategy provides the foundation for the tactics and is the framework in which the communications programme sits, and is monitored by whether it achieves its objectives. It is also important to remember that objectives and strategy can be limited by finances and existing programmes.

The management philosopher Drucker (1954) saw strategy as an indication of the organization's positioning for the future; the 'what' rather than the 'how'. This suggests that it is more important for an organization to improve its effectiveness rather than focusing on the 'how' of what it is done.

Strategic planning involves:

- determining an organization's mission
- determining an organization's profile
- assessing an organization's environment
- matching the organization's profile to environmental opportunities
- choosing the best options consistent with the organization's mission, choosing long-term goals, and developing short term objectives
- implementing the programme and evaluating it.

The following is an example of how the public relations consultancy Be Communications used an objective and strategy to lead a campaign involving regional music events.

Case Study

Using music to promote Red Stripe lager

Source: Courtesy of Be Communications

Red Stripe lager is a Jamaican lager-style beer associated with the reggae scene and brewed under licence in the UK. The organization's goal was to increase the consumption of lager among the 18–30-year-old group. It developed an ongoing annual Red Stripe Music Awards where a regional gig series showcased emerging artists culminating in a national final.

PR Objective

To use its historic link with music to encourage Red Stripe as the lager of choice among regional English music lovers aged 18–30 during October to May 2008-9.

The PR strategy

By communicating Red Stripe support for emerging artists through the regional Red Stripe Music Award (see Figure 6.2).

Fig 6.2
Red Stripe Music Awards

Source: Courtesy of Be Communications

Implementation

The public relations team developed the music awards, comprising a four-month long regional gig series, where emerging artists and bands were given the chance to play at credible live music venues and potentially win slots at the summer's best-loved festivals. Over 1,000 bands entered in 2009 with over 100 bands and artists playing at 27 regional showcases around the country. The final took place at the HMV Forum in May 2009 and was headlined by Mercury Music Prize winners, Gomez.

The public relations consultancy, Be Communications, managed and attended each gig working with venue managers, local promoters, and bands to ensure all gigs were promoted at every level. Media coverage was positive and extensive and Myspace and Facebook numbers doubled over the campaign period, with a substantial increase in Red Stripe Lager sales.

Go to the Online Resource Centre to access the link to the Red Stripe Music Award video

6.2 Theoretical context

Grunig (2006) believes that public relations should have a place in the strategic management of an organization rather than merely being a 'messaging, publicity, and media relations function'. He believes that the application of the key theories to developing a communications programme (situational theory of publics, the four models of public relations, and evaluation of communications programmes) links public relations to strategic management.

Public relations and strategic management

Grunig (2006) found that it is when public relations analyses the social, political, and institutional environment of an organization (as discussed in chapter 4) that it participates in the organization's strategic management and brings an outside perspective to its decision making. Grunig (2006) argues that public relations has real strategic value when it helps organizations to achieve their goals which have been developed through interaction with publics.

Dozier et al (1995: 48) believe that communications must contribute to strategic plans but can only do this if the dominant coalition, that is the decision makers in the organization, values and supports communications and understands the two-way flow as the preferred communication objective.

Dozier et al (1995: preface) see asymmetrical communication as persuasive and symmetrical communication as negotiation.

> **Excellent communication describes the ideal state in which knowledgeable communicators assist in the overall strategic management of organizations, seeking symmetrical relations through management of communication with key publics on whom organization survival depends.**

Dozier et al (1995) believe that excellence in communication is achieved through working towards the symmetrical public relations model in executing communications programmes. This means that the practitioner tries to get to know the publics and then advises senior management on how to manage conflict and promote mutual understanding in order to achieve communications objectives.

Conversely, the one-way press agentry and public information models simply transfer information from the organization to the publics. This means that the opinions of the publics do not influence the decisions made by senior management.

In the two-way asymmetrical model the communicator gathers information from publics and uses this information to develop messages that are most likely to persuade publics to behave as the organization wants. However, this information is not used to change or influence the organization's behaviour.

Getting the messages to the publics requires more tactical knowledge than strategy. This tactical ability is needed after an organization's strategy has been employed which focuses on the relationships desired from publics. Then the objectives are process or action objectives, such as getting people to attend an event, obtaining media coverage, or setting up a website, getting traffic to the website, and publishing a newsletter.

In a proposal there can be an overarching communications objective followed by additional objectives called process objectives or specific action objectives, for each public.

Persuasion and the public relations models

Persuasion is often used with activists in order to get them to do what an organization wants. Persuasion follows the asymmetrical model whereas the symmetrical model uses theories of conflict resolution and negotiation to increase the dominant coalition's understanding of publics.

The asymmetrical model is when publics are persuaded to accept the position of senior management and the organization does not change. Persuasion has three different effects (Perloff 2003).

1. It can shape attitudes by linking with positive images, such as trying to influence young people's attitudes to smoking by showing beautiful women or handsome men smoking.

2. It can reinforce a position they already hold such as strengthening their resolve. For example, the Central Office of Information (COI) 'no tobacco' campaign (chapter 1) worked on persuading people to increase their attempts at quitting.

3. It can be used to change attitudes such as perceptions of different cultures.

Aristotle believed that persuasion was convincing the audience to make the best decision about a matter. Perloff (2003) argues that persuasion assumes people have free choice and that people are responsible for the choices they make in response to persuasive messages. He argues that persuasive communication can be used by moral and immoral persuaders and it is the intention behind it which decides whether it is ethical or not (see Chapter 2 for more on how people make decisions).

The symmetrical model is considered more ethical than the other three (press agentry, public information, and asymmetric) as it is working at achieving cooperation, rather than persuasion, between an organization and its publics.

In order for the symmetrical model to work the practitioner needs to ensure that the organization is prepared to change its own behaviour and will negotiate with publics to reach a position that is a win-win zone. This open dialogue may mean that the publics may not reach the position that the senior management want, simply because it is cooperative where both sides will need to change their behaviour.

Senior management focus on an organization's mission and long-term goals to plan strategy. The organization's mission, that is, its purpose and direction, is affected by its relationships with publics in the organization's environment.

Applying theory to practice

Overall, Rogers and Storey (cited Windahl and Signitzer 2009) observe that because communication operates in a complex social, political, and economic mix and travels in an unpredictable way, it cannot be expected to generate any satisfactory results without guidance; hence, there need to be communication objectives which influence and guide the programme. Puska et al (cited Windahl and Signitzer 2009) note that objectives can follow different routes such as:

1. A behavioural change approach which helps people to identify risk factors, learn about a new way, and motivate them to change their behaviour. For example, once people become aware about the link between exercise and heart disease they are more likely to improve their lifestyle.

2. A communication behaviour approach which requires a change in what publics know through gaining their attention, changing their attitudes, and then their behaviour. For example, hearing about people from other disadvantaged families succeeding at university can encourage these families to realize it is also a possibility for them and encourage their enrolment.

3. An innovation diffusion approach which uses early adopters of innovations to communicate benefits. For example, those who decide to try out a new restaurant can be profiled and used as ambassadors to promote it.

The following case study by Turk Telekom in 2009 shows how public relations created a change in behaviour by getting people to switch from paper accounts to to e-billing through a strategy which created an environmental link.

Case Study

'Save a Tree, Plant a Tree': new billing technology

Source: Courtesy of Turk Telekom

Turk Telekom (TT) is the biggest provider of integrated telephone services in Turkey. It pioneered e-billing technology to reduce the cost of paper invoices and was one of the first companies to issue e-bills in Turkey. In 2008, e-billing was recognized as legitimate and legal documentation in Turkey but legalization and the technological launch were only the beginning. Consumer acceptance of online billing statements and conversion were essential to the success of the programme. What would motivate people to make the switch?

The answer was a public relations programme by which paper savings would be converted into ecological benefits. 'Save a Tree, Plant a Tree' was born. Research ascertained attitudes about target publics and Turk Telekom's reputation in order to develop messages and identify publics.

Business goal

The business goal was to convert 500,000 (approximately 8.2 per cent) of the company's six million ADSL users of paper bills to using e-bills within one year. From a marketing services standpoint, there was a goal to plant a tree for every 1,000 accounts that converted to e-billing.

Communications objective

To encourage ADSL users to be aware of the environmental impact of paper statements and how paper could be saved if they made the switch to e-billing.

Communications strategy

By associating Turk Telekom with a tree planting programme which expanded awareness about environment protection and the impact of paper statements on communities.

Implementation

At the first stage of the project, Turk Telekom transferred its own archives from paper to electronic, saving 1,500 tons of paper each year—equivalent to 24,000 trees (see Figure 6.3).

A reputation building approach to the corporate and business communications project was then launched.

- A communications campaign blitz offering 10 minutes of free calls every month for a year to those customers who chose e-billing was in virtually every newspaper in Turkey.
- Flyers were created as statement stuffers and other versions of the flyer were distributed in taxi cabs in major cities such as Istanbul and Ankara.
- Public service announcements were placed on public and private television, and the topic was covered in talk shows.
- At the International Brand Conference, TT gave away cordless telephones to customers who then and there transferred their billing from paper to electronic statements.
- At the CEBIT fair—the largest IT expo in Turkey—TT created a special stand just for the introduction of the e-billing system.
- Backyard campaigns were also conducted at the local level, involving townships and mayors of selected cities, in accordance with the research findings.

Creativity

Turk Telekom branded 34 forests and made them their own, with TT designing and placing huge, eye-catching signs at the entrance to each forest. The media ran news on how this

Fig 6.3
Turk Telekom created their own forests when e-billing

Source: Copyright OUP

new service from Turk Telekom was having a positive impact on Turkey's natural resources thereby motivating people to switch to electronic billing.

Results

Just before the 'Save a Tree, Plant a Tree' programme began, IT was printing 23.5 million billing statements per month, using 350 tons of offset paper, 125 tons of company archive materials, 125 tons in customer copies, and 100 tons in envelopes.

The corporate and business communications programme results surpassed the objectives, converting 850,000 Turk Telekom customer statements in the first six months alone, saving more than 4,200 tons of paper on an annual basis.

Turk Telekom is planting more than 100,000 trees. The multiplier effect of engaging customers at the local level has boosted consumer concern about the environment, substantiated by post-research of customer attitudes about Turk Telekom's role as an environmentally responsible corporate citizen.

6.3 Influences

A communications programme resembles a communications model where there is a sender, receiver, channel, message, and a feedback mechanism and it is affected by all the issues that influence communication.

Planning a campaign looks at environmental scanning or intelligence gathering in order to really understand the organization and its publics so that communication can be developed that will appeal to specific publics.

Hierarchy of effects model

Communications objectives are often developed through focusing on informing people first, followed by influencing their attitudes, and finally their behaviour. This originated from what is called the hierarchy of effects model, developed in 1961 by Lavidge and Steiner. The model represents the process of initial unawareness to the final stage of actual purchases that people went through when they were exposed to advertising. It assumes a logical and sequential movement of publics from an attitudinal stage towards a final behavioural stage (Fill 2006).

Cognitive

The cognitive stage is getting people to think about the issue, problem, or product where people develop their knowledge. It means creating awareness and getting the public's attention so that they are motivated to become informed. This involves learning about something.

Affective

The affective stage is getting people to feel something and appeals to emotions. It creates an attitude towards the product, problem, or issue such as preferring something or disagreeing with an idea.

Conative

The conative stage is when people do something. They have moved from changing their attitude to behaving in a certain way like voting, attending an event, or buying something.

Grunig and Hunt (1984) applied this thinking to public relations in the situational theory of publics and recommended setting cognitive objectives first in order that people understand the issues. The following example applies the hierarchy of effects model.

Case Study

BT ChildLine campaign and the hierarchy of effects model

Source: Courtesy of Grayling

The UK telecommunication organization, BT, has supported the charity ChildLine since its inception in 1988, providing fundraising, office space, and a memorable helpline number—0800 111. There is a natural synergy as communication is at the heart of both organizations.

Cognitive

One of BT's objectives in being involved is to engage and motivate its 100,000 employees and ensure that 80 per cent of them are aware of the organization's support for ChildLine. The project is incorporated into the daily workplan of employees with regular briefings and fundraising initiatives.

Affective

Employees have become extremely enthusiastic about fundraising and many volunteer at the call centres with some of them now even training to become counsellors (see Figure 6.4).

Fig 6.4
Organizations support charities to engage and motivate employees

Source: Copyright OUP

Conative

The association appeals to BT employees and creates high enthusiasm among staff, motivating them to raise funds and donate, including payroll giving. Nearly all (99 per cent) of BTs employees are aware of the partnership with ChildLine, with those participating in the fundraising and volunteering having higher productivity than other colleagues.

Another advertising model that is also used to guide public relations programmes is called **Dagmar**—which stands for 'defining advertising goals for measured advertising results' developed in 1961 by Russell Colley (Fill 2006).

This model is similar to the hierarchy of effects and looks at how people can be persuaded to buy a particular brand. It addresses the initial unawareness factor and highlights the fact that people need to have a feeling of conviction in order to stimulate them to behave in a certain way. The model focuses on showing the need to move people through the stage of unawareness to awareness which must then be developed, maintained, and strengthened in order to provoke interest and stimulate involvement.

It works to avoid competing messages, such as other advertising brands, by strengthening people's interest and understanding, then on to develop their beliefs so they are then moved to act.

Objectives and strategy in online public relations

As with all communications programmes, the objectives for online projects need to coincide with the organization's goals and values. This is crucial for an online programme as the internet makes an organization very visible So it must be seen to act according to the values it communicates. Therefore, employees need to be fully briefed and understand what is happening so they can reinforce the organization's strategic direction.

An online strategy should include new and old media and a mix of activities, bearing in mind that the online community may shift the programme to different platforms and channels (Phillips and Young 2009: 183). There must be constant monitoring and reporting of online activities, even if there is nothing dramatic happening at the time as it can take off suddenly.

6.4 Application to industry

Writing SMART objectives

For objectives to be effective they should meet the criteria of being Specific, Measurable, Achievable, Relevant, and Time-bound which forms the acronym SMART.

Specific: objectives must be written in a clear and precise way to provide a focus and clear outcomes. As online media is mediating all public relations, objectives should take in the global, time-shifting, interactive, two-way nature of the internet.

Measurable: objectives must state a specific amount or result to be achieved, this can be measured in numbers, statistics or proportions and be across many media platforms, channels, and contexts.

Achievable: objectives need to be realistic and have the resources required such as the budget and staff.

Relevant: objectives must link to business objectives and focus on communication.

Time bound: objectives must have a clear timeframe which allows monitoring and evaluation (Watson and Noble 2007), although with the internet there is never a final moment so there must be awareness that outcomes will be ongoing.

There are variable interpretations of this SMART acronym. Gregory (2009) uses the R for 'resourced' although this could be included with 'achievable'. Watson and Noble (2007) add another R for 'relevant' and another T for 'targeted'. Others use the A for 'agreed' and add an E for 'ethical' and R for 'recorded' to make SMARTER.

An objective has to take into account many factors and Table 6.1 shows a simple process to guide its development:

Table 6.1 Developing objectives for a public relations programme

Review business goals
Review or develop a business communication brief:
This will outline, from the business goals point of view, the issue that a communications programme is to address. It lists target publics, dates, budgets, and how the organization sees the communications issue and what it expects from public relations
Identify communications issue(s) based on the situation analysis:
Note the environmental influences which could be positive and negative.
Note timing issues.
Estimate resources as objectives must be realistic and fit to a budget and team.
Note competing programmes and issues.
Identify publics from the situation analysis and stakeholder analysis:
Who is involved (internal and external).
Who is affected.
Prioritize depending on their influence and power within the organization/external to the organization.
Confirm opinion leaders, gatekeepers, and decision-makers.
Overall objective:
There can be one overall communications objective which states the communications outcome of the programme, along with publics and timing.
Overall strategy:
An overall strategy can state how the above communication goal will be reached. It provides a framework for the programme and is usually the theme. For example, the Red Stripe campaign used the Red Stripe Music Awards as their communications strategy.
Action objectives:
Each objective must have a single outcome, that is, what will happen, when it will happen (dates and timings are important), and how it can be measured (through statistics or numbers for example).
These should be sequential from getting people to think about something, to developing an attitude and opinion and then working to behaviour change.
It must state a specific public or several publics.
Check against SMART.
Check against business objectives.
Action strategies:
An action strategy should address how each action objective will be delivered.
Implementation:
Identifies the detail on how each objective will be delivered (see chapter 7).
Evaluation:
This relates to ongoing measurement of achieving the objectives (see chapter 8).

Case Study

Creating a new sector of shoppers

Source: Courtesy of Kavanagh Public Relations

The following is an outline of an award winning campaign showing its objectives and strategies. The Aldi campaign in 2009 succeeded in creating a new sector of Aldi shoppers, as well as retaining its original shoppers. Note that it links to the business objectives and follows a sequential pattern of cognitive objectives, attitudinal objectives, through to behavioural objectives.

Aldi is a global discount retailer. Its goal is:

To provide our customers with the products they buy regularly and ensure that those products are of the highest possible quality at guaranteed low prices.

The business objective was to increase its customer base, through attracting new customers who were shopping at more expensive supermarkets. Although Aldi was seen as a deep discounter where price was the most important factor in attracting customers, it needed to sustain this market as well as to attract more shoppers through positioning itself as offering value and quality.

The retail chain carried out extensive stakeholder research into the mindset of shoppers and found that first-time buyers buy one or two products and realize the goods are of good quality, at their second visit they pick up a basket and realize they are buying quality at a good price. At the third visit they use a trolley to do the family shopping. Based on this research, Aldi found that if you get a customer in to the shop to buy one or two items they will return; the challenge was getting customers over the threshold.

To achieve this they turned to public relations, hiring the consultancy Kavanagh PR. Their research found that frugality was resonating with Aldi's messages on quality and saving. The public relations objectives followed a process of providing publics with information, changing their attitudes, and changing their behaviour.

Overall communication objective

To sustain existing customers and build market share through giving ABC1 shoppers who think of discounted shops as 'cheap and cheerful' a compelling reason to switch retailers.

Overall strategy

By developing new attitudes towards Aldi by using the credit crunch as a compelling reason to switch retailers through focusing on discounted quality products where the message of 30 per cent cheaper is no compromise when comparing to quality.

It was vital that Aldi retain its existing customers but it also needed to appeal to new customers. A new area was the ABC1 shoppers who went to more expensive stores. The credit crunch highlighted the need for frugality and Aldi harnessed this message in its strategy, linking to frugality and quality.

Action objectives and strategies (using hierarchy of effects model)

1. Cognitive objective

To present Aldi discounted products as an overall discount figure to financially aware consumers at the beginning of the credit crunch both to existing consumers and potential consumers.

Strategy

By leveraging the financial crisis through the Aldi MD launching a campaign strapline called 'Aldi saves nation £1 million a day'.

The Aldi MD, who had never given media interviews before, was made available to the media, taking journalists on an educational Aldi shopping tour highlighting the integrity of the business and profiling the discounts and the numerous and diverse food industry product awards such as best cheese, best pizza, best jam, best mince pies, etc.

The 'saving the nation' message was profiled in the financial press and on TV news as a positive message regarding the credit crunch.

2. Affective objective

Change attitudes through personalizing the nationwide savings message to intelligent and aware stakeholders.

Strategy

By profiling Aldi as a quality discount shop for intelligent and discerning shoppers who want to save money during uncertain financial times. This led to a 'Savvy Shoppers Shop at Aldi' theme through a trendy interactive online microsite which calculated individual shopping savings and created a 'tell a friend' option resulting in a highly popular viral campaign.

An informal Aldi IQ test of retail shoppers showed that Aldi shoppers, compared to shoppers at other retailers, were more aware about the concept of price promotion and 'good quality at good value' and were not swayed by brand. This persuaded new Aldi customers that they were intelligent shoppers.

3. Behavioural objective

To get consumers to participate in comparing well-known brands of everyday products such as tomato ketchup and crisps to Aldi products.

Strategy

By a 'taste the nation' blind product tasting trial, comparing well-known brands of popular products such as tomato ketchup and crisps to Aldi products. This encouraged shoppers to

Fig 6.5
**Shoppers search for the
best deals**

Source: Copyright OUP

try for themselves. It reinforced the messages of quality and savings and consumers realized they could have quality and cheaper groceries and did not need to pay for the 'shopping experience' available in more expensive outlets.

Outcome

A full media content analysis showed that the message was consistent and engaged with the creative themes. Overall this campaign secured a change in attitude and behaviour and increased sales by 44 per cent and raised Aldi's market share. In addition, the message 'the Aldi effect' became a stock phrase in the media for any company which was combining frugality and quality (see Figure 6.5).

PR Tool

Negotiation technique

Source: Courtesy of Mindtools *http://www.mindtools.com*

Preparing for a successful negotiation ...

Depending on the scale of the disagreement, some preparation may be appropriate for conducting a successful negotiation.

For small disagreements, excessive preparation can be counter-productive because it takes time that is better used elsewhere. It can also be seen as manipulative because, just as it strengthens your position, it can weaken the other person's.

- **Goals:** what do you want to get out of the negotiation? What do you think the other person wants?

- **Trades:** what do you and the other person have that you can trade? What do you each have that the other wants? What are you each comfortable giving away?

- **Alternatives:** if you don't reach agreement with the other person, what alternatives do you have? Are these good or bad? How much does it matter if you do not reach agreement? Does failure to reach an agreement cut you out of future opportunities? And what alternatives might the other person have?

- **Relationships:** what is the history of the relationship? Could or should this history impact the negotiation? Will there be any hidden issues that may influence the negotiation? How will you handle these?

- **Expected outcomes:** what outcome will people be expecting from this negotiation? What has the outcome been in the past, and what precedents have been set?

- **The consequences:** what are the consequences for you of winning or losing this negotiation? What are the consequences for the other person?

- **Power:** who has what power in the relationship? Who controls resources? Who stands to lose the most if agreement isn't reached? What power does the other person have to deliver what you hope for?

- **Possible solutions:** based on all of the considerations, what possible compromises might there be?

Style is critical ...

For a negotiation to be 'win-win', both parties should feel positive about the negotiation once it's over. This helps people to keep good working relationships afterwards. This also governs the style of the negotiation—histrionics and displays of emotion are clearly inappropriate because they undermine the rational basis of the negotiation and because they bring a manipulative aspect to them.

Despite this, emotion can be an important subject of discussion because people's emotional needs must be met fairly. If emotion is not discussed where it needs to be, then the agreement reached can be unsatisfactory and temporary. Be as detached as possible when discussing your own emotions—perhaps discuss them as if they belong to someone else.

Negotiating successfully ...

The negotiation itself is a careful exploration of your position and the other person's position, with the goal of finding a mutually acceptable compromise that gives you both as much of what you want as possible. People's positions are rarely as fundamentally opposed as they may initially appear—the other person may have very different goals from the ones you expect!

🌐 **Go to the Online Resource Centre to access a link to a quiz on your negotiation style**

In an ideal situation, you will find that the other person wants what you are prepared to trade, and that you are prepared to give what the other person wants.

If this is not the case and one person must give way, then it is fair for this person to try to negotiate some form of compensation for doing so—the scale of this compensation will often depend on the many factors discussed above. Ultimately, both sides should feel comfortable with the final solution if the agreement is to be considered win-win.

Only consider win-lose negotiation if you don't need to have an ongoing relationship with the other party as, having lost, they are unlikely to want to work with you again. Equally, you should expect that if they need to fulfil some part of a deal in which you have 'won', they may be uncooperative and legalistic about the way they do this.

Summary

Objectives are an integral part of a public relations plan. They fit into any planning model and are the second part of the Cutlip et al (2006) four-way planning model which includes identifying publics, objectives, and actions.

They must address the business goal of the organization and be developed in the context of a public relations programme. They need to consider what is already on the media agenda, the influences which may be important, and the key publics, as well as the diverse and available channels of communication.

Therefore, objectives must be the result of an extensive situation analysis or environmental scanning analysis. There can be an overall objective for the public relations programme and then a series of action objectives which can also target particular publics.

Strategy is the approach or theme that directs the course of activity for each objective. For example, the Aldi campaign used the credit crunch theme as a compelling reason for shoppers to change their retailer.

There is a diverse spread of theory that a practitioner needs to consider in order to develop objectives. These range from theories which illuminate the factors involved in the communication process as well as the communication outcomes. They focus on how information travels, whether publics are active or passive in receiving information and acting upon it, and also how much they influence the organization.

The theory also illuminates how objectives can be developed in an effort to influence thinking, attitudes, and behaviour. Objectives are directed at stakeholders and in order to know how to engage them and to address their concerns there are various processes which help to analyse the influence and activity they have. Clear objectives are also needed in an effort to guide the evaluation process so that they benchmark progress.

In developing objectives it is important that they are SMART, that is specific, measurable, appropriate, resourced, and timely. Tactics can then be developed to deliver these objectives and a programme implemented.

Public relations crosses boundaries within an organization and must take account of influences from each area. In addition, public relations can be increasingly used in strategic management which ensures that the communication helps to deliver the overall business goal, taking into account stakeholders and their influence.

Discussion points

A. Objectives

Access the *PR Week* showcase of PR case studies and download several case studies.

Review their objectives. Do you think these are satisfactory? What makes them objectives? Are they SMART?

B. Business objectives

Identify three large organizations and access their websites. Can you identify their mission statements and their business objectives? Do you see any mismatches?

C. Identify three key media stories

Is there evidence of a public relations strategy?

Are the organization's objectives being communicated?

What communication objectives would you create? How are they different?

References

BBC (2010) 'Why the Vatican's Media Strategy is Failing', News BBC, 14 April. Available at: http://news.bbc.co.uk/2/hi/8621197.stm

Choo, G. (2009) in R. Tench and L. Yeomans (eds) *Exploring Public Relations* (2nd edn). London: Prentice Hall

Cutlip, S., Center, A., and Broom, G (2006) *Effective Public Relations* (9th edn). Upper Saddle River, NJ: Pearson

Davis, A. (2007) *Mastering Public Relations* (2nd edn). Houndmills: Palgrave Macmillan

Dozier, D., Grunig, L., and Grunig, J. (1995) *Manager's Guide To Excellence in Public Relations and Communication Management*. Mahwah, NJ: Lawrence Erlbaum

Drucker, P. (1954) *The Practice of Management*. New York: HarperBusiness

Fill, C. (2006) *Marketing Communications: Engagement, Strategies and Practice* (4th edn). Harlow: Pearson

Gregory, A. (2010) *PR in Practice: Planning and Managing Public Relations Campaigns: A Step-by-Step Guide* (3rd edn). London: Kogan Page

Gregory, A. (2010) 'Strategic Strategy and other Confusions CIPR Skills Guides'. Available at http://www.cipr.co.uk

Grunig, J. (2006) 'Furnishing the Edifice, Ongoing Research on PR As a Strategic Management Function', Journal of Public Relations Research 18/20: 151–6

Grunig, J. and Hunt, T. (1984) *Managing Public Relations*. New York: Holt, Rinehart and Winston

Grunig, J. and Repper, F. (1992) 'Strategic Management, Publics, and Issues' in J. Grunig (ed) *Excellence In Public Relations and Public Relations Management*. Hillsdale, NJ: Lawrence Erlbaum

Henry, A. (2008) *Understanding Strategic Management*. Oxford: Oxford University Press

L'Etang, J. (2008) *Public Relations: Concepts, Practice and Critique.* London: Sage

Mindtools http://www.mindtools.com/SommSkll/NegotiationSkills.htm

Missionstatements.com (2009) Available at: http://www.missionstatements.com/

Parkinson, M. and Ekachai, D. (2006) *International and Intercultural Public Relations: A Campaign Case Approach.* Boston, MA: Pearson

Perloff, R. (2003) *The Dynamics of Persuasion: Communications and Attitudes in the 21st Century* (2nd edn). Mahwah: NJ: Lawrence Erlbaum

Phillips, D. and Young, P. (2009) *Online Public Relations: A Practical guide to developing an Online Strategy in the World of Social Media* (PR in Practice) (2nd edn). London: Kogan Page

Steyn, B. (203) 'From Strategy to Corporate Communication Strategy: A Conceptualization', Journal of Communication Management 8/2: 168–83

Watson and Noble (2007) *Evaluating Public Relations: A Best Practice Guide To Public Relations Planning, Research and Evaluation* (2nd ed). London: Kogan Page

Windahl, S. and Signitizer, B. with Olson, J. (2009) *Using Communication Theory: An Introduction to Planned Communication* (2nd edn). London: Sage

Implementation and budgeting

(7)

Learning outcomes

1. Be able to understand what implementation means and how timing and budgets are its key drivers.

2. Be able to develop an implementation plan with tactics within a strategic framework, and according to communications objectives and ongoing evaluation.

3. Be able to use creativity to tailor implementation plans to different business areas or foci, such as corporate communications, internal communications, or sponsorship.

4. Review historical aspects of public relations implementation and apply concepts to modern-day public relations.

5. Be able to explain how teams are formed, the role of different team members, and how these affect the implementation process.

6. Be able to develop relevant tactics for objectives explaining how they would be created, anticipating their outcomes, and ongoing potential and evaluation as well as planning their timescale and budget.

Practitioner Insight

Clive Booth
Director, Lansons Communications, London
& Chairman, Royal College of Radiologists
Clinical Radiology, Patients' Liaison Group, UK

Clive is a former global director of public affairs and media relations for one of the world's largest professional associations, before which he was head of corporate affairs for Lewis PR. Previously a parliamentary candidate he is a Fellow of the Chartered Institute of Public Relations and the Royal Society of Arts and Commerce. At the start of his career he worked on Accountancy Age and Financial Decisions and then spent six years at the *Financial Times*.

How do you approach implementing a campaign?

Firstly agree the objective. What is it that this activity needs to achieve? Some of the best PR consultancy I've offered to clients is to help shape their thinking ahead of a PR campaign. It's quite rare to meet a client who always knows exactly what success looks like. The means of achieving it are usually relatively simple, once you know what results are needed.

As we all instinctively know, it's not always the volume of media coverage that matters, but the quality. Nor is front page coverage always the yardstick by which impact should be judged. Lehman Brothers, BP, and Enron all made the front pages for days, but not for the right reasons.

How can you ensure creativity against a tight budget?

Clients often think they need creativity but what they most need is a successful result. Often the best campaigns are methodically planned and executed with ruthless efficiency.

Social media channels are terrific. For instance in 1980s Britain 40 per cent of the adult population always watched the evening news on TV, 25 per cent read a newspaper every morning. Yet by 2009, take an event like the death of Michael Jackson and pretty much everyone I know had it tweeted to their mobiles within 20 minutes of the news breaking in California.

If mass market, consumer communication is what you need then the internet is probably the best channel. If financial analysts need to be persuaded that a hostile takeover bid is in shareholders' interests then you can probably target all 20 of them, at the same time, in the same room in front of a well-rehearsed CEO and chief financial officer.

What is an example of an impressive campaign?

I am resistant to celebrity endorsement and there are many cases where these go wrong. The stories of ordinary human beings are the most compelling.

I led a campaign to promote a new medical device, in which a cerebral pacemaker had been fitted into a Parkinson's Disease sufferer to counteract the tremors caused by the disease.

The TV news crew and I were moved emotionally when we filmed the outstanding effects on a patient's life. 'Tim' shook so uncontrollably he fell out of his chair yet when he turned his device on he could talk and hold his granddaughter with just a hint of slurred speech.

What tactics are essential, and why?

It's essential to understand the motivation of your audience hence Apple is a successful brand because it appeals to a demographic wanting to be cool.

One of the best tactics of all is to get others to do your PR for you. Once again Apple scores top marks. Having seen your neighbour's iPhone didn't you immediately covet it? Campaigns in which endorsement by our own peer group are the main advocates are very hard to fault.

What advice would you give about implementing campaigns?

Be methodical. Plan. Consider what if? Talk the plan over with others and ask if you've missed something. Consistently good communicators are consistently good listeners.

7.1 Definition of implementation

Once the public relations objectives of a communication proposal are defined according to the overall strategy, the next stage is to deliver them through a series of tactics outlined in an implementation plan along with budget and timings. According to the Collins English dictionary, a tactic is 'a move or method used to achieve an aim or a task' (Black et al 2007: 544).

Implementing, or carrying out, a proposal is where ideas are put into practice. It is delivering what is stated in the objectives, addressing the target publics, and developing in the context of the strategy. The strategy provides the framework in which an implementation plan is developed.

Tactics

An implementation plan outlines all the tactics and when and how they will be achieved. It may include tactics such as a media event to launch a new product; a large organization may, or may not as the case may be, call a shareholders' meeting to announce its successful financial results; an author may have a book signing event to launch a new book; a new airline may promote itself by running a competition which offers free flights; a politician may hold a garden party to meet constituents and raise funds for the campaign. A blog is also a tactic and very effective in initiating and nurturing relationships with publics and a viral video is a tactic that achieves peer-to-peer communication. The use of third parties, such as opinion leaders, is a common tactic to gain endorsement for a product or service.

Developing an implementation plan starts with reviewing the situation analysis, the objectives and the strategy, and the stakeholders. A stakeholder analysis which also considers what the organization needs from the stakeholders can identify where barriers might be, and the actions that need to be taken. This can be used to develop the tactics (see Table 7.1).

Table 7.1 Stakeholder analysis grid

Public/ stakeholders	Their interests/ needs	What the organization needs from them	Influence/risk	Recommended actions

An implementation plan must be appropriate not only to the public but also to the organization. Stunts may work well for consumer products, but not so well for more serious products such as medicines which have regulations to ensure a responsible approach is taken in consumer promotions. A conservative organization such as a pharmaceutical company may prefer to use doctors or scientific researchers to act as their opinion leaders and provide an in-depth scientific view. However, they can also use a celebrity to promote different aspects of the campaign, such as encouraging people to eat healthy foods, or to raise awareness of a particular illness.

Cost, time, and feasibility

According to Gregory (2006) the development of an implementation plan is affected by:

1. Cost: all tactics must be planned using a budget which is a finite resource.
2. Time: a tactic needs time to be developed and carried out, and should link it to other aspects of the plan as well.
3. Feasibility: a tactic must be specific, fit the context of the message, and be appropriate to the organization

This means that cost, time, and feasibility must be monitored during the implementation of each tactic and this will help to evaluate the ongoing success of the programme.

Tactics

It is the creativity that affects how tactics are developed and applied to the different areas, and it is how well they are adapted to deliver the objective, that makes them successful. The following is a grouping of commonly used tactics.

1. Media releases

Media releases communicate that a tactic is going to happen. This may be an event, which has to be planned in order to announce its various stages to the media. A media release can also be used as an invitation—there is plenty of room for creativity in a media invitation. For example, an invitation can be printed on a product, inserted into balloons and then sent to the media, emailed as a screen saver, or delivered on a memory stick. A screen saver can carry powerpoints, images, and interactive messages and is also ideal for internal communications where employees can interact with corporate messages on a regular basis.

Surveys are often an effective way of leading a media release. Carrying out surveys for organizations can get their brands into the media by focusing on particular newsworthy angles that the research has drawn out. However, practitioners need to be aware of the media cynicism to surveys. The *Irish Times* (Hegarty 2008) discusses the explosion in snappy surveys over the last decade and argues they are statistically inaccurate with worthless information. Despite this, Hegarty concedes that surveys remain a regular feature of the media and generate their own news.

Offering broadcast quality footage, also called a b-roll (see chapter 4), which present a newsworthy angle and may be otherwise difficult for the media to obtain owing to cost or access, work as a type of broadcast release, and can help to encourage media interest. This can mean offering b-roll footage of a celebrity activity which can be given to all journalists. For example, in a campaign promoting responsible drinking, Bacardi were able to provide media with footage of journalists driving with Michael Schumacher at a branded media event (see chapter 13 for more details on this case study).

2. Media tours

Media tours can mean taking journalists to a location to understand the organization or visit a factory to see how products are being made, or they can be a visit to a tourist destination if that location is being promoted. Aldi arranged media tours of its shops, but made it more interesting by having their CEO run the tours and offer financial information about the organization, as well as new insights into retail food business trends. This generated very positive and effective media coverage and corporate positioning (see chapter 6).

● Go to the Online Resource Centre to access media releases on surveys and their media coverage

3. Awards

Awards or prizes can raise media awareness of the organization or the issue. This involves preparing for the award, announcing the award, and then following up the receiver after the award. An award can become an event if someone important to the organization can present the award, or an award can announce what an individual or a group has achieved, and encourage media coverage by focusing on that individual or team. For example, Red Stripe lager ran a music strategy to encourage lager consumption (see chapter 6). Its tactics included music awards for a regional gig series to encourage shows and associated promotion at different music venues around the country.

4. Press rooms

Press rooms are arranged at events or conferences where the media can access information and have a place to interview people and write articles. These rooms are usually
accessible only to journalists and often run by a public relations practitioner on behalf
of the event. They may be sponsored by an organization. Virtual press rooms are located
in special sections of an organization's website and are called online press rooms and
are where an organization can post their media information including video footage
and high-resolution photographs. It can also be used as a channel to deal with media
requests.

In an international study of virtual press rooms Alfonso and Miguel (2006) found
that there is opportunity to take more advantage of internet tools to build solid
relationships with the media. The researchers recommend there should be releases,
financial data, reports, biographies, and historical data as well as good classification
of information and its location. They suggest that these virtual press rooms be used to
make available high-resolution images as well as having quality charts, illustrations,
graphics, and logos which can be downloaded for the media. In addition, there should
be a high-quality video that can be used by TV broadcasters and can be downloaded.
They recommend that even low-quality footage can be viewed by a TV professional
with a view to their ordering high-quality versions. Speeches and statements from
company spokespeople could also be included. In addition, RSS feeds—an expanding
technology among blogs and online media—could be offered within virtual press
rooms rather than emails.

Alfonso and Miguel (2006: 272) note that a virtual press room is really a request
centre and provides an opportunity to use interactive tools where media can engage in
dialogue and reciprocal communication can be encouraged through loyalty tools such
as alerts, online interviews, or newsletters, as well as ensuring updated content and this
also encourages media loyalty. The researchers also found that it was likely more media
contacts would be made and relationships built if a named professional operated the
press and liaised with journalists.

5. Events

Many tactics can be packaged into an event such as a media conference, an internal
meeting, a fundraising event (think of the UK Red Nose Day), an award, an anniversary, or a marketing initiative such as the launch of a new product. An event creates
attention for the organization. These must be planned according to the organization's
objectives to ensure that they deliver the appropriate messages. A conference can attract many delegates and is attractive for a sponsor who wants to reach and influence
the same people.

Well thought-out invitations to an event are crucial in order to encourage attendance
and these should be from the head of the organization or another very important
person. Reply addresses or automatic email responses to the invitations are needed to
be able to evaluate responses. Other promotional tactics to potential invitees may be
needed to encourage their interest.

⊕ Go to the Online
Resource Centre to
access a link on
arranging a royal visit

A royal visit is a large event which must be planed about nine months in advance with the royal diaries and arranged with the royal's private office. It must also fit the agenda of the royal invitee. See more on event planning and management later in this chapter.

6. Promotional weeks and days

Linking to already established dates or running special weeks or days offers an angle to launch a campaign; these could even be existing events. For example, Devon County Council used the event of British Summer Time going back to Greewich Mean Time in order to launch a campaign for safe cycling as it would be getting darker earlier. Promotional weeks can be created although this is becoming an overused PR activity in which the media are becoming less interested. In 2009 the World Cancer Research Fund wanted to increase awareness that there was a link between bowel cancer and eating processed meat. They used the new school year as a hook to create timeliness to warn parents not to include ham in their children's lunchboxes. Another example of timeliness is the Kleenex campaign which launched an interactive online hayfever map during hay fever season to alert people to high pollen areas and subsequent awareness of its tissues (see chapter 5 for more on this case study).

7. Stunts

These are a particular kind of a photo event (see chapter 1) where the story is really the picture and it is usually the newspaper picture editors and television news programmes who are invited. Stunts need captions prepared in advance along with the full names and titles of those pictured and their purpose.

8. Placement on television and radio

The producers of television soaps, documentaries, and radio programmes are often open to discuss health and social themes which offer an opportunity to involve an organization or its product. In addition, product placement in television soaps can be effective. Any of these ideas must fit into the implementation timeline as product placement and themes need about six months of preparation time. There are also opportunities to profile a building or location by providing it to television to be used for any travelling TV shows such as dancing programmes, antique road shows, and real estates shows.

9. Publications and competitions

A publication—which can be a website, a DVD, a viral film, a book, and on a smaller scale even a leaflet or a poster—is a key tactic to mark a particular event, product launch, or the opening of an attraction (see Figure 7.1).

Competitions help to ensure editorial coverage and give several media opportunities. Announcing the competition includes information about the organization and the prizes—which may be linked to the organization—as well as announcing the winners

and participating in further publicity. Most media outlets run competitions but there are special rules such as the prize value. These rules vary for different media, for example some magazines run regular 'reader offers' which means products are offered to readers and will be written about. Radios regularly run competitions which have the opportunity to reach large audiences and gain instant feedback (see chapter 3).

10. Third parties

Involving third-parties is a powerful communication tactic; these can be in the form of sponsorship, links, or simply associations. For example, the Land Rover campaign described in chapter 5 protected its brand through profiling its sustainability. This was implemented through developing partnerships with their numerous stakeholders, such as Greenpeace.

11. Sponsorship

An organization may sponsor a sport, activity, or an event in order to increase its profile and link an organization, product, or brand with the values of the sponsored item or event. This can provide a halo effect, generating goodwill, and is also an opportunity to offer hospitality to publics. Whatever is sponsored must fit the objectives of the organization or brand and, in turn, sponsorship is valuable in providing financial support and subsidy to sports, cultural, and/or entertainment events. Areas for sponsorship can include artistic and cultural events, children's activities, education, sport, and supporting initiatives that benefit the wider community.

   The sponsored—that is the event, organization, sport, or charity—must ensure that the sponsor reflects their philosophy; there must be compatibility and an understanding of each other's corporate values.

Public relations frequently activates sponsorship; that is, an organization which is sponsoring an event or activity calls in public relations to communicate its sponsorship. (See the information about BT ChildLine in chapter 6.) It is therefore important to record what the sponsorship has agreed which includes how much branding is allowed by the sponsor. The sponsor's logo may have to be evident in all photographs and in television coverage, however these are also bound by rules and there can be different cost levels for more exposure. Additionally, it is important to be aware that a sponsor should not overwhelm the event with its own messages.

For example, Siemens, a leading computer technology company with specific services for corporate finance, sponsors GB Rowing which links to Siemens' key values of innovation, performance, corporate responsibility, and employee engagement. It wanted to promote its computer technology and services to businesses and make the most of its partnership with GB Rowing, so ran a campaign orchestrated by the London PR consultancy, Threepipe.

Siemens linked its sponsorship of GB Rowing with the charity Stroke Association, which was also targeting the business community, in a joint effort to raise awareness of the risk of stroke and guidelines for its prevention, such as healthy living. A 'Stroke to-Stroke Week' highlighted the crucial role of regular exercise in preventing stroke, by challenging individuals to row 10km. Consumers signed up to the campaign website to take part and raise funds for the charity.

The campaign was launched to its target publics through the business media receiving a 'Stroke in Business' research report which analysed responses to stress across the UK business sector, making the link between a lack of exercise, stress levels, and the risk of stroke (see Figure 7.2).

Areas of implementation

Tactics are implemented within the context of the type of public relations being carried out. The following is an outline of some of the areas for which tactics are tailored.

1. Corporate

These relate to promoting the overall organization rather than a specific product or service and usually focus on strengthening the financial interest in the organization.

Fig 7.2
Siemens' photo of rowing squad

Source: Courtesy of ThreePipe

Public relations can ensure that the annual report communicates to a diverse range of shareholders how well the company is managing financially. Instead of the report being a traditionally uninteresting and factual accounts document, it can be developed into a publication with interesting visuals of the organization. Additional information can give insights into the organization and be presented in an engaging format with exciting visuals.

Inviting media to the annual general meeting, where the company's financial situation is announced, can help to provide positive media coverage of the organization, especially if media can interview key business leaders who positively communicate the organization's messages.

Shareholders meetings keep investors of a company informed and involved and are called by management but may be arranged by public relations practitioners. Company spokespeople can be trained to address any issues or questions at these meetings. By constantly monitoring the organization, practitioners can ensure that relevant activities can be communicated to the shareholders so that they feel involved in the organization.

2. Internal communications

An organization communicates with its own employees to ensure that they support the organization, are fully informed of its ongoing business, and follow its procedures and instructions. Communication is generally through newsletters, which can be in both online and print formats, and are increasingly interactive using questionnaires and voting opportunities. The official monthly magazine of the British army, *Soldier*, is published by the Ministry of Defence. The magazine is crucial to the army and has adopted a 'lad's mag' style and format to ensure its readers engage with the topics such as personal administration, pensions, health issues, and the military system.

Go to the Online Resource Centre to access a link to the *Soldier* magazine

3. Financial relations

Financial relations involves briefing investors, shareholders, and the media about the financial aspects of an organization. Tactics include one-to-one meetings, shareholders meetings, annual report events, seminars, or tours of the company. Organizations also spend time developing relationships with financial analysts who inform the media about the organization.

4. Public affairs

Public affairs involves working with the government or regulatory bodies to make changes to legislation or regulations which affect an organization. Macmillan Cancer Support successfully lobbied the government to abolish prescription charges for cancer patients in England and Northern Ireland (CIPR 2010) and gave the media survey results and case studies of cancer patients unable to afford treatment, which created emotional media stories. It orchestrated questions to be asked in Parliament and encouraged campaigners to send a template letter to local Members of Parliament asking them to write to the Public Health Minister, and held face-to-face meetings with ministers (CIPR 2009).

5. Business to business

Business to business is when organizations deal with other organizations, rather than individuals, to sell or buy services or products. They may have a product or other resources that an organization wants to buy. For example, a contact lens organization needs to liaise with optometrists in order to educate them about their contact lenses, then optometrists can stock them and inform their customers about the products. The organization will liaise with professional media such as *Optician* magazine, which is read by optometrists rather than the general public, in order to communicate to them about their products and services. Another example of business-to-business is food wholesalers who would communicate to supermarkets directly as well as through *The Grocer*, a trade magazine that includes articles about the launch of new food products.

Trade conferences are also effective in getting the organization's message to reach the business contacts of the organization. They require speakers and delegates (people attending). The conference will host presentations under a theme such as changes in the industry, new research, or responses to economic pressures.

Exhibitions are frequently used by organizations and many organizations sponsor an event and have an exhibition stand at the event. They may also have a hospitality tent where they can meet potential clients. Hospitality is important to a business and many organizations entertain potential clients and key buyers of their products. For example, at the Cheltenham Race Week every March, organizations, such as the real estate agency Knight Frank, have a marquee in which they host potential prominent clients who may be interested in selling or buying property.

Case Study

Business to business for a legal firm

Source: Courtesy of Montpellier PR

The largest law firm in Gloucestershire, England, Rickerbys, wanted to maintain its position as the first port of call for corporate and commercial clients against stiff competition. It seized the opportunity of communicating to businesses about new legislation the government was introducing—the 2008 Companies Act—which would change how companies conducted business. Although companies were aware that they must understand this Act, the sheer volume of information was daunting.

Montpellier PR created a public relations objective to profile Rickerbys as experts in company law to businesses. This meant they would be noticed by their target publics—the large businesses which needed corporate legal advice. They developed the strategy of ensuring they were seen to communicate the new legislation on company law in an interesting and digestible form to leading businesses in the region. The tactics were then created to deliver the objective via the overarching strategy.

Tactics

1.   A newsletter which was dubbed a 'Business Alert', acted as a guide to the new company law. The newsletter presented a digestible form of new legislation and incor-

Fig 7.3
Business Alert newsletter helped to guide solicitors through company law

Source: Courtesy of Montpellier PR

porated comments from opinion leaders to make it more credible, such as a leading spokesperson from the Institute of Directors (see Figure 7.3).

2. Associated media fact sheets summarizing key information were provided to journalists, along with media interviews with Rickerbys' solicitors. This resulted in extensive media coverage of the law firm, profiling it as a law firm for companies seeking legal advice.

3. A seminar—profiled as an 'Open Seminar'—was created in the style of *BBC Question Time* where a top panel of high-profile speakers take questions from invited guests. The panel comprised Rickerbys' solicitors as well as the Institute of Directors, senor banking executives, a leading accountancy firm, and the local editor-in-chief of the Thompson newspaper group.

This involved creating partnerships with these organizations which profiled Rickerbys even more strongly among the business community. Recruiting the local newspaper group as a media partner meant that Rickerbys had a strong media position from the beginning, thereby increasing their opportunity of media coverage. Invitations were sent to a list of prestigious businesses which was announced in the media and profiled the elite panel. The event organization included catering, branding of the room with Rickerbys' stationery and posters, and producing a detailed timeline of the seminar.

Results

The campaign secured business from potential clients, cementing Rickerbys as experts with existing clients, and positioning them as a leading law firm for corporate and commercial legal advice. Rickerbys demonstrated that it had an understanding of the government's new business legislation and could enable companies to navigate their way through it.

The business alert fact sheets and newsletter gave Rickerbys a high-profile corporate platform so that it was seen as a credible corporate law firm for large corporations. This helped Rickerbys to develop opportunities with existing clients as well as to get business from new clients. Rickerbys continued the innovative format for the seminars and newsletter in a new series of intellectual property seminars. and cemented a relationship with the media which has become the platform for further collaborations.

7.2 Theoretical and historical context

Implementation of a public relations plan uses many different tactics applied in creative ways. Drawing on the past shows what public relations can achieve and how tactics can be adapted to all situations.

Watson (2008: 19) describes the 'great displays and games' that took place in imperial Rome. He identifies the 'fairs and jousts' as public relations activities of medieval England. Early religious communications such as worshipping, attending church, songs and sermons, paintings and statues designed to inspire faith could also be described as public relations activities.

Watson (2008: 19) writes about how public relations created the canonization of a well-known saint in England:

> In late 10th century England, a little-known and long-dead bishop named Swithun was canonised and became one of the most-widely culted saints in the country. Behind the creation of the cult of Saint Swithun were communication and political strategies with aspects of brand creation and extension, fund-raising, message creation and delivery, and stakeholder engagement using tactics such as word-of-mouth, the creation of special events and music, and use of specially commissioned publications.

Although Watson says this communication was not strategically planned as it is now, public relations practises similar methods which have been adapted to mass communication.

How tactics apply to the four communication models

The four communication models developed by Grunig and Hunt (1984) and described in chapter 2, are really defined by their implementation. The press agentry model is a one-way model of communications and is concerned with publicity, often through exaggerating the facts to attract as much attention as possible. Feedback is largely unimportant and its effectiveness is largely shown by how people respond to the messages, such as buying tickets or attending an event. Barnum the circus promoter used publicity to get people to attend his circus. The posters and news articles he used to achieve this made exaggerated claims, calling his travelling circus the 'Greatest Show on Earth'. Weeks before the show he would attract visitors with newspaper articles and pre-circus events in the town.

Mark Borkowski, of Borkowski PR, is considered the modern-day Barnum and in 2009 he placed posters in Edinburgh locations for an online exhibition of publicity stunts at the Edinburgh Festival over the last 20 years (Borkowski 2009). Borkowski dubbed this exhibition a Twithibition and made it accessible via Twitter and on http://www.markborkowski.com/improperganda/.

The public information model is a one-way process from organizations giving their publics information it thinks they need to have such as facts, figures, and advice. It comprises bulletins, announcements, posters, and leaflets and does not depend on feedback except for people to follow its advice or instructions. The UK Department of Health campaign on swine flu was an example of this.

The two-way asymmetric model aims to persuade people to do what the organization wants and may include ways to get publics involved but still delivers a message that benefits the organization but does not seek to benefit the public. It involves messages going in both directions but favours communication from the sender. Its aim is to persuade people to change their opinion and research, often opinion surveys, is usually carried out to find the current public opinion and how it can be changed.

Go to the Online Resource Centre to access a link to the swine flu campaign

The two-way symmetric model aims for mutual understanding when both parties engage in dialogue and negotiation to ensure the outcomes are favourable and fair to both sides equally. A meeting, roundtable, or interactive online seminar can be a good tactic for both parties to talk and exchange ideas and come to an agreement.

Ethics

Ethics is important in guiding how the tactic is both developed and delivered. Messina (2007), who explores the ethics of persuasion, believes we should be governed by a Kantian philosophy of ethics, meaning that all people should be treated as ends in themselves and never as a means. Implicit in this rule is that persuasive communication must include enough information for audiences to make voluntary, informed, rational, and reflective judgements.

Therefore, when developing tactics it is important that all information must be truthful, authentic, and demonstrate respect and equity. If there are times when all details cannot be given because of the need to serve the public interest then Messina (2007) recommends asking questions such as

- How would I feel as the subject of the act in question?
- What would others think?
- Could the activity be generalized, and would the consequences be justified?

(See chapter 11 for more on ethics.)

7.3 Influences

All implementation requires careful planning, monitoring, and controlling of team activities. Very little can be achieved without teamwork and teams need to have a goal. Smith (2000: 15) presents four different types of teams:

1. Pseudo teams: members have to work together but have no interest in doing so and therefore they perform poorly.

2. Traditional teams: members work together but have no interest in helping each other and motivating each other to improve, they struggle and the team's performance is slightly better than that of the average member.

3. Cooperative teams: members are a real team, they have a goal, are accountable as individuals and as a group, use teamwork skills and share leadership responsibilities and analyse how they work together.

4. High performance teams: members perform at a high level as they are a cooperative learning group. They have a high level of commitment to each other and the group's success.

What makes an effective team?

Smith (2000) finds that there are certain characteristics that make teams effective.

1. A single or common goal that they work towards.
2. Individual and group accountability which means that everyone takes responsibility for the performance as well as having group accountability.
3. They interact and work is done face-to-face.
4. Teamwork is evident through effective communication which means good problem solving and decision making.
5. They reflect on how the team is working, making improvements together and they celebrate their success.

Successful teams are usually diverse which could mean members have complementary skills and therefore there are more resources to draw on. Managing a diverse group requires skills in working with others, the understanding of what is needed, and the ability to appreciate different perspectives.

A team's development may be viewed in four distinct phases (Acas 2009).

- First is the 'forming' phase where everyone is getting to know each other. Enthusiasm for and commitment to the new team is high but competence is low. Teams can become stuck in this stage if they are too polite.

- Second is the 'storming' phase when the team members begin to voice their opinions and where conflict starts and has to be managed. Relationships in the team may become stormy as everyone struggles to fine the best way to work together. It is in this stage where there may not be so much commitment as a result of conflict and this adds to the conflict.

- Third is the 'norming' phase where the team starts to accomplish its goals and reach its potential.

- Fourth is the 'performing' phase where the team is fully mature and effective and is accomplishing its goals. Development of team members is seen at this stage.

- Fifth is the 'adjourning' stage where the project is completed and the team dissolves.

Teamwork usually involves some sort of a struggle for teams to realize their potential. They can become stuck in the early stages, or become complacent in the later stages. Teams may also need objectives clarified, additional resources provided, training and team building exercises.

Emotional intelligence is a requirement of all teams, and this means recognizing one's own feelings and those of others. High emotional intelligence is demonstrated through an ability to motivate oneself and manage emotions in both oneself and in relationships.

Generally, a team needs to establish its direction, be formed through what individuals can offer the team, and set clear immediate and long-term goals. Smith (2000: 26) recommends that all teams have guidelines or a code that they all agree to, such as that shown in Box 7.1.

> **Box 7.1 A team code helps to establish direction**
>
> **Team code**
> - Attend all meetings
> - Carry out actions assigned
> - Email everyone not just one member
> - Share all information
> - Be positive
>
> *Source:* Smith (2000: 26)

Go to the Online Resource Centre to access a movie on how the Blue Angels ensure teamwork

Brainstorming and creativity in developing tactics

The creativity in developing a public relations tactic means taking something that has been done before, applying it to the issue, and ensuring it fits the public and the organization.

For example, a book can be published for an anniversary or the launch of a product, it can be written by a celebrity or a specialist. The tactic's success comes from how well it is adapted. As Green (2001) mentions, thinking big is not necessary, everything is a small idea which is just built on through a series of 'mini-steps'.

Creative thinking can be stimulated by finding out the latest trends and this can be done using Google Zeitgeist—a snapshot in time of what people are searching for on Google all over the world. When developing the implementation aspect of a programme, Green (2001) recommends applying the 'what', 'where', 'when', 'why', and 'who' to a task and also recommends getting to solutions by asking 'why?' at every stage of programme development.

Brainstorming was pioneered in the 1950s by Alex Osborn (cited Green 2001) and is now a common technique to get people generating ideas. Brainstorming is effective as it generates enthusiasm and a variety of ideas but it must still be structured with specific objectives and each participant needs to make a contribution. The basic rules of brainstorming mean that there should be no criticism of ideas, wild and exaggerated ideas should be encouraged, others' ideas are built on, and it should be ensured that everyone has equal status.

Green (2001: 81) argues that a brainstorming process should be established at the outset outlining what is to be achieved, criteria to evaluate the ideas, and resources and timings for implementing the ideas. Green claims that research shows that individuals working by themselves are more effective than brainstorming, but brainstorming helps to create team participation in the programme.

Osborne (cited Green 2001: 78) developed the following rules for brainstorming:

- brainstormers are placed in an informal setting
- brainstormers are encouraged to run wild intellectually
- no one should criticize anyone else's idea

- the more unusual or crazy the idea the better
- ideas can be combined and recombined
- all brainstormers' views are sought
- all brainstormers are of equal status.

Fitzpatrick (2009) recommends generating ideas without criticism in order to ensure creativity and then assembling ideas into groups. For the next step he recommends analysing each idea by everyone wearing three metaphorical hats as opposed to de Bono's six hats as ways of looking at ideas. The first hat is red and is the emotion around an idea, that is if everyone likes it or not. The second, a yellow hat, involves making a list on the flipchart of what everyone thinks is good about the idea.

Finally, the black hat helps everyone to consider the concerns about an idea and these should then be listed on the other side of the flipchart. This method avoids argument because only one element of the idea is considered at a time.

Presenting implementation plans

All implementation must link to the communications objectives, be clearly defined, and be defended or rationalized as to their purpose. Their outcomes should be outlined and they should also be sustainable, that is they should be able to be used for another purpose or have spin off effects. Additionally, how they will be measured must also be clear.

Assumptions

When developing a tactic, it is important to assess the assumptions made as these are the areas of vulnerability. For example, it is an assumption that the media will come to a launch event and therefore it is important to look at improving the likelihood of them attending.

Another assumption is believing that a product will be ready in time for the planned launch. There will be a high impact on the event if the product is not ready therefore the probability of this occurring must be kept low by making sure the launch event is not planned too early. A risk assessment looks at the likely outcomes of a project and will review whether resources are adequate, the organization's needs and whether they will change, the equipment, and if the correct and trained staff will be available. (See chapter 10 for more on risk assessment).

Surveys and research reports

The popularity of public opinion surveys is greatly influencing how public relations programmes are being implemented. Surveys are becoming increasingly common in raising awareness of organizations or highlighting issues on which organizations wish to focus. For example, in July 2009 the National Association of Estate Agents wanted to raise their profile in the media and conducted a survey asking people about whether it was harder to get a mortgage. It carried out a survey through the marketing agency,

Tickbox (2010), and gained media coverage showing that almost 25 per cent of people said they did not qualify for any available mortgages. The organization presented itself as supporting buyers by calling for lenders to relax their restrictions.

Another example from Tickbox (2010) was the Federation of Wholesale Distributors (FWD) which represents the interests of UK wholesalers trading in food, drink, tobacco, household, and related non-food products markets who supply independent retail outlets and caterers of all types. The FWD wanted to lobby government into acting upon the interminable rise of the supermarket at the cost of independent high street traders. With leading authorities on retail behaviour, the organization created a research report on the impact the growth of supermarket chains is having on local community and national identity. This report was used for political lobbying and the Office of Fair Trading requested a copy for its ongoing review of retail competition policy.

Implementation plan

Table 7.2 shows an example of how a tactic can be presented in a communications proposal and is applied to the new branding of the Queensberry Hotel in Bath, implemented by Montpellier PR in Cheltenham.

Table 7.2 **Developing a tactic**

Communications objective	
To communicate the new branding of the Queensberry Hotel, Bath in order to consolidate existing clients, develop new clientele over the next six months and increase ongoing customer awareness and contact. Strategy: By leveraging the easy and innovative interactive technology aspects of the new branding to facilitate bookings and client interest.	
Tactic	Develop an interactive media centre showing new branding of hotel.
Rationale An outline of what the benefits are to the organization, individuals, or stakeholders in delivering the project	This visual interpretation of the objective will transform the hotel but it will remain loyal to its traditional clientele.
Definition What the tactic comprises	Interactive media centre photography online where prospective visitors can research the hotel and make bookings. Simple navigation, content quick to download, simple, and stylish. High-quality images of each style of room available. Secure portal to book online and check availability.
Timing and budgets	Account executive: the anticipated hours spent multiplied by the hourly rate of the account executive. Account Director time: the anticipated hours spent multiplied by the account director hourly rate of the account executive. Start dates and completion dates were set.
Outcomes What will be delivered at the end of the project? Eg a report, a building, improved service levels etc.	Interactive media centre allowing easy and quick bookings, and presenting an up-to-date vision of the hotel resulting in positive customer feedback and an increase in bookings and room sales. Media coverage on rebranding of hotel and the innovative way to make bookings.

Go to the Online Resource Centre to access a link to the Queensberry Hotel

Maximizing How it can be used across other areas or expanded on	Used for ongoing bookings. Contact with clients to offer news and promotions. Can be easily updated.
Evaluation How to measure the success of the project. NOTE: the success criteria must be measurable.	Client feedback. Room sales Ease of use by booking staff Media coverage
Assumptions The assumptions made—these need to be reviewed through a risk assessment	Clients will use it to book online. The technology will work as expected. Media will cover it owing to interesting technology used and focusing on the rebranding aspect of a well-known hotel.

7.4 Application to industry

A simple management process, such as the following, is needed for any project:

1. Agree the tactic.
2. Plan the project—time, team, activities, resources, and financials using the activity template.
3. Communicate the plan to the team.
4. Agree and delegate actions.
5. Manage and motivate the team.
6. Check, measure, review progress, adjust plans. Ensure there is always a point in the middle of the project in which to make changes.
7. Complete the project; review and report on performance.

Event planning

Tactics need to be well planned and managed to ensure they are implemented successfully with a good outcome. An event is a tactic and how it is managed affects its outcome. There needs to be enough time to organize the people, venue, and materials and could take anything from a few weeks to a year depending on the nature of the event. The more advance warning people have of what is happening, the more chance of achieving a good turnout. A budget must be agreed to cover the costs of running the event and any associated communications materials (such as leaflets, posters, and information sheets).

Planning an event is like putting together a very specific communications plan and the same principles apply. There may be forthcoming events which can be used to achieve objectives rather than running a stand-alone event. Surveying members of the public can help to decide how the event might work best. Planning needs to consider the date, venue, and format and a checklist can include:

- How long should/can the event be?
- A minimum or maximum number of attendees.
- What are the key elements?
- Who should present to have the most impact?
- Who will facilitate sessions or steer the agenda?
- Is presentation equipment needed?
- What accessibility and health and safety issues are required?

The organization, target public, and availability of key speakers will help to inform the choice of venue, date, and time but there are other factors such as term times and religious holidays to consider. The venue needs to be visited to check whether it is appropriate and can be branded through posters, logos, and stationery to profile the organization. This is important even if the location is abroad; it is too late to plan an event when the team arrives to run the event.

Once the date, venue, and format are confirmed it may help to put together a detailed timeline to help to plan the event. Catering and equipment needs early planning as do branding materials and handouts. Successful event management is all about detail and allocating clear responsibilities.

Whoever leads the event will affect the invited media and any invited VIPs or celebrities may have a special role and need to be briefed on this. There may be arrangements for them to do a photocall (see chapter 1), a speech, and meet particular people. Just before the event there are checks such as the sound facilities and rehearsal of speeches.

Resources

Time and budget and how they are used affect the success of the tactic. Although costs start to be incurred from the beginning of the project, there is more flexibility at the beginning when costs are low therefore changes are best made at this time.

Time

A diagrammatic way of showing a schedule will help to visualize the project and its timings. A Gantt chart is a horizontal bar chart which was named after its developer, Henry L. Gantt, in 1917. The chart illustrates a project schedule with a timeline showing what should have been achieved and what still needs to be achieved; this is a useful way of showing blocks of activities and helps to manage the project and its costs along the way (see Figure 7.4 on page 206).

Budget

The other key resource is the finance which determines what can be carried out for the money allocated. There are four elements of a budget:

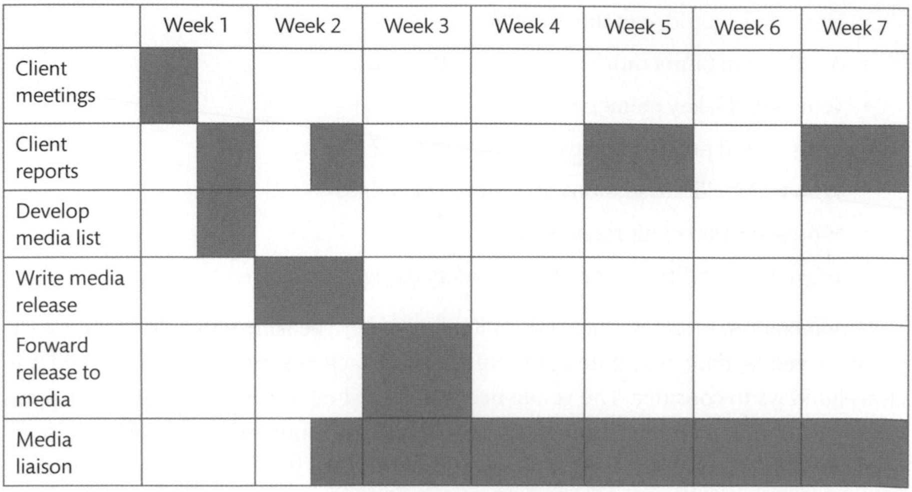

Fig 7.4
Example of a Gantt chart showing the preparation of a media release

	Week 1	Week 2	Week 3	Week 4	Week 5	Week 6	Week 7
Client meetings	■						
Client reports		■			■		■
Develop media list		■					
Write media release			■				
Forward release to media				■			
Media liaison			■	■	■	■	■

Go to the Online Resource Centre to access a link which gives examples of Gantt charts

1. Fee

This is the cost of people based on their time and skills. Each practitioner in a PR consultancy who works on a project will have a different hourly or daily rate depending on their seniority and level of responsibility. Even if the project is in-house a labour cost still has to be estimated to know the value of the project. This fee is an estimate of the amount of time the different team members will need to spend on the project.

White (2002) interviewed many consultancies on fees and found that clients judge the fees they are charged against the value of the people, the level of advice offered, the creativity of the ideas presented, and the time and expenses involved in managing and completing activities. In addition, some areas charge a higher premium; public affairs and financial practitioners may have a higher rate as they are considered specialists and more valuable. Similarly, certain specialist areas such as healthcare command higher rates.

2. Office overheads

Office overheads are also called fixed costs or house costs and include running costs such as office space, heating, electricity. Usually these are estimated as 10–15 per cent of the overall budget.

3. Materials

These are the key purchases that are either made or bought such as slides, photographs, videos, exhibition centre space, conference hall hire, publication printing costs. It can also include buying in services such as any advertising. As these are paid by the consultancy before it invoices the client and are usually charged at a higher rate than they cost, which pays for the interest accrued on the money spent. This handling charge or mark up is usually between 10–15 per cent.

4. Expenses

These are also called disbursements or out-of-pockets or incidentals and include the additional costs expended in the course of the project: telephone calls, stationery, meet-

Box 7.2 Working out a budget for a project

Fee	Time	£
☐ Development of recommendations	2h AE + 1hAM +.5h AD	Hourly rate
☐ Development of media list	2h AE + .5h AM	
☐ Draft media release	6h AE +1h AM + .5h AD	
☐ Release distribution x 25	2h AE	
☐ Media liaison	5h AE +1h AM	
☐ Client reports x 3	2h AE + 1hAM +.5h AD	
☐ Client meetings x 2	4h AE +4hAM+2h AD	
☐ Overall management	2h AM + 2h AD	

Subtotal

Costs

1.	Materials (photos)	£
2.	Expenses (media monitoring service, couriers, tel calls)	£
3.	Office overheads – 12.5% of total fee	£

Subtotal £

TOTAL £

Key: AE = Account executive; AM = Account manager; AD = Account director. The fee is calculated on the hourly rates of these practitioners.

ing room hire, media monitoring, and other aspects required for the project. They are usually charged as direct costs. Box 7.2 shows how to work out a budget for arranging a media announcement.

Case Study

Rebranding Maldives Airport

Source: Courtesy of Montpellier Public Relations

The following case study presents an implementation plan to rebrand Maldives Airport (see Table 7.3).

Table 7.3 Implementation plan

Business objective The Maldives Airport Company is an airport management company which needed to ensure its financial future through a combination of more landing fees, aircraft fuel, aircraft maintenance, air traffic control, catering, and duty free products. It needed to encourage more planes to land and use the airport en route to their destinations and ensure its airline services were top quality with employees committed to its new direction.	
Communications objective To rebrand and differentiate the airport within six months making it inspiring and exciting for employees and customers and increase use by airline customer group by 25%.	
Strategy By creating a visual rebranding of a progressive airport linking to the airport's 40th birthday and innovative online services.	
Tactic	Use visual interpretation to rebrand Maldives Airport.
Rationale	Branding would be inspiring and exciting to employees and customers and also in terms of business to business marketing to the airline group that is encouraging airline business.
Definition	In all airport signage, promotional material, and online accesses use a visual metaphor of a palm tree leaning over representing a plane taking off, with the strapline 'Your Journey: Our Business' which underpins the internal and external communication messages.
Timing and budgets	To link to airport's 40th year celebrations using pre-allocated budget divided into costs for design, IT development, media communications, and internal communications.
Expected outcomes	Reflects the airport as a destination associated with a modern progressive and prestige experience for air passengers. Underpins the internal communications changes necessary for customer-focused and energized workforce of 1,000. Demonstrates to airlines that the airport can offer some of the best airport services in the Indian Ocean region.
Maximizing	Link the branding to an online portal for airlines and private pilots which would differentiate it from other airports in the region. Include SMS alerts for passengers for departures. Link to tourism events on the island.
Evaluation	Employee surveys every two weeks. Use of online portal by pilots and tourists weekly. Increased use of airport within six months.
Key assumptions	The workforce will be positive towards the rebranding.

The campaign was implemented as described above and has led to greater development of the online portal and other interactive services for both pilots and tourists. The rebranding helped to imbue greater pride in its customer focus for the workforce (see Figure 7.5).

Fig 7.5
Rebranding the Maldives Airport

Source: Courtesy of Montpellier PR

PR Tool

Event checklist

Table 7.4 shows a checklist which can be tailored to any event.

Table 7.4 Planning an event

Time line	Activity
6 to 12 months before	Ensure the event ties in with the messages and accurately reflects what the organization is and wants to achieve, choose a theme Decide event's purpose (raise funds, visibility, celebration, etc) Visit potential sites Get cost estimates (hire, food, drinks, sound/lights, entertainment, design/printing) Create sponsorship opportunities Invitation list Check proposed date for potential conflicts Contracts for site, entertainment, permits, insurance Create a media plan and media material, including spokespeople
3 to 6 months before	Begin monthly meetings Get logos from corporate sponsors for printing Final copy for invitations, return card, posters Finalize invitation list Order invitations, posters, tickets, etc Arrange catering Confirm celebrities, spokespeople

Time line	Activity
2 months before	Announce event to media, noting celebrities, etc Send invitations to attendees Finalize transportation/hotel accommodations for staff, VIPs, honorees Confirm media participation Rehearse with all those involved at event site Review budget, actions, and timeline
1 month before	Follow-up invitations Confirm staff and activities, eg registration, greeting, etc Confirm celebrities, speakers, and other participants and ensure they understand what is expected Complete welcome packets or conference bags Meet with all suppliers to coordinate event Review script/timeline Assign seats, including VIPs, speaker's platform Confirm accommodation, transport, and directions for participants; ensure contact details are on website Prepare welcome packet for VIPs, chair, and key staff Schedule deliveries of special equipment, rentals Meet with chair, caterer, and key staff to finalize the above
1 week before	Meet with suppliers and client for last-minute details Complete email follow-ups Confirm number attending Finish seating/table arrangements Finalize staff including hosting, registration, filming Schedule pickup or delivery of equipment Reconfirm site, hospitality, and transport Deliver timelines to celebrities, speakers, and participants Finalize catering Follow-up calls to news media for advance and event coverage Schedule rehearsals
Day before	Check all equipment and supplies to be brought to the event Go through timeline Arrange a cash kitty for additional expenses on the day
Event day	Arrive early Arrange equipment, seating, and supplies Be sure all VIPs are in place and have speeches Reconfirm refreshments/meal schedule for volunteers Review final details with caterer and other staff Set up registration area Check sound/light equipment and staging before rehearsal Hold final rehearsal

Source adapted from: The Great Event (2009)

Summary

Implementation focuses on how a programme is achieved. It delivers the objectives according to a strategic framework and within the resources, which are primarily time and money. Although implementation tactics may seem diverse they are often standard communication practices which use creativity to make them relevant to a particular business and its communication objective as well as to the target publics. Publics can be analysed using a stakeholder analysis to identify them, assess their needs, understand what the organization needs from them, and what influence they have on the organization.

Implementation often relies on media relations to communicate to publics what is happening such as an event, awards, competitions, or results of a survey. Media tours of interesting aspects of an organization can also be effective. Many ideas can be turned into events to become a media conference, fundraising activities, anniversary celebrations, and product launches.

Other implementation activities include creating promotional weeks or days to provide a focus or angle. Stunts can offer the media photographic opportunities, ideas can be developed into themes for television programmes such as soap programmes, and product placement can include venues as well as products featuring in television shows. The use of third parties is a common tactic to get publics aware of an issue by using someone to represent it to their own publics. Sponsorship links an organization or product to an event or a charity and develops an associated link with them. Public relations is usually involved in activating sponsorship to ensure appropriate profile-raising communication is achieved.

Implementation is tailored to different areas of public relations such as corporate PR which affects the overall image of an organization. Business to business involves communicating with other organizations and includes trade exhibitions, trade media and trade conferences. Internal communications targets the publics within an organization such as the employees. Staff newsletters, competitions, and an intranet are key components of this area. Public affairs involves influencing regulations or legislation so that organizations can achieve their objectives. Implementation in the financial area will involve working with the annual report and communicating with investors and shareholders, and these often mean creating various forms of meetings.

Many activities implemented today have historical origins; for instance, religious activities used public relations to attract followers and establish churches. Now activities are more strategically planned and influenced by mass communication. In addition, it is vital that practitioners consider ethics when implementing public relations; this means they should ensure that people are provided with enough information to make informed and rational choices which encourage reflective judgement.

Implementation requires teamwork to ensure effective project management and there are four different types of teams defined by how well team members work together, ranging from pseudo teams—where members have to work together but have no interest in doing so and therefore perform poorly—to high performance teams—where members perform at a high level and commit to each other and the group's success. Teams are usually more effective when members have complementary skills and therefore more resources to draw on. Overall, managing diverse groups requires the ability to work with others and therefore knowing how teams work is an important factor. A team's development includes a forming stage followed by a potential conflict stage called storming and then a stage called norming, when actions are beginning to be carried out, followed by the performing stage when goals are accomplished, and then ending in the completion stage.

Emotional intelligence helps people to manage emotions both in themselves and in their relationships. In order to ensure a team has direction, it is recommended a team code is formed at the beginning of the teamwork which outlines expectations and agreed actions. Creativity is another important component of teams and developing ideas together can enhance team skills and draw out ideas. Creative brainstorming can ensure that ordinary ideas are given a new perspective and tailored to different projects.

When developing an implementation activity, an analytical outline can ensure how a tactic fits an objective and the resources needed to create it as well as what is delivered, how it can be evaluated, and reviewing any assumptions made as these can clarify any risks involved. All implementation needs a plan as well as checklists. In addition, timelines such as Gantt charts which show a start and finish date can help to plan actions. A budget schedule alongside these also helps to monitor resources including hourly rates of team members (also called fees), as well as costs which include office overheads, materials that are purchased for the project, and expenses which are incurred during the project.

Discussion points

A. Tactics

1. Go to the Online Resource Centre and download a case study. Identify the tactics in the case study.

2. Do they fit the objectives? If they do not, how could they have been improved to match the objectives?

3. How have cost, time, and feasibility influenced the development of these tactics?

B. Teamwork

1. Think about a team in which you have been a member. It could be a sports team, a debating team, even a small project team at university, a family team.

   What was the team's goal?

   What made it an effective team?

   What category of team was it?
   - pseudo
   - traditional
   - cooperative
   - high performance.

2. Think about group work. Was the team hating each other or really enjoyed each other? What made it different?

3. Think of a leader you know—it could be a politician or someone more familiar to you. List their leadership skills.

C. Project management

1. Go to the Online Resource Centre to access an implementation plan of a project which shows planning implementing and completing.

2. How are resources used during the processes?

3. Note when the cost was highest and when it was lowest. What does that tell you about changes you can make?

D. Brainstorming

1. Arrange a team of 12 members and present the information around a news topic and identify the communications issues.

2. Develop a brainstorming session to create public relations activities. Use the three hat approach and record your results. Review the brainstorming process.

3. How valid were the solutions proposed?

4. Do you think it created team participation?

5. How could the brainstorming have been improved?

References

Acas (2009) *Team Development*. London: Acas. Available at: http://www.acas.org.uk/index.aspx?articleid=842

Black, D., Crozier, J., Grandison, A., Mckeown, C., Summers, E., and Weber, P. (eds) (2007) *Collins English Dictionary*. Glasgow: HarperCollins

Blokdijk, G. (2007) 'Project management 100 success stories, best practices in project management?', ebook

Borkowski, M (2009) 'Improperganda: The Great Edinburgh Stunt #Twithibition', Mark Borkowski's Mark My Words, A Varied Study in Improperganda, 9 August. Available at: Borkowski http://www.markborkowski.com/improperganda-the-great-edinburgh-stunt-twithibition/

CIPR Category 7 (nd) 'Public Affairs: Prescription charges campaign'. Available at: http://www.cipr.co.uk/content/category-7-public-affairs

Fitzherbert, N. (2009) 'Hats off to de Bono's theory', September, Professional development, CIPR. Available at: http://www.cipr.co.uk/content/news-opinion/features/professional-development/hats-de-bonos-theory

Green, A. (2001) *Creativity in Public Relations* (2nd edn). London: Kogan Page

Gregory, A. (2006) *Planning and Managing Public Relations Campaigns* (2nd edn). London: Kogan Page

Hegarty, S. (2008) 'This Just In—90 Per Cent Agree Media Surveys Are Worthless', *Irish Times*, 29 March, p 2

Messina, A. (2007) 'Public relations, the public interest and persuasion: an ethical approach', *Journal of Communication* 11/1: 25–9

Pawinska, M. (2005) 'Market Research: Speed or substance', PR Week, 10 June. Available at: http://www.prweek.com/uk/news/search/479668/Market-Research-Speed-substance/

Smith, K. (2000) *Teamwork and Project Management* (2nd edn). New York: McGraw Hill

The GreatEvent.com (2009) Event Planning Checklist. Available at: http://www.thegreatevent.com/content/ap.asp?id=4

Tickbox Press Coverage (2009). Available at: http://www.tickbox.net/press.php?SES=eb5edf6f399315a0a7de a156025d2ea6

Watson, T. (2008) 'Creating the Cult of A Saint: Communication Strategies in the Tenth Century England', PR Review 34: 19–24

White, J. (2002) 'Fee Setting in Public Relations Consultancies: A Study of Consultancy and Client views of Current Practice in the UK', Journal of Communication Management 6/4: 355–67

8

Learning outcomes

1. Identify the need for evaluation in public relations and how it applies to all stages of a programme.

2. Understand how evaluation links to a planning model and identify opportunities for changing the plan as the programme proceeds creating a circular evaluation process.

3. Be conversant with research tools that are needed for evaluation such as surveys, media content analysis, and media evaluation processes.

4. Be able to compile evaluation into a model that shows outputs, outtakes, and outcomes by applying it to a case study.

5. Recognize that what is evaluated and how it is evaluated is changing because of financial imperatives and new developments in online capabilities.

6. Be able to use a research tool to evaluate online media for an organizzation.

Practitioner Insight

Sarah Pinch
Communications Director
University Hospitals Bristol
NHS Foundation Trust

I am responsible for the communications department in the largest research and teaching hospital Trust in the South West of England, University Hospitals Bristol NHS Foundation Trust. We employ almost 8,000 staff working across nine city centre hospital sites, with a turnover in excess of £450 million.

I trained as a journalist and producer with the BBC and enjoyed 11 years working on local and national radio and TV. I left in 1990 to move into Public Relations and have since set up teams and departments in my new business roles. I left FirstGroup plc in 2008 to join the NHS. I am chair elect of the West of England CIPR and a national council member and am passionate about the professionalization of communications and the region in which I live and work.

How valuable is evaluation in your organization?

If my team and if I cannot deliver clear evaluation for our work then it is not taken seriously. The need to ensure good research—before and after projects—is considered standard for good quality. It is one of my ambitions that communications is taken as seriously as finance or human resources and ultimately garners a board position. So I have to ensure that the work undertaken by my team is thoroughly evaluated—before, during, and after. As a public sector organization we are spending public money. Although the communications and marketing budget is tiny as an overall percentage of the Trust's turnover, I believe this is appropriate for an organization that provides healthcare as its frontline resource; but however small our allocation of resources, we must demonstrate its appropriate use.

What changes are influencing evaluation?

The National Health Service is moving into a challenging time with the recession hitting the public services. I am determined that our communications budget holds its own and this means we need to regularly profile the value of our work and the effective use of resources. We have already, for example, delivered over 20 per cent savings on our internal staff magazine through careful evaluation of methods of production, distribution, and negotiation with suppliers.

The ability to quantify and demonstrate the impact of all our communications activity is the life blood of future investment and in maintaining the level of interest in and the priority and attention given to communications by the Trust Board.

How does evaluation influence the profile of PR?

To me evaluation influences how seriously communications is taken. Working alongside board members and sitting on the executive group are only afforded to communicators who can clearly demonstrate their contribution to the wider reputation and strategy of their organizations. I think the industry is realizing how important this is, especially as budgets tighten and communications needs to demonstrate that it delivers excellent value for money. The communications industry needs to emphasize the need for evaluation and share good practice and help to develop evaluation models as well as recognize that evaluation is a time consuming and often difficult process.

What evaluation methods do you use?

We have developed our own models. For example, we have a strong model for our media relations evaluation and we use specific models for all our other work. Our website campaigns have bespoke evaluation tools that sit alongside the development of their objectives.

We are constantly reviewing progress to ensure we are meeting objectives—and at the end of project we evaluate against them to ensure that we have delivered. This review means we can change the plan as different elements come into play such as when new regulations are introduced.

We publish our evaluation for the Trust Board against a set of key performance indicators for each area of our work: stakeholder management; marketing and branding; media relations; online communications; events and fundraising; and internal communications. Furthermore, each member of the team has their own objectives and key performance indicators against which they are measured on a quarterly basis.

8.1 Definition

> Probably the most common buzzwords in public relations in the last ten years have been evaluation and accountability.
>
> (McCoy and Hargie 2005: 3)

Public relations must be justified and its results measured in order to know if it is achieving its objectives which must be specific, measurable, achievable, relevant, and timebound (SMART). As with any other management function, public relations must set a direction, allocate and manage resources, and monitor progress. The evaluation in public relations is the analysis of an active communications model. A basic communication model comprises:

1. Sender—who sends the message, or the source of the information and this is affected by the culture, knowledge, and attitudes of the sender.

2. Message—what is being disseminated and has its own content, style, and language.

3. Channel—how it is being disseminated, whether this is to be read, seen, or heard.

4. Receiver—who is the receiver and what is the effect, how the message will be interpreted and evaluated.

Windahl et al (2009) argue that this sender, receiver, message, channel, and receiver model is linear and does not show the dynamic aspects of communication. Evaluation which considers all the communication models (see chapter 2) and the interaction of the different publics involved (see chapter 5) would provide more depth of information upon which decisions could be made.

Chapter 4 reviewed intelligence gathering (environmental scanning) as a planning process. The same sort of research is carried out for evaluating a programme while it is being developed and implemented so that it can be amended if necessary creating a circular process. This is called formative evaluation.

> **Evaluation is essentially a process to assess the quality and effectiveness of a project. It is a key element of any communications strategy—campaigns, media, agencies and our communications delivery model must all be evaluated to measure success.**
>
> **In doing so we can learn from our experience and feed back into the planning process to continuously make improvements and build on progress.**
>
> (Home Office cited COI 2009)

Finally, finding out how effective the programme has been in reaching its stated objectives is done through assessing its results and this is called a summative evaluation. It analyses who has understood and acted on the messages: the organization's relationships with its publics, the growth of opinion leaders, advocacy, reputation, image, strength of brand, and change in attitudes and behaviour. Too often summative evaluation analyses only media coverage and does not show the effects of a campaign on its publics, or the online activity.

Public relations evaluation uses the same research tools as for any other project and these are growing owing to the opportunities provided by the internet. Research tools include surveys, questionnaires, media content analysis, opinion polls, behaviour studies, and readership surveys which were outlined in chapter 4. These are used in primary and secondary research which was also discussed in chapter 4. Primary research is new research such as questionnaires, surveys, and interviews and these can also be carried out online with the high-quality research tools now available.

Secondary research collects and analyses existing information, such as research reports, and applies it to the campaign. Many research studies are conducted and made available which can help to develop the campaign—there are social media reports and market research reports available online through Mintel, CACI, the CIPR, and the COI. The research results are then analysed to identify the effectiveness of the campaign.

The PRE model (planning, research, and evaluation) presented by Cutlip et al (2006) (see chapter 4) gives public relations a structure from which it can develop an evaluation. Watson and Noble (2005: 90) have developed it into the following five-step circular evaluation which uses both primary and secondary research.

Circular evaluation

1. A full review which conducts research and gathers information to form a situation analysis.

2. Set SMART objectives that are aligned with the organization's goals and identify indicators of performance (see chapter 6).

3. Decide the strategy and implementation taking into account that these must be measurable activities. This stage must also pre-test the techniques employed.

4. Formative evaluation as ongoing measurement checking that the programme is on track, and changing it as necessary.

5. Summative evaluation to analyse whether the programme's objectives have been achieved.

When evaluating public relations programmes there are many variables to consider, such as how people are motivated, what influences their thinking and behaviour, and to what extent and for how long. Does more or less information make a difference, and what type of information is the most effective and is this dependent on how it is delivered? How much are people influenced by each other and how much does interactivity change the message?

In 2005 the CIPR noted the following complexity of public relations evaluation.

*   Measurement of all organizations is problematic and it is difficult to separate one area of management, PR, from other activities.

*   By good planning practices and objective setting, outcomes can be measured with greater facility.

*   PR activity takes place in a complex arena and this should be recognized by considering relationships in greater detail rather than simply identifying a single element such as monetary factors.

Evaluation model

An early model of evaluation by Lindenmann in 1993 demonstrated three levels of evaluation: output, outtakes (or outgrowths), and outcomes.

The first stage of identifying whether people are aware of a new communication is through accessing their level of available knowledge through outputs such as media information. The second stage is called outtakes which show that attitudes are developing and this is usually identified through opinion polls. The final stage is outcomes which identify a change in behaviour, for example a campaign to eradicate head lice succeeded in getting parents to check their children's hair for lice every week (see Case Study).

This was taken further by Macnamara (2005) who developed it into a pyramid of evaluation which encapsulates the hierarchy of effects model (see chapter 6) which shows public relations as following a cognitive, attitudinal, and behaviour persuasive pattern.

Macnamara's pyramid evaluation model shows how to evaluate a programme continuously from its beginning to the end and this shows how it is performing and what needs to be changed (see Figure 8.1 and Table 8.1 below).

The levels of evaluation based on Macnamara's pyramid model

1. The inputs form the situation analysis and comprise the research for creating messages, the identification of publics, and the way the persuasive messages will be delivered. It is used to form the objectives and the implementation. Research for this stage finds out what the public is thinking and doing through focus groups, surveys, and media analysis including blogs and wikis.

    It pre-tests implementation activities and reviews research reports and academic papers. Many of these can be found online through public relations organizations—such as the CIPR—and a diverse range of government organizations—such as the Central Office of Information, Department of Health—and non-government organizations—such as the telecommunications regulator Ofcom. Many demographic studies, such as ACORN, are also online. Market research organizations, for instance Mintel, IPSOSMori, and Nielsen, make parts of research reports available, with the possibility of buying more content. Case studies are also evaluated before a program is started to identify best practice. If an organization wanted to implement an action it could collect case studies of a number of organizations which have carried out a similar proposed activity and then identify what would work best.

    Research tools such as surveys and focus groups find out what the public is thinking; while a media analysis reviews all the media coverage on a topic or organization. Both provide a benchmark for the campaign. This is a measurement that can be used to set objectives at the beginning and to compare to the campaign's ongoing media coverage and progress.

2. The outputs show how much awareness is being raised during the campaign and measures what has been transmitted in the campaign and who has received it. Media monitoring is the most common form of evaluating public relations but is quantitative and looks only at the number of press clippings or length of airtime. It shows how much coverage was achieved but not the quality achieved or its messages.

    Media content analysis identifies messages in the media, where the coverage has been read, seen, or heard and by whom, the publications produced and who reads them or accesses them; this includes websites and the number of hits. The research for this stage is therefore counting, tracking, and observing media coverage and activities, messages and their likely interpretation by different publics, readership, viewers' listeners' and users' demographics, monitoring of website hits, downloads, and interactivity, attendance at events and any other responses that were elicited.

3. Outtakes identify the attitudes developed as the campaign progresses. Research includes opinion polls and may use focus groups to find out how much attitudes have changed. Surveys can be used at or after events to evaluate the outcomes and are a key research tool.

4. Outcomes identify if behaviour has changed. It is calculated through what has been achieved such as sponsorship, fundraising, adoption of an idea, products bought, lobbying results, and any measured change in people's opinion and attitudes that may affect behaviour.

Because there are so many variables in a public relations campaign there are many arguments about what to evaluate and how to evaluate it. McCoy and Hargie (2003) argue that public relations looks largely at changing attitudes and behaviour and therefore it is mostly persuasive. They observe that the two-way symmetric model, where both parties have equal outcomes and have participated equally in the programme, is rare.

However, McCoy and Hargie (2003) also argue that it is simplistic to think that public relations creates awareness and forms favourable attitudes and subsequent behaviour change. They suggest that practitioners set more realistic public relations objectives and evaluate these. These include getting a campaign to set an agenda, which is get a topic talked about, which may stimulate interpersonal discussions and may then lead to attitude and behaviour changes. For example, a technology campaign would encourage people, including the media, to talk about upcoming technological developments in order to create a desire and need for a new innovation.

Table 8.1 **An example of how to measure output, outtake, and outcomes**

Objective	Implementation	Output measurements	Outtakes	Outcomes
To launch a product	• Arrange conference to launch product • Place product information in media • Create social platform through new website, blog, and social media	• Number of delegates at conference • Amount of media coverage (readership and content analysis) • Number of website hits • Number of links to blog and social media	• Participation in conference activities • Readership and retaining of messages • Opinion poll showing attitudes	• Requests for information • Sales of product
To ensure employee involvement and participation	Announcements through intranet Working parties to inspire groups Organize competitions	Access of messages Participation in working groups and competitions	Attitudes through participation in discussion groups	Improved retention and enthusiasm and participation in projects

'Pyramid Model' of PR Research

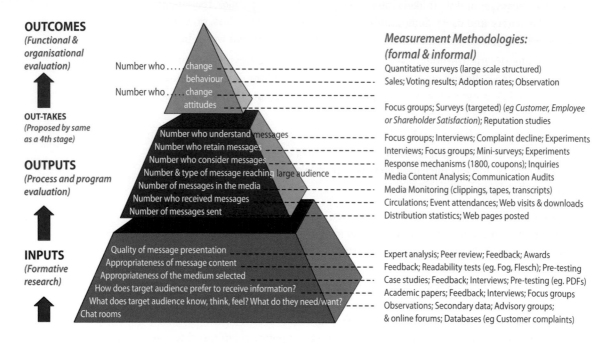

OUTCOMES
*(Functional &
organisational
evaluation)*

Number who .... change behaviour

Number who .... change attitudes

OUT-TAKES
*(Proposed by same
as a 4th stage)*

Number who understand messages
Number who retain messages
Number who consider messages
Number & type of message reaching large audience
Number of messages in the media
Number who received messages
Number of messages sent

OUTPUTS
*(Process and program
evaluation)*

INPUTS
*(Formative
research)*

Quality of message presentation
Appropriateness of message content
Appropriateness of the medium selected
How does target audience prefer to receive information?
What does target audience know, think, feel? What do they need/want?
Chat rooms

Measurement Methodologies:
(formal & informal)
Quantitative surveys (large scale structured)
Sales; Voting results; Adoption rates; Observation

Focus groups; Surveys (targeted) (*eg Customer, Employee
or Shareholder Satisfaction*); Reputation studies

Focus groups; Interviews; Complaint decline; Experiments
Interviews; Focus groups; Mini-surveys; Experiments
Response mechanisms (1800, coupons); Inquiries
Media Content Analysis; Communication Audits
Media Monitoring (clippings, tapes, transcripts)
Circulations; Event attendances; Web visits & downloads
Distribution statistics; Web pages posted

Expert analysis; Peer review; Feedback; Awards
Feedback; Readability tests (eg. Fog, Flesch); Pre-testing
Case studies; Feedback; Interviews; Pre-testing (eg. PDFs)
Academic papers; Feedback; Interviews; Focus groups
Observations; Secondary data; Advisory groups;
& online forums; Databases (eg Customer complaints)

Key Steps/Stages in Communication:

© Copyright Jim Macnamara 1992, 1999, 2002, 2005

Fig 8.1
**Pyramid model of public
relations research**

Source: Courtesy of J.
Macnamara (2005) *Jim
Macnamara's Public
Relations Handbook*
(5th edn). Sydney:
Archipelago Press

Gregory (2006) highlights objective and subjective aspects as markers of a successful campaign. The objective aspects are those which are measurable, such as time and money. The evaluation of a campaign's success is dependent on whether it came within budget. A campaign that goes over budget may not be considered successful, even if the outcomes are very positive. For example, it may be a great idea to use a celebrity to support a product launch, but if their fees are too high it may not have been worthwhile. Campaign costs must always be reviewed against budgets. The hire of an ideal venue needs to be weighed up against budget, travel costs need to be assessed, hospitality costs need to be in line with what is allowed. Budget is often affected by time, if the team have to work too long on a project it will incur high fees and not be of value to the organization.

Similarly, if there were any delays the campaign may not be a success: these can range from speakers being late to address a conference, a product not produced in time, media not being followed up in time, speakers not being briefed correctly, and the product and website launched too late. It also includes a lack of response. For example, the Betfai campaign (see chapter 2) launched a microsite as the Betfai team took to the streets of London during the London mayoral elections. If the microsite development had been delayed it would have affected the campaign. The Kleenex tissue campaign (see chapter 5) needed to be launched during the hay fever season, along with its interactive online map. PR practitioners must therefore ensure an accurate budget that estimates both

Fig 8.2
Teamwork can be evaluated

Source: Copyright OUP

length of time and costs and is regularly reviewed for any changes (see chapter 7 for budget development).

Subjective aspects are more difficult to measure as they concern people and their personal input: creativity, efficiency, and teamwork. The CIPR (2005) found that the input of an individual practitioner made a difference to a campaign but it was difficult to measure and even identify the practitioner's attributes that influenced the campaign. Criteria for successful teamwork (outlined in the previous chapter) can be monitored to highlight how it is progressing and address any changes. Furthermore, the increasing amount of research on how effective leadership affects decision making and team building is encouraging more monitoring of these areas (see Figure 8.2).

Media evaluation

Although many research methods are the same for all aspects of the campaign, they can be applied differently in different combinations. For example, media evaluation uses qualitative and quantitative methods and applies content analysis, monitoring and observation. Below is a method to evaluate media coverage.

Table 8.2 Reviewing the success of media coverage against objectives

Message	What was the message agreed to be communicated?
Benchmark	Analyse previous coverage and use to compare with ongoing coverage.
Prominence: page/section/ time/day	The potential media readership, viewership, and listeners. Online audience is affected by the value of the site in terms of visitors, links, and topicality.
Readership/listeners/viewers numbers and demographics	Check with RAJAR figures for radio listening and BARB figures for broadcast media. Online figures are measured through monitoring hits and links.

Message	What was the message agreed to be communicated?
Opinion leader	Who are the spokespeople listed, what is their position? Are they known or chosen by the organization? What influence do they have? Were they credible or persuasive? Where else do they feature? Are they positive or negative?
Type of article	Is it positive or negative—it can be given a rating. How was media coverage generated—directly from organization or as a response to other coverage or conversations (agenda setting?).
Reporter	Is the reporter a specialist in this area, are they known formally and formally to the organization? How do they write—is it opinion or factual. Do they seem to have an agenda? Do they have a relationship with the organization?
Visual impact	Are images included? What sort of images? What impact do they have?

Case Study

Campaign evaluation: Parkinson's UK

Source: Courtesy of Grayling PR

An evaluation of Parkinson's UK Brain Donor Appeal shows how a complex, well-thought out campaign with potentially difficult messages can be communicated clearly and powerfully. To mark Parkinson's Disease Awareness Week in April 2009, Parkinson's UK launched an inaugural Brain Donor Appeal, urging people to donate their brain to the Parkinson's Brain Bank after their death in order to contribute towards vital research for a cure.

According to new research from YouGov commissioned by Parkinson's UK, the people have misconceptions about brain donation, with only 27 per cent having considered it compared to 63 per cent feeling comfortable about donating a heart or kidney. The survey also revealed that one in three people knew someone affected by Parkinson's.

Celebrities who became involved in the campaign were Jane Asher (President of Parkinson's UK and actress), Jeremy Paxman (journalist and TV presenter), and John Stapleton (TV presenter). Journalists were taken around the Brain Bank, which could also be seen online, and media filmed interviews at the Brain Bank while a web TV show encouraged debate on brain donation. The campaign was simple but generated widespread national print and broadcast media coverage and subsequent interest in donations of brains (see Figure 8.3).

Evaluation

This campaign was evaluated through its media coverage, the number of website hits, calls to the helpline, government support, and fundraising. The Brain Donor Appeal achieved coverage across national and regional print, broadcast, and online media in just five days.

Outputs

- The story was the second news item on BBC Breakfast News—reaching (1.13 million viewers).

- There was a double-page spread in the *Daily Mail*—reaching over two million readers.

- Every national newspaper covered the story—some covered it twice.

- The story appeared in over 60 regional newspapers and generated dozens of interviews for the regional broadcast media.

- On the launch day of Parkinson's Awareness Week the charity had 7,880 web visits compared to a maximum of 2,500 hits a day.

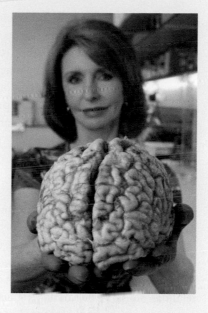

Fig 8.3
A brain held by Jane Asher, President of Parkinson's UK Campaign

Source. Courtesy of Grayling PR

Outtakes

- The Brain Bank received over 5,500 email requests for information packs.

- The Helpline had one of its busiest weeks ever dealing with 850 enquiries in five days.

- A direct mailing appeal was sent to existing supporters to mark the 40th anniversary on the same week as the Brain Donor Appeal.

Outcomes

- The Brain Bank had more than 700 people signed up and four brains were donated.

- In Scotland, 59 MSPs gave their support to the Brain Donor Appeal.

Go to the Online Resource Centre to access a link to the Parkinson's Brain Bank and to view Jane Asher's visit to the Parkinson's Brain Bank

8.2 Theoretical and historical context

Public relations evaluation draws on many different disciplines including psychology, marketing, advertising, and mass communications theory. In the 1920s psychological research measured attitudes based on psychological studies into attitude and opinion (Gregory and Watson 2008). In fact, much of public relations and its evaluation were based on its ability to change attitudes and public opinion. For example, the Torches of Freedom campaign focused on the negative attitudes towards women lighting up their cigarettes in public. By creating an association with the suffragette movement it was successful in changing public opinion towards women smoking in public places (see chapter 1).

In the 1940s and 1950s social scientists evaluated the impact of public relations through using mass communications theory and linked it to public relations research such as that by Grunig and Hunt (Gregory and Watson 2008: 337). In the 1960s evaluation took on a more commercial perspective based on the impact public relations had on business. In addition, media coverage was being analysed and later measurements of publicity could be provided by computer programs. At the same time academic articles on the use of opinion polls, focus groups, and readership studies were measuring PR effectiveness.

Business performance

The 1990s showed more input from business disciplines as there was more emphasis on developing objectives which could be linked to results and to the organization's overall strategy. There was a lot of research on measurement and evaluation, objectives, and techniques (Lindenmann 2006). Now terms such as key performance indicators (KPIs), which identify a measurable element of a goal, are used in evaluation to see how public relations can generate revenue, reduce costs and risks in an attempt to ensure value for money or return on investment (Gregory and Watson 2008). However, there remains uncertainty in public relations about how to define its value as well as how to define its evaluation.

Dashboards

Go to the Online Resource Centre to access link to a dashboard

Computer technology has allowed more visual representations of business data which can be presented on one screen. A car dashboard presents complex information in one place, showing fuel consumption relating to speed, battery, and engine performance. In the same way information about an organization can be brought together in one visual document, combining sales and overhead costs, targets in sales, marketing, and finance (Watson and Noble 2007). Now all this can be adapted for public relations to show public relations targets and tie these to specific business performance criteria.

Paine (2006) outlines how to design a public relations dashboard:

- rank priority of publics
- choose measures of effectiveness for each public
- compare current year's performance with other years and with other organizations
- choose tools for measurement and seek integration between tools.

Balanced scorecards

Balanced scorecards were first developed by Kaplan and Norton in 1992 to show more about the organization's strategy and business performance than simply the profit and loss and return on investment. They are similar to dashboards but are more integrated with the organization's operations and strategy (Gregory and Watson 2008).

Balanced scorecards have developed further to show more integrated features such as a team's performance or business success. By showing the link between communications and corporate objectives and the changes as the programmes unfold, it allows all team members to identify their role and make changes accordingly. The hardest part is ensuring the scorecard has the correct information, such as the success factors and value drivers, and then matching them to the organization's KPIs.

Dashboards and scorecards put organizational data into an organization-wide format. However, they can work as a tool that aligns communication strategy with business objectives and presents data in a concise and readable manner (Watson and Noble 2007).

Evaluating relationships

It is evident that PR can contribute to an organization through creating long-term relationships with its publics. According to Watson and Noble (2007) PR has moved away from changing public opinion to focus on building, nurturing, and maintaining relationships between an organization and its publics. Ledingham (2003) also argues that the main change in public relations over time is recognizing that there is more focus on relationships, not just communication. However, it is the management of these relationships that requires communications and behavioural initiatives.

How effective these relationships are can be measured through qualitative methods such as interviews and focus groups. However, is important first to define what a relationship is and what aspects should be measured.

Researchers identified key aspects which are recognized as making relationships successful. Hon and Grunig (cited Ledingham 2003: 185) suggested equality, trust, satisfaction, and commitments as relationship outcomes between an organization and its publics. Ledingham and Bruning (cited Ledingham 2003: 185) found that people who ranked an organization highly with regard to its relationship dimensions were more likely to use that organization's services rather than a competitor. These factors can be evaluated by developing questions so they can be rated by both the organization and the public, as shown in Table 8.3 below (Grunig IPR). Although the questions here are exploring the public's perception, similar questions can be asked of the organization.

In online public relations, the success of public relations in building relationships can be seen as getting traffic to a site, engaging users in it, and sharing content. For example, Google paid £1.6 billion for YouTube in 2005. However, the value of YouTube was not the computer program and machinery, which was worth only several thousand dollars; Google really paid for relationships which share knowledge, that is, it paid for traffic to the site. Several years after the deal, Google's YouTube is the only major social video sharing site. When relationships are the most vital aspect of an organization, evaluation must look at measuring those—any other evaluation is insignificant.

Table 8.3 **Evaluating the quality of relationships**

Characteristics of relationships	Suggested questions for publics to evaluate relationship with organization
Control mutuality Means the public does not feel dominated by the organization but has a say in the decision-making process. The organization and the public have some control over each other.	To what extent do you believe the organization is attentive to what the public says? Do you have any control over what the organization does that affects you?
Trust The public and the organization are confident and open with each other.	Has the organization done anything fairly, unfairly? Does the organization deliver what it says it will?
Commitment The public and organization will maintain the relationship.	What are examples of commitment from the organization?
Satisfaction The public and organization feel happy with each other and this is reinforced by their behaviour.	How satisfied are you with the relationship?

Source: Grunig (IPR)

8.3 Influences

Online media news and comment is rapidly developing and is no longer dependent on daily newspaper or television news deadlines. Tools, such as Twitter, mean there are real time conversations about organizations, people, brands, events, and issues. Subjects are found even before journalists write about them. The change in public opinion can be followed as it happens. Additionally, an organization's priorities and an individual's foremost thoughts are online and therefore very public.

A Twitter search, using tools like Twitterfall or Tweetdeck, can be very effective to learn people's thoughts and reactions immediately. They are public, gather together all available searchable information and can come together to form reputations and shape relationships. Online tools like Google Analytics and Omniture allow measurement and show what people are doing online and are likely to do, that is they can show their intent. For example, online monitoring tools, such as Tealium, have the ability to provide information about the visitor's past and whether or not there is a direct link which takes the visitor from one site to another. These tools can record what social and traditional sites a person goes to before they buy something online or whether they do anything else interactive such as vote or blog (Tealium 2010). They can also identify how many leads from a site were a result of its social media programs, such as YouTube videos. They can report on which specific stories or articles about the company resulted in the most site traffic and which created feedback and this information can then be used to allocate resources towards social media marketing efforts (Tealium 2009).

Learning to adapt to this rate of operational change is an example of how quickly media outputs must be monitored and responded to. For example, when a media release is issued it may be discussed immediately on Twitter and can change the media agenda. This means practitioners may need to respond quickly and provide more information or engage in the conversation and answer questions.

Monitoring

The impact of social media and online PR can be measured through assessing the traffic to a site, online sales, leads, or conversions. Online monitoring means individuals are finding out more about what others are thinking and doing more quickly, and this qualitative analysis is being posted as user content on web pages creating more online discussion.

Digital media is developing new methods of evaluation. Internet tools such as blogs and wikis can be used to evaluate programmes as they can accumulate comment and feedback and impact on events and communication activity. Organizations that offer such services include news monitoring by Google (Google Alerts), Technorati, CyberAlert, and eWatch. There are companies that focus exclusively on online/social media. These cover blogs, wikis, Twitter, social networks, bulletin boards, and discussion lists. Meanwhile the traditional press clipping agencies and other media evaluation organizations still monitor print coverage such as newspapers and magazines and re-digitize the content for it to be to analysed.

Real-Time Web is driving a need for more and faster services. Topsy (http://topsy.com) is a real time search engine that stands out because it focused on real time links as opposed to real time content. Instead of seeing what people are talking about on the real time web, it shows the most popular and prominent links that are being shared on the real time web; it can even be sorted to see the most shared links over the past hour, day, week, or month (Killer Start Ups 2010).

Paine (2007: 3) argues that measuring what consumers are saying is not that different from traditional media analysis and there is still the focus on outcomes, outputs, and outtakes. There are many services, often free, which monitor the outputs, such as blogs, resulting from social media campaigns. Online surveys can be used to identify outtake, that is, the public's perceptions (Paine 2007). Outcomes identify the increase in traffic and actions resulting from a campaign and these can be determined through monitoring the site as well as through surveys, purchasing, and online and offline responses.

There are many ways to find out how people use media. Morgan Stanley, the financial investment organization, developed a research report on the latest media trends among teenagers, titled 'Media and Internet: How Teenagers Consume Media' (Hill-Wood et al 2009). What made this refreshing is that they used a 15-year-old summer work intern to describe how he and his friends consume media. Although it is not statistically accurate Morgan Stanley claimed it gave them 'one of the clearest and most thought provoking insights' on teenage media use. The following is a brief outline of the report.

On newspapers

No teenager that I know of regularly reads a newspaper, as most do not have the time and cannot be bothered to read pages and pages of text while they could watch the news summarized on the internet or on TV.

On social media and Twitter in particular

Facebook is popular as one can interact with friends on a wide scale. On the other hand, teenagers do not use Twitter. Most have signed up to the service, but then just leave it as they realize that they are not going to update it (mostly because texting Twitter uses up credit, and they would rather text friends with that credit). In addition, they realize that no one is viewing their profile, so their 'tweets' are pointless.

On music

Teenagers listen to a lot of music, mostly whilst doing something else (like travelling or using a computer) … but they are very reluctant to pay for it (most never having bought a CD).

8.4 Application to industry

Evaluation by the PR industry

PR evaluation has been evolving for more than 85 years although as argued by Gregory and Watson (2008), adoption of evaluation methodology in the industry has been slow in practice.

In 2009, the International Association for Measurement and Evaluation of Communication (AMEC) and Benchpoint Ltd surveyed 520 PR professionals largely from the US, Germany, UK, Ireland, India, and Canada. Results found that most of the practitioners believed evaluation to be an integral part of public relations and that there is more evaluation carried out than ever before.

However, not all agreed on how to evaluate and there is no one agreed methodology or criteria. Although the industry is realizing that relationships with publics are increasingly important, most practitioners are not analyzing it, they are focusing on media coverage and moving towards evaluating opinion and awareness.

Evaluation tools

According to the AMEC research (2009), the tools practitioners use the most are monitoring and counting press clippings and assessing their message content. The next most popular evaluation tool is advertising value equivalents (AVES), which means how much an advertisement in the same media would have cost. However, this is an unreliable measure as it does not measure attitude, opinion, or behaviour change, nor does it measure agenda setting or any other aspect of a campaign such as relationship building. More rigorous tools include internal reviews, benchmarking, and specialist media evaluation tools; opinion polls and focus groups are also popular.

Overall, the research showed that practitioners are divided into two groups: the ones who measure outputs such as clippings and AVEs, and the ones who tend to have a more analytical approach through using research such as internal reviews and opinion polls which are also more costly.

In summary, the survey found that most practitioners see the cost of evaluation as a major barrier, followed by it being time consuming. They also report that they lack expertise in their own evaluation ability and question the overall value of evaluation.

Evaluation criteria and tools used

The following identifies the evaluation criteria and tools used by the practitioners in their external and internal communications, according to the AMEC research (2009).

1. Criteria used to evaluate external communications

Practitioners use a variety of criteria to asses their activities. They use more than one and there is no universal agreement on which criteria to use (see Table 8.4).

Table 8.4 Criteria used for evaluating external communications effectiveness

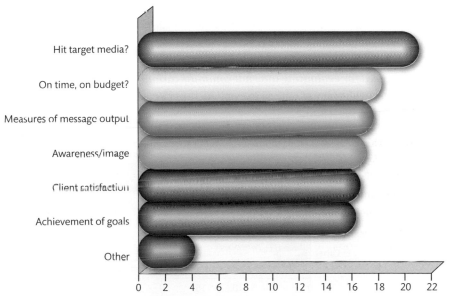

2. Tools used to evaluate external communications

Practitioners also use a variety of research tools to evaluate the effectiveness of external communications, and many use more than four tools and some use all of them (see Table 8.5).

Table 8.5 Tools used for evaluating external communications effectiveness

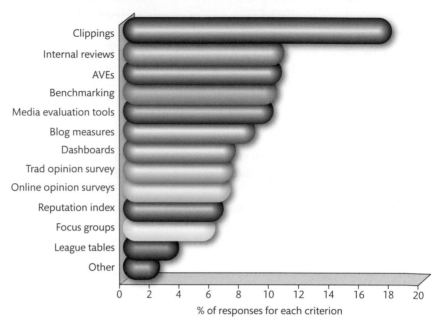

3. Criteria used for evaluating internal communications effectiveness

Practitioners use a variety of criteria to evaluate the effectiveness of their internal communications (see Table 8.6).

Table 8.6 Criteria used for evaluating internal communications effectiveness

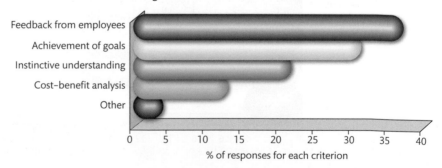

4. Tools used for evaluating internal communications effectiveness

The tools practitioners use include employee surveys, internal reviews, feedback from colleagues, and focus groups (see Table 8.7). These all achieve strong approval ratings.

Table 8.7 **Tools used for evaluating internal communications effectiveness**

Go to the Online Resource Centre to access a link to the global survey

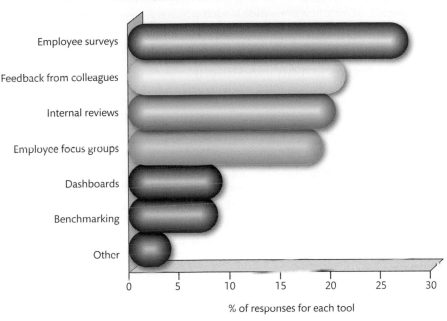

% of responses for each tool

Source: Tables 8.5–8.7 courtesy of The International Association for Measurement and Evaluation of Communication (AMEC) and Benchpoint Ltd

New approach to evaluation

In Europe in June 2010, new global measurement principles of public relations programmes were announced. The leaders of five global PR and measurement and evaluation bodies and 200 delegates from 33 countries at the second European Summit of Measurement, adopted a new framework of global programme measurement called the Barcelona Declaration of Research Principles. The organizations involved were the Global Alliance, IPR Measurement Commission, AMEC, PRSA, and ICCO.

The seven new measurement principles are expected to replace outdated programme measurement models and include.

1. Goal setting and measurement are fundamental aspects of any PR programmes.
2. Media measurement requires quantity and quality. Press clippings in themselves are not enough.
3. Advertising Value Equivalents (AVEs) do not measure the value of public relations and do not inform future activity.
4. Social media can and should be measured.
5. Measuring outcomes is preferred to measuring media results.
6. Business results can and should be measured where possible.
7. Transparency and replicability are paramount to sound measurement.

These principles mean that public relations is focusing on the importance of evaluation and is expected to create new evaluation models which will create a more consistent approach throughout the industry.

Evaluating the return on investment

Organizations are looking closely at how to measure the benefits of what public relations achieves against its cost. With the driving force of financial imperatives there is an emphasis on outputs, particularly media coverage, as this is tangible evidence of a campaign. This has led to public relations evaluation going back to the unreliable method of advertising value equivalence which equates media coverage in terms of the cost of advertising space or airtime and provides a financial figure for the evaluation.

The term Return on Investment (ROI) is the ratio of how much profit is made from an actual activity against its actual cost. It is used to guide the strategies and investments of many marketing and financial projects and is now focusing on communications. However, the actual profit can be difficult to identify if it does not have a direct monetary value. For example, a public relations campaign can change opinion or attitudes but these may not be seen to have an immediate or direct financial effect.

The COI (2009: 3) notes that government communication, unlike commercial organizations, does not focus on creating value for its shareholders but has complex objectives and must take a long-term perspective on influencing citizens. For example, it could be working to reduce alcohol abuse, encouraging more people to take up teaching, or attempting to reduce tobacco use.

The COI announced in November 2009, that although financial analysis is only one measure for government communications programmes it should still play an important part in evaluation. It estimates the ROI by identifying the contribution that it will make and identifies the outcomes and how they can be measured and then applies financial values to them.

Go to the Online Resource Centre to access a link to how the COI estimates return on investment for its communications programmes

Table 8.8 **Tobacco control campaign**

Outcome	Measurement	Financial costs
Improved health	Number of smokers	N/A
	Number of deaths from smoking-related illnesses	Value of a prevented fatality
Saving to the NHS	Number of admissions to hospital for smoking related illnesses	Treatment costs (from academic study)
Reduction in accidents	Number of domestic fires caused by cigarettes	Costs associated with domestic fires (from academic study)
Savings to employers	Number of sick days due to smoking related illnesses	Average cost of a sick day (from academic study)

Source: Courtesy of Central Office of Information (COI 2009: 52)

An example of how to work out the return of investment is the UK Government's Tobacco Control campaign (COI 2009) shown in Table 8.8 opposite. This reduced the number of smokers between 1999–2004 by more than a million. It meant that there were fewer smoking-related deaths and created a saving in NHS costs of £170 million.

The following case study demonstrates how a campaign was evaluated to identify outtakes, outputs, and outcomes.

Case Study

Campaign to check for head lice

Source: Courtesy of Pegasus PR

Hedrin—Once A Week Take A Peek Getting Ahead of Head Lice. 2008–2009

Executive summary

The 'Once a Week, Take a Peek' campaign enlisted support from schools, healthcare professionals, and pharmacists to educate parents on the need for weekly head lice checks, giving education and advice on how to identify and manage head lice infestations. Over 120,000 advice leaflets were requested from the campaign website and 115 news articles appeared. The campaign helped Hedrin position itself as the authoritative voice within the head lice market, growing its market share and position as brand leader.

Situation analysis

One in 10 primary school children suffer from head lice at any one time and research amongst parents highlighted a lack of knowledge. Head lice are also hard to treat owing to time-consuming treatment options and resistance to traditional insecticide-based treatments. Hedrin eradicates head lice without pesticides or time-consuming combing. However, new products with a similar action increased the need for Hedrin to be seen as the most credible and authoritative brand.

Objectives: March 2008–March 2009

- Promote the Once a Week, Take a Peek (OAWTAP) educational campaign, and generate at least 30,000 requests for information.

- Secure at least 50 items of media coverage, generating at least 20 million opportunities to raise awareness of the educational campaign, particularly with parents of children aged 4–11.
- Position Hedrin as the most advanced and effective head lice treatment available, encouraging pharmacy, school, and medical recommendations.
- Generate consumer product demand, protecting the existing market share and supporting retail listings.

Campaign strategy

- Position Hedrin as the leading authority on head lice to maintain market share.
- Use the OAWTAP educational campaign as a platform to champion the role of parents in the battle against head lice.
- Use the media to raise awareness of increasing resistance to traditional head lice treatments and Hedrin's efficacy.
- Build Hedrin brand credibility and trust and drive recommendations by raising awareness of clinical trials, case histories, and association with experts.

Implementation

1. Educational tactics

- The campaign used a memorable strap line (Once a Week, Take a Peek) to encourage weekly checking.
- Educational leaflets were available via the campaign website, and provided clear advice to appeal to busy people and avoid information overload.
- A campaign microsite was developed as a valuable source of information—http://www.onceaweektakeapeek.com.
- Creation of a 'Superhero Mum' cartoon character helped to champion the role of parents in the crusade against head lice.
- Information was tailored to parents' existing knowledge.
- A Medical Advisory Board advised on the campaign materials and members acted as spokespeople.
- The campaign championed the role of parents in the battle against head lice—communicating their responsibility.
- The campaign was promoted through the media, in online discussions, at pharmacy workshops, by word-of-mouth, briefings with key opinion leaders, and at relevant industry events.

2. Media tactics

- Roundtable media event and meetings briefed consumer, pharmacy, medical, and education media for the September back-to-school period, presented new clinical research highlighting Hedrin's efficacy and the OAWTAP campaign.

- Emotive case studies and surveys encouraged media to write about head lice, eg a survey that found three-quarters of parents want tougher penalties for those parents who do not treat head lice.
- A social media campaign recruited brand ambassadors to talk about the brand and give advice.

3. School and pharmacy tactics
- Three month project putting the OAWTAP campaign concept to the test, involving a Northampton primary school, parents, and local pharmacies all working together.
- Campaign materials were provided and text service to inform parents of head lice outbreaks in the school.
- Case study created following project was communicated to media and made available for healthcare professionals, schools, and pharmacies to roll out on a local level around the country.
- Success evaluated through parent questionnaires pre and post the project—88 per cent felt better informed about head lice treatment and prevention as a result of the initiative and 74 per cent now check at least once a week.

Evaluation

1. Outtakes
The educational campaign generated at least 30,000 requests for information with leaflets ordered by consumers, schools, and pharmacies. Feedback via the campaign microsite included positive feedback from schools on their successful head lice eradication as well as equivalent feedback from pharmacists.

2. Outputs
Extensive media coverage created 115 items of coverage including 11 articles in national newspapers and positioned Hedrin as the most advanced and effective head lice treatment available as nearly all (94 per cent) of the media coverage mentioned the Hedrin brand, with comments from the Hedrin expert advisory panel.

Coverage was also secured in the pharmacy, education, and medical press, raising awareness of Hedrin's efficacy and unique mode of action.

3. Outcomes
Consumer product demand increased sales and grew the market share despite new competition.

PR Tool

A model for online evaluation

A representation of what the world is thinking about an organization can be found through carrying out a semantic analysis of all the web pages—which reach an organization's publics—on the same day.

Then identify the organization's own web pages and record the difference between what is on that site and what people are talking about and doing on the other pages. However, to measure social media, a large sample is needed in order to review many different conversations. A public relations practitioner must then plan to reduce this communications gap by engaging in the social media world through blogs, wikis, news sites, etc.

Online evaluation can be analysed as follows.

1. Outputs

This is also known as reach and asks who is talking about an organization.

Quantity: How many authors are generating these mentions? What are they saying about the organization and the sector? Where are they occurring, eg Twitter, social networks, blogs, discussion forums.

Quality: What social influence do the authors have? Do they influence opinion? How do authors change as there are new influencers?

Look at the organization's site: How many hits does it have?

2. Outtakes

This is also known as attitudes and notes whether they have changed. It analyses the topics or themes that are the focus of related blogs. They need to compare with what an organization wants and what is actually on the organization's website. What is the tone, what are the keywords? What is changing? (Paine 2007).

3. Outcomes

This is the level of engagement with the site resulting from social web and shows a change in behaviour. For example, it identifies which sources drive behaviour such as a purchase, a download, or a vote. It looks at the intent in blogs, Facebook, Twitter, SEO, emails, and so on and what has been downloaded from the organization's sites, eg brochures, images and reports and who has registered or bought from the site. Online evaluation can be done through news monitoring services such Google Alert, Technorati, CyberAlert, and eWatch. There are also companies that focus on online/social media and cover blogs, wikis, Twitter, social networks, bulletin boards, and discussion lists (Murdough 2009).

Summary

Evaluation is important to public relations and should be carried out throughout the lifecycle of the programme. That is, from the beginning at the planning stage to the end where results are collected.

More online research tools and more information online mean that more research is possible. Evaluation requires reviewing this research and using it to identify how to develop a campaign as well as monitor its progress and outcomes against the key performance indicators derived from the objectives.

Public relations is a complex discipline and evaluating it is difficult because it is integrated, often seamlessly, into other management areas. Therefore setting specific public relations objectives and looking at relationship building is critical to being able to monitor it accurately.

Ideally, it is best to isolate the communications model, identifying the sender, the message, the channel, and the receiver and assess what is going into each of these stages and the progress of it. However, all the dynamics within this model need to be reviewed which includes online activity, how publics are motivated and interacting, and the relationships developed with the organization.

The ideal process of evaluation reviews the ongoing development of the programme in an effort to influence how it is delivered , as well as its results. The same research tools are used in evaluation as for a situation analysis. In order for PR programmes to be evaluated Watson and Noble (2008) have recommended a five-step circular process for programme developement:

1. A full review to gather information at the beginning.
2. Setting specific objectives.
3. Deciding the strategy and implementation.
4. The ongoing formative evaluation which means the programme can be altered.
5. Evaluation of the results measured against the objectives.

An effective evaluation format is the pyramid model of public relations research developed by Macnamara (2005). This shows the progress during the different levels of communication. The first level is inputs which includes confirming messages, media information, event arrangement, brochures and social media. The next level is outputs which monitors changes in awareness through media coverage, events and other activities followed by outtakes which measures the subsequent changes in attitudes and the final level is outcomes which measures behaviour changes.

Each level has a particular research methodology which can be applied to ascertain the programme's progress. For example, the output stage monitors the number of people who received messages and the methodology would be measuring circulation figures of different media, attendance at events, and website downloads. The outtake stage uses more qualitative methodology such as focus groups and opinion surveys to find out changes in attitudes. The outcome state identifies how much behaviour changes and this can be measured through adoption rates, purchases, and large quantitative surveys.

There are many debates about what public relations means and some believe that it should only measure agenda setting, that is, how effective is it in getting something talked about in the media.

Other crucial aspects of evaluation are budget and timing which should be clarified during the planning stage. Other less measurable factors are relationships, as well as creativity and teamwork. However, the final analysis is the effectiveness of the campaign against its objectives. Although research methods may be the same for many aspects of a programme, they can be applied differently and often in different combinations.

Public relations evaluation has its own history and arises from psychological research, social sciences, and business disciplines. Now business indicators are driving evaluation and this can be presented visually in onscreen displays which show all elements of a programme and assesses them against financial imperatives.

However, it is relationships that are being considered as crucial to public relations and there is increasing research on how they can be evaluated. Online public relations relies on relationships and getting traffic to a site and increasing its popularity. However, the question on how to measure relationships is difficult to answer, but increasingly important as these can be a significant part of an organization's value.

Online public relations and media are influencing evaluation. This is because of the immediacy of information where reputation can be affected instantly, locations and time zones are less meaningful and the increasing availability of better online measurement tool. For example, faster online tools mean people's actions and their shared links can be seen before they purchase or download anything.

However, according to research on the industry, evaluation by public relations practitioners still focuses on media monitoring with new research tools only slowly gaining acceptance. Nevertheless, business is increasingly demanding that public relations demonstrates a tangible financial return. There are many ways this can be shown, such as creating financial values for every outcome. The plethora of evaluation tools makes this an exciting area but it also means looking at programme development more closely in order to build in up-to-date measurable factors at each stage.

Discussion points

A. Outputs, outtakes, and outcomes

Go to the Online Resource Centre and review a case study.

1. Identify its inputs.

2. Then list its outputs, outtakes, and outcomes.

3. Review how much evaluation took place in the campaign. What was evaluated?

4. What evaluation measures would you have added?

5. What research tools would you have used?

B. Evaluation debate

Arrange a debate in class where you have a judging panel and two teams.

1. One team is the client and the other the consultancy.

2. The client must announce that it has decided that evaluation is too expensive and will only look at outcomes. The consultancy team must provide an argument for ongoing evaluation at the different stages in order to show performance.

C. Online evaluation

Find the latest online evaluation tools.

1. Use these to evaluate your favourite organization through researching what other organizations and individuals are saying about them online.

2. Then go the organization's website and check if what is being said online matches their messages. Identify any dissonance and see if you can find what is influencing this. How do you think the organization should get involved in this chat?

D. Blogging

Reflect on your favourite hobby or interest.

1. During a week identify the key bloggers on this topic.

2. What makes them influential?

3. Does their importance change over a week and if so what is influencing this change?

References

COI (2009) 'Home Office: Evaluating Communications—A Best Practice Guide: Version 1 January'. Available at: http://coi.gov.uk/blogs/bigthinkers/wp-content/uploads/2009/11/coi-payback-and-romi-paper.pdf

Cutlip , S., Center, A. and Broom, G. (2006) *Effective Public Relations* (9th edn). Upper Saddle River, NJ: Pearson

Gregory, A. (2006) *Planning and Managing Public Relations Campaigns* (2nd edn). London: Kogan Page

Gregory, A. and Watson, T. (2008) 'Defining the Gap Between Research and Practice in Public Relations Programme Evaluation—Towards A New Research Agenda', Journal of Marketing Communications 14/5: 337–50

Grunig, J. (nd) 'Qualitative Methods for Assessing relationships Between Organizations and Publics', IPR. Available at: http://www.instituteforpr.com

Hill-Wood, E., Wellington, P. and Rossi, J. (2009) 'How Teenagers Consume Media: Media & Internet', July, Morgan Stanley Research Europe. Available at: http://media.ft.com/cms/c3852b2e-6f9a-11de-bfe5-00144feabdc0.pdf

Killer Start Ups (2010) 'Topsy.com What Are You Talking About Right Now?'. Available at: http://www.killerstartups.com/Social-Networking/topsy-com-what-are-you-talking-about-right-now

Ledingham, J. (2003) 'Explicating Relationship Management as a General Theory of Public Relations', Journal of Public Relations Research 15/2: 181–98

Lindenmann, W. (2006) 'Public Relations Research for Planning and Evaluation', May' Institute for Public Relations. Available at: http://www.instituteforpr.org

Macnamara, J. (2006) 'The Fork in the Road of Media and Communication Theory and Practice'. Paper presented to the Summit on Measurement, Institute for Public Relations, Portsmouth, NH, October. Available at: http://www.instituteforpr.org/research_single/the_fork_in_the_road_of_media_and_communication_theory_and_practice/

McCoy, M. and Hargie, O. (2003) 'Implications of Mass Communication Theory for Asymmetric Public Relations Evaluation', Journal of Communications Management 2003 7/4: 304

Murdough, C. (2009) 'Social Media Measurement: It's not impossible', Journal of Interactive Advertising 10/1 (Fall)

Paine, K. (2007) 'How to Measure Social Media Relations: The More Things Change, The More They Remain the Same', Institute for Public Relations. Available at: http://www.instituteforpr.org

Phillips, D. (2007) 'In Reply to Frank Ovatt', 22 June, LeverWealth. Available at: http://leverwealth.blogspot.com/2007/06/in-reply-to-frank-ovatt.html

Tealium (2009) 'Social Media Measurement That Matters'. White Paper, January, Tealium Inc. Available at: http://www.tealium.com/resources/Social_Media_Measurement_That_Matters.pdf

Watson, T. and Noble, P. (2007) Evaluating Public Relations: A Best Practice Guide to Public Relations Planning, Research and Evaluation. London: Kogan Page

Wright, D., Gaunt, R., Leggetter, B., Daniels, M., and Zerfass, A. (2009) 'Global Survey of Communications Measurement 2009—Final Report September', Benchpoint/AMEC. Available at: http://www.benchpoint.com/summit.pdf

PR communications for business

9

Learning outcomes

1. Understand that all forms of media and business communication are affected by changes in the elements of a communication model and is largely persuasive, following the three elements of communications: ethos, logos, and pathos.

2. Be able to review and prepare information which is easy for the reader to recognize its function, assimilate its meaning, and act on its objectives.

3. Be aware of the ethical and legal aspects of media and business and their relevance to public relations.

4. Recognize and apply the key elements of grammar, punctuation, and style to business and media writing to ensure its clarity and persuasiveness.

5. Be able to formulate a variety of business reports by learning about their common guidelines and formats.

6. Be aware of the different interpersonal skills required and how to use them in meetings, presentations, and social business occasions.

Practitioner Insight

Chris Genasi
CEO Eloqui Communications
Past President of the Chartered Institute of Public Relations
Author of several books on PR including Winning Reputations—How to be Your Own Spin Doctor and Creative Business

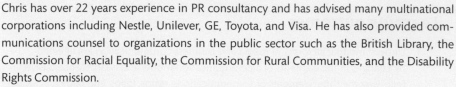

Chris has over 22 years experience in PR consultancy and has advised many multinational corporations including Nestle, Unilever, GE, Toyota, and Visa. He has also provided communications counsel to organizations in the public sector such as the British Library, the Commission for Racial Equality, the Commission for Rural Communities, and the Disability Rights Commission.

Prior to founding Eloqui in 2003, he was at Weber Shandwick, the world's largest PR firm, where he was Global Director of Strategy and before that, Chief Executive of the European Corporate Practice. Chris worked across Europe and in the US, specializing in strategy development, issues management, and reputation building campaigns.

Chris was named by *PR Week* as one the UK's most influential PR practitioners and is a past president of the Chartered Institute of Public Relations.

What is the difference between business and media writing in public relations?

When you are writing for a business audience, it is essential to provide clear advice that is both practical and realistic. The emphasis should be more on facts and examples of where others have succeeded. A lot of media writing is based on opinions or speculation. I think business writing needs to be much more fact-based and pragmatic, offering advice that can be applied easily by any business leader.

What are key legal issues in business communications?

If you are a listed company about issuing information that could be seen to be influencing the share price directly, you need to make it clear that your communications are not a future statement about likely share performance. A standard template at the end of all press releases will cover this. It is also important not to disclose any confidential information or be defamatory about competitors or individuals working in competing companies.

What are key legal issues in media communications?

Journalists have a range of legal constraints they need to be aware of and PR people similarly need to know when they can and cannot comment—for example, when a legal case is pending.

What makes a good business meeting?

- A clear understanding by all of the purpose of the meeting—before the meeting and re-stated when the meeting starts.
- A detailed agenda.
- A strong chair who stops people talking too much and who keeps the discussion focused.
- Clear actions, in writing, for who will do what next and by when.

How has the web changed how people communicate in public relations?

It has changed things dramatically. A story now can evolve throughout the day with sentiment shifting as people blog in response to a news announcement. A piece of good coverage in the morning can be turned into a negative situation by the evening (and vice versa), if the online chatter takes a dislike to the morning news.

The web also impacts on the timing of stories– stories may break in other countries and are picked up by the UK before the UK version has been issued. The other major change is that there is now a whole new community of people to reach online-bloggers, and other websites with similar interests, will put out comments on your stories. It is essential to build relationships with these new 'corporate journalists' and commentators and treat them with the same respect as traditional journalists.

What advice would you give to young practitioners about business and media communications?

This is a great and growing area to go into. The internet means that PR has an even bigger future in business communications, as more and more business leaders realize that PR can deliver great value for money.

I recommend focusing on one specialism—whether it be a sector or a type of communications. If you have specialist expertise, you are more likely to be able to charge a premium for that service, whether in terms of salary or consultancy fee. Finally, I would suggest concentrating on those sectors where the big money is—the City, Financial Services, the public sector, and so on. Find out where the big PR budgets are and concentrate your career on those sectors.

9.1 Definition

Communications is what business is all about. We need to communicate to sell something, to buy something, or persuade people to change their attitudes or behaviour. We communicate in many different ways. Visual media is a powerful way of communicating and can range from watching television to watching a live presentation. We can also listen to someone speak either on the radio or in person and music is effective in being able to evoke emotion.

Writing is a key form of communication in business but it can incorporate the other modes of communication, for example one can write in order for something to be read, acted, or sung.

Business communication is the same as any communication in that we need to understand the models described in chapter 2 which identify the sender, the receiver, and the variety of communication channels which can be face-to-face, written documents, the internet, radio, and television. The Osgood and Schramm model identified both encoding, which is how language is used; and decoding, which is how people make sense of what has been communicated. All the communication models look at the influence of noise, which is anything that distorts a message and can range from transmission difficulties to personal influence such as tiredness or boredom. The Westley and MacLean model showed the influence of feedback, which is what the receiver communicates to the sender. This can range from body language, such as frowning or clapping, to letters, blogs, or television voting.

How effective communication is depends on the relationship between those who are doing the communicating. Therefore, public relations relationships are built to make the information more appealing. In turn, the information must be tailored to the relationship built.

In personal communication, most of the meaning does not come from words; it is formed through visual signs, called non-verbal signals. For example, a firm handshake, good eye contact, and a positive tone of voice shows a willingness to communicate positively. Personal space is very important in business and getting too close to others or 'invading their space' can be annoying or intimidating.

According to Hall (cited Hartley and Bruckman 2002: 42), people work with four zones of distance:

- intimate friends converse with a distance of 45 cm between them
- casual acquaintances have more distance separating them which is 45–90 cm
- socializing is done at 120–365 cm between participants
- public speaking is more than 365 cms from an audience.

However, different cultures have different distances with which they are comfortable.

Writing

Writing is more objective, formal, and abstract than speaking. To achieve its objectives it should be easy to read and understand, be correct, have enough information and create a desire to read it. It is important to consider the subject and reason for the writing in order to develop the correct style. For example, a subject such as medical research will have a serious reader whereas an announcement about a rock concert will be more informal.

In public relations there are three key types of writing: business writing, media writing, and promotional writing. Using a personal writing style for a business situation will not have the effect wanted. Equally, writing for the media demands a particular style in order for the media to want to read it (see chapter 3). Promotional writing in brochures and even websites appeals directly to an identified public.

Media writing

The most common form of media writing is a media release which is written in a specific way to attract the journalist (see chapter 3). It follows a pyramid structure which gives the who, what, where, when, and how in the first paragraph and then follows with more information and a quote. It must have a heading, a date, a punchy first paragraph followed by more information in short and concise paragraphs. The end finishes with the name of a person to contact for more information.

A media backgrounder is rather like an appendix as it provides information referred to in the media release but is not needed to understand the media release, although it helps a deeper undersatnding. Media writing can also include biographies which are summaries of the people involved in the media story.

Media writing includes:

Media releases	Backgrounders	Invitations	Biography
Factsheets	Websites	Research reports	

Business writing

Business writing is more formal and usually follows a set format, or style, of the organization, which is called the house style. Most documents are written on a regular basis such as the annual report or after a scheduled event, such as a meeting.

Business writing includes:

Letters	Reports	Proposals	Invitations
Budgets	Action plans	Presentations	Research reports
Annual reports	Meeting minutes		

Promotional writing

Frequently public relations practitioners need to write newsletters, leaflets, copy for advertorials, and copy for websites. For example, a newsletter style depends on who is reading it, what it is expected to achieve, and how often it appears. The layout must ensure that it reflects the topic and is attractive to read as well as ensuring the most important articles are well profiled with content determined by the reader's need to know

Fig 9.1
Anglian Water poster to encourage car sharing

Source: Courtesy of Anglian Water

as well as being in an interesting style targeted to the reader. There are different types of newsletters depending on who they are expected to reach (see Figure 9.1).

Promotional writing includes:

Websites	Brochures	Advertorials
Leaflets	Posters	Newsletters

Websites are used to deliver newsletters so there are now fewer printed versions. A UK charity, the British Heart Foundation (BHF), which promotes and protects cardiovascular health, publishes a monthly e-newsletter to which anyone can subscribe by completing the online subscription. The e-newsletter covers the BHF work in fighting heart disease, in pioneering research, services for heart patients and their carers, news for health professionals, BHF events and campaigns, BHF shops, and new features on the BHF website. By offering products to sell it also works as a fundraising tool (British Heart Foundation 2010).

The public relations consultancy, Weber Shandwick, publishes a quarterly newsletter which appears on their website featuring the latest news in public relations and reinforces the organization as a leading international consultancy.

The extensive high technology available means that professional designers now have the tools to make websites interesting and interactive (Phillips and Young 2009). These websites can host blogs which encourage dialogue, chat, or discussion forums which allow direct communication and feedback between organizations and their stakeholders so need to be attractive, accessible, and user friendly.

Discussion or message boards use asynchronous communication so that publics can post messages that others can read and can respond to later. Organizations can use these to provide information pertaining to the discussion (Mersham, Theunissan, and Peart 2009: 157).

Go to the Online Resource Centre to access a link to the latest Weber Shandwick newsletter

9.2 Theoretical content

The art of communication is in finding the most effective means of sharing ideas and information. Public relations writing is largely persuasive and the three basic principles of persuasion were established by the Greek philosopher and scientist Aristotle (384–322 BC). These principles are discussed in Aristotle's book *Rhetoric* and are outlined below.

> Go to the Online Resource Centre to access a link to the translation of Aristotle's book *Rhetoric*

Ethos

Ethos is the communicator's personal character which establishes credibility. In a speaker this can be portrayed as how they relate to the audience. It is vital that audiences see the speaker or writer as credible and then they will be receptive to what they say or write and more likely to accept it. For example, a speaker paid to endorse a product would not be seen as credible as someone who has used the product themselves and is giving their own opinion of the product's value. Viral campaigns are effective as they generate this 'word of mouth' communication and get a lot of people talking about a product. Also documents written in a recognized format and using a business letterhead appear more authoritative and credible.

Pathos

Pathos is the effect the communicator has on the audience's emotions. The emotional influence on the audience can convince an audience of the message. Aristotle said of pathos:

> **so change men as to affect their judgements, and that are also attended by pain or pleasure.**

(European Rhetoric 2010)

A good speaker can appeal to emotions; stimulating and connecting to the minds of their audience. The US President, Barack Obama, connects to his publics by being warm and enthusiastic, compared to the UK's ex-prime minister Gordon Brown who is more restrained and analytical.

Although business writing is logical and does not seek to be emotive, people still react with emotion to most things. For example, students are more likely to feel positive about enrolling in a university which presents information showing that it has high graduate employment. When preparing communication it is necessary to find what creates an emotional reaction; this could involve focusing on financial implications, political or religious feelings, or other values.

Logos

Logos is the use of facts and logic to create a reasoned argument, based on evidence which has been considered and evaluated. For example, a document or a presentation is more persuasive if there is a clear presentation of the facts, an objective analysis of the information, a conclusion based on this information, and recommendations aris-ing from it (Hartley and Bruckman 2002: 149). For example, a university can appeal to students by showing the high employment rates of their graduates.

Presenting information

According to neurological and psychological research, the brain continuously antici-pates, organizes, and reorganizes the information it receives (Hartley and Bruckman 2002: 144). Therefore the retention and understanding of messages is dependent on how they are presented. Much of this is unconscious and people can be easily misled by the way information is presented. For example, how information is asked can influence an answer, which is why leading questions are seldom used in surveys.

It is important that all writing is well structured as people find it hard to remember information which is not structured. Based on Hartley and Bruckman's (2002: 144) exercise of structuring a list, below is an alphabetical list of invertebrates which is hard to remember or even understand as it is not structured in any meaningful way.

1. cockroach	3. earthworm	5. mussel	7. slug	9. spider
2. cricket	4. lobster	6. oyster	8. snail	10. worm

Hartley and Bruckman (2002: 145) point out that it is easier to understand and remem-ber if items are put into groups. In this case we can sort these invertebrates by what sort of bones they have.

1. No shell: slug, worm, earthworm

2. Hard shell: snail, mussel, oyster

3. Tough coatings: cricket, lobster, spider, cockroach

Applying this technique of sorting information when writing means that the informa-tion is more likely to be read and remembered.

The weighing up of different and conflicting information is an essential aspect of business writing. Critical thinking is required to develop clear and often persuasive messages, which can range from presenting an analysis of a situation, recommending a proposal, or presenting the progress of a campaign. A practitioner gains credibility when they demonstrate that they can present, both verbally and in written form, objective advice based on critical thinking which has been formed through the synthesis and analysis of complex information.

As with any writing it is important to know the readers and what will motivate them. They need to be encouraged to read what has been written, therefore it helps to set out a document in an appropriate format. For example, a meeting report, or minutes, has a standard and recognizable format. The date of the meeting and its purpose is noted at the top, the attendees are listed, the body of the meeting report reviews any outstanding minutes from the last meeting and then it covers the new topics, based on its agenda and outcomes from the meeting.

The key to business writing

1. Planning

This is planning, organizing, and structuring information so it makes sense and is easy to read. The best way to structure information is through chunking information, that is, breaking it into small sections and then ordering it and signposting it through headings and paragraphs to make it easy to follow.

2. Style

Most organizations have a house style which means they use standard formats for all their business writing. There may be a particular format for meeting reports, another for proposals, and another for letters and so on. This also concerns the type of font used, layout, headed paper, and may require the use of standard phrases. Many public relations practitioners are involved in developing the house style for an organization and ensuring it is adhered to.

3. Layout

How a document looks is vital to its credibility as it reflects the organization. A clear layout uses headings, paragraphs, margins, spacing, and font sizes to create a visually attractive and easy to read document.

The framework of business writing

1. Legalities

In business, practitioners will come across masses of information about their organization or their client and most of it will be confidential. Usually organizations have public relations practitioners sign documents to confirm that they will observe these confidences but even so confidentiality is considered an expected professional behaviour (Jones and Benson 2006: 199).

This observation of confidentiality is called a duty of confidence. The information it concerns may be in business proposals, interim reports from investigations or research, on new product developments, or about customers. This information is considered to be trade secrets and should never be shared with anyone who is not involved in the project.

2. The protection of ideas

Public relations is all about ideas and a duty of confidence should cover these from being copied or developed by others. A concept or a novel plan, when implemented can make an organization very successful, yet the thinking and the creativity behind these ideas is hard work and a duty of confidence should cover these from being copied or developed by others, although it is difficult to enforce. Once an idea is discussed it may be extremely easy for someone to implement and even improve on it, and therefore the creator of the idea could 'lose' it or in effect have their idea 'stolen'.

3. Copyright

Copyright is really the right to control the copying of someone's work by others. Practitioners must be careful about copyright and must not quote or paraphrase someone else's work without referencing it.

Jones and Benson (2006: 213) state that copyright owners have the following rights:

- to copy the work
- to issue copies of the work to the public
- to rent or lend the work to the public
- to perform, show, or play the work in public
- to communicate the work to the public
- to make an adaptation of the work, or to do any of the above things in relation to an adaptation.

Therefore, none of these activities can be done unless copyright permission is granted. All these aspects are important in public relations, for example information cannot be copied from any published material without gaining permission, any quotations or paraphrasing must be referenced, and approval must be gained for any images used. Often a public relations event may include a short play or theatrical show to communicate a point or provide entertainment but if it is not an original piece then copyright approval will need to be obtained. Permission must also be granted for using the words of a song or for adapting them or the music.

4. Libel and slander

Defamation means saying or writing something that lowers an organization's or individual's reputation. Libel is defamation which is written or broadcast and also includes the internet. Slander is considered face-to-face words and gestures. Deformation must have been published (or in the case of slander, spoken) to a third party. It must be understood to refer to the person who is complaining about it and the allegation must have a defamatory meaning.

This can be anything that affects their personal or business life, and can just be a comment which allows them to be ridiculed. The test for defamation is not based on what the speaker or writer intended; it is based on what the ordinary reader is likely to think of the person who had been spoken or written about. Defamation also includes anything that is said that suggests untrue negative aspects about someone's reputation.

Any statement in a book, journal, or newspaper or any other published matter (an advertisement, email, Twitter, Facebook, or website, for example), runs the risk of being defamatory if it contains an untrue allegation or imputation which disparages the reputation of another (Jones and Benson 2006: 164).

For example, in 2009, Abramovich, the owner of Chelsea Football Club, won libel damages over an Italian newspaper which alleged that he had a serious gambling problem. *La Repubblica* had reported that Abramovich had lost a substantial amount, including his yacht, in a poker game. These allegations were not checked with Abramovich so he had no chance to respond before they were published (Holden 2010).

5. *Approvals*

When writing anything on behalf of an organization the practitioner must always ensure it has the organization's approval before it is submitted to its public, which includes the media. In many organizations media information is checked by its legal team to ensure that there is no confidentiality broken and also that it is in line with the organization's overall business objectives.

In addition, any written quotes from spokespeople must be approved by the person who said them before the document is released to the media. All media and business information needs to be reviewed by a senior employer; this could be the corporate affairs manager, the communications' director, and frequently the company lawyer before it is released to a third party.

When submitting information for internal approval it is advisable to record on the actual document signatures to show the approval process or create an email notification that can make it clear which document is being approved. This is important as often there can be many versions of one document and they can get muddled. Most organizations have a procedure for approvals and public relations practitioners need to adhere to them.

9.3 Influences

Writing well means understanding sentence construction, paragraph construction, grammar, and punctuation as well as how to layout and format a document. All writing must show a sequence of paragraphs which divides a subject into different topics. Paragraphs can be of any length and a variety of lengths can be used to maintain interest.

In media writing, paragraphs are very short, sometimes just one or two sentences. In reports they can be much longer although it is advisable to have a new paragraph with each new topic to aid clarity and makes the document easy to follow.

In a business report, the first paragraph is the introduction, the second the body, and the third the conclusion. There may be more paragraphs within each of these to identify a new area in the topic. Often the paragraphs have a subheading which helps the structure and layout. Picking up one paragraph from where the other left off is the best way to write rather than starting on a completely new topic. This can be done by using key phrases from the previous paragraph creating a link to form a unified whole.

Style in business writing must be appropriate to the organization, it must be accurate, and it must be brief. It must take into account what the recipient already knows, needs to know, and wants to know. It must be clear with a good structure often using subheadings and not too much detail.

Making meaning

PR is often accused of writing 'gobbledygook'; where the meaning is unclear, often caused by the writer trying to impress the reader with their own knowledge. Examples of gobbledygook (courtesy of Plain English Campaign):

'At base level, this just comes down to global strategic consulting.'

'My organization believes in integrated policy projections.'

Apart from 'gobbledygook' some people like to use long impressive sounding words and phrases that they don't even understand. The following is a list of these compiled by the Plain English Campaign.

ballpark figure	be proactive not reactive
bring it to the table	mission critical
move the goalposts	think outside the box
blue-sky thinking	pushing the envelope
there is no 'I' in team	knowledge base
core competencies	win-win situation
client focus	deliverables
incentivize	take it to the next level

Creating precise meaning

Long-winded official writing is ineffective in communicating meaning. The following four examples from the Plain English Campaign demonstrate how to cut through all explanations to create precise understanding.

1. High-quality learning environments are a necessary precondition for facilitation and enhancement of the ongoing learning process.

   Improvement
   Children need good schools if they are to learn properly.

2. If there are any points on which you require explanation or further particulars we shall be glad to furnish such additional details as may be required by telephone.

   Improvement
   If you have any questions, please phone.

3. It is important that you shall read the notes, advice and information detailed opposite then complete the form overleaf (all sections) prior to its immediate return to the Council by way of the envelope provided.

   Improvement
   Please read the notes opposite before you fill in the form. Then send it back to us as soon as possible in the envelope provided.

4. Your enquiry about the use of the entrance area at the library for the purpose of displaying posters and leaflets about Welfare and Supplementary Benefit rights, gives rise to the question of the provenance and authoritativeness of the material to be displayed. Posters and leaflets issued by the Central Office of Information, the Department of Health and Social Security and other authoritative bodies are usually displayed in libraries, but items of a disputatious or polemic kind, whilst not necessarily excluded, are considered individually.

Improvement

Thank you for your letter asking for permission to put up posters in the library. Before we can give you an answer we will need to see a copy of the posters to make sure they won't offend anyone.

Sentences use different devices to create a sense of immediacy or action and this influences the writing style. For example, the present tense uses direct speech, that is, when the words of a speaker are quoted. Direct speech is often used as a quotation in the second or third paragraph of a media release to add credibility to the first paragraph. Indirect speech is usually written in the past tense and summarizes what someone has said. It is often used further down in a media release. A report is more formal and focuses on what has happened and rarely uses direct speech.

Active or passive

In writing for the media, active expressions are used more than passive ones. This is because active words usually sound more direct, and more interesting than passive words. A passive voice sentence is often longer than an active one and can be in any tense. To make your writing more lively, change a passive sentence to an active one by finding the subject which follows the word 'by' and then switch that to the beginning. For example:

The marks will be changed <u>by the exam board.</u> (Passive)
<u>The exam board will</u> change the marks. (Active)
More examples
The trees were cut down by three axe men. (Passive)
Three axe men cut down the trees. (Active)
The product will be launched by a celebrity at a public function. (Passive)
A celebrity will launch the product at a public function. (Active)

Although active sentences are clear and direct it is sometimes appropriate to use a passive expression when formality is required. It may also be used in reports so that whoever is doing the action is not noted because it is unimportant or irrelevant to the report. For example, the sentence: 'The students will have their essays marked by part time lecturers' does not need to be made more interesting as it is simply a formal announcement.

Grammar

Knowing about grammar and how to use different parts of a sentence helps to make writing more concise and effective. All writers need to know the definitions and use of basic grammar such as nouns, pronouns, adjectives, and verbs in order to avoid mistakes that can undermine any writing.

Go to the Online Resource Centre to access a link to a gobbledygook generator

Go to the Online Resource Centre to access the link to a grammar quiz

Go to the Online Resource Centre to access definitions and examples of these grammatical tools

9.4 Application to industry

In business, **reports** are the most common forms of writing as they can be used for many different purposes. A report communicates ideas and information and has different styles and conventions depending on its purpose and subject. It is a factual document which may include data from one source or it may be an analysis of a collection of data. A report provides information, encourages understanding, answers questions, is accurate, is objective, and can be any size, ranging from one page to a full research report.

For example, a report can be an outline of how a campaign is running, an update on budget expenditure, or the results of a research project. A media content analysis report will analyse what has been reported in the media about an organization or product. To make it easy to read it may include a table showing the coverage against different criteria. A progress report acts as a record on how a public relations programme is reaching its objectives. Action plans can also be a report which updates the team on all aspects of a programme and are often weekly. In addition, reports written following a meeting are called meeting minutes, and capture what has been agreed, what has been done, and what needs to be done.

Legalities

A report is also a legal document. This means that it can be used in a court of law as evidence of what has been agreed. Therefore, there is a strong need for a report to be clear and accurate. Despite their differences, Seely (2002) states that reports have the following common elements:

1. They set out a series of facts based on a review of evidence.
2. The information is verifiable.
3. The information is set out in a format that is useful to the reader.
4. They are usually aimed at readers with a specific interest in the subject.

Public relations proposals are a type of report, they analyse a situation, they list objectives, and they provide solutions and ask for agreement. They can be meeting reports, proposals, and status reports. Most reports show what was done, how it was done, what the results are, what conclusions can be drawn, and what recommendations can be made. Reports are not a letter and do not need to be signed by anyone but they must note who they are to and who they are from.

The goal for a report is for it to be presented as clearly and as concisely as possible to the required readers. Each type of report has a recognized format which signals the type of information being presented and also takes into account the organization's house style.

Structure of a report

All reports have at their beginning, a small section which shows who receives the report. For example, a meeting report will go to all those invited to the meeting (even if they were absent) as well as anyone else who would benefit from reading it. The beginning section also shows the date of the report, or meeting, who it is from, and the topic such as the budget for the meeting. The report itself should be written on the organization's letterhead to give it authority and credibility and also to reinforce its official purpose.

Following this is a short introduction which outlines in brief what the report is about and what it expects to achieve in terms of agreement or awareness. For example, the first paragraph of a progress report will state that it intends to outline the development of a public relations programme, what it has achieved, and the next steps. If additional budget is required that would be identified in this introduction. Longer reports have an extended introduction and this is called an executive summary. It summarizes the whole report in a page or several pages, so that the rest of the report provides greater depth of information.

The body of the report provides the information needed and should use subheadings which make it easier to read. The conclusion gives a concise summary of the information which outlines what is required from the reader. This could mean arranging a meeting or gaining agreement on the recommendations presented. A report can include tables, images, and charts to illustrate a point that is mentioned in the report. It can also have appendices, which is detailed information referred to in the report but does not form part of the report's body.

To ensure that readers absorb the key points the layout must allow the report to appear uncluttered. Features such as headings and subheadings guide the reader through the report, emboldening of subheadings show a clear layout, bullet points emphasize aspects, lists and numbering help the reader to remember the information, and white space, margins, and consistently indented or aligned paragraphs make it look uncluttered. There should be a space between paragraphs and subheading, and a long report should have a contents page listing all the headings and subheadings. A clear font is essential and only one font should be used per document, and the selection of font is often a question of house style.

Reports can use quotations, paraphrasing, and summaries of other work in order to support recommendations or add credibility, they can also give different views on a subject. Quotations from other sources must be the same as the original. Paraphrasing means changing writing from another source material, often making it a briefer version of the original material. Summarizing is the same except that it includes only the main points. In all cases it is necessary to reference the original source.

Go to the Online Resource Centre to access a link to guides on how to improve your writing

Business plans

All organizations have a business plan and these are a form of a report on which the whole business is based and which also identifies the organization's goals. It is important for a practitioner to understand the format of a business plan and be able to link it to the public relations programme. The practitioner may also be involved in writing a business plan and will be expected to present a public relations proposal in the format of a business plan. The following is a four-part format of how a business plan is written.

1. The executive summary

The executive summary gives a concise summary of the overall business plan and should only be about a page in length. It focuses on the competitive advantage the organization (or products or services) has, that is the strategy and the unique selling points, it introduces the profit that can be made and the timescales. This is usually the last aspect to be written but appears first in the document.

2. Background

This should use lots of subheadings, it usually refers to diagrams, lists, and charts which are in the appendix. It identifies the size of the market for the business and what is influencing it, discusses the actual organization, and then puts it into a context of other similar products or organizations. It refers to what its publics want and what is influencing them such as finances, time of year, competitors, and regulations. It also gives an historical background to understand the business and the key people involved and the relationships the organization has with them. This section also provides details on the product, services, or organizations such as its advantages, its sales and expected sales, and the audience segmentation. Examples may be used and the competition and the organization's advantages over the competition is discussed.

3. The strategic action

This section explores the best way to achieve the objectives and lists timings, costs, and resources which must be written down in an organized way so that it forms logical action steps with measurable outputs and values. This shows what is expected over time in terms of costs and returns.

4. Recommendations

This identifies the action needed and the resources required.

Annual reports

An annual report provides financial information as well as content about the organization's environmental and social impact. Although primarily for shareholders, it is usually available to anyone who is interested in the organization, such as employees, consumers, competitors, educators, and investors. It comprises a purpose statement of the organization, a chairman's report, the general manager's report, an organizational chart showing the senior managers, performance achievements and the financial statements, and in some cases consolidated statements of accounts. The annual report includes photographs of the CEO and senior managers as well as photographs of other staff and activities, relevant to what is reported, such as a team or factory or third party involvement. In addition, the report needs to be made easy to read with visual representation of the accounts using bar charts, pie charts, flow charts, graphs, and tables.

Table 9.1 shows a 28-week schedule which identifies the steps for an annual report.

Go to the Online Resource Centre to access a link to an annual report

Table 9.1 Schedule for an annual report

Weeks	Practitioner's tasks	Design/production tasks
1–2	Agree on and research the areas to be covered in the report Meet with key managers to agree on objectives Prepare cost estimate	
2–5	Select graphic designer Meet designer to discuss objectives Agree on design brief	
6–10	Collect operating and financial information Get executive input Get printing quotes	
11	Meet with designer to review concept, schedule, and budget Obtain photo-subject suggestions and locations	Present budget estimate, production schedule, recommended printer and photographer
12–14	Discuss possible future use of photographs Complete photo schedule Arrange locations a list and contact people at each one	Submit word counts for all text sections Commission photographer, designer and printer
15–16	Review and revise budget estimate Write first draft of various reports	Complete design concept to include envelope, photos, and charts Deliver financial section text
17–18	Finalize mailing arrangements with share registry and printer Review design with photos and charts	Before photographer leaves a remote location, approve digital photos by email
19–21	Final revision of text Proofread envelope design	Send text, photos, charts, and cover designs for final layout Send envelope design for printing
22	Proofread first pages of main text Order mailing labels to be sent to printer	Send financial copy for layout Review envelope proofs if necessary
25	Supervise proofing of final pages Proof and get financial approval of charts	Send financial setting approval to designer/typesetter, arrange for proofed pages to be sent to printer
26	Check and obtain manager approval of page proofs and revised digital proofs	Review final proofs Make final corrections on page proofs Review corrected page proofs
27–28	Attend printer and inspect advance copies of report If not satisfactory, advise production	Give colour approvals on press Check on mailings and bulk deliveries

Source: Courtesy of Mersham, Theunissen, Peart: Public Relations and Communications Management: An Aoteoroa/New Zealand Perspective © Pearson 2009

Online content development

Data and text are the most common forms of information included in online business media communication although sound and images are also included, and hyperlinks are used instead of appendices.

All information must be integrated into the website so there is the same overall style which fits the organization's corporate identity. As in any report all information must be broken down into segments. Graphics support messages but many do not suit the business objectives. To help to ensure that the site is visited means that regular changing of content is needed as well as interactivity and building of relationships. This can be through featuring members of the organization and ensuring continuous development in discussion groups, question and answer forums, and bulletin boards plus interesting images. Information in business statements is relatively constant but online sites also need ongoing and changing information to ensure interest.

For example, a commercial and domestic security services in Gloucestershire, All Cooper, wanted to present itself as the leading service provider in a cluttered market and reflect its brand values of trust, service, and design solutions for the full gamut of security needs, including data networking, surveillance, and access control. The consultancy Montpellier PR created the strapline 'Trust is Everything' and designed the logo which represented a wedding ring to signify the trust (marriage) between the security company and the client (see Figure 9.2).

Montpellier PR also created the website with clear, large, and easy-to-read text carrying the logo and the strapline. In addition, more straplines were used as titles of pages to strengthen the brand and its values of trust. The website, http:// www. allcooper.com, became an e-portal through which home and business users could research the services in confidence and also access their own security services, such

Fig 9.2
Public relations communicated All Cooper's brand value of trust

Source: Courtesy of Montpellier PR

as the key recovery service if they lost their keys. The website was a strong public relations tactic and was launched to coincide with the security company's 20th anniversary celebrations.

Brochures and other promotional writing

A **brochure** is often called a **leaflet** and used to arouse interest, answer questions, and provide sources for further information (Bivens 2006: 197). They are short documents usually on one piece of paper that is folded once or in threes, when longer they are called **booklets**. The size and shape depends on its purpose; it could be pocket sized or opened out as a poster. A two-fold brochure has two creases and means that there are six panels. It is important in the layout to establish the front panel which has a clear headline and gives the purpose of the brochure, and the last or back panel has the contact details. The second panel is the first panel inside the brochure and refers to its headline and should be the most engaging page and carry the more important information. Each panel is a separate entity, information does not link to the next page, it should be in chunks with subheadings so that each piece can be read independently. However, the brochure should appear as a unified whole with words and graphics.

The way the brochure is arranged or formatted should match its purpose and its readers. It could be a question and answer format, have short paragraphs or be diagrammatic. The brochure may also be integrated into other materials such as the website, and should be similar in style, content, and format. Other promotional writing includes flyers, which are a single sheet and more like a print advertisement, and posters which are a larger version and used for display.

Advertorials are considered paid for editorial. They usually reflect the same format and style of editorial but the space has been paid for and therefore the copy is written and approved by the organization. However, the journalist or staff copywriters may write the text to ensure it is in line with their own editorial but the practitioner may need to approve the copy. This means approving its accuracy and ensuring the messages are clear and the correct visuals are used along with correct corporate logos, colours, and trademarks, as appropriate. However, the style is much more promotional than editorial and the headline needs to be catchy.

Presentation skills

Presentations in public relations may be to a live audience or may be a video conference, a chatroom, a radio or television broadcast, or a telephone presentation. Presentations can vary, they can be purely spoken, use various media, use PowerPoint, or be impromptu talks, lectures, or speeches. Public relations often requires practitioners to give impromptu presentations to their own organization, to a client, and to the media.

A presentation owes its success to preparation. This means identifying the reaction you want from the audience, developing a structure, knowing how it will be delivered, how long it will take and then rehearsing in order to be in control and more able to elicit the desired audience reaction.

Preparation

Identify the audience, their age, what they do, and what they want or will expect. What is in the presentation for them?

Think about the rule of threes.

1. The introduction. Tell them what they are going to be told about, how long it will take, and when they can ask questions. The impact the speaker has is decided in the first 4–7 seconds. A presentation can start with a controversial question, a quote or a loud noise to attract attention.

2. The body of the presentation. This is the core content and is outlined in the introduction.

3. The conclusion. This reviews the points made in the body of the presentation.

Each of these three sections is divided into threes to keep a structure. This means three parts for the introduction, three parts for the body, and three parts for the conclusion. Once the outline is developed add more information such as examples, statistics, and hyperlinks.

PowerPoint and the rule of sixes

When using PowerPoint there is a 6:6:6 rule of effective and professional PowerPoint presentations. That is, six slides, of no more than six bullet points, of up to six words per bullet point. The first slide should contain the title of the paper, the presenter's name, and the institutional logo. The PowerPoint can have a design, animation, and background, as long as they are not gimmicky, clichéd, or too cluttered. It is best not to use capitals as it makes a slide too hard to read—people read through identifying the shape of a word and capitals give all words a similar rectangular shape.

Delivering the presentation

The presentation should start with a strong opening; this could be a question to establish rapport, respect, and authority. The presenter's body language affects how people respond so instead of trying to look at everyone, the presenter needs to divide their audience into thirds and visualize a plant in each section. Then move their eyes to and from each imaginary plant. This ensures there is no staring at one person but covers the whole audience. A presenter should also look at an individual's nose, instead of looking directly at an individual's eyes; this still gives the impression of looking at their eyes but is less confrontational. The presenter should also smile throughout the presentation. It is helpful to get audience participation; even simply getting someone to come up to the front of the room can improve the dynamic. Other ways of achieving participation are getting people to raise their hands to answer a survey-type question; asking the audience to do something physical such as clapping, standing, or jumping; or asking them to find out the opinion on the topic from the person beside them.

Also, it is necessary to use the same language as the audience uses, for example, use scientific language for scientists, but avoid jargon. If a presenter's voice is too quiet they will need to throw their voice. This can be practised through thinking of the voice as a small ball and when speaking throw it out of the mouth to the back of the room. Practising speaking using lots of different energy will help the speaker to communicate enthusiastically and show excitement.

Index cards are good prompts to jot down key points. Alternatively, the PowerPoint print-out is useful which allows notes to be written alongside each slide; however, many sheets of paper can make the presenter look unprepared and be distracting.

Rehearsing a presentation is necessary in order to know it well. This can also help to identify if there is too much information. It is important to get the audience wanting more information—don't be guilty of giving them too much. Rehearsal is effective through reading a sentence, then putting the script down and speaking it out loud. This should be continued until the end. However, if it becomes tedious it can be left for a while and continued later.

All members in a team presentation must make sure they pay attention to whoever is speaking. It is very distracting if one of the team members in the presentation is looking bored or gazing out the window, appearing disinterested in what the speaker is saying. An effective way to end a presentation is when the last speaker hands over to someone else to conclude as this rounds off the presentation.

Meetings

Business meetings are another form of group presentation and have a standard procedure. They follow an agenda which is distributed to attendees in advance of the meeting and also state the time and place of the meeting and topics to be discussed. Attendees are those who are invited, it is not correct simply to turn up uninvited at a meeting but is important to go if invited. The meeting is run by a nominated leader called a 'chair' who takes attendees through the agenda and brings in other information on these topics. Invitees send the chair information they want discussed or provide information on the agenda topics and the chair will bring up this information at the meeting and ask the relevant attendee to speak about it. When attendees want to speak they need to ask the chair if they can and then address the chair. It is inappropriate to have conversations with other members during a meeting, unless this is facilitated by the chair.

Most meetings start with a review of attendees. Non-attendees should have sent their apologies to the chair, and these are announced at the start of the meeting and noted in the minutes. The meeting then gains agreement from the attendees that the minutes from the last meeting are accurate. Matters arising from that meeting, such as the progress on actions, are then discussed followed by other topics listed on the agenda.

All meetings allow for a topic at the end of the meeting called 'any other business', this means that issues relevant to the meeting but not on the agenda can be raised. Often meetings only discuss any other business that has been sent to the chair several days in advance of the meeting.

The meeting concludes when the chair announces that the meeting has come to an end and agrees a date for the next meeting. During the meeting someone must take notes to record how each topic on the agenda has been discussed and note any actions arising from them. The minutes will then go to every participant to read them and agree that they are an accurate version of the meeting.

Social business

Public relations involves building relationships with stakeholders. Many business meetings take place as informal events without any written agenda and a practitioner may find themselves taking clients to the opera, or going to dinner at a smart restaurant, or just socializing at a media function. Nevertheless, there will be business obligations and it is important before going to an event to know what is the desired business outcome and what is expected. Practitioners need to ensure that they know the start time and what to take with them, who else will be there and to have planned ahead as to what to wear.

A public relations practitioner is expected to have social skills and often these simply mean being able to listen to others, asking people about themselves, and getting them to start talking. It can be ideal to make a comment about what is going on and ask a question—as long as it is an open question where people have to answer more than yes or no. Also, as Yeung (2008) suggests, a listener needs to show reciprocity through disclosing some things about themselves which encourages rapport. Usually a dinner or social function with business associates starts off with social chit chat and then proceeds to a business discussion. It is important a practitioner has some social conversation such as what is in the media and have an opinion. However, it is not a good idea to pretend to know about a subject and in that case it is much better merely to show a polite interest.

If someone looks interested by smiling and having shoulders straight, chin up, and a positive posture and expression, people are drawn to them. Conversely, a frown or a look of anxiety will keep people away but showing an interested expression when someone is talking suggests listening. Business conversations can be daunting therefore practitioners need to focus their attention on the other person and make an effort to listen effectively to what they are saying while also contributing to the conversation.

When nervous, people tend to take short and fast shallow breaths. Breathing from the diaphragm will help to address this, that is, taking slow deep breaths from the stomach. Inhale to a count of four and exhale to a count of four. Breathe in through your nose and the abdomen will rise. Several minutes after doing this can give a feeling of being more relaxed and confident.

PR Tool

A Style Book

Source: Courtesy of Sharon Wheeler

Most organizations have their own particular style or way of writing and presenting their material and this is part of managing the image of the organization. The following is a style book which gives guidelines to ensure acceptable clear and concise writing.

Abbreviations: unless they're well known, such as BBC and IRA, spell them out in full the first time. Don't put full points between letters. With police and military titles, use them in full the first time, then abbreviate—Superintendent Sharon Wheeler becomes Supt Wheeler. Latin abbreviations, such as etc, eg, and ie, have no place in copy. Be careful about shortening Gloucestershire to Glos—you can't do that in copy, and in headlines it depends on the context and how serious the story is.

Addresses: leave out house numbers, but obtain road name, district, and town.

Advice/advise: see licence.

Affect: *affect* is used as a verb—'It won't affect our chances.' *Effect* is almost always a noun—'this will have no effect on the outcome.' The only exception is the verb *to effect*, meaning to bring about (to effect a change).

Americanisms: when a word ends in 'ize' this is generally the American spelling. British spelling tends to use 'ise'—make sure you use socialise/realise/apologise and so on. Check your computer's spellchecker is set to English (UK). This book uses 'ize' spellings because that is the house style used by the publisher, Oxford University Press.

Apostrophes: apostrophes are used to denote the possessive (Sharon's style book, football clubs' fines) or to indicate a missing letter (can't, wouldn't).

Note: its for the possessive (the cat scratched its back) but it's for it is. Also note: women's, children's as these are already plural. You don't need an apostrophe for MP's when you mean MPs or 1990's unless you're talking about something belonging to that year.

Brevity: every word must pay its way:

- was freed NOT walked free from court
- met NOT met with
- firstly NOT in the first instance.

Capital letters: use sparingly—for proper names (Sharon Wheeler, University of Gloucestershire), roads (Acacia Avenue), special names and titles (Cheltenham Borough Council, the Prime Minister). Note, though, the city council, the planning committee. Use initial capitals for titles of books, plays, and films (Return of the Native, The Merchant of Venice, Apocalypse Now)—and you don't need quote marks round them.

Cliches: avoid them like the plague. Don't even touch them with a bargepole ...

Colon: a colon introduces a series or a list and is not used not after the verb 'to be' or after prepositions.

Common mistakes:

- all right NOT alright
- a lot NOT alot
- different from NOT different to or than
- less than one and with quantities, fewer than with people or individual items—less than £50, fewer than 20 people
- compare is usually followed by with, unless you are likening something (shall I compare thee to a summer's day)
- centre on NOT centre around
- register office NOT registry office

- St John Ambulance NOT St John's Ambulance
- councillor—someone elected to a council to represent you. Counsellor—someone who counsels you
- people don't die of AIDS—they die from an AIDS-related illness.

Currency: this is one of the occasions where figures below ten don't have to be written out in words. Style is £5 or £5 billion. If you refer to amounts in other countries' currencies, such as dollars, or euros, the same applies, but it's usual to add the sterling amount in brackets afterwards.

Dates: 11 November not 11th of November or November the 11th.

Disabled: people are not disabled. They have a disability.

Hyphens: use as follows:

- to make the meaning of a word clear: re-form and reform, re-sign and resign
- when two vowels come together awkwardly: re-elect, pre-empt
- to separate lower case and capitals: anti-American, pro-British
- to make it clear where the accent falls on a word: co-respondent, re-elect
- with prefixes: all, anti, ex, far, fellow, non, pro, self, and semi
- in compound words: half-share, out-of-date.

Inverted commas: use double quote marks for quotes. Try to avoid using single inverted commas for partial quotes—can you use reported speech instead? Use them sparingly to avoid confusion.

Lie and lay: *to lie* means to recline, to lie down; *to lay* means to place an object somewhere.

Less: applies to objects and not to quantity—'There is less wind today than yesterday.' BUT ... it is not 'There are less people here today than yesterday.' The correct word there is fewer—'There are fewer people here today than yesterday.'

Licence: c is for nouns, s is for verbs. 'The licensing authority ...' 'Applying for a licence ...' This applies to all such words, including advice/advise and practice/practise.

Myself: almost invariably misused. It is not 'John and myself are going for a walk'—it's 'John and I ...' It is not 'The awards for best lecturers have gone to John and myself ...'—it's '... have gone to John and me.'

Numbers: One to ten written out in words. If it's 11 and above, use figures. Try to avoid starting a sentence with a figure. If you really have to, it's 'Twelve men have been arrested ...'

Over-used words: ban, blast, rap, bid, probe, boost, shock, sensation. Avoid journalese.

Per cent: put percentages into context—instead of saying '25 per cent of the population eat chocolate daily', say 'a quarter of the population eat chocolate daily.' Note that per cent should always be written out, rather than using %.

Practice/practise: see licence.

Quotation marks: see also inverted commas. Don't close quote marks if the quotation continues in the next paragraph. Full stops, commas, question marks, and exclamation marks should be placed inside the quotation marks.

Sexism: a female over the age of about 18 is a woman, not a lady or a girl. Use chairman/chairwoman, or spokesman/spokeswoman—chairperson or spokesperson is clumsy. It's firefighters, not firemen, and cleaner, not cleaning lady.

Split infinitive: there is great debate about this, but the general rule is don't! Make it 'to attack quickly' rather than 'to quickly attack'. The best-known split infinitive is Star Trek's 'to boldly go ...'

Stage: we don't stage demonstrations. We don't stage protests. We only stage theatre productions. Otherwise we demonstrate or protest.

Substitute: something is substituted FOR not BY.

Suffering: people do not suffer from Parkinson's disease, or AIDS, or anything else. They have it. After all, you don't suffer from red hair, or being left-handed or being short-sighted.

Tautology: this is saying the same thing twice over in different words. Something can't be very unique! Backing NOT full backing. Priority NOT top priority.

There/their/they're: often confused. *There* is an adverb (in or at that place or position): 'There you are', 'Put it down there', OR a noun (that place): 'She lives near there.' *Their* is a possessive pronoun, meaning 'of themselves'. 'That's their house over there.' *They're* is a contraction of they are—note the apostrophe to denote the missing letter!

Titles: always include people's first names, then refer to them by title—Sharon Wheeler, then Ms Wheeler. Exception is sport. Paul Gascoigne, then Gascoigne, or when someone has been found guilty in court. If it's a light story, or one involving children and teenagers, use first names.

Try: you try to do something, not try and, as in 'We will try to reach a peaceful solution.' You wouldn't dream of saying 'We are trying and reach a peaceful solution.'

Your/you're: often confused. *Your* means belonging to you: 'Is that your notebook?' *You're* is a contraction of you are. Note the apostrophe to denote the missing letter!

Summary

Business and media communication can be verbal or non-verbal and has variable effects depending on the sender, message, channel, and receiver. All these are affected by how we use language, how it is transmitted, and the relationship between those who are communicating. This takes into account cultural differences as well as the reason for the communication.

Writing is the key form of communication in public relations and can be very persuasive and powerful. Media and business writing have their own particular style to attract their target publics.

Communication follows the three elements of communications: ethos which means it must establish credibility, logos which means it must create a reasoned argument and therefore based on evidence and show objective analysis, and pathos which means it appeals to the emotions, therefore the practitioner must identify what emotional reaction needs to be created.

Public relations writing must be planned in order to be easy to read, use a recognized style that fits its purpose and its organization, and have a layout that makes it attractive to read and reflects the organization.

All communication must fit into a legal and ethical framework. Business writing must be aware of legalities, such as observing confidences about business practices and information. In addition, practitioners are expected to have a duty of confidence about business ideas or developments. Copyright must also be adhered to as any published writing and visual material has an owner and therefore their information cannot be used without their approval. There is also a legal framework that protects an organization's or individual's reputation, and broadly speaking, it is considered libel if anything defamatory is written and slander if anything defamatory is said. To ensure that the organization is represented correctly, anything submitted to the media must first be approved legally by the organization, this includes any quotations used.

Effective writing must be planned with recognizable layout and style for its purpose. Media writing generally uses short and punchy paragraphs, sometimes with only one or two sentences as opposed to business writing which may have longer and more complex paragraphs. Paragraphs help the reader to move thorough information by starting one where the other left off which helps to unite the whole document. Subheadings are also useful in this and can be used as a point of reference later.

Grammar used well makes a document more readable and more credible, therefore an understanding of nouns, pronouns, adjectives, and verbs will help the practitioner to construct a strong writing style. In addition, using active expressions makes sentences more effective and more interesting than those with passive expressions. In addition, simple expressions, rather than convoluted impressive sentences, have more impact and create a precise understanding.

Reports are a common form of writing and set out verifiable facts in a useful format for the reader and aimed at readers with a specific interest in the subject. They are a legal document and have an official purpose such as being a report on a meeting, a research project, a media analysis, or a proposal. They have a set format which always highlights who the report is to and who it is from, its date, and its purpose. The introduction, body, and conclusion are always very clearly marked in order that the reader is guided through the report.

A business plan is a form of report and must form an integral part of a practitioner's research when developing a situational analysis. Familiarity with the contents of a business plan will help the practitioner to develop public relations objectives which relate to the overall business goals.

Online information follows the same rules as other written information but uses sound, images, and hyperlinks and interactivity. In addition, the content needs to be changed and updated regularly to ensure that it stays attractive to readers.

Presentations are usually based on written material and developed into PowerPoint slides and other visual material. They rely on structure and audience knowledge to be effective. Presentations have the rule of six—six bullet points and six words per point. However, practitioners are often required to be able to present effectively in a business meeting and in social business situations which require interpersonal skills as well as knowledge of business settings and formalities. Business meetings have their own specific style of behaviour, such as being managed by a chairperson, and all participants are expected to adhere to this. In addition, meetings follow a written agenda and a meeting report—called minutes—summarizes the meeting and the actions agreed by the participants.

The way information is presented and written is a crucial part of an organization's image. Therefore most organizations have a style book which provides guidelines on how to present the information so that it represents the organization. A practitioner is frequently involved in the developing of a style guide. This is because a practitioner is expected to know the organization and its objectives and be able to ensure that its communication is acceptable, clear, and concise as well as reflecting and improving its reputation.

Discussion points

A. Making summaries

Access Twitter and identify research reports summarized in brief and the web link to them. How effective is the short Twitter summary in making you want to read the report?

Go to websites of environmental organizations such as National Heritage and the Royal Society for Protection of Birds and check the summaries of their research reports. How effective are these in making you want to access the report? Could they be shortened further to use on Twitter?

B. Personal space

Select three people in your seminar, one who you know well, another who you know reasonably well, and another you do not know at all.

Stand facing each other and start talking. Do you notice any difference in the distance you stand apart? See if you can continue the experiment with other people you meet.

C. Meeting skills

Use your classroom seminar time to improve your meeting skills. Use the following criteria and complete the grid in Table 9.2 at the end of the seminar, circling the number and adding comments, then ask a peer to mark it and compare results,. See how you seem to your peer(s) in the seminar and assess how your peers see you.

Criteria

1. Punctuality—being on time and greeting people.

2. Participation—raising issues, being engaged with the topic, contributing to the discussion, looking interested.

3. Listening/not interrupting.

4. Reaching a consensus—recommending ideas or solutions.

Table 9.2 **Criteria for meeting skills**

Criteria	Own evaluation	Peer evaluation
Punctuality	1 2 3 4 5	1 2 3 4 5
Participation	1 2 3 4 5	1 2 3 4 5
Listening	1 2 3 4 5	1 2 3 4 5
Reaching a consensus	1 2 3 4 5	1 2 3 4 5

D. Writing

Take an average sized article from the newspaper. Identify the grammatical parts of the sentence. How does the use of grammar make the article concise and interesting?

References

Bivins, T. (2005) *Public Relations Writing* (5th edn). New York: McGraw Hill

European Rhetoric (2010) 'Aristotle's Rhetoric'. Available at: http://www.european-rhetoric.com/rhetoric-101/modes-persuasion-aristotle

Hartley, P. and Bruckmann, C. (2002) *Business Communication*. London: Routledge

Holden, M. (2010) 'Chelsea's Abromovich Wins Gambling Slur Damages, Reuters Online. 18 March. Available at: http://uk.reuters.com/article/idUKTRE62HIQQ20100318

Jones, H. and Benson, C. (2006) *Publishing Law* (3rd edn). Abingdon: Routledge

Mersham, G., Theunissen, P., and Peart, J. (2010) *Public Relations and Communication Management: An Aoteoroa/New Zealand Perspective*. Auckland: Pearson

Phillips, D. and Young, P. (2009) *Online Public Relations: A Practice Guide to Developing an Online Strategy in the World of Social Media* (2nd edn). London: Kogan Page

Plain English Campaign (2010) http://www.plainenglish.co.uk/

Seely, J. (2002) *Writing Reports*. Oxford: Oxford University Press

Sussans, J. (1998) *How to Write Effective Reports* (3rd edn). Hampshire: Gower

Yeung, R. (2008) *Confidence: The Art of Getting What You Want*. Harlow: Pearson

part
C

The broader context

Issues and crisis management

10

Learning outcomes

1. To be able to define an issue and crisis, consider what contributes towards creating them, and when they can arise, based on an understanding of the internal and external environment and case studies.

2. Understand and apply risk benefit analysis and probability/likelihood models in order to identify issues and crises and assess their priority and impact.

3. Be able to apply the steps to managing an issue and a crisis by reviewing different approaches and influences such as globalization, advocacy, and digital media.

4. Understand the lifecycle of an issue and the possible intervention at each of its stages as well as identifying issues arising during the growth stages of small and medium enterprises.

5. Examine the changing environment of increasing transparency and activism and how issues are multi-faceted and require creating an involving approach with stakeholders.

6. Be able to participate in developing plans that can be tailored to a wide range of issues and crises.

Practitioner Insight

Adam Lewis
Director Immediate Future

Adam is a director of Immediate Future, the London-based social media and online PR agency specializing in measurable social media activity for blue-chip companies worldwide. Adam provides strategic communications counsel across a broad range of disciplines, including digital, corporate communications, and issues management. He specializes in integrating social media into communication programmes.

Adam has advised some of the world's biggest brands including Shell, Bacardi Ltd, Sony Ericsson, Vestas, and Coca-Cola. Adam has directed campaigns which have won multiple industry awards including PRCA, European Excellence, and Hollis. Previously Adam was a director in the digital, design, and brand team, Burson-Marsteller and also launched the sponsorship practice for Burson-Marsteller UK. He has worked with Luther Pendragon and in-house at healthcare company BUPA.

How do you define an issue?

An issue is an event that may have a negative impact on corporate reputation if it reached the 'outside world'. It requires an issues management process to assess the potential impact on the business, identify relevant stakeholders, and develop a communications plan to deal with them.

What issue have you worked on that has been the most interesting/successfully managed/challenging?

We can't discuss the details of our work in this area as it is confidential. Some of our best work has been helping client to keep issues out of the media. This can be done by carefully planning the key messages and then getting the strategy right in terms of the way it is communicated to stakeholders.

What are the key actions to deal with a crisis?

A crisis is characterized by three things: surprise, lack of information, and a loss of control. You can never predict when a crisis will break but you can prepare by establishing systems and teams to be deployed when a crisis breaks. The crisis management team has to manage the response of the business crisis both in terms of operations and communications.

How has social media affected issues and crisis management?

Bad news can travel very quickly in the socially networked world we now live in. Furthermore, it can't be controlled. This requires that businesses adapt their crisis management plans. For example, they need social media listening tools to pick up conversations that might be a pre-cursor to the crisis breaking out to the wider world. They need a plan to use their own social media channels (ie YouTube channels) to communicate their response to a crisis.

Do you think issues management should be an integral part of a communications plan?

Yes. An issues management process should be a core part of the communications strategy of any business. The best laid, proactive PR plans can be derailed by a reputational issue hitting the media.

What advice would you give students who wanted to get into issues and crisis management public relations?

Generally speaking, crisis and issues management specialists have a lot of experience. My advice would be to build up a good grounding in PR and communications first (in particular media relations) before thinking about specializing in crisis or issues management.

10.1 Definition

An organization is increasingly open to scrutiny by its publics and is expected to be open about its social and ethical accountability. People have expectations of what an organization should do and when these expectations are not met this can lead to what is called an issue. With better education and greater awareness of what is going on globally, helped by communication technology, people have more knowledge about business and how it affects the world and are therefore more able to assess an organization and its impact. There is now more pressure from publics to make sure organizations are not only profitable but are also socially aware, have ethical practices, and are environmentally responsible. The phrase, 'people, planet and profit' sums up the areas in which organizations are expected to achieve equally. When an organization is seen to falter in any aspects of this area, which is also called the triple bottom line, there is a risk of an issue occurring which can damage an organization's reputation and thereby affect its overall success.

In addition, organizations are under pressure to communicate what they are doing and to deliver constant and updated information for the 24 hour media. They also need to be aware of the fast development of individuals networking online to form pressure groups and gain support. Public relations practitioners have to work quickly to prevent and resolve issues by building lasting relationships between stakeholders and the organization to ensure an investment for the future.

An issue can be considered a genuine or potential risk to an organization's reputation and must be managed to prevent any damage. Regester and Larkin (2002: 43) define an **issue** as 'a gap between corporate practice and stakeholder expectations.' That is, the difference between what a corporation does and says and what its stakeholders expect it should be doing and saying.

Gregory (2002: 144) defines an issue as being when the reputation, finances, or trading of an organization is damaged or interrupted. Both issues and crises are potentially damaging. Unmanaged issues become threats to an organization's reputation, its most valuable asset.

Heath (cited Pratt 2001: 337) saw issues planning as part of an organization's strategic planning that requires issues monitoring and analysis and ensures organizations not only influence their publics but also change their own practices as they become more responsive to their publics' interests.

Usually a **crisis** is an issue that has not been resolved, has had negative effects or is a situation that has developed suddenly. Fearn-Banks (2001: 480) defines a crisis as 'a major occurrence with a potentially negative outcome affecting an organization as well as its publics, services, products or good name.'

Griffin (2008: 80) defines a crisis as something that happens suddenly and is an acute risk to reputation, it 'leads to intense scrutiny and puts your organization in the spotlight for all the wrong reasons.'

Seeger et al (2001: 156) argue that the chaos and organization, 'disruption and renewal' of a crisis are a necessary part of an organization's lifecycle and can be viewed as an opportunity for development.

Developing corporate responsibility programmes is an integral part of issues management as it builds the organization's reputation and addresses ongoing issues. Corporate responsibility is discussed in detail in the next chapter.

When can an issue or crisis arise?

Issues can be identified from a situational analysis and categorized as emerging from political, economic, social, and technological backgrounds (see PEST analysis on the music industry in chapter 4). Pratt (2001) argues that the first rule of issues management is to understand the internal and external environment of both the organization and its products and services. This analysis can help to look for triggers that may lead to emerging issues. For example, an issue can arise if there are demographic changes which mean that there is no longer a market for a product. Technological developments can mean something can be created which is better than an existing product or service. A car with an improved safety profile may outsell its competitors, creating an issue for them.

Environmental factors such as an earthquake, storms, or lightning strikes can damage an organization, its buildings, or impact upon it through affecting the people and services around it (see Figure 10.1). For example, the Indian Ocean tsunami in

Fig 10.1
Natural environmental factors can create a crisis for an organization

Source: Copyright OUP

2004 created a crisis in the tourist industry through causing a massive loss of lives and homes as well as destroying hotels and the infrastructure of the affected countries.

Potential changes in legislation may mean an organization needs to change. For example, impending new health and safety regulations can mean that buildings need to be updated. Competition can mean that an organization's products or services are outdated, seen as more expensive, or less efficient, a faulty product or service can also become an issue, for example a medicine could be launched with side effects which had not been previously identified. Published research can highlight the deficiencies of a product or service, or even announce a competitor. A change in the performance of an organization can lead to an issue as can mergers or takeovers and other organizational or staff changes can trigger dissatisfaction.

Scandals generally lead to an organizational crisis. For example, in late 2009 the world-class golfer, Tiger Woods, believed to be the world's wealthiest athlete and estimated to earn about $100 million a year in endorsements, confessed to marital infidelity. A study found that during the scandal, the companies which had sponsored Woods dropped in value, meaning a crisis not only for Woods' own reputation but also for the organizations and their investors (Eurosport 2009).

Differentiating issue management from crisis management

Issues management and crisis management are closely related in the pre and post-crisis stages (Seeger et al 2001: 157). In the pre-crisis stage there is research monitoring, identifying, and communicating about an issue and developing perceptions in order to minimize the threat. The post-crisis stage examines what happens and usually leads to new practices being developed.

Griffin argues that although there seems to more space and time with issues management than with crises management this can often be false comfort. Although some issues can become crises the issues can damage an organization's reputation if left too long. Issues management deals with chronic risks and crisis management deals with acute risks but both 'protect and enhance reputation through the potentially bad times' (2008: 111).

Regester and Larkin (2005: 42) define issues management as being more anticipatory than crisis management as it needs to identify the potential for change and influence decisions relating to that change before the issue has had a negative effect on the organization. They see issues management as predicting issues and getting to know publics in order to close the gap between stakeholders' (publics) expectations and the organization's activity. Alternatively, crisis management is more action-oriented and reactive, dealing with a situation after it has affected the organization.

Issues management involves looking into the future to identify potential trends and events that _may_ influence the way an organization is able to operate but which currently _may_ have little real focus, probably no sense of urgency and an unclear reference in time.

(Regester and Larkin 2005: 42)

PR practitioners need to be responsible for anticipating issues, putting together issues management teams, and presenting the best ways to deal with issues. All these activities involve:

- Being aware of the organization's goals and monitoring the environment to assess what could affect these.
- Identifying the issues and developing different scenarios for each issue in order to explore the possible outcomes and how to mitigate or prevent them.
- Identifying and prioritizing publics and building relationships and ongoing collaboration, especially with the most important and influential publics.
- Identifying spokespeople for the organization and ensuring they are well trained and briefed in issues management.
- Running regular scenario planning with budgets and timing in order to identify and manage emerging issues.
- Ensuring processes are in place such as media information and statements, internal and external communication, and monitoring to report progress of issues management to the organization.

Issues are not always negative

Regester and Larkin (2005: 42) argue that issues are not always negative as they can identify new opportunities within the organization and can be harnessed to shape the organization positively. They claim effective issues management can increase market share, enhance corporate reputation, save money, and build relationships with stakeholders.

Griffin (2008) suggests that issues management should be about focusing on the positive aspect of any risk or change in the organization rather than looking at the negative aspects. He also encourages organizations to own an issue and shape it. Griffin cites the issue where anti-Nestle campaigners argued that mothers in third world countries were mixing its infant formula powder with contaminated water. Nestle engaged with their concerns and developed guidelines (which limited its own promotions) and participated in a World Health Organization code of marketing for breast milk substitutes. Griffin argues this was a defensive stance and was not only difficult to enforce worldwide but focused on what was negative about infant formula rather than what was positive. Griffin argues that it was only when Nestle met with activists at student union meetings and presented the value of infant formula products that it took control of its reputation.

Issues management means that practitioners need to know how to control the issue and the news agenda to create a positive outcome. For example, British Airways handled the crash-landing of a Boeing 777 at Heathrow in January 2009, by moving the organization away from the issue. It praised and detailed the captain's skill in landing the plane and emphasized the flight crew's role in saving the lives of 136 passengers, thus preventing it from being seen as a corporate disaster.

Issues vs crises

The development of an issue or a crisis can mean that the organization may have to create a new product or modify an old product. New legislation will have to be accommodated which can mean new safety measures or more testing on products, it may mean providing more education on procedures and allowing the public to learn more about safety procedures and product testing. In this way stakeholders will have more information which will help them to develop more realistic expectations.

Crisis planning requires a crisis management team which should include senior management and experts in public affairs, legal matters, operations and security, and finance, and all trained in group decision making and media relations. Griffin (2008) believes that issues management teams can be much smaller, as immediate action is not required by people running the business (see Table 10.1). A smaller planning team then works through facilitating ownership of the issue by the organization, empowering decisions, and guiding the level of responsibility.

Fearn-Banks (2001: 480) defines crisis management as strategic planning to prevent and respond to a crisis or negative occurrence, 'a process that removes some of the risks and understanding and allows the organization to be in greater control of its destiny'.

Table 10.1 **Identifying issues and crises**

Issues PR	Crisis PR
Addresses potential matters which are a threat to the organization but which may also be a positive influence in leading to changes	Addresses existing disasters facing the organization
Deals with ongoing matters	Deals with acute risks
Not action-orientated—focuses on anticipating and planning, requires ongoing research and monitoring	More action-orientated
More time to consider a plan	Reactive, deals with situations after they have become public knowledge
Looks to future to identify potential trends and events that may influence it	Situation must be dealt with immediately
Publics consider issues as negative aspects of an organization	Window of goodwill if it is an accident—a crisis may have the public on side if it is an accident
Plans in a developmental stage	Clear focus with finite actions and publics
Key teams developing clear guidelines and drawing on expert knowledge in the organization.	Needs a large active senior management team with specialist expertise and all trained and able to respond using prepared statements
Language is clear and not emotional	Emotive language used
An issues may never happen and can be prevented or it can become a chronic issue with ongoing consequences	A crisis has happened and has an effect on the organization's development
An issue can influence an organization's development	

Case Study

A crisis in the natural health industry

Source: Courtesy of Pegasus PR

A carefully constructed crisis management campaign by Pegasus PR for the Health Food Manufacturers' Association (HFMA), the leading trade association for the natural health in-dustry manufacturers and suppliers in the UK, succeeded in positioning this organization as the main source of comment for the sector.

Twenty-four hours warning

In 2008, the HFMA was presented with 24 hours warning that a negative review would be published by the Cochrane Collaboration, on the use of antioxidant vitamins and minerals for the primary prevention of mortality. The Cochrane Collaboration is a consumer advo-cacy group which claims to summarize the results of available healthcare studies and the effectiveness of healthcare interventions.

This review had the potential to have a negative effect on the health food industry. The HFMA had to defend the industry and position itself as the authority for the sector.

Research

At the start of the campaign a media audit revealed that there was low awareness of the HFMA as an industry commentator. In addition, its impartiality was questioned as it represented companies across the wider natural health sector.

In order to address these weaknesses in the face of the impending crisis, an HFMA expert panel was established to provide unbiased, timely, and accurate commentary for the media on issues relevant to the industry. Statements were prepared and approved by the HFMA legal team.

Briefing of expert panel

The HFMA expert panel were briefed and trained to respond to the media attention expected to occur on publication of the Cochrane review. An HFMA statement which gave an expert opinion in response to the report was forwarded to the media. Media interviews were also given by the HFMA Expert Panel.

Setting the agenda

On the day of the Cochrane review publication there was blanket media coverage of the HFMA's key messages on all media, which showed that the HFMA had set the agenda, and the HFMA panel carried out interviews. Immediately following the publication, HFMA sent the media a more in-depth scientific response which received high media coverage.

The HFMA's decision to proactively rebut the Cochrane review in advance of its publication assisted in overcoming any negativity of the story. Following this up with a scientific paper enabled more in-depth coverage resulting in a more considered approach. Most importantly, the HFMA was positioned as the leading source of impartial and thought-provoking commentary for the sector.

As a result of the campaign, the HFMA and its expert panel was positioned at the forefront of the minds of the media, making it a voice piece for the sector and the first point of call for journalists in the event of a breaking natural health story.

10.2 Theoretical and historical development

The phrase 'issue management' was first introduced by an American, Howard Chase, in 1976, who believed that organizational change was needed to address issues and a network of relationships was necessary to deal with issues in an organization. His research identified the processes of anticipating, analysing, and preparing for an issue in order to enable the organization to respond or even gain some advantage (Jaques 2009).

Chase Jones Model

The Chase Jones model developed in 1977 forms the basis of issues management today, and comprises five primary steps (see Table 10.2) which require interaction with stakeholders (Jaques 2008).

Table 10.2   **Five primary steps to issues management according to Chase Jones model**

Identification	Analyse trends
	Compare to organization's goals and objectives
Analysis	Identify origin of the issues
	Review existing research and current actions
	How does it affect organization? Review strengths and weaknesses of the organization
Strategy	Is the organization reactive?
	Can it influence the environment and lead the issue
Action	Allocate resources to achieving the action
Evaluation	Monitor the situation against desired results, noting the progression of the issue and its effect

Source: Jaques (2008)

Regester and Larkin (2002: 17) state that issues management is 'about assessing and communicating the possible hazards associated with a particular process relative to the safeguards and benefits which it offers.'

However, the impact of an issue varies with different people therefore a stakeholder analysis needs to be carried out to see how each public is affected and how they interpret the issue (see chapter 5). People have their own attitudes formed by social and cultural factors which influence their behaviour and are difficult to change. For example, in November 2009 the UK government launched a campaign to tackle the issue of the high number of teenage pregnancies. According to experts, the reason that UK teenage pregnancy is twice that of Europe is because British teenagers do not talk about contraception or sex in the same open way as do their European counterparts (Dade 2009).

Identifying how much an issue affects an organization decides how it can be prioritized, that is how urgent it is and how much should be spent on it. The following provides some guidelines and models for identifying the impact of an issue and the process to go through in analysing it.

Guidelines to issues analysis

1. Identifying an issue

The practitioner needs to find out the threats and weaknesses of the organization and what is going on in the environment around it. The issue could be natural, man made, or environmental. Categories such as corporate, local, and global help to categorize this as does a PEST analysis. Griffin (2008) emphasizes the need to categorize and prioritize an issue. He divides them into corporate issues arising from the running of the company and concerns products, corporate governance, and performance; global issues which concern other companies and may include environmental concerns, health matters, and ethical sourcing; local issues which affect a defined affected group such as employees or a community.

2. Analysing the risk based on probability and impact

Once identified, an issue may not even occur. However, it is vital the organization knows the risk that issues pose to the organization. A way of working this out is by balancing each risk against the likelihood of it occurring and the impact it will have on the organization. It requires a lot of intelligence gathering and also the use of a SWOT analysis (see chapter 4) to assess the organization itself and its ability to deal with the issue.

Analysing the risk based on impact and probability helps to define its priority The impact can then be categorized as low, medium, or high depending on what is motivating the risk. For example, a major earthquake in the UK has a high impact but low probability and unlikely to occur, therefore it will be a low priority. An example of whether to proceed with legal action faces the cell phone company, Nokia. The organization is no longer the sector leader over rivals in terms of product development and in 2009 Nokia alleged Apple had infringed its patents. Although there is a risk of a legal minefield with ongoing costs and legal technicalities it could be to Nokia's advantage, according to analysts. This is because Nokia has been developing handsets from the very beginning of the industry and built up a huge stock of patents which Apple may well have used to some extent (Young 2009).

Assessing the impact of an issue through comparing its probability to its impact using the diagram in Figure 10.2 can help to assess its risk to the organization.

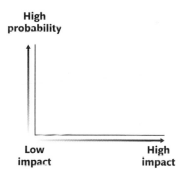

Fig 10.2
Risk analysis

3. The response of the organization

How much damage the issue can cause means knowing the vulnerabilities and likely response of the organization. This can be clarified by knowing the timings involved, the likely costs and the actions to take. The timings include knowing when the issue may occur, when the organization should respond, when it is able to respond—that is, when factors are in place to prevent an issue—and when it can no longer respond. It is also important to be aware of the warning signs of the issue. For example, a staff complaint is a warning sign but on the internet it can gain a huge following so should be dealt with immediately. Therefore, it is important to know which issues need to be addressed and when.

The cost is a factor in identifying the impact of an issue; if too much expense is required to address the issue it may not be feasible to do so. Before anything is started a budget needs to be agreed in order to be able to address an action.

The actions to take include knowing what the organization can do to prevent the issue from happening or from creating damage. Much of this depends on the vulnerabilities of the organization worked out through the SWOT analysis and that may be the time to address any weaknesses. Actions include identifying, briefing, and training the organization's spokespeople to communicate with the media. Media materials must be developed; and these include statements, video footage and photographs, website development, all of which must have the organization's legal approval. Third parties need to be encouraged to show their support and relationships created with them well in advance of any issue.

4. Fallout

Every risk analysis must identify the lasting effects of an issue. Once it is dealt with does not mean an end to it, it could lie **dormant**. Conway et al (2007) argue that the dormant stage no longer happens as an issue can lurk on the internet. Once an issue appears on the internet it stays there forever, creating an ongoing residual risk for anyone researching the organization or issue. Table 10.3 can be used to record risk identification and its effects.

Table 10.3 **Analysing risk**

Issue	Likelihood	Impact	Response of organization	Fallout
	When may it occur Where may it occur	Who/what will be affected? Over what time?	Who is taking control? Media statement and material. Spokespeople (including third parties) briefed Identify and monitor organization's weaknesses	Ongoing damage Who/what may be affected Online presence

Risk benefit analysis

Risks are always taken in an organization and practitioners need to be aware of how choices are made about a risk. There is never a zero risk rate as it is always balanced by a benefit. The development and associated activity of all products and services of an organization carry some element of risk, so managing an issue could be simply about reducing its risk. Many corporate decisions are made with the knowledge that risks are being taken.

How to manage a risk is based on a risk versus benefit (reward) model. **Risk management** depends on the source of this information about risk. This model charts the potential rewards of strategic options against the associated risks and assesses the strategic options in order to allocate resources. It is also an effective way of comparing different types of projects in order to see what sort of benefit they give the organization over their risk (see Figure 10.3).

⊕ Go to the Online Resource Centre to access more charts showing the reward against the risk

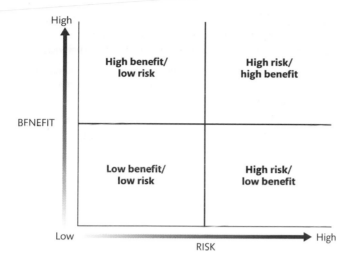

Fig 10.3
Risk benefit analysis

Risk or benefit in the music industry

Table 10.4 shows an analysis of the risk/benefit in changing how a music producer can reach new markets. Some of the tactics have a high risk owing to their cost or other factors determined by those doing the risk analysis. That is why issues and risk assessment should involve a diverse range of specialists throughout the organization in order to create a more accurate assessment of how much impact an issue is likely to have.

Fig 10.4
The music industry needs to find new ways to earn

Source: Copyright OUP

Table 10.4 **Risk benefit analysis for the music recording industry in reaching new markets**

Benefit	Low risk	Medium risk	High risk
High benefit	Attract fans through promotions Create and sustain online community	Develop new markets	Hide subscriptions to music in mobile devices
Medium benefit	Ensure media play music		Sue companies responsible for offering 'free' downloading
Low benefit		Reach DVD buyers through communicating with 'games' buyers	Make it difficult to download any music

Lifecycle of an issue

An issue, according to a model developed by Hainsworth and Meng cited by Regester and Larkin (2005: 49), follows a lifecycle of potential, emerging, current, and resolution points (see Table 10.5).

Table 10.5 **Lifecycle of an issue**

Potential	Priority depends on its likelihood of happening and its impact. Be prepared.
Emerging: Appears in the media	Requires media monitoring and communicating with the media. Talking to advocacy groups and the media. But be aware that the issue can grow. Monitor the commercial, regulatory, and social environment. Prepare for action.
Becomes current	Action is required and is when the pressure is on the organization to resolve the issue.
Resolution	It may have been prevented, reduced, or dealt with if it became a crisis.

Source: Based on Regester and Larkin (2005)

Fearn-Banks (2001: 480) lists five stages of a crisis:

1. Prodromal—watching for warning signs.
2. Prevention—preparing and preventing to avoid the crisis.
3. Containment—limit the duration and damage of the crisis.
4. Recovery—returning to normalcy.
5. Learning—evaluate and determine what has been lost and gained to help identify future warning signs.

Case Study

Dealing with a crisis in the water industry

Source: Courtesy of Anglian Water

This case study explores Anglian Water's response to a water quality issue which required all water to be boiled (a 'boil warning') in the Pitsford area of Northamptonshire.

Preparation is crucial to responding effectively to any incident. Issues with water quality are a huge concern for Anglian Water, and to tackle this they have developed a stakeholder pack and emergency response strategy for their areas of operation. The issues plan, developed over the last 15 years, is constantly updated. Anglian Water's aims are to minimize the health risks to the public from any incident and the reputational damage to the firm. Their first objective in any incident is to get the message across to their customers and reassure government that the problem is being managed effectively and is under control.

Stakeholders

As a water company, Anglian Water is in contact with a large number of stakeholders, including MPs and district councils. It aims to have good relationships with its stakeholders so that trust is already established if an emergency arises and Anglian Water keeps contact details of all key stakeholders, including politicians, regulators, media, business customers, and vulnerable customers in their operating region. The crisis plan has assigned responsibilities and written responses ready for different events.

After issues with water quality were revealed in Pitsford, the emergency plan meant that in a few hours senior managers had personally contacted all the media in the affected area and political stakeholders in the region.

Media relations are critical; you can talk to all your customers but if you don't have the right messages in the media, then all is lost. (Andrew Mackintosh, Head of Group External Communications, Anglian Water)

As well as providing regular information to the media throughout the incident, Anglian Water monitored websites to ensure accurate information was communicated. For example, during the Pitsford incident the first live interviews were at 6 am, and by 10 am it was reported in China.

Anglian Water gave personal and regular media updates which helped stakeholders get to know and trust the 'face' of the company, and kept messages consistent. Over the next ten days, customers also received letters and mobile units in towns maintained full visibility and reassured the general public.

A priority was to get messages and help through to the most vulnerable customers, including the young, elderly, and those that needed direct assistance. Following the incident

the local council committed to keeping a more comprehensive record of those who would need direct assistance in the future. Information was communicated in a number of languages and police contacts were used to identify the minority group's community leaders and target specialist media. On day three Anglian Water was able to meet identified ethnic groups to explain the issue. Since the event it has significantly extended the number of languages their emergency plan covers.

The Drinking Water Inspectorate (DWI) is the regulator for the sector and has the power to prosecute and fine companies which are at fault. The DWI confirmed that there would be no prosecution as a result of the incident and cited the quality and speed of Anglian Water's response as an important factor in their decision.

Anglian Water's Top Tips for Emergency Stakeholder Planning:

1. The key thing is readiness, having a plan ready and establishing those relationships beforehand is essential.

2. Keep your response fully transparent and visible. Be seen to be taking the problems seriously, taking responsibility and taking action. A visible and timely response has an enormous impact on minimizing reputational risk.

3. Help the media. Create a plan to feed regular information to the media to avoid them having to look for issues to cover.

Issues in a developing organization

Environmental scanning (outlined in chapter 4) identifies issues that the organization must address. The category of **small or medium enterprises (SMEs)**, which are enterprises employing fewer than 250 workers and have a turnover not exceeding €50 million, are the main businesses in Europe; they drive much of the business innovation and competition (European Commission 2005).

PR practitioners manage issues in these organizations and when an organization is growing issues can arise at each of its developmental stages. Many of these issues are resolved by management but understanding each stage helps to identify the potential of a crisis and how the organization will need support.

Greiner's growth model, developed in 1927 (van Assen et al 2009), helps to identify the specific problems that may occur in any stage of a fast-growing organization. In addition, it is easier to identify an issue by knowing where the organization is in the growth stage and whether it is close to a crisis, and then actions can be taken to ensure these transitory stages are smooth. Van Assen et al (2009) describe the following challenges which face the management team of a growing SME:

1. Creativity stage

This is the time during which the product and its market are being developed. Comunication within the organization is frequent and informal. As the organization grows and becomes more complex it then needs to be managed. There can be internal communications issues around leadership at this stage and a business manager needs to be employed.

2. Direction

This is a more functional time for the organization where there is more structure and financial management and more formal management. There can be issues with how work is shared and most organizations move towards delegation.

3. Delegation

As the organization grows it forms into many different sections. The overall control of these becomes difficult and can lead to a fragmented company. At this stage it is best to find ways to coordinate everyone, rather than control them.

4. Coordination

This stage is when the organization gets bigger and needs to merge with other product groups and centralize its support. The organization may fall into bureaucracy and red tape therefore people need to be more flexible.

5. Collaboration

The organization becomes team-orientated with teams interacting. However, future growth is generally by collaboration with other organizations.

6. Alliances

Organizations try to grow through extra organizational solutions, and mergers etc.

The changing environment

Organizations are required to be increasingly transparent to their publics. Watson et al (2002) argue that organizations therefore need to develop new ways of working with these publics. Organizations are now expected to collaborate with their publics when making business decisions that affect their needs or interests. This collaboration with publics is increasingly important as people are investing in organizations based on their triple bottom line.

Refusal to collaborate or being unaware of the need to do so creates poor communication and has severe effects on an organization's reputation. Watson et al (2002: 55) describe how Shell in 1995 had to abandon its plan to dump the Brent Spar offshore platform at sea as it was seen to be doing this without the public's knowledge and was open to criticism by Greenpeace.

A well-known example of advocacy was the 2005 McLibel trial which ran over ten years. A group of London campaigners produced a leaflet which claimed McDonald's was selling food linked to heart disease and cancer, that it cut down rainforests and also abused its workforce. McDonald's began court proceedings against five people who were responsible for the publication. Two of the environmentalists decided to fight in the courts. Although McDonald's won two hearings, the drawn out litigation caused damage to its reputation and gave the environmentalists a media opportunity to create global support generated by a David vs Goliath scenario. In addition, the organization's business practices were exposed as McDonald's internal policies and procedures were opened up to public scrutiny. During the trial, volunteers helped to create and maintain the now famous http://www.McSpotlight.org website which provides regular and negative reports on McDonald's social and environmental position. Furthermore, a film, *McLibel*, was produced about freedom of speech and the power of multinational corporations.

@ **Go to the Online Resource Centre to access the link to the social and environmental reports on McDonald's**

Watson et al (2002) observe that publics are now questioning scientific truth and also making judgements about companies based on their own emotional reactions. Therefore, they argue, organizations need a 'mutual gains' approach which acknowledges the publics' concerns and involves them in the organizational decision making. Watson et al (2002) recommend the following five-stage issues negotiation process to build relationships with those who affect the value of the organization.

1. Identify and analyse the concerns and motivations of all stakeholders and clarify the organization's goals for the organization itself and its publics.

2. Include all relevant stakeholders and allow their involvement.

3. Explore and understand the different viewpoints of publics and share that through informal and formal discussions. Ensure that each side understands the other and works within agreed parameters, and agree to do things jointly; this would include not briefing journalists without the other party knowing.

4. Negotiate through sharing the information gathered.

5. Continue with the relationships and develop ongoing levels of commitment required from all parties.

According to Watson et al (2002) public relations should take a more involving approach with all its publics and its plans for the future. This means focusing on communication and forming partnerships to solve issues as they arise, and bringing all its publics together to share one voice.

10.3 Influences

Globalization is a major influence in any organization. The media's demand for more information, its global reach, and ongoing coverage means that issues can be turned into an international cause. As mentioned above, the Anglian Water case study was first discussed in English media interviews at 6 am and reported in China by 10 am the same day. In addition, any issue can be highlighted and given impetus through social media. One person's campaign against higher prices can lead to the campaign being fuelled by supporters reacting to similar issues. Also what can seem like a local matter can be broadened to existing global issues such as climate change. Griffin (2008) identifies climate change as an issue that needs long-term thinking and argues that it is an issue which all large organizations need to address with long-term strategy.

Stakeholders monitor organizations for their ethical standards and advances in multimedia technology mean that mobile phones and cameras can be used to report from inside an organization or show the services of organizations. For example, hidden cameras have been used to portray poor standards in care homes and mobile phone cameras have been used to film police abuse. This technology has a global reach and has the power to influence people to rise up and drive an issue forward.

A local product can affect the global reputation of a brand and this is more apparent with the increasing emphasis on brands as a marketing tool. The product is increasingly associated with the corporate brand, therefore when a product is considered poor the corporation itself is damaged.

The rise of activism

Regester and Larkin (2005) point out that there is an anti-corporation movement which is responsible for the increase in activism and in empowering its supporters. In addition, consumers are more active than ever before, exerting greater personal choice and questioning new developments. Activists are constantly researching and exposing lies and misleading claims. There is a need for organizations to have open discussion and take an active role with any pressure group ranging from the formalized Greenpeace to the hundreds of protestors or eco-activists demonstrating against the third Heathrow terminal.

Watson et al (2002) take it further than simply a two-way symmetrical discussion, they recommend organizations enter into partnerships with activists to achieve their objectives. For example, the Land Rover case study (see chapter 5) described how Land Rover collaborated with Greenpeace and other sustainability opinion leaders about its technologies, such as the hybrid engine.

Increasingly, practitioners are becoming advisers to legitimate activists groups. The power is no longer with commercial organizations but becoming more equally distributed.

The role of the internet

The internet can change an issue or create an issue and one quarter of crises are related to the internet, according to Herbst (cited Conway et al 2007: 214), so organizations have to know how to manage them.

The internet can distribute large amounts of information which can be selected and compared simultaneously; it operates at low cost, is instantaneous, and reaches a mass audience. An internet audience can be more powerful than any mass audience, strengthened further by being anonymous and accessible over 24 hours.

According to Conway et al (2007), organizations are losing control over their communications as there is an increased exposure of corporations on the internet and an increase in crisis potential. The virtual publics accessing and distributing information are difficult to identify and stakeholders can emerge offline, be uncontrollable and constantly change, challenging conventional communication.

Conway et al (2007) describe the internet as working in a 'push pull' manner. It acts as a push mechanism by distributing information, especially rumours, without altering them thus maintaining a consistent message which appears credible. It acts as a 'pull' medium to gain information and allows for interactivity, community-oriented networking through chat rooms and newsrooms for example. The internet's lack of identified gatekeepers and its low cost creates the potential for an issue to be communicated. Anyone can post on the internet and many damaging and often unfounded rumours about celebrities can emerge. Therefore, people with low power and low impact can become influential.

Conway et al (2007: 215) outline four major internet crises:

1. A reinforcing crisis where the internet is used in addition to traditional media to reinforce stakeholders' opinions. For example, in April 2010, the massive oil spill from an explosion aboard Deepwater Horizon, an offshore drilling rig in the Gulf of Mexico, which killed 11 people, was covered on the internet with television footage replayed and creating widespread coverage and ongoing interest, thereby reinforcing public awareness about the crisis.

2. An absurd crisis which emerges from the internet's uncontrollable and diverse content, ie a crisis from an unfounded opinion such as a rumour. Celebrities are often subjected to these crises.

3. An affecting crisis when corporations are scrutinized by virtual stakeholders and become the subject of negative discussion.

4. A competence crisis which is when online experts, despite their own limited resources, can damage an organization. For example, online protestors, can create DDOS (distributed denial of service) attacks where a website is bombarded by requests for pages, often taking it offline (see chapter 5).

An issue that emerges online can be managed in the same way as any other issue. That is, identify the issue, analyse it, decide the approach and action, and then evaluate the results and ongoing situation. Organizations need to ensure regular scanning, monitoring, and analysis of the internet as an integral part of their corporate communications in order to identify any potential issue sources.

In preparation for a crisis, Genasi (cited Conway et al 2007) recommends preparing a **dark site**—an empty place on the net fully equipped and waiting to be used if a crisis occurs. This allows the organization to react quickly to a crisis event by providing information online, ie a central information point for the public and stakeholders which can be easily updated. This is also important for the media who will be searching for updated information and their use of it can shape the public's perceptions. Also an up-to-date website that is credible enhances corporate credibility and its attempt to take the crisis seriously.

The internet has become an essential factor in issue and crisis awareness. An organization needs regular online monitoring and analysis, stakeholder management on the internet, an internet dark site, and preparation of an internet plan and allocation of resources. According to research by Conway et al (2007), online monitoring by organizations is irregular; and although integration of the internet into corporate communications is important only a minority have it as part of their crisis communications strategy.

10.4 Application to industry

Scenario planning should be a critical part of issues management as it helps to deal with an issue or a crisis. This means testing out different situations that may occur which highlight the weaknesses of the existing information and helps to plan for the issue.

To develop scenario planning it is best to raise the issue and suggest several ways it could develop and ways that it could be addressed and then use an issues management team to ask questions that challenge assumptions (van Assen et al 2009). This will identify what is not known about how to deal with the crisis and highlights the vulnerabilities of an organization. It allows time to develop responses and can avert a crisis. Updating the scenario should be a regular part of planning for issues and crisis management.

Case Study

Crisis management for a chemical company explosion

Source: Courtesy of Montpellier PR

Crisis communications helped to save the reputation of a chemicals company following an explosion and the destruction of its manufacturing facility in a peaceful Cotswold village.

> I think I need your help; the production facility has exploded, luckily no casualties but I need you guys to help me out. (Managing Director, BioLab UK)

BioLab UK is part of the global BioLab family of pool, spa, and home care products and a subsidiary of the New York Stock Exchange (NYSE) quoted chemicals group Chemtura Inc. In the UK, the business had a leading position in the market for pool and spa chemicals.

A fire in the production line had sparked an explosion which ripped through the facility. As a consequence fire engines were called out, roads were blocked, and nearby residents were evacuated for fear of toxic fumes as a three-mile high plume emanated from the site and was carried across rural areas (see Figure 10.6).

The Environmental Agency reported pollution of nearby waterways, with the loss of trout and other wildlife. From the first alert Montpellier PR's crisis programme swung into action; this required director-level support to tackle the incident and its strategic communications requirements, whilst allowing the core team to tackle ongoing trade communications, and promote the 'business as normal message'.

Fig 10.6
The explosion created clouds of smoke across the Cotswolds

Source: Copyright OUP

The parent company, Chemtura Inc, was due to announce its quarterly results to the NYSE. Widespread negative coverage in the US, picked up from news agencies, would adversely affect the stock price.

Objectives

- Provide the communications lead for the US/UK incident team and ensure full media communications and regular updates.
- Protect NYSE quarter year stock announcement by parent Chemtura Inc.
- Address concerns of local community including business neighbours and affected residential areas.
- Manage communications with the trade supply chain, trade outlets, and consumers.

Planning

Immediately, the crisis framework was agreed with the senior management team on-site and lines of communication established with the US communications team, together with the CEO of Chemtura, HR management, legal, insurance, operations, and sales functions. The whole organization was to be involved and kept informed.

The media frenzy needed to be satisfied with regular dialogue and Montpellier PR researched all elements including the environmental impact. In addition, responsibilities were allocated to the UK MD, commercial and operations director.

All media and communications were handled through Montpellier PR's incident room. A US team was flown in within 48 hours to help with operational and HR issues and were briefed prior to arrival.

An intranet was established with password protection to ensure that all senior team members could participate and be briefed on the status of communications coverage and approved statements, including TV, radio, and press comments/coverage were accessed.

Daily US/UK conference calls, with on-site and remote meetings kept everyone informed including solicitors, insurance underwriters, and loss adjusters.

Stakeholders

Statements were prepared and approved to address communications with stakeholders, principally:

- employees at the site and other UK facilities
- local community (business neighbours on the industrial estate and residents affected)
- statutory authorities (parish council, district and county council, Health & Safety Executive, Environment Agency, Severn Trent Water) landowners, police, fire, and emergency planning authorities
- trade customers
- end-users.

Media relations

The media relations strategy required the MD to be briefed by the consultancy director and to take media calls and requests for interviews with TV and radio stations and newspapers.

Activities included drafting statements; briefing executives; selecting and briefing media spokespeople, preparing possible questions and answers, ensuring a constant media contact; coordination of all communications activities for UK and lead counsel to the US communications team.

Community relations

A community hotline was set up immediately for public enquiries and linked with public information provided from the health authorities; this clarified issues and quelled rumours.

All businesses and relevant villages were visited and details down to insurance claims were discussed. Letters to local press were monitored along with residents' interviews on TV and radio, with appropriate responses produced.

Human resource issues

Because the entire facility (ie production) was lost due to the explosion, it was vital that staff were reassured about their status because production had to be outsourced to other sites, primarily in South Africa, France, and Germany. The consultancy worked with the human resources teams to advise staff and work through the consultation process required to ensure that communications were timely and addressed both legal requirements. A strategy was developed to handle communications regarding potential redundancies/redeployment of staff.

Environmental communications

Montpellier PR was the point of contact for communications with the Environmental Agency communications group established to monitor contamination to the water system.

Trade communications—'business as usual'

In parallel with the incident management activities, full-time support was dedicated to issues programmes and media handling—the core trade activities, including newsletters, trade and consumer media relations, features, advertising, and support communication. This allowed a focus of activities on a twin track which contained the incident but also fed information to the trade and consumer communications team.

Evaluation

With crisis management programmes, the volume of media interest is often difficult to gauge. The key objective was to provide open communications within agreed message frameworks. Once it was clear that there were no casualties, protection of the stock price was a key objective to be met by the controlled communications strategy.

The Biolab managing director praised the crisis management:

> Without Montpellier PR there was no way we would have coped. The division of labour with Montpellier taking the lead on communications not only greatly assisted my team but has been seen as an immensely professional operation by our Stateside colleagues, who have had previous experience of serious chemical explosions.

The end result

- Containment of media coverage to the region with no media coverage in the US and consequently no adverse effect on the parent company stock price.
- Reassurance of local communities with community relationships restored with continued support for the local school.
- Strengthening of relationship with local media.
- The 'business as usual' trade message was received and covered by trade media, which minimized production and delivery issues at a time when competitors were busy in the market attacking BioLab accounts.
- Within three months, BioLab fulfilled 85 per cent of orders and in four months was on top of all orders, supported by trade communications.

PR Tool

Crisis plan

Monitoring

1. Identify and work with stakeholders to avert issues and gain their support.
2. Watch for crisis triggers such as share prices, terrorist threats, fire threats, advocates, and try to deal with these early.
3. Continuously assess issues and risks; use risk assessment analysis models.
4. Identify third-party spokespeople who will support the organization.

Material

1. Develop statements for each potential crisis.
2. Develop background media material about the organization, eg what it does, years established, number of employees, annual report, key personnel, etc. Include video footage and photographs of the organization and key personnel.
3. Develop a dark website.
4. Develop messages for each anticipated crisis.

Go to the Online Resource Centre to access a link to video footage on how to say sorry during a crisis

Training

1. Involve everyone at every level within the organization.

2. Arrange one on-site simulation exercise a year as well as crisis media training for spokespeople.

3. Develop core team crisis comprising senior members and define their roles in a crisis, members should include the CEO, managing director, directors, company lawyer, insurance advisors, and the communications practitioner who is experienced in communicating with the government, investors, and the community.

4. Identify spokespeople within the organization as well as third parties and their roles, responsibilities, and contact details.

5. Identify internal and external stakeholders which includes employees, third parties, and the media. Identify how to reach them at anytime.

6. Develop the communication flow to be used for alerting stakeholders within the first our of a crisis starting with employees and others within the organization

7. Practice scenario planning to ensure updated solutions are in place for a crisis.

Crisis activities

1. Focus on speed of message.

2. Inform internal employees.

3. Establish three key messages and distribute to all staff. These should define the crisis and state the action to be undertaken by the organizaton.

4. Have the spokespeople accessible to the media and briefed on the three key messages.

5. Ensure spokespeople are constantly updated and briefed on any changes to the situation.

6. Distribute messages to media focusing on the three key messages.

7. Add information to the background media material and the 'dark site' which can be released to the media.

8. Prepare a media briefing room if needed which must be accessible to media, this could be a hotel—ensure refreshments and toilet facilities are available.

9. Keep records of every media interview and arrange media monitoring services to record all media, including the internet.

10. Consider how to handle the issue after the initial activity is over—it may be an opportunity to present the organization in a positive light if the crisis has been handled well.

11. Alert staff to a standard memo that will be recognized when needed. It should be clear and concise and enable swift completion and circulation as an email (see Box 10.1).

Box 10.1 **Memo to all staff regarding a crisis**

Date:
Crisis concerning:
Departments/people aspects of organization it affects:
Organization's position:
Action taken to date:
Organization's statements:
Organization's spokesperson and contact numbers:
Staff responsible for dealing with crisis:
Special instructions:
Other information available:
Key contact(s):

Summary

An issue can be a gap between what publics expect of an organization and what it is saying. A crisis can be the impact of an unresolved issue or it can be instantaneous and without warning, such as a fire or a tsunami.

A practitioner needs to monitor an organization constantly for issues and that means identifying triggers that may lead to them. These triggers can be anything concerned with change arising in the organization or its external environment. Understanding how to assess a risk means analysing its probability versus its impact.

Risk management is identifying the risk and its likely impact, deciding a strategy, implementing it, and then evaluating it. All research tools used to develop a situation analysis can be used in analysing issues. These include existing qualitative and quantitative research, a SWOT analysis, a PEST analysis, and surveys.

The responses of the organization need to developed, such as spokespeople, third party support, and overall leadership. Any issue has a 'fallout' or residual effect and this is particularly evident on the internet where an issue can stay 'alive'. Therefore ongoing monitoring and issues management is an integral part of any practitioner's role.

Choosing how to deal with a risk or even whether to allow a risk is an organization's decision. All activities have some risk and analysing whether activities should proceed can be based on a risk benefit analysis. Most importantly, risk management involves being timely. It is crucial that issues are not left to wait, it is vital that there is a plan, good relationships with opinion leaders, publics and the media, and clarity and transparency when providing the media with information.

Increasingly, organizations are expected to be transparent to stakeholders and to engage in public consultation on organizational decisions. This is especially important as consumers and investors are deciding to deal with organizations based on their social, financial, and environmental profile.

Advocacy is stronger as publics feel more empowered and so organizations need to relate to stakeholders and their issues. Watson et al (2002) recommend a relationship-building process which means that all stakeholders and the organization negotiate together on issues, forming a joint investment in the changing future. Globalization can turn local news into global media and social media can fuel support and provide impetus for any issue.

Stakeholders are monitoring organizations for ethical standards and demand ethical and trustworthy behaviour. It is essential that organizations take responsibility for an issue and lead on it. It is also vital that practitioners maintain their own integrity to maintain trust with stakeholders and the organization. Multi-media technology is allowing more and more views inside organizations be extended to the outside world.

All issues have a lifecycle but the internet is changing how issues develop and how they are resolved; its accessibility, low cost, and immediacy challenges conventional communication. Although an issue follows a lifecycle of potential, emerging, current, and then possibly occurring as a crisis, the internet means that it may not enter into or stay in a dormant phase because it will always be online.

Dealing with issues means good assessment, a SWOT analysis, risk to benefit and likelihood to impact analyses and scenario planning. A crisis plan brings all those together quickly where the full involvement of all stages is necessary. Organizations are increasingly aware that they cannot be in isolation; they are an important part of the community and this is discussed in the next chapter.

Discussion points

A. Analysis of an issue

Identify a current crisis in the media.

1. What stage is it in?

2. What spokespeople would you put forward?

3. Research the media and identify what is being said about it. What is the prevailing view? Which views seem to be directing the issue? Why do you think that is?

B. Risk assessment

In pairs, identify some weekly activities you both like doing, for example, these could be playing a sport or driving a car.

1. Identify the severity of this risk using the risk/benefit graph.

2. Identify the priority of this risk through using the probability/impact graph.

3. Do you and your partner agree on the risk benefit and the probability/impact of each risk? How do you differ? What does this tell you about risk assessment generally?

C. Online crises

Go online and identify the four internet crises defined by Conway:

1. a reinforcing crisis

2. an absurd crisis

3. an affecting crisis

4. a competence crisis

What makes them different from each other?

What criteria have you used to define them?

Do you think these are appropriate criteria for identifying internet crises? Explain your answer.

References

Conway, T., Ward, M., Lewis, G., and Bernhardt, A. (2007) 'Internet Crisis Potential: The Importance of a Strategic Approach to Marketing Communications', Journal of Marketing Communications 13/3 (September 2007)

Dade, C. (2009) 'UK Government Launches Campaign to Reduce Teenage Pregnancies in Digital Journal', 30 November. Available at: http://www.digitaljournal.com/article/282961

European Commission (2005) 'The New SME Definition: User Guide and Model Declaration, Enterprise and Industry Publications'. Available at: http://ec.europa.eu/enterprise/policies/sme/files/sme_definition/sme_user_guide_en.pdf

Eurosport (2009) 'Tiger Woods sex scandal cost shareholders up to $12 billion', 29 December. Available at: http://uk.eurosport.yahoo.com/29122009/58/tiger-woods-sex-scandal-cost-shareholders-12-billion.html

Fearn-Banks, K. (2001) 'Crisis Communication: A Review of Some Best Practices' in R. Heath (ed) Handbook of Public Relations. Thousand Oaks, CA: Sage

Gregory, A. (2006) Planning and Managing Public Relations Campaigns (2nd edn). London: Kogan Page

Griffin, A. (2008) New Strategies for Reputation Management. London: Kogan Page

Jaques, T. (2008) 'The Man Who Invented Issue Management', Journal of Communication Management 12/4: 336–43

Pratt, C. (2001) 'Issues Management: The Paradox of the 40-Year US Tobacco Wars' in R. Heath (ed) Handbook of Public Relations. Thousand Oaks, CA: Sage

Regester, M. and Larkin, J. (2005) Risk Issues and Crisis Management: A Casebook of Best Practice (3rd edn). London: Kogan Page

Seeger, M., Sellnow, T., and Ulmer, R. (2001) 'Public Relations and Crisis Communication: Organizing and Chaos' in R. Heath (ed) Handbook of Public Relations. Thousand Oaks, CA: Sage

Van Assen, M., van den Berg, G., and Pietersma, P. (2009) Key Management Models: The 60+ Models Every Manager Needs To Know (2nd edn). Harlow: Prentice Hall

Watson, T., Osbourne-Brown, S., and Longhurst, M. (2002) 'Issues Negotiations: Investing in Stakeholders', Corporate Communications, An International Journal 7/1: 54–61

Young, B. (2009) 'Nokia's Latest Patent Strike on Apple, a Risk, But May Pay Off', UKTechnology, 30 December. Available at: http://www.reuters.com/article/idUSTRE5BS2J820091230

11 Ethics, legalities, and corporate responsibility

Learning outcomes

1. Develop reflection through reviewing different scenarios to assess the importance of ethics, truthfulness, and transparency to an organization's reputation and how persuasion fits into this context.

2. Define corporate social responsibility and how programmes can be created which benefit the community and the organization as well as drive public relations programmes.

3. Value the importance of reporting corporate responsibility to stakeholders to demonstrate financial and corporate citizenry.

4. Know how to analyse the drivers behind corporate responsibility such as globalization, speed of communications, regulations, and stakeholders.

5. Understand how corporate responsibility in an organization can generate changes in attitude and behaviour through differentiation, promotion, engagement with employees, and stakeholder self identity.

6. Be able to develop a code of ethics for an organization taking into account the regulatory and business framework within which an organization operates.

Practitioner Insight

Rachel Dyson
Corporate Responsibility Manager
Anglian Water

Rachel entered corporate responsibility through a financial route when she started as a project investment manager for Invesco Asset Management Ltd, in Ireland. She moved to Microsoft Research in the UK as project manager and then became the investor relations manager for Anglian Water. Rachel pursued her real passion for working on environmental and community issues when appointed as its corporate responsibility manager in 2007.

What is your role at Anglian Water?

Working with the Head of Corporate Responsibility and the team I manage the delivery of Anglian Water's corporate responsibility and community strategy and in particular work to establish Anglian Water as central to the life and well-being of local communities and the environment throughout the region. Anglian Water provides high-quality clean drinking water as well as wastewater services. We operate in the driest region in the UK with a rapidly growing population, therefore my role focuses on engaging people to value water and not waste it .

What is an example of what you do?

Promoting and coordinating the company's community engagement activities through our employee volunteering and education programmes, community investment, and charitable donations. For example, we run a very successful RiverCare programme in partnership with Keep Britain Tidy and the Environment Agency where employee volunteers and local residents get together to adopt stretches of river to keep it clear of rubbish.

How is sustainability part of your work?

Sustainability is crucial to our business because we are continually supplying more homes with water and yet there is no more rain falling. Rather than building a new reservoir which is not sustainable, we first want to do all we can to engage customers to be water wise as well as. We realize that for people to value water, they must realize that it belongs to the environment and is a finite resource.

However, change in behaviour happens more effectively if people don't have to think about it, that is, a behaviour change has to be made easy. For example, we have managed to encourage a high percentage of our customers to use a water meter which makes them conscious of their water use.

What is the value of corporate responsibility?

Companies with good corporate responsibility programmes are making a real change to create a sustainable world. Anglian Water is a big landowner and has a responsibility not to affect the environment negatively but to protect it. We actually go beyond the legal requirements to enhance the environment. For example, the Rutland Water Park and Nature Reserve that Anglian Water created from its reservoir introduced the ospreys back after an absence of more than one hundred years (see Figure 11.1). However, CR is not a philanthropic exercise; there is no point in it unless it adds value.

What advice would you give a student who is thinking about working in CR?

Have a passion for it. One could argue that in a few years there will be no corporate responsibility jobs as they are becoming embedded in how businesses operate, but there will always be a role for corporate responsibility although it may eventually have a different name. It is important to be aware that the focus of corporate responsibility may change as research and opportunities mean that issues evolve over time.

Fig 11.1
One of nine new lagoons being built at Rutland Water for waterfowl. The new lagoons will ensure birds will not be detrimentally affected by the need to abstract more water from the main reservoir

Source: Courtesy of Anglian Water

11.1 Definition

Publics are paying more and more attention to an organization, expecting them to give something back to the community and communicating about their business decisions more than ever before. This situation is being recognized worldwide and organizations are becoming accountable to their communities and the environment.

The global head of sustainability services for a leading worldwide accounting and advisory organization, KPMG, announced in its international company report on corporate sustainability that organizations must be accountable.

In a world of changing expectations companies must account for the way they impact the communities and environment where they will operate.

(Will Bartels, KPMG (2008))

These expectations are largely driven by the availability of communication technology which allows greater communication, globalization, and rapid transfer of information. It also means that everyone can communicate to a wide audience, people inside an organization can speak out about it privately, and people feel empowered to engage in online discussions and use these as a platform to build themselves as experts.

The ethical, environmental, and social impact

As a result, organizations are realizing that they have to be aware of their ethical, economic, environmental, and social impacts and issues that concern their publics. When ethics are applied to all aspects of running a business they cover decisions made by the board, how employees are treated, how business is conducted, how products and services are created and sold, as well and how the organization is run as a whole. PR practitioners must therefore understand the role of ethics, the concept of truth and truthfulness, and how these affect an organization's reputation and form the basis of its corporate responsibility programme.

Persuasion

Public relations has a vital role in developing the communication channels between an organization and its stakeholders and must be seen to be trustworthy. However, most public relations on behalf of an organization or an individual is usually persuasive in an attempt to communicate key messages. Persuasion has negative connotations and is considered to be manipulative, even though it is an intrinsic part of life and evident in advertising and public communication campaigns (Fawkes 2007). For example, the UK government's swine flu campaign in 2009 persuaded people to catch sneezes in tissues and then dispose of them in order to limit the spread of the disease.

Fawkes (2007: 328) puts forward the idea that persuasion is a form of negotiation that publics, with their increasing knowledge and media literacy, are more than capable of participating in. This means that if people have a sense of equality and are not being manipulated, public relations may be more of a two-way symmetrical practice than is realized. Messina (2007) states that even to communicate at all means persuading someone that they are worth listening to, looking at, or have written something worth reading. Arguably, if people are being made aware of how to deal with issues that affect them, such as life-damaging illnesses, then persuasion has a noble role.

Ethics

Moral judgements are formed through the effort of guiding conduct by reason; it is not about personal taste but more about impartial consideration of each individual's interests (Rachels and Rachels 2010). Ethics is derived from a moral philosophy which has many different perspectives. In the eighteenth century the philosopher, Emmanuel Kant, developed what is now called Kantian ethics. Kant thought that human beings had an intrinsic worth as they were guided by reason, unlike animals, and therefore could ensure that moral goodness existed. This means treating people as an end, not a means to an end, that is, promoting their welfare and rights and treating them with respect without manipulating them or deceiving them, but respecting their own rational capabilities and letting them make their own decisions.

Another philosophical perspective on ethics was developed in the early nineteenth century by the philosopher Jeremy Bentham, and called **utilitarianism**. It judges circumstances by their consequence, that is the amount of happiness or unhappiness created and everyone's happiness has the same value. Therefore utilitarians choose the action with the best overall consequences, which has given rise to the expression 'the greatest good for the greatest number', which means that the end justifies the means (Rachels and Rachels 2010).

Public relations needs a code of ethics as practitioners hold confidential information, are in a position of trust, safeguard a client's reputation, are the source of ethical messages, and have a professional code of conduct which must be upheld. Ethical issues in public relations could concern persuading the media with expensive gifts, making something seem better than it is, giving only partial information to stakeholders; or not revealing a conflict of interest, such as representing two competitive clients, or covering up a bad practice rather than encouraging corporate transparency.

Obligations of the public relations practitioner

Sieb and Ftizpatrick (1995) identify four categories of duty to identify the specific obligations facing public relations practitioners:

1. Duty to self.
2. Duty to the client or organization.
3. Duty to the profession (public relations institutes have a code of conduct which presents ethical guidelines for practitioners, these were discussed in chapter 1).
4. Duty to society.

The International Public Relations Association (IPRA), which is the professional body for senior public relations practitioners, positions itself as providing intellectual leadership for the public relations profession. It has therefore developed codes and charters which provide an ethical framework for public relations and it is expected that all members abide by these and encourage their adoption worldwide. The Code of Venice, adopted by the IPRA in 1961 and amended in 2009, provides guidelines for professional conduct. In 1965 the IPRA adopted the Code of Athens which asks practitioners worldwide to respect the Charter of the United Nations and the moral principles of the Universal Declaration of Human Rights.

It is crucial for practitioners, as member countries of the United Nations, to abide by the Charter which means observing fundamental human rights. Also, through their professional work, practitioners can help people to meet their intellectual, moral, and social needs so that they can benefit from having met their physical and material needs. Furthermore, practitioners have the potential to be in contact with millions of people and therefore have a power which must not be misused.

The IPRA has also developed other global ethical codes for practitioners including the Code of Brussels in 2007 for public affairs practitioners which builds on the earlier Codes of Venice and Athens and focuses on transparency, integrity, confidentiality, and honesty (IPRA 2010).

Go to the Online Resource Centre to access the IPRA code of ethics

Telling the truth

Ethical communications means that people should be given enough information to make voluntary, informed, rational, and reflective judgements. This explains why lying is wrong; it treats people as a means to achieving something and prevents them from making choices through reasoning (Messina 2007). To ensure public relations is ethical, even though persuasive, it is important for the practitioner to examine their own practices of truthfulness, authenticity, respect, and equity (see Box 11.1).

However, telling the truth can be a problem for organizations if it means that company secrets would be revealed thus causing them to lose competitive advantage. Fitzpatrick and Bronstein (2006: 93) discuss the various interpretations of truth

---

Box 11.1 Ethical test to assess public relations practice

The following is a test used to examine the ethical basis of decisions.

1. Transparency
Do I mind others knowing what I have decided?

2. Effect
Who does my decision affect or hurt?

3. Fairness
Would my decision be considered fair by those affected?

and transparency and compare the ethical and legal views on truth. They state that 'from an ethical standpoint being truthful means not lying' whereas truth from a legal perspective means that the information can be verified and is not misleading.

Corporate confidentiality can be an issue for all organizations and the practitioner needs to know the regulations affecting their particular sector in order to know when confidentiality is legally required. For example, financial regulations demand that an organization cannot reveal that it will be floated on the stock exchange as this will affect its share price unfairly. Pharmaceutical organizations are restricted in what they can say about their medications and to whom they can say it. In the UK, for example, pharmaceutical companies are not allowed to reveal that a medicine may have other benefits apart from those for which it is licensed.

The importance of transparency

Stakeholders are not only demanding truth but also transparency. Gower (2006) claims that telling the truth is not enough for an organization to have a trusting relationship with its stakeholders. He argues that transparency in an organization is not only keeping people informed about what is going on but also letting them know the reasons behind the decisions and actions of the organization. This presents the argument that an organization which is being truthful by telling its employees they are going to be made redundant does not mean it is trustworthy. After all, the organization may not have been transparent about issues which made it create the redundancies.

Truthfulness also concerns the expectations that publics are led to have about an organization; these expectations should be delivered. Not delivering can undermine the trust people have in an organization, therefore an organization must be careful not to create false expectations or mislead people. Scandals can bring a company down if they are seen to be acting against what an organization has led people to expect. For example, the world's top golfer, Tiger Woods, had an image as a family man with an honest and upright moral image and earned huge advertising and sponsorship revenue based on this. When in 2009 his marital infidelities were played out in public, his image fell apart and his publics, which included his sponsors, felt as if they had been misled.

Truth and reputation in the fashion world

Any organization's reputation is fragile. Even if it needs to go to court to prove it has acted truthfully and ethically, the organization's reputation can still be damaged, owing to comments and misrepresentation. In 2009, the giant French fashion designer, Chanel, was accused by one of its knitwear suppliers of stealing a design (AFP 2009). During a drawn out trial Chanel had to steady itself against negative public comments from the supplier.

The French court threw out accusations against Chanel, and ruled that Chanel had not stolen the design but had only broken a contract with the supplier. Chanel had to pay only several thousand euros in damages, instead of the millions requested. Chanel then sued for damages to its reputation and the supplier was ordered to pay just under a million euros in compensation (AFP 2009).

Truth, ethics, and values

All the arguments about truth, ethics, and value make up an organization and how it relates to its publics. An organization's approach to what it is responsible for, to whom it is responsible, and why, is underpinned by its ethical values and by the policies and programmes in place to make those values operational. Most of these come under the term of corporate responsibility and are an integral part of issues management and crisis prevention.

These non-financial measurements of progress are often an important part in the overall assessment of an organization's performance. Organizations have grown through selling services or products to different publics, but for organizations to continue to grow they need to be sustainable. That is, they need to ensure that what they are doing is not only for their own commercial profit but benefits their consumers and the community. In addition, organizations need to be able to function without damaging their social and environmental interests.

Increasingly stakeholders are judging an organization by how it adheres to ethical decision making and organizational codes of conduct as well as other social and environmental decisions. How an organization makes decisions also reflects its own values, bound by government legislation, industry regulations, and its codes of conduct which are more formal manifestations of ethics.

Corporate responsibility

Corporate responsibility (CR) can be thought of as the public's opinion about the social and environmental impacts of an organization's business operations and its voluntary contribution to the well-being of its global and local communities. For example, Nike was vilified for its abuse of Nike workers in Vietnamese factories (see chapter 1 for more details). The Vietnam Labour Watch then investigated these working conditions and released a report which created an ongoing worldwide campaign against sweatshops and the companies which use them (Kenyon 2000).

According to a report in the *Economist* (2008b) there is some thinking that CR could be seen as merely a publicity exercise. However, the report also noted a link between an organization's principles and its commercial competence that decides the kind of image it has. It must be strong on its values and commercial competence. An organization with strong values but which is badly managed and doesn't make a profit means it will not do well; equally, a company that is highly competent commercially but has no CR may do well but is in an increasingly vulnerable position.

A strong commitment to CR and strong commercial competence means a good chance of success. A report on corporate social responsibility for the *Economist* (2008a), argues that it is worth identifying CR as something distinct from good business practice. CR makes an organization look outwards and think imaginatively about the risks and opportunities it sees.

Additionally, CR may be an indication of how business will be carried out in the future. When CR influences decisions on everything from where it sources its raw products to its business strategy this becomes embedded in the organization, thereby influencing every decision (Economist 2008a).

Online ethics

The rapid development of the internet is bringing up more ethical issues which practitioners have to address. Hallahan (2006: 120) argues that ethical online public relations should provide publics with the opportunity to communicate. This means ensuring that they have the tools and ability (computers, wireless connections, training, and access) to participate in online communication. Hallahan (2006: 121) also warns about ensuring accuracy of content which means checking information that is often fragmented and from different online sources. Additionally, as there is so much information on the internet it is important to be aware of the issues of misappropriating content.

Hallahan (2006: 124) also highlights the issue of online information being dependable. This means that if an organization is reaching people through the internet it must have updated information and ensure that its hardware and software are functioning properly. This is particularly important during a crisis. Also, if organizations invite their publics to be interactive there should be meaningful and timely responses to opinions and requests.

The use of web tools for evaluation can also create ethical issues on privacy and practitioners need to question whether it is ethical to track website visits and other activity. The internet allows segmentation of audiences through this process and there is an ethical issue on how much information can be collected about users and how this information is used. Practitioners need to review their organization's online practices and online developments to ensure that they are maintaining ethical practices in a rapidly changing environment. See chapter 12 for more on online public relations and its ethical issues.

Go to the Online Resource Centre to access a link to a video about CR in the recession

11.2 Theoretical and historical context

The increasing demand on organizations to perform financially and be good **corporate citizens** has resulted in corporate responsibility programmes where organizations focus on how they are affecting the world around them. This is largely based on their impact on climate change, community health, education and development, as well as demonstrating business sustainability where they achieve strong economic growth without jeopardizing future prospects (KPMG 2008).

Figure 11.2 shows that there are many ways an organization impacts the world and is in turn affected by its stakeholders who include government, NGOs, suppliers, shareholders, its local community, environment, and the marketplace. Stakeholders generally look to the outer circle of the diagram to see how the organization has performed in terms of its products and services, its impact on the environment and on local communities, and how it treats and develops its workforce. **Financial analysts** look

Fig 11.2
How an organization impacts the world and is affected by the world

Source: Courtesy of Mallen Baker http:// www.mallenbaker. net/csr/index.php

to the financial performance and the quality of management as these can be used to indicate likely future performance (Mallenbaker.com accessed 2010).

Reporting on CR

Companies are now reporting on their corporate responsibility which allows their stakeholders to know how business is not only affecting its community and the world at large but also how it is contributing to it. An international survey in 2008 by KPMG tracked the reporting trends of CR in more than 2,200 of the world's largest companies. It found that in 2008 nearly 80 per cent have released reports on their corporate responsibility compared to about 50 per cent in 2005 (KPMG 2008).

The Department of Environment, Food and Rural Affairs (Defra) stresses the importance of CR in its reporting guidelines for UK Business (2006). In the report's foreword, the Director General, Digby Jones, said:

Responsible businesses are at the heart of society. Companies that understand their links with the communities they operate in, and their impact on the environment, are most likely to prosper in the long-term. At the same

time, interest from stakeholders in firms' environmental performance is at an all-time high.

CR is driven by increasing organizational transparency which is affected by the globalization of organizations, the speed of media, as well as active and educated audiences. Organizations are a part of the society they represent and have a major impact on social and physical environment and must take responsibility for this position. CR is moving forward influenced by global guidelines and consumer pressure.

According to the KPMG survey (2008), three-quarters of the world's top 250 organizations have a corporate reputation strategy with defined objectives. Now almost two-thirds of these companies engage with their stakeholders in a structured way, whereas in 2005 only one-third did so. It is expected that other organizations will follow in this practice of ensuring that stakeholders are informed and will consult them increasingly.

Influence from the United Nations

The United Nations Global Compact has a framework of ten principles (see Box 11.2) that member organizations use to guide their corporate commitment to social environmental issues. The importance of transparency and accountability in the global market was highlighted in 2008 when the UN Global Compact marked nearly 100 companies as inactive or delisted them from their active pool of participants for not communicating with them on their CR (KPMG 2008). However, an increasing number of companies in more than a hundred countries follow the United Nations' guidelines on CR and most large companies now have specific CR programmes (Perez 2009: 177).

The *Economist* report on CR (2008b) outlines the different attitudes of key countries to CR. It claims British business has innovative CR, formed through NGOs and think tanks but is not so strong on implementation. American firms have impressive execution, such as Wal Mart; CR in Japan is seen as emerging from traditional Japanese business, and Japanese firms already pay a lot of attention to the environment and to relations with local communities; Russia is less interested in CR whereas Brazil has a network of businesses committed to CR; India has a history of philanthropy especially with family-owned companies already providing services such as a schools. China is becoming the new CR frontier; although Chinese companies within China focus on growth and less on CR, those seeking global markets are already aware that they must pay attention to CR. For example, the report claims PetroChina was targeted by campaigners for disinvestment in the Sudan (Economist 2008b).

🕲 **Go to the Online Resource Centre to access the link to a video about CR in the recession**

Box 11.2 UN Global Compact's ten principles

The UN Global Compact's ten principles in the areas of human rights, labour, the environment, and anti-corruption enjoy universal consensus and are derived from:

- The Universal Declaration of Human Rights
- The International Labour Organization's Declaration on Fundamental Principles and Rights at Work

- The Rio Declaration on Environment and Development
- The United Nations Convention Against Corruption

The following text is extracted from the Compact:

> The UN Global Compact asks companies to embrace, support and enact, within their sphere of influence, a set of core values in the areas of human rights, labour standards, the environment, and anti-corruption.

Human Rights

Principle 1: businesses should support and respect the protection of internationally proclaimed human rights; and

Principle 2: make sure that they are not complicit in human rights abuses.

Labour Standards

Principle 3: businesses should uphold the freedom of association and the effective recognition of the right to collective bargaining,

Principle 4: the elimination of all forms of forced and compulsory labour;

Principle 5: the effective abolition of child labour; and

Principle 6: the elimination of discrimination in respect of employment and occupation.

Environment

Principle 7: businesses should support a precautionary approach to environmental challenges;

Principle 8: undertake initiatives to promote greater environmental responsibility; and

Principle 9: encourage the development and diffusion of environmentally friendly technologies.

Anti-Corruption

Principle 10: businesses should work against corruption in all its forms, including extortion and bribery.

Source: http://www.unglobalcompact.org/AboutTheGC/TheTenPrinciples/index.html

Climate change

The issues of climate change are now mainstream owing to various UN climate directives and efforts of high-profile advocates such as the US past vice-president Al Gore. Organizations worldwide are trying to understand risks and opportunities in a carbon-constrained world. For example, the UK committed to reduce total greenhouse gas emissions by at least 80 per cent below 1990 levels by 2050 under the Climate Change Act 2008 and companies have to calculate their carbon footprint in line with Defra guidelines.

Go to the Online Resource Centre to access a link to Defra's Environmental Key Performance Indicators: Reporting Guidelines for UK Business

A leading provider of water and wastewater services in the UK, Anglian Water, is working to Defra's guidelines, and reducing its total net greenhouse gas emissions by 50 per cent from a 2010 baseline by 2035. Nearly a quarter (22.5 per cent) of the energy Anglian Water uses comes from renewable sources in addition to generating its own energy through Combined Heat and Power engines. Its carbon dioxide emissions come from wastewater process emissions, purchased electricity, self-generated renewable electricity, transport emissions, fuels used at operational sites and offices, water process emissions, and biosolids to land emissions.

Anglian Water used diverse methods to reduce its emissions and these included installing hundreds of smart meters to improve the accurate measurement of electricity consumption; developing a carbon model to calculate the emissions from the building and operating of new assets; generating electricity from renewable sources and saving electricity, making a key wastewater treatment works self-sufficient in renewable power, and launching a 'think energy' campaign which reduced energy consumption and raised employee awareness.

How far should CR go?

There is the question of how far companies should go beyond managing their own impact. For example, Mattel was forced to recall almost 20 million items made in China because of lead paint on toy cars and tiny magnets that could be deadly if swallowed. Nike recalled 235,000 football helmets because the Chinese-made chin cup had a defective strap and caused at least two concussions and a broken nose (Fortune 2008).

Stakeholder communication is now CR

With the growth of CR, practitioners can be involved in helping an organization communicate its corporate responsibility performance to its key stakeholders such as customers, employees, investors, suppliers, and community groups. Communicating CR to publics is an increasingly significant strategy and can help an organization to attract finance, encourage innovation through building understanding with stakeholders, attract and retain workers, and enhance its reputation.

Stakeholder groups are also expected to play a more active part in reporting and shaping the type of information that is disclosed as well as its format and timing, according to the KPMG report (2008). Rapidly advancing communications technology can help organizations to connect with their stakeholders in more innovative and effective ways such as through social media forums and other discussion groups and engage them in scenario planning to identify corporate responsibility risks. See chapter 10 for more on risk assessment.

Using CR to link people to an organization

More and more people are deciding on what to buy and who to buy it from based on an organization's social and environmental criteria (Perez 2009). Therefore, CR has become a way for a company to differentiate itself from its competitors. It can do this by being part of an organization's promotional initiatives, linking to social causes to generate a perception of a socially responsible organization to which consumers relate. An example of this is BT ChildLine (see chapter 6) where employees fundraise and volunteer for the ChildLine charity.

In a competitive marketplace where many products are similar, people are making buying choices because they identify with one organization more than another. Also, consumers are buying products to express something about themselves. Perez (2009) argues that CR can help an organization to generate a degree of identification with its publics in order to encourage their interest and commitment towards it. Therefore, CR programmes need to examine the shared values, shared personality traits and characteristics, common objectives and needs of both the organization and its stakeholders. Perez (2009) suggests generating a positive attitude and behaviour towards an organization and subsequent identification with it through:

1. Carrying out social responsibilities and communicating these as CR initiatives that relate to how consumers perceive the organization.
2. Develop a corporate brand based on CR as this reinforces the consumer's relationship with the company.

For example, Anglian Water is one of the largest employers in the east of England and, employees are given many opportunities to contribute to the communities they serve. Anglian Water's CR includes an education programme to encourage people to see water as a vital resource and develop responsible attitudes to its usage and waste disposal and to promote environmental concerns. This education fosters environmental action and brings benefits to customers, employees, investors, business partners, and the wider community (see Case Study in this chapter).

The future

Human rights are now a fast-changing issue for business. The UN recognizes that although governments have the primary responsibility for human rights, the business community has a responsibility to uphold human rights both in the workplace and within its 'sphere of influence'. The UN states that behaving responsibly is allied to recognizing that a good human rights record can support improved business performance. Consequently, this has led to the discussions between business, governments, and society on the expectations and responsibilities of big business towards human rights.

The UN claims that behaving responsibly means complying with local and international law; addressing consumer concerns, especially as consumers are increasingly aware of where goods come from and where they are made; treating workers with dignity, building good community relationships particularly as global companies are very visible owing to communications technologies; and respecting the national laws of the countries in which they operate; as well as being aware of human rights and embedding these into the organization's values.

According to the UN Global Compact (2010) successful and sustainable businesses make a crucial contribution to supporting human rights by providing jobs, goods and services and most go further in supporting human rights. Principle one of the UN

Global Compact's ten principles states that 'businesses should support and respect the protection of internationally proclaimed human rights'. See Box 11.3 for the UN examples of how companies are supporting and respecting human rights through their daily activities.

Box 11.3 Examples of how companies are supporting and respecting human rights through their daily activities

In the workplace:

- by providing safe and healthy working conditions,
- by guaranteeing freedom of association,
- by ensuring non-discrimination in personnel practices,
- by ensuring that they do not use directly or indirectly forced labour or child labour, and
- by providing access to basic health, education and housing for the workers and their families, if these are not provided elsewhere.

In the community:

- by preventing the forcible displacement of individuals, groups or communities,
- by working to protect the economic livelihood of local communities, and
- by contributing to the public debate. Companies interact with all levels of government in the countries where they operate. They therefore have the right and responsibility to express their views on matters that affect their operations, employees, customers and the communities of which they are a part.

In security:

If companies use security services to protect their operations, they must guarantee that existing international guidelines and standards for the use of force are respected.

Source: http://www.unglobalcompact.org/AboutTheGC/TheTenPrinciples/principle1.html

---

⊕ **Go to the Online Resource Centre to access a link to the United Nations human rights issues pages to find out about how to implement human rights in an organization**

11.3 Influences

The United Nations states that an organization should strive to ensure that its operations are, at the very least, consistent with the legal principles applicable in the country of operation. It urges an organization operating outside its country of origin to promote and raise standards 'in countries where support and enforcement of human rights issues is insufficient'.

Ethical values of an organization and its publics are usually incorporated into the legal business framework of its country which determines how it must trade, what financial restrictions it has, and how it can communicate to its publics. In public relations, practitioners need to ensure that they are working within an organization's legislation, regulations, and codes.

Legislation is a law, or a set of laws. In the UK these have been passed by Parliament at Westminster. On the other hand, regulations do not have to go through that process; they can be directly imposed by an approved person, organization, or trade body.

Office of Fair Trading

The UK's **Office of Fair Trading** (OFT) is an independent **regulatory body** that plays a leading role in promoting and protecting consumer interests while ensuring that businesses are fair and competitive. For example, in 2010 the OFT imposed a penalty after the employees from the Royal Bank of Scotland shared confidential information about the pricing of its loans with Barclays Bank. This allowed Barclays to set the pricing of its own loans which suggested some customers could have been charged more for their borrowing (*Guardian* 2009).

Powers are granted to the OFT under consumer and competition legislation to arm businesses with knowledge to protect themselves against unlawful practice and encourage self-regulation rather than having laws which dictate their practices. The OFT works with sector regulators, government, the courts, the Competition Commission, the European Commission, local authority trading standards services, and businesses, consumers, and their representatives.

Office of Communications (Ofcom)

Practitioners need to know about the **Office of Communications** (Ofcom 2010) which is the regulator for the UK communications industries. It has responsibilities for television, radio, telecommunications, and wireless communications services. Ofcom is required by the government to draw up a code or codes setting standards for programmes, sponsorship, and fairness and privacy, and also includes advice to broadcasters on how smoking and other drugs can be portrayed in the media.

Trading Standards Institute

The **Trading Standards Institute** protects consumers and is a not-for-profit professional body formed in 1881. It has members in the public and private sectors in the UK and abroad and encourages honest enterprise and business and helps to safeguard the economic, environmental, health, and social well-being of consumers. Trading standards authorities are responsible for enforcing new regulations based on an EU Directive which aims to protect consumers from unfair trading practices. The new law bans unfair advertising, marketing, and other commercial practices used by businesses in their dealings with consumers.

Go to the Online Resource Centre to access a link to finding out more about the UK Parliament and enacting laws

Go to the Online Resource Centre to access a link to the Ofcom Code (2009)

Advertising Standards Authority (ASA)

The **Advertising Standards Authority** is the UK's independent regulator of advertising across all media, including TV, internet, sales promotions, and direct marketing which, in addition to consumer protection law, helps to keep UK advertising responsible. It develops advertising codes which lay down rules for advertisers, agencies, and media owners to ensure ads are legal, decent, honest, and truthful, as well as socially responsible and in line with the principles of fair competition. It deals with complaints, and has advertisements withdrawn if a complaint is upheld. The Advertising Standards Codes are separated into codes for TV, radio, and all other types of advertisements, including teletext and interactive advertising. Public relations practitioners need to know about advertising regulations in order to ensure that their organization is not advertising inappropriately or misleading its publics and thereby being seen as unethical.

In addition, the codes contain specific rules for certain products and marketing techniques. These include scheduling times of TV advertisements, rules for alcoholic drinks, health and beauty claims, children, medicines, financial products, environmental claims, gambling, direct marketing, and prize promotions.

An example of a breach of advertising regulations was a TV advertisement for an Old El Paso fajitas kit, which showed a family cooking, preparing, and eating fajitas. A viewer believed the ad was misleading because the tortillas shown were larger than those provided in the Old El Paso fajitas kit. The company claimed the advertisement was originally Australian and had used the larger Australian tortillas and adapted the footage for use in the UK. Although on-screen text stated 'Kit contains smaller tortillas than shown', the ASA ruled that this contradicted the more prominent visuals, which showed tortillas larger than those supplied with the kit. The ASA concluded that the advertisement was likely to mislead viewers about the contents of the product and was deemed to breach the TV Advertising Standards Code (ASA 2009).

Regulatory bodies

Most trade and manufacturing sectors have their own regulatory body which means they regulate themselves instead of having laws to dictate their practices. For example, the Association of the British Pharmaceutical Industry (ABPI) is the trade association for more than 90 companies in the UK which produce prescription medicines. Its member companies research, develop, manufacture, and supply more than 80 per cent of the medicines prescribed through the National Health Service. It has developed a code of practice which influences legislation affecting the industry and has rules governing communication about medicines to all publics. PR practitioners must familiarize themselves with this code in order to communicate ethically with these publics.

However the code of practice does not take into consideration online interaction, for example, **Sidewiki technology**. This online tool can be downloaded via a Google toolbar and means that members of the public can write comments directly next to a brand's website and the brand cannot delete them. However, strict regulations limit how much pharmaceutical companies can interact with the public and is creating some big PR

🌐 **Go to the Online Resource Centre to access a link to weekly ASA adjudications**

challenges, according to *PR Week* (O'Reilly 2009). Other companies can respond to comments alongside any web page, but the pharmaceutical industry cannot interact with the public so freely. Therefore, although sidewikis can change the way people view a pharmaceutical organization's information online, the organization has no control over it.

Changes in one country's regulations can also create confusion in another country. The US Food and Drug Administration, which regulates medical treatments and their promotion, changed its rules to allow direct-to-consumer marketing in 1997. This led to advertising and PR campaigns promoting prescription drugs and celebrities endorsing particular medicines during chat show appearances. However, medicines that need a prescription cannot be marketed directly to the British public and therefore the American campaigns were not able to be used or mimicked in the UK.

⊕ **Go to the Online Resource Centre to access a link for more about legislation**

Commercial law

In addition to international and country laws governing organizations in general, there are specific requirements and legal structures which cover the different types of businesses and commercial transactions and the sectors in which they operate. This affects an organization's legal obligations, its liability and how it communicates.

1. Incorporated companies

An **incorporated company** is registered at Companies House, a government branch which acts a registrar of companies. There are two main types of incorporated companies—private limited and public limited.

Private limited company (Ltd)
A **private limited company** is one where the liability is limited. A sole trader has unlimited liability but in a limited company the liability is limited to the value of the shares issued. This means that any debts belong to the company and not the owners. To form a limited company it must be registered at Companies House and have formal legal documents including a Memorandum and Articles of Association. There need be only one director and they have to prepare annual accounts and submit these to Companies House where they are kept on record. All these accounts are available for anyone to see at a small fee.

Public limited company (Plc)
Like a private limited company, a **public limited company** (plc) has shares, but the key difference is that these shares can be bought by the public. Anyone buying shares is therefore a shareholder or investor. Offering shares is a means by which companies are able to obtain finance to invest in the company, therefore shareholders are important to a plc because they provide the investment to keep the company financially secure and maintain or even increase its value. Customers are also important as they buy the product.

When carrying out public relations for a plc is important to consider both these publics. If the reputation of the organization is poor the shares of the company will fall and sell for less and less, therefore affecting its overall value. A company's reputation also affects whether people will buy its products or services. Plcs are legally bound to produce annual reports and accounts and submit them to Companies House. A plc must have at least two directors and a fully qualified company secretary who is responsible for the accounts and the legal dealings of the company. It is important for a PR practitioner to know that a company's board of directors provides the company with direction and advice and ensures that the company fulfills its mission statement. The board of directors frequently sets the company's overall policy objectives and therefore needs to be involved with any ethical or corporate responsibility initiative or implementation. Examples of British plcs are British Airways plc, British Gas plc, and British Telecommunications plc.

2. Unincorporated companies

An **unincorporated company** is a business that is not registered with Companies House. There are two main types:

Sole trader

A **sole trader** is the simplest type of business—it has no legal requirements. It can just be one person who sets up a business and any income or profit are their own, except for the tax they pay on the income. Any debts incurred are the personal responsibility of the sole trader.

Partnership

A **partnership** is like a sole trader but with ownership between partners. A partnership has a legal partnership agreement which shows the rights and responsibilities of the partners. 'Sleeping partners' are those who own a share of the business but are not involved in the day-to-day running of it; they are usually a partner because they have helped finance the business. Just like a sole trader, a partnership has unlimited liability.

11.4 Application to industry

A CR report in the *Economist* (2009) noted that in the recession which started in 2008, CR budgets were not cut as much as predicted and claimed that consumer interest in sustainability was likely to remain strong, even in economically difficult times. This may be because companies are seen to be making the world better while making money at the same time.

For example, Mars and Cadbury (which both make confectionary products) have separately announced plans to increase the amount of cocoa they source from sustainable sources. Ikea is concerned about ongoing sources of wood—its main raw material—and is planning to use more wood from responsibly managed forests (*Economist* 2009).

Case Study

Looking after England's rivers

Source: Courtesy of Anglian Water

This case study shows the enormous ramifications of a CR programme which affects stakeholders from employees to the government in building its CR profile as well as achieving its business objectives.

Anglian Water, a leading provider of water and wastewater services in the UK, is located in the east of England and serves the needs of around six million industrial, commercial, and domestic customers. Anglian Water's corporate responsibility is about making sure it manages key elements of its day-to-day business and long-term planning in ways that are sustainable. It seeks to demonstrate to all its stakeholders (customers, communities, investors, employees, regulators, and other agencies) that it makes sound business decisions that ensure their needs are met, now and into the uncertain future.

In the Anglian Water region there are over 3,326 kilometres of rivers and also the UK's only wetland national park, the Norfolk and Suffolk Broads. These waterways support a variety of plants and animals and commercial businesses and they improve the local communities' quality of life. The environment is central to Anglian Water's business and to their customers' quality of life. It takes water from the environment, treats it, and supplies it to their customers. It then collects and treats their wastewater before returning it to the environment.

In the east of England, Anglian Water operates over 1,100 wastewater treatment works producing high-quality water to protect the river environment. The RiverCare programme is an opportunity for local communities to do their bit to protect and enhance their river environment. The focus was on partnerships with the communities with whom Anglian Water works and establishing self-sustaining groups able to take lasting local action in partnership with their district council, wildlife trust, local Environment Agency (EA), and Anglian Water staff.

Working with partners

RiverCare is funded by Anglian Water, managed by Keep Britain Tidy—an environmental charity—and supported by the EA, all working together in partnership. Having the EA's support at a corporate level is critical in raising the project's profile and the EA has also provided the expertise of its teams.

At a local level, stakeholders comprise local authority officers, councillors, police, wildlife trusts, EA staff, and the media. Effective partnerships with these stakeholders provide the local support network necessary for each RiverCare group to take effective local action against their given issues.

ⓦ Go to the Online Resource Centre to access a link to the RiverCare interactive website

The project supports volunteers to improve their local river environment by helping them with the removal of litter, fly-tipped debris, and non-native species. Community volunteer activities are coordinated primarily by two full-time staff.

There are 45 RiverCare groups operating across the Anglian Water region—comprising more than 900 regular volunteers empowered to deliver local environmental improvements. During 2008, volunteers participated in numerous RiverCare events removing hundreds of bags of litter and thousands of bulky items from river environments across the region. Research has revealed an 8 per cent increase in customers' satisfaction with river water quality due, at least in part, to the RiverCare scheme.

Community and organization integration

The project is guided by a RiverCare Steering Group of senior managers from Anglian Water and Keep Britain Tidy. It is fully integrated with the wider CR policy with targets and progress against those reported in its annual community and environment report. The Anglian Water Executive Board and a CR steering group monitor progress on all CR activities promoted within and outside the company.

Anglian Water funds and supports RiverCare managers to establish their community group and run events, carry out river risk assessments, provide equipment for the groups, and develop partnerships with local authority officers, councillors, wildlife trusts, Environmental Agency staff, and the media.

Reporting through key performance indicators

The project's performance is monitored through key performance indicators and against individual 'input', 'throughput', and 'output' targets each month and submitted to the Anglian Water Executive Board. The communications strategy is constantly updated.

Employee involvement

Anglian Water has an employee volunteering programme which gives employees time to volunteer for community activities, including RiverCare. Anglian Water staff volunteer at Rivercare clean-up events, give presentations to local stakeholders, and establish RiverCare community groups of their own. Anglian Water staff have also organized events with EA staff which has strengthened relations between the two organizations and enhanced joint working.

Internal communication

Articles are written for the company intranet, staff magazine, and weekly e-bulletins sent to participating staff with inspiring stories encouraging involvement from staff members. Knowledge is shared between board members at the Steering and Working Group meetings and the lessons learned are reported to the company's community investment programme.

Fig 11.3
An example of the art made from dumped supermarket trollies

Source: Courtesy of Anglian Water

Community communication

A 'Trolley Art' media campaign was launched using sculptures of riverside wildlife made from discarded shopping trolleys pulled out of rivers (see Figure 11.3). It communicated project details to local communities, encouraging them to set up their own group. The Trolley Art campaign and its awards created extensive media coverage with the subsequent publicity significantly enhancing the RiverCare brand and the reputation of Anglian Water. Website visits to http://www.rivercare.org.uk doubled and a dozen new community groups were established as a direct result of the interest generated.

The communications team undertakes media work promoting the project, profiling Anglian Water as funders and key partners, and encouraging more people to become involved. Both Anglian Water staff and the Keep Britain Tidy team share good environmental practice.

Business to business communication

The success of RiverCare is communicated to the utilities sector and wider audience by entering industry specific awards and by sharing knowledge through WaterUK.

RiverCare is not only a partnership between the organizations which run the project, but also with local people. As stated above, in 2006 independent market research for Anglian Water revealed an 8 per cent increase in customers' satisfaction with river water quality. RiverCare has also helped to improve customers' wider perception of Anglian Water's services and views on less positive subjects such as bill increases and disruptive capital investment works.

RiverCare has also provided a rewarding means of developing employees' skills through volunteering and meeting their personal and professional development objectives. Staff associated a 'feel good factor' with volunteering for RiverCare and feel a greater sense of pride in working for Anglian Water because it is an organization that goes above and beyond its statutory responsibilities to protect and enhance the local environment.

Engaging young people

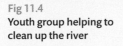

Go to the Online Resource Centre to access a link to more examples on the RiverCare 'local projects'

A great deal of additional benefit is achieved through the coverage the groups gain in the local media. This raises awareness about the issue of litter dumped in waterways and therefore inspires others to take action. More than 40 media hits are attained in the local press by the groups each year. Every RiverCare group has its own success story such as the one below involving young people.

A key priority for RiverCare is to engage young people with the project and encourage them to take pride in their local environment (see Figure 11.4). A RiverCare group was set up in the town of March in Cambridgeshire, working specifically with young people from the town and successfully engaging them in positive riverside environmental projects. The group now holds many clean-ups each year.

RiverCare supports the Northampton Sea Cadets and the Waveney Valley Canoe Club, encouraging their younger members to engage with their environment in a positive way. Between them, these two groups removed over 50 bags of litter from their water courses during 2008.

RiverCare also worked with Grantham Police to engage teenagers in an area of high youth crime. The teenagers were supported in cleaning-up Grantham Canal and in doing so they gained a sense of ownership and responsibility for their local community and river environment.

Fig 11.4
Youth group helping to clean up the river

Source: Courtesy of Anglian Water

PR Tool

How to develop a code of ethics

Source: Courtesy of the Institute of Business Ethics http://www.ibe.org.uk

The following outlines how to develop a **code of ethics** for an organization

1. Get endorsement from the board

Corporate values and ethics are matters of governance. The board must understand the business case for an ethics policy and code, recognize their role in its success, its relevance to what they do and how, and be committed to monitoring its effectiveness.

2. Find a champion

It is good practice to set up a board level (ethics or corporate responsibility) committee, preferably chaired by a non-executive director, or to assign responsibility to an existing committee such as one involved in risk management. A senior manager will need to be responsible for the development of the policy and code and the implementation of the ethics programme.

3. Understand the purpose

It is important to clarify the relationship between and understand the organization's approach to corporate responsibility, ethics, compliance, and corporate social responsibility strategies.

4. Find out what bothers people

Merely endorsing an external standard or copying a code from another organization will not suffice. It is important to find out what topics employees require guidance on, to be clear what issues are of concern to stakeholders, and what issues are material to the organization's business activities, locations, and sector.

5. Be familiar with external standards and good practice

Find out how other companies in your sector approach ethics and corporate responsibility. Understand what makes an effective policy, code, and programme from the point of view of the business, the staff, and other stakeholders. How will the code be embedded into business practice?

6. Monitoring and assurance

Consider how the success of the policy will be monitored and to whom the business will be accountable regarding its ethical commitments. How will it be evident that it is working? What are the key indicators/measures of an ethical culture for the organization?

7. Try it out first

The draft code needs piloting—perhaps with a sample of employees drawn from all levels and different locations. The Institute of Business Ethics welcomes requests to comment on drafts.

8. Review plan

A process of review that will take account of changing business environments, strategy, stakeholder concerns and social expectations, new standards, and strengths and weakness in the ethical performance.

Summary

Organizations and stakeholders are becoming more aware of ethical, environmental, and social impacts of a business. The availability of communications technology is driving greater communication between the two groups. In addition, organizations are becoming an integral part of a community. Yet with communication comes the expectation of truthfulness. Publics are expecting transparency of information from organizations that allows them to make decisions.

Therefore ethics in an organization means ensuring that people have information which allows them to make rational and reflective judgements. Even though public relations uses persuasive forms of communication, practitioners need to ensure it is truthful, authentic, and respectful of its publics. However, there are also issues of corporate confidentiality which need to be considered when communicating and understanding the particular sector and these can allow practitioners to communicate appropriately.

With increasing scrutiny by publics, organizations have to ensure that they are not only successful commercially but also benefiting the community. CR is a reputational issue as the social and environmental impact of an organization is affecting business in the future and becoming a consideration in all its decisions. These can range from where an organization sources it raw products to forming and implementing its business strategy.

CR is now being increasingly reported by organizations through their annual reports, on their websites, and through specific CR reports. Much of this initiative has been driven by the UN which is demanding CR from large companies. Three-quarters of the world's top organizations have a CR strategy and an increasing number are following UN guidelines which inspire other companies to do the same.

Globalization, rapid media changes, and active and educated stakeholders are driving the need for CR and the requirement for transparency from organizations. CR is implemented differently throughout the world depending on the country but organizations are guided by the UN's Ten Principles in the areas of human rights, labour, the environment, and anti-corruption.

CR can also be used to differentiate a company from its competitors thereby creating a perception as a socially and environmentally responsible organization. This can also help publics to identify with an organization, sharing its values and influencing their buying choices. It is therefore important that public relations practitioners communicate CR programmes to stakeholders and also incorporate them into the corporate brand.

The issue of climate change is now an intrinsic part of CR programmes and the UK has legislation to ensure this happens. In addition, communication with publics is seen as part of a CR programme and innovative communications technology can engage people in social forums and scenario planning. Equally, human rights is a growing area for CR and the UN expects businesses to take responsibility for this by ensuring employees and the community are not negatively affected by the business.

Ethical aspects of business are usually incorporated into an organization's legal framework and it is crucial that practitioners understand the specific legislation and regulations which affect its communications. There are also organizations that affect how business is managed, such as the OFT which is an independent regulatory body and protects consumer interests and ensures businesses are fair and competitive. The media is also regulated and this is done by Ofcom which has codes for the standards of media content and scheduling.

There are also commercial laws that affect how an organization is run, depending on how it is constructed. For example, whether a company is registered with Companies House, is incorporated as a private limited company or a public limited company and has specific legal considerations. A public limited company has shares which can be bought and those who buy them are called shareholders, who are a significant public for the organization and are affected when the overall value of the organization changes or is expected to change. Therefore a public limited company must have a strong reputation to ensure its value stays strong.

A code of ethics for a company is an essential aspect of any organization and the practitioner will be involved in developing this. It must have a clear purpose and reflect the organization's CR approach and be specific to the organization, addressing real concerns from its publics, including employees. A code of ethics also provides an opportunity to ensure that the CR aspects of a business are monitored and evaluated, reviewing stakeholder concerns and issues.

CR is a growing area and has enormous ramifications and builds reputations as well as achieving business objectives. It is important that CR is embedded in the company and this needs ongoing involvement of the company's board.

Discussion points

A. Types of organizations

Find six organizations that interest you.

Can you classify them as incorporated or unincorporated? Are they sole traders or partnerships? Or are they a limited company or a public liability company?

What legal aspects would be different in each of these companies? As a public relations practitioner what factors do you need to be aware of?

B. Regulations

Identify the sectors in which these organizations work. Then find the industry code or regulations that govern them. Do they have their own company code?

C. Corporate responsibility

Using the same six organizations, find their corporate responsibility programme. What does it cover, eg communication with stakeholders, social interests, education and development, community involvement. How can you identify its key stakeholders from its CR programme?

How is the CR reported, eg in the annual report, on the website, in an awards programme such as Business in the Community?

D. Ethical tests

Think about a decision you have made after some consideration.

Put it to the following ethical test:

1. Transparency

   Do I mind others knowing what I have decided?

2. Effect

   Who does my decision affect or hurt?

3. Fairness

   Would my decision be considered fair by those affected?
   List each out of ten. How does using an ethical test affect your decision?

References

Advertising Standards Authority 'ASA Adjudication on General Mills UK Ltd'. Available at: http://www.asa.org.uk/Complaints-and-ASA-action/Adjudications/2009/12/General-Mills-UK-Ltd/TF_ADJ_47842.aspx

AFP (2009) 'Chanel Cleared in French Counterfeit Case', News On Political Scandals, 12 November. Available at: http://www.politicalscandalnews.com/article/Chanel%20cleared%20in%20French%20counterfeit%20case/?k=j83s12y12h94s27k02

Bartels, W. (2008) 'KPMG Corporate Responsibility Survey', Foreword, p 2. Available at: http://us.kpmg.com/RutUS_prod/Documents/8/Corporate_Sustainability_Report_US_Final.pdf

Defra 'Environmental Key Performance Indicators: Reporting Guidelines for UK Business'. Available at: http://www.defra.gov.uk/environment/business/reporting/pdf/envkpi-guidelines.pdf

Economist (2008a) 'Corporate Responsibility is Largely a Matter of Enlightened Self Interest', Economist 386/8563 (19 January): 22–4

Economist (2008b) 'Going Global: CSR is Spreading Around the World but in Different Guises', Economist 386/8563 (Special section 19 January): 20–1 Available at: http://web.ebscohost.com/ehost/delivery?vid=9&hid=1057sid=fe7c4f45-499e-4d8-a

Economist (2009) 'A Stress Test for Good Intentions', Economist 391/8631 (16 May): 69–70

Fawkes, J. (2007) 'Public Relations Models and Persuasion Ethics: A New Approach', Journal of Communication Management 11/4: 313–31

Fitzpatrick, K. and Bronstein, C. (2006) Ethics in Public Relations. Thousand Oaks, CA: Sage

Gower, K. (2006) 'Truth and Transparency' in K. Fitzpatrick and C. Bronstein (eds) Ethics in Public Relations. Thousand Oaks, CA: Sage

Griffin, A. (2008) New Strategies for Reputation Management. London: Kogan Page

Hallahan, K. (2006) 'Responsible Online Communication' in K. Fitzpatrick and C. Bronstein (eds) Ethics in Public Relations: Responsible Advocacy. Thousand Oaks, CA: Sage, pp 107–30

Institute of Business Ethics (2008) 'Developing An Effective Code of Ethics: Eight Steps for Preparing a New Code' Available at: http://www.ibe.org.uk/codesofethics/codes2.html

International Public Relations Association (2010) IPRA Codes available at: http://www.ipra.org/detail.asp?articleid=31The Economist

Kenyon, P. (2000) 'Gap and Nike: No Sweat?', BBC News, 15 October. Available at: http://news.bbc.co.uk/2/hi/programmes/panorama/970385.stm

KPMG (2008) 'International Survey of Corporate Responsibility'. Available at: http://www.kpmg.com/CN/en/IssuesAndInsights/ArticlesPublications/Pages/Corporate responsibility-survey-200810-o.aspx

Mallenbaker.net (2010) 'Corporate Social Responsibility'. Available at: http://www.mallenbaker.net/csr/definition.ph

Messina, A. (2007) 'Public Relations, The Public Interest and Persuasion: An Ethical Approach', Journal of Communication Management 11/1: 29–52

Fortune (2007) '101 Dumbest Moments in Business'. Available at: http://money.cnn.com/galleries/2007/fortune/0712/gallery.101_dumbest.fortune/index.html

Ofcom (2010) http://www.ofcom.org.uk/tv/ifi/codes/bcode/

O'Reilly, G. (2009) 'Google Sidewiki Could Damage Corporate Brand Reputations', 20 October. Available at: http://www.prweek.com/uk/news/search/947139/Google-Sidewiki-damage corporate-brand-reputations/

Perez, R. (2009) 'Effects of Perceived Identity Based on Corporate Social Responsibility: The Role of Consumer Identification with the Company', Corporate Reputation Review 12/2: 177–91

Rachels, J. and Rachels, S. (2010) The Elements of Moral Philosophy (6th edn). New York: McGraw Hill

Seib, P. and Fitzpatrick, K. (1995) Public Relations Ethics. Orlando, FL: Harcourt Brace

Tench, R. and Willis, P. (2009) 'Creativity, Deception or Ethical Malpractice: A Critique of the Trumanisation of Marketing Public Relations Through Guerrilla Campaigns', Ethical Space, The International Journal of Communication Ethics 6/2: 47–55

United Nations Global Compact (2010) Available at www.unglobalcompact.org/AboutTheGC/TheTenPrinciples/principle1.html

UNGC (2007a) 'Global Compact Annual Review'. Available at: http://www.unglobalcompact.org/docs/news_events/8.1/GCAnnualReview2007.df

UN global compact (2007b) 'Making the Connection, the GRI Guidelines and UNGC Communication in Progress'. Available at: http://www.unglobalcompact.org/docs/news_events/8.1/GCAnnualReview2007.df

Wearden, G. (2010) 'Royal Bank of Scotland Fined £28.6m for Breaching Competition Law', 30 March Available at http://www.guardian.co.uk/business/2010/mar/30/rbs-fine-competition-law-barclays

Go to the Online Resource Centre to access a link to a movie showing how an innovative water pump brings life to villages

12 Online PR

Learning Objectives

1. Understand the context of online media, its origins, and its composition and how this has led to its social media capabilities.

2. Be able to understand the pervasiveness and usability of the web and the relationship it has on everyday life and how it affects people's lives.

3. Be able to explain how people use the internet to obtain information and how it has changed behaviour such as multitasking.

4. Be able to review how an organization's value can change owing to how the internet affects reputations and the development of publics.

5. Be able to explain how social media replaces mass communication and networked relationships and how it has led to participation, openness, community conversations, and connectedness.

6. Be able to define online social media and how to develop a social media strategy through reviewing the skills and practices in case studies.

Practitioner Insight

David Phillips
Practising online consultant with
Publicasity

David Phillips FCIPR, FSNCR is a practising online consultant with Publicasity (Consumer PR), Living Group (financial PR), and Gosh PR (lifestyle and travel) and is a director of the online PR research company *Klea* Global.

David is a long-time advocate of online public relations and first spoke about it to the Chartered Institute of Public Relations in 1995. He is the author of three books about public relations and the internet and has written many papers.

David is a Fellow of the Chartered Institute of Public Relations and a Fellow of the Society of New Communications Research. He is also a professor of online public relations at Escola Superior de Comunicação Social, Portugal and lectures at the University of Gloucestershire.

What has been the main way that the internet has changed public relations?

The mid twentieth-century hijacking of PR to serve marketing, spin, and publicity (advertising) has done a lot of damage to the practice of PR. The internet, with its emphasis on the need for competitive transparency, the dangers of an 'always on everywhere' internet making organizations porous, the internet acting as an agent of message change both automatically and through the intervention of external actors, incredible richness in content and its glocal 'Real Time Web' reach, has brought to the fore the need for PR practice to be fundamentally about relationships.

What would you advise practitioners to focus on when talking to organizations about social media?

Forget the term 'social media', it is a distraction. The real focus is on the extent of the public digital asset. Tens of thousands of pages of information about the client organization is already online. The key for all organizations is how the asset is being managed and by whom. When the CFO knows he has yet another asset to worry about, the return he can achieve from it will focus the mind of the Board in terms they understand from day-to-day management of shareholder assets.

What do you think are the key trends in online PR?

I think that the biggest change is that the internet has escaped from the PC. Mobile internet, iPad, and chips in everything from the hearing aid to the microwave oven are pretty fundamental. These developments affect relationships between organizations and their constituencies.

What are the best ways to monitor online media?

There are two schools of thought. One is to select the media to monitor (measure, evaluate, and assess) such as print press, online media, blogs, social networks, etc. The alternative is to monitor it all in real time using sophisticated tools which can identify the many different types of online channel. Always, there is a need for a benchmark and so competitive analysis has a significant role to play.

How can practitioners keep abreast of developments in online PR without feeling overwhelmed?

Well, I guess I wish I knew. In the agencies I work with we tend to have a single repository of news, we go to a lot of conferences and we monitor experts closely—and, we play with the toys—every week.

12.1 Definition

Online public relations is that part of public relations practice which empowers an organization's internal and external publics to use the internet for optimum benefit to the organization. Online public relations is utterly pervasive in PR practice. It acts on every public, stakeholder, and influencer. According to Phillips and Young (2009) it acts on two levels of relationship and often both at the same time.

- the internet has direct influences on publics
- the internet mediates influence on publics.

No one controls the internet; it is an agent in its own right. There is considerable scope for the well-informed and skilled communicator to influence channels for communication online and the content made available for interaction.

History

The internet has been around for a long time. In the 1950s computers could pass data from one to another. Some years later, Licklider (1960) proposed a network of computers, connected to one another by wide-band communication lines working as libraries together with information storage and retrieval and other similar functions.

That started the idea of a web of computers which could transfer data over telephone wires, cable, optical fibre, and radio waves (by satellite then and now on the mobile phone network).

Within a few years, Donald Davies at the British National Physical Laboratory developed a network based on what he called **packet-switching**. This gave the embryo internet the kind of reliability we now take for granted. Information is cut into small packets of data with an address; this means that each packet can use any route to get to its destination and can be stored and sent many times and then re-assembled with the other packets when it arrives at the end destination.

Early email

In the early 1970s a system called Bulletin Boards was developed for sending written messages that could be stored, read, and replied to all on one 'page' and by 1978, with the advent of Usenet, came additional capability to hold online discussions in near real time. In 1979, an American company, CompuServe, became the first service to offer electronic mail capabilities. That led to the birth of email and in 1980 it offered real-time chat which is now known as instant messaging. In two years Bulletin Boards, Usenet, email, and instant messaging brought social media to everyone who had access to a computer.

Next came the internet

In 1977, a three-computer network test was conducted between sites in the US, UK, and Norway. This test provided a basic system that could be used by everyone who wanted to send data and messages from any computer to any other computer. This set of electronic rules is called Internet Protocols commonly known as TCP/IP. Several other TCP/IP prototypes were developed at multiple research centres between 1978 and 1983. From then on, there were almost no systems for providing information that could not be shared between different computers and computing systems. The internet had truly arrived.

At this time, the internet was used by academics, national defence industries, and big companies with lots of information they wanted to shift round the world. There was also a tiny band who wanted to talk to people round the world using the rather drab formats with green screens and a blinking cursor. There were by now new computers called 'Personal Computers'. These were used for word processing and other business functions and could be hooked up to the (painfully slow pre-broadband, dial-up) telephone network to get onto the internet, send and receive emails, and chat to friends. Everything was now in place for the next big thing.

The World Wide Web

In March 1989 a scientist called Tim Berners-Lee wrote 'Information Management: A Proposal'. It began with the understated sentence: 'This proposal concerns the management of general information about accelerators and experiments at CERN', and created the biggest social and economic revolution for centuries.

Go to the Online Resource Centre to access a link to Berner-Lee's internet proposal

The Web arrived on 6 August 1991 when Berners-Lee published his technical papers; his breakthrough was to marry hypertext and a single structure for text to the internet. In his book, *Weaving the Web*, he explains that when he finally tackled the project himself he developed a system of globally unique identifiers for resources on the Web and elsewhere: the Uniform Resource Locator (URL) and Uniform Resource Identifier (URI); the publishing language, HyperText Markup Language (HTML); and the Hypertext Transfer Protocol (HTTP).

The first web browser called Mosaic came in 1993 and allowed graphics to be integrated into web pages. A year later among the 2,738 websites was Dave and Jerry's Guide to the World Wide Web (later renamed *Yahoo* without the exclamation mark) and Birmingham City Council, an early local government site initially hosted by the University of Birmingham at http://assist.cs.bham.ac.uk:8080/ (it is now at http://www.birmingham.gov.uk).

The Web is about 5,000 days old. It has grown at near exponential rates; its flexibility is such that content from almost all the other protocols can use it and it has never broken down. Today it is also the internet protocol that carries more data than any of the others so far invented.

Web 1.0

When the internet first developed, people put online what was already in traditional media. This came directly from radio, video, film, and print and there was little change in its formatting; information was simply pasted onto a website or recordings added. There was limited opportunity for users to interact and provide feedback or content in this one-way push of information. This was known as **Web 1.0**.

Web 2.0

Web 2.0 includes chatrooms, online forums, blogs, collaborative sites such as wikis, photosharing sites, videosharing sites, and so on. It actively encourages user contribution, interaction, and user-generated comment. Web 2.0 is helped by IT developments such as the availability of blog software which means people do not need programming skills. Social networking sites use software that can be programmed to act, find, and retrieve content a user wants. Search engines are also a vital part of Web 2.0 as they store information about websites and match them to the user's search criteria (Macnamara 2009).

Web 2.0 is conducted in the form of dialogue as conversation. It is not a top-down monologue as is the mass media but enables communities to form and have a two-way exchange to reach mutual objectives.

The internet meets PR

By 1999, the Public Relations Consultant's Association and the Chartered Institute of Public Relations formed a joint Internet Commission and began to consider improved online services and practitioner engagement.

The web influences

The web affects everyone. For example a 92-year-old grandmother can have internet-mediated care, the delivery of frozen ready meals can be ordered on the website by her family, and her carers can have schedules accessed online and via their mobile phones. In addition, she can be a broadcaster—via Skype— to her grandchildren around the world who are likely to be writing content, publishing photos, and broadcasting their own and other people's videos and sound tracks on social networks. Her life can be mediated by the internet even if she does not use it herself, by having a panic button, fall sensors, door, window, and smoke alarm sensors accessed online by her family from a cell phone, laptop (using wifi and cellular connectivity), or even a PC at a WiFi hotspot, they can also speak to her using a mobile or computer connected to an internet/Bluetooth 'squawk box'. Such interactions are possible without the internet, but the case, immediacy, and low cost of relationships and their management is unprecedented.

The internet in personal and organizational communication can be used as follows:

- online commerce (buying food)
- confirm contracts (confirming email)
- an intermediary between organizations and constituents (friendly, caring, and reliable drivers)
- managing employees (schedules for carers)

Timeline of social media *(not to scale)*
Social media technologies that facilitate conversation

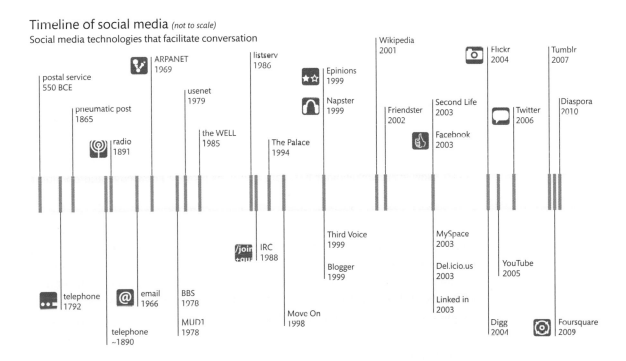

Fig 12.1
Timeline of social media

Source: Courtesy of idfive

- different forms of communication (PC, mobile phone, sensors round the house, Bluetooth)
- one on one messaging service to manage the unusual (to send SMS messages to cell phones)
- a range of communications capabilities
- many platforms (PC, laptop, mobile phone, sensors, gaming machines like Wii and Xbox), range of communication protocols (web, email, SMS, VoIP), technologies (broadband, WiFi, cellular, Bluetooth) and channels (website, email, sms, Skype, social networks) and they are used almost without thinking about them
- anyone, even a 92-year-old grandmother, can create content and be a publisher.

The internet delivers diverse, ubiquitous, and pervasive communication. It can be seen that the practitioner working for an organization providing any of these services or simply interacting with ordinary citizens has to consider the scope of influence these interactions have. They are part of that bundle of relationships that affect reputation.

12.2 Theoretical context

The mass media has been fragmenting at an astonishing rate. In only 30 years it has gone from a handful of television channels, radio stations, local and national newspapers, and magazines. Organizations and businesses believed that they had reasonable control of what was said and believed about their activities. Now the new communications channels are becoming available to everybody. This means anyone can see into a company, there is less confidentiality with its documents, its patents, its innovations, and its employees who are also likely to be communicating about the company on social media.

The organization has increased transparency and porosity (Phillips and Young 2009). Now every stakeholder has, can, and does provide knowledge and opinion to online social networks. In addition, anyone can create a website, they can have it hosted for free, and they can add discussion lists and chat facilities.

Just as weblogs (blogs) and other social media allow (or have the potential to allow) organizations an effective environment through which to have discussions and communicate directly with publics and stakeholders (without the mediation of traditional gatekeepers), so they allow users, clients, opponents, and competitors to communicate freely with each other, with the potential to create a conversation that is significantly beyond the control of the subject.

Lack of control a concern

This lack of control is a recurring concern for practitioners using digital media. A study by Seoa et al (2009) analysed how non-governmental organizations (NGOs) used digital media, such as websites, blogs, podcasts, and wikis, which allowed interactivity and independent distribution of information. The key public relations functions of the

NGOs were promoting the image of their organization, fund-raising, engaging and interacting with the general public, forging and facilitating networking with other NGOs, and providing journalists with easy access to materials regarding the organization.

Although the practitioners of the surveyed NGOs agreed on the importance of new media for public relation activities, they had concerns about reliability, message control, and the scope of online audiences (Seoa et al 2009). Most of them said that the prestige of getting stories into the mainstream media is still very important, as publics do not always think of new media outlets as being as credible as well-known media programmes. Some expressed concerns that messages posted to blogs or other social media are easily modified and misused by others and this may keep some NGOs from engaging in digital public relations.

This study also suggests how characteristics of organizations influence the ways practitioners use new media for external communication. Seoa et al (2009) suggested that NGOs should consider expanding their online public relations to include more diverse modes of new media and to recognize the potential of new media tools for enhancing two-way communications with publics and present their public relation strategies accordingly. In particular, organizations with less capacity and tight budgets should make more extensive use of new media modes, which can offer more efficient ways of promoting an NGO image and raise funds.

The media with no middle

According to Clay Shirky, the New York University professor of new media and the author of *Here Comes Everybody*, the internet changes everything about the news industry. Shirky (2008) argues that the central problem of digital media is that there isn't a central problem. It's the disappearance of the centre which is undermining the old industrial newspaper industry with its top-down hierarchies and centres of power.

The digital revolution means that audiences are, or can be, small. A single author blog can be just as effective and informed. Indeed, many journalists are very evident in many media genre and it is not difficult to follow the tweets or blog posts of top journalists from all over the world.

There is an almost endless supply of experts and charlatans who can provide copy for an almost endless number of readers. The time and timing of publication can be much more flexible. As for editorial control, there are millions of people who are prepared to act as editors by commenting on every forum, blog, or Twitter post, web page video or picture. Internet technology does away with the oligarchy of newspaper publishers, enabling anyone to publish almost anything they like in real-time at minimal cost on an always-on global network using a vast range of media. The range of media, once a few newspapers and magazine titles, TV channels, and radio stations, is now huge and diverse. With the internet anyone can read newspapers from across the world, and listen to radio stations and watch TV channels. But most people don't.

Most people go to search engines, websites, Facebook and Bebo and the music network MySpace or perhaps Last.FM, online games, blogs, instant messenger (GTalk, IM, AOL, etc), bulletin boards, wikis, Twitter, and lots more. It is big and diverse and,

Go to the Online Resource Centre to access a link to Professor Shirky's blog

furthermore, most people multi-task. They vote for X-Factor wannabes on a cell phone, watch it on TV, add comments on Facebook and all at the same time (and a few will be using **instant messaging** to mates as well) (BBC 2009). The core reality of the internet is its absence of a centre. The distributed internet has done away with the centralized structures of power of the old industrial world. There is no single media circulation or 'advertising impressions'. And without a core, news and views can't be controlled by a central power. It can no longer be owned. It can no longer be controlled.

The online asset

Go to the Online Resource Centre to access a link to the top sites list

An organization's value is related to its online presence. Perloff (2003: 45) argues that values are more global and abstract than attitudes. He gives the example of freedom as a value, which he explains includes attitudes towards censorship, entrepreneurship, political correctness, and smoking in public. People have hundreds of attitudes but dozens of values. Beliefs are more specific and can be considered the building blocks of attitudes, which are a mix of belief and feelings.

In a Google search it is not uncommon to see 'Results 1–10 of about 509,000 for XXXX organization (0.44 seconds)'. It is also easy to see how many of these pages have been indexed by Google in the last day. All the web pages mentioning an organization represent a huge internet asset and these are the sort of assets that include the recommendations and comments of the online community. Many link one with another. They add to the ranking of the organization when it is searched; and to its depth of presence in all manner of media, yet very little will have been provided by the organization or its traditional stakeholders. These search results are an online asset which does not appear on a balance sheet and yet it is the stuff of online relationships, shared values, and reputation (Phillips and Amaral 2009).

Creating relationships building reputation

These shared values act as a magnet as people cluster round shared values online. Given the opportunity, many people will also interact to share and add their own values thus enhancing the relationship.

Relationship values are the building blocks of reputation, and relationships add tangible values to products and services (Amaral and Phillips 2010). Reputation creates value from tangible and intangible assets. When an organization, product, service, or person has a good reputation it will be chosen first and foremost above competitors; it will attract more customers and they will contribute more to be a customer or 'friend'. Reputation transforms value into wealth. Social media is powerful because it is a simple way in which people can form and enrich shared values, develop relationships and organizations and people of good repute.

Conversely, Grunig (2009) believes that instead of publics forming around values, it is values, concepts, and ideologies that influence the problems that people recognize and how they define them. Online content monitoring techniques can help to code how important the problem is and whether people feel they can do anything about it, how much involvement they have in addressing it, how motivated they are in seeking information, as well as identifying their values, concepts, and ideas. Therefore, practitioners can tell management about problems and issues as it makes decisions.

Social media

There is no better place to share values than where an individual can add comments, news, views, greetings, share photographs, and perhaps real-time conversation. In this place, values can be shared with people of like mind and with similar interests, the kind of values that we most like to be associated with. This is like Facebook or Bebo, Orkut or MySpace and any number of similar social network services. It is here that after the first invitation to a friend to visit these expressions of values that friends recommend other friends to join, look, enjoy, comment, and invite each other to the 'online home' of their values. It will be a place where each is comfortable and among familiar news, views, comments, icons, and other representations of values.

Where there is discordance, people ignore or avoid such values or they become involved and react to values they do not agree with. These comments—where there is a common interest and understanding—are passed on, re-interpreted, and talked about in a network spread far and fast (Benkler 2006).

Single channel communication is no longer mass communication; it is a private conversation in the corner. There is resistance to external influences that try to impose values. The values evident in a badly targeted or ill-timed or intrusive advertisement engender resentment. Such intrusions are disliked. Mass advertising in the conversations space is tolerated only as far as it provides something such as a 'free' service, is highly relevant and timely, or a welcome distraction. This is how social media works. It replaces mass communication with networked relationships focusing on participation, openness, community, conversation, and connectedness.

There are still plenty of places online where mass communication works and works well. Websites are a good place for mass communication and offer 100 per cent control (until someone adds a Google Sidewiki comment: http://Google.com/sidewikii).

Go to the Online Resource Centre to access a link to Google Sidewiki

What does social media mean?

Social media is the term given to online technologies which allow users to interact with each other in some way. In his online book, Anthony Mayfield (2009) describes social media as a group of online media, which share most or all of the following characteristics:

1. **Participation:** encourages contributions and feedback from everyone who is interested. It blurs the line between media and audience.
2. **Openness:** open to feedback and participation, encourages voting, comments, and sharing of information with few barriers to accessing and making use of content—password-protected content is frowned on.
3. **Conversation:** offers a two-way conversation rather than content being transmitted or distributed to an audience.
4. **Community:** allows communities to form quickly and communicate effectively sharing common interests.

5. **Connectedness:** thrive on their connectedness, making use of links to other sites, resources, and people. Mayfield (2009) describes the six major forms of social media as follows:

- *social networks:* allow people to build personal web pages and then connect with friends to share content and communication, eg MySpace, Facebook, and Bebo;
- *blogs:* online journals, with entries appearing with the most recent first;
- *wikis:* websites that allow people to add content to or edit the information on them, acting as a communal document or database—the best-known wiki is Wikipedia4, the online encyclopaedia;
- *podcasts:* audio and video files that are available by subscription, through services like Apple iTunes;
- *forums:* areas for online discussion, often around specific topics and interests and are a popular element for online communities;
- *content communities:* communities which organize and share particular kinds of content—the most popular content communities tend to form around photos (Flickr), bookmarked links (delicious), and videos (YouTube).

6. **Microblogging:** social networking combined with bite-sized blogging, where small amounts of content ('updates') are distributed online and through the mobile phone network. Twitter is the leader in this field.

Social media is migrating to mobile devices with a very high proportion of social interactions being conducted via mobile applications (apps).

Social media strategy

Social networks can get organizations to engage with wider audiences and strengthen relationships with existing customers. The greatest number of followers on Facebook, Twitter, and YouTube are from grocery, fashion, and retail brands according to research from Famecount (cited Warc 2010). According to this research, Starbucks is the most effective brand in engaging with consumers online. It has more than 7.5 million Facebook fans, more than 900,000 Twitter followers, and 6,588 followers on YouTube. Brands have different online strategies. For example, Coca-Cola's strategy is dubbed a 4R approach—reviewing, responding, recording, and redirecting and has most of their online engagement on Facebook with 5.7 million netizens tracking its activity.

Wholefoods, the online natural organic grocery chain, has built its social media success on Twitter and encourages followers by uploading deals for this group only. RedBull uses subscriber status on YouTube to view interviewees, advertisements, and clips from extreme sports (Warc 2010).

Social media and the two-way symmetric model

Grunig (2009) sees social media as making public relations practice more global, strategic, two-way, interactive, symmetrical, and socially responsible. He sees that public relations using the open social media sites, Twitter, and interactive online community represent the two-way symmetrical model. He believes it is forcing practitioners to think globally about public relations practice. In response to those who claim that public relations loses control with digital media, and argues that the control of messages historically has been illusory along with the false belief that publics can be created and influenced.

Grunig (2009) states that the practitioner is a participant in an organization's decision making, rather than a conveyer of messages about the decisions. He believes that it is actually the publics who build the relationships with other publics and control the messages, to which they are exposed, not the organization or the media that disseminated the messages intended for them. Publics control their exposure to the messages and how they understand and control how much information they give to others as they move to active publics communicating with each other.

He argues that publics occur because of the consequence of an organization's behaviour on people. This could include loss of a job, changes in government legislation, or publics seeking help from an organization for obtaining medication, jobs, etc. Public relations may well try to reach the non-active publics but the messages will have minimal effect as the publics are not seeking this information. Grunig (2009) refers to his research which shows symmetrical communication is more successful than asymmetrical in building relationships with publics. Also, research shows that reputation, brands, and images are what publics think and say to each other, what they interpret, and not something organizations can create or manage.

Therefore the only way public relations can manage what people think about an organization is by participating and managing the behaviour of an organization and its communications with publics in order to cultivate relationships with them. Grunig (2009) believes that an organization and its publics are embedded in internet-mediated social networks but public relations is still about an organization's relationship with its publics. He argues that the internet has empowered publics; they are less constrained by information that is given to them, and can seek it and connect with it and interact with more information sources, not just from journalists. Digital media makes it easier to form and establish relationships. Grunig (2009) believes that digital media makes conversations formed through social networks as easy as interpersonal dialogue and urges practitioners to take advantage of the interactive and dialogic and global characteristics of the new media where it focuses communication towards the two-way symmetrical model.

Campaigning with social media

Amnesty, the international human rights charity, aims to increase awareness of human rights across the globe and in 2008 it created the blog, protectthehuman.com which became a platform for a community of digital activists. AmnestyUK launched a social media campaign to stop violence against women. A media audit identified its internet presence in a 'cloud' of social spaces, networks, and websites. These included Facebook, MySpace, Flickr, YouTube, and Twitter as well as blogs. It analysed how these linked and drew a map of Amnesty's social universe.

AmnestyUK developed a programme with digital experts. Amnesty was already a member of the End Of Violence Against Women Coalition and in partnership they launched a campaign which focused on International Woman's Day. The key message was that one in ten UK women experience rape or other violence; they also promoted the message that one in four local authorities lack the specialized support needed for female victims of violence.

The campaign's key actions

Using the mapofgaps.org (set up by Equality and Human Rights Commission and the End Violence Against Women Coalition) which showed support services needs in each postcode area, people were encouraged to write to their MPs about the campaign. AmnestyUK used protectthehuman.com as its landing page and the campaign was launched with a post on the blog explaining how people could help. A Twitter network built its social platform with followers growing from around 300 in December 2008 to more than 3,000 by mid-March 2009.

The campaign worked to get Twitter followers to change their Twitter **avatars** to the 1:10 logo and to tweet the message at 1.10 pm on 6 March 2009 (International Women's Day): 'Each year, around one in ten women in Britain will experience rape of other violence. Act now http://oneten.org.uk.'

Amnesty created a pledge on PledgeBank.com saying they would post the campaign's messages if other people agreed to do the same. Pledge Bank is a free site to help people to get things done, 'especially things that require several people'.

Amnesty posted on Facebook, MySpace, and Twitter, and to individual and group blogs which showed an interest in women's rights, and asked them to post similar messages. They also asked Twitter followers to use the hash tag #oneten to mark all Women's Day-related tweets.

The impact was profound.

- 3,000 mentions of #oneten on Twitter on 6 March
- @amnestyuk was the third most retweeted user and gained 600 new followers that week
- #oneten was in the top ten trending topics on 6 March and oneten.org.uk was the most tweeted link on that date—this data could be viewed on Twitscoop
- Protect the Human Blog had 900 Twitter referrals, 1,700 Facebook referrals, 78 comments, 12,000 page views and 8,500 unique visitors
- MapofGaps showed that 215 people emailed their MP on 6 March and nearly 3,000 emails were sent on the issue
- Twitscoop was used to measure Twitter mentions of one:ten that day (Source: Twitscoop).

Go to the Online Resource Centre to find out more about Twitscoop

The overall result was that in May, the Home Office launched a public consultation to develop a 'violence against women' strategy. AmnestyUK fed into this, demanding that the strategy tackles destructive social attitudes around violence against women and that it plans services for minority ethnic women facing violence such as genital mutilation and honour crimes.

12.3 Influences

The volume of internet traffic is predicted to rise by 400 per cent between 2009 and 2014, according to Cisco, the IT networking specialist (cited Warc 2010b). Most of this will be consumer use (88 per cent) compared to only 13 per cent for businesses. The main drivers will be video, including television and user-generated content and video on demand. Therefore practitioners need to consider the use of visual media when using the internet.

Social media implementation

It is no longer good enough to have a site that can be used by traditional search engines such as Google, Yahoo, or Bing to search for specified keywords. The search has shifted to other devices not bound by web browsers such as Internet Explorer, Firefox, and Safari (Roussos 2010).

Many organizations have developed a strong Google presence and focused on Twitter but have not embraced Facebook. Roussos (2010) argues that the objective is to embed content in areas where people gather to share information and initiate conversations about products, services, and brands. By tapping into distribution channels other than Google and Bing means expanding on internet opportunities. According to data from Hitwise (2010), Facebook's share of internet traffic recently surpassed even search engine giant Google.

Stafford (2010) cites a survey from StollzNow Research which revealed that 75 per cent of respondents believe companies should listen to what people say on social networks about their products, and follow up with individual conversations. The same survey indicated that customers will abandon a company if they read negative reviews about them on a social network or blog.

Being a practitioner using social media requires a set of skills and practice as social media interactions are time consuming and need to be sensitive to the community. In addition, the practitioner will, through practice, begin to understand the work rate and techniques needed to be accepted into online communities. The language and approach needs to be culturally in tune with the online community, using the language of the community with an awareness of the driving forces of such communities.

Social media implementation

1. Guidelines

Before any social media is used it is important to access the CIPR social media guidelines which cover the laws which affect social media such as:

- Consumer Protection from Unfair Trading Regulation 2008
- Advertising Standards Authority
- intellectual property—including copyright and trade marks
- disclosure/confidentiality

Go to the Online Resource Centre to access a link to the CIPR social media guidelines

- defamation
- invasion of privacy.

2. Strategic purpose

There has to be a purpose behind using these communication channels and the overall strategy needs to be integrated with the strategic goals of an organization. Before a social media is included in a strategy, assess the size and type of audience and the practicalities of appealing to the social media community. The competition can be very stiff. There are more than 1.5 million local businesses with active pages on Facebook and the internet doubles in size every two years.

3. Use multi-online media

There is a significant amount of cross posting and interaction. A tweet in Twitter.com may quickly appear in a Facebook page and could reference the client's blog post. In effect, by cross referencing the post in different media, new and wider communities can be reached.

Leverage all media such as video, blogs, eBooks, articles, SMS messages, instant messaging, and apps and postings on multiple networks to increase the exposure of messages. This also means that the title and content is **keyword rich** and descriptive. All the social networking accounts should be connected and a Really Simple Syndication (RSS) feed can syndicate a blog to targeted and popular social sites. Social media still expects measureable success such as hits, visitor loyalty, visitor recency, traffic referred by site (Roussos 2010).

4. Social media sites have rules

Detailed knowledge and application of social media facilities is important as all social media has a set of rules. Usually called **Terms and conditions**, practitioners must advise clients on these and work within them.

5. Design and branding

Knowing the purpose and approach to the online community will also dictate what design and branding will be appropriate and relevant. Knowing the community and purpose of using social media and content and rate of interaction will help to make this activity a success. However, this is not an ideal medium for 'PR campaigns' or one-way communication because a dialogue needs to develop over time. Building relationships with online communities takes time and the organization must be responsive to messages and regularly update their website and postings.

The goal is to fit into the demographic as well as send content in the same way that those members are receiving and sending content. Every discussion invites new changes for networking with others (Roussos 2010). Ensure discussions create interest, trust, and learning which encourage conversation and participation among other members rather than promotional messages. These should ensure continual conversation and feedback should be given to other comments. By being credible and trustworthy a social media user can then talk about products and services if they are compelling and offer readers something. In this way stories can spread virally and can be retweeted.

12.4 Application to industry

The internet has enormous potential for the practitioner. According to research by Pointer et al (2009: 251), practitioners could make more of the internet but are slow to adopt it. For example, blogs could be used as a new avenue for identifying issues, environmental scanning, and engaging other bloggers. An organizational blog can also be used to improve relationships by speaking to its publics. Pointer et al also argue that blogs are a chance to monitor WOM and informal conversations about publics and could be used more as a listening post than a conversational post. Additionally, blogs can be used to target specific publics because they are an ideal platform for two-way communications during a crisis.

Creating online media management policies

The practitioner will always advise clients to have very definite social media policies in place, not least as guidelines to employees. But having a policy in place is not enough: there is a need to ensure that everyone follows those rules, or else risk reputation or legal trouble. Here are five actions to help create and implement a social marketing code of conduct:

Action 1. Work closely with legal and PR teams

Online public relations need to be transparent and honest with the public. Recent history is loaded with examples of companies whose social marketing ran foul of public sentiment. In March 2010, Greenpeace launched a campaign with the aim of shocking the general public into taking action against Nestlé for using palm oil from non-sustainable sources and affecting the habitats of orang-utans (Greenpeace 2010).

Apart from investigative reports on Nestlé's practices, Greenpeace launched a spoof Kit Kat commercial showing a Nestlé employee eating an orang-utan finger in a KitKat pack. Nestlé tried to get Google to take down the video on YouTube on the grounds of copyright violation but this fuelled more activist activity and the video went viral on Vimeo and was re-posted on YouTube. Nestlé also responded irately to criticism left on their Facebook page; however a week later Nestlé took more reasonable actions to rectify what had turned into a damaging online and offline storm.

Social media allows activists to engage with supporters on a big scale without substantial spend thanks to the viral effect of social platforms like YouTube, Twitter, and Facebook. This helps to move the balance of power away from big brands such as Nestlé to anti-corporate activists such as Greenpeace. With activists tapping into viral loops anti-corporate campaigns will become increasingly more controversial and hard-hitting.

⚏ Go to the Online Resource Centre to access a link to more on the Nestlé KitKat storm

Working with the public relations or corporate communications departments will help to ensure:

- clear communication about the organization, brands, people, and other subjects which are part of the online PR strategy
- there is a coherent response to dispel confusion in the market
- a swift and effective response to criticism in the public.

The public relations activities have to remain ethical to avoid untoward or unwanted scrutiny and some organizations may need to involve their legal department. There is also a need for practitioners to ensure that each department (marketing, public and corporate affairs, legal, and IT) is following the same set of guidelines and rules.

It is now important that organizations hold regular sessions about social media and word-of-mouth public relations and other corporate conversations online. It is important to discuss the issues that everything put online is there forever, what is confidential and what can be released, and that content is open to scrutiny and needs to be handled responsibly.

Action 2. Circulate and publish policy documents

With social media, internal communications is a critical part of the process. Internal stakeholders see what is going on just as much as anyone else. The organization's guidelines about social media and word-of-mouth interactions will change and once they have there is a need to share them with the rest of the organization.

Some organizations have an intranet website or private wiki for social media as part of e-marketing communication. That is where most organizations put training materials and educational materials. These resources act as repositories where the PR and other communicators can also publish documents, such privacy policies, to make the commitment to ethics more transparent. There is also a good case for publishing these materials online.

Action 3. Authorize and monitor social media relations

Some organizations have tens of thousands of employees, but not everyone is authorized to speak for the company. Before an employee can engage in social media, the PR team should be mandated to ensure the person has:

- training
- experience
- authorization for specific channels
- authorization for specific types of messaging.

Before giving the authority to employees, public relations teams will also ensure the person has the means to use the channel. Blogging, for example, requires writing ability and spare time. Hosting a YouTube channel requires a repository of videos or the means to create them.

Action 4. Require partners to follow your policies

Making sure that communication partners and agencies are adhering to the same policies and rules as the in-house team is important.

Action 5. Monitor industry news

Missteps, such as KitKat and others, are recurring themes in PR news.

Monitoring comments associated with the client across the media (print, radio, TV, web sites, blogs, social networks, wikis, discussion lists, micro-blogs, video and picture sharing sites, etc) is now relatively easy and inexpensive. These services also provide evaluation metrics.

Monitoring online PR news and comment helps the practitioner to learn from mistakes and successes and what can happen if the PR team loses sight of ethics. They also show which tactics can really upset the public.

Case Study

How BT uses social media for internal communications
Source: Courtesy of Richard Dennison, BT Online

BT sees social media tools as a huge opportunity to transform the way employees interact with each other, the company, customers, partners, and suppliers. They set up a social media site which was intuitive and simple, with no technical barriers to participation. It reflected social behaviour and was fashionable and therefore encouraged use.

The tools launched initially were an enterprise-wide wiki called BTpedia (see Figure 12.1), based on the concept of Wikipedia, which allows any BT person to publish articles or edit articles published by others. They also launched a blogging tool. Both were well received and within a matter of weeks there were several hundred articles in BTpedia and around 300 blogs.

The best application was a social networking tool called 'MyPages'. MyPages provided every BT person with their own place on the intranet. In it they could create web pages and allow others to edit them (wiki pages); set up photo sharing pages and file stores; set up wiki calendars; create as many blogs as they wished; and connect themselves with other people in the organization through 'friends'. Employees could manage all this functionality through a single 'portal' which created high adoption rates. Within a couple of weeks over 1,500 people had activated their MyPages.

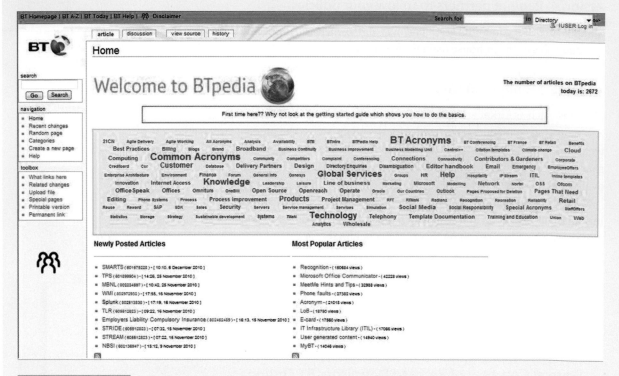

Fig 12.2
BTpedia

Source: Courtesy of BT

Corporate talk becoming a conversation

BTs internal communications consultants had to let go of controlling the messages which become owned by the BT and edited by the BT community. The internal communications practitioners also have to communicate to the employees in channels they don't own and cannot control, such as employee blogs. Communications became a 'conversation' rather than a managed activity.

The responsibilities are shifting between those responsible for intranet management and intranet users (see Figure 12.2). Today, more and more content is produced and owned collaboratively—with no clear ownership, who manages a piece of community-owned content through its lifecycle and ensures it is deleted or archived? In addition, what regulations can be applied to user-generated content?

To help users to find and keep up to date with so much user-generated content, BT published a combination of 'tagging', where publishers and users attach key words to content which are then searchable by others, and RSS, where content is published into appropriate feeds to which users can subscribe for updates via a feed reader client on their PC or via an RSS server. This requires both publishers, whose audience may never visit their site but read content in their feed readers, and users, who are used to viewing structured content on the sites upon which it is published, to behave in very different ways.

One of the most positive impacts has been in the area of accountability. Management and communications teams have to think more about the final outcomes of what they do as the employee channels provide a perfect platform to hold them accountable for what they

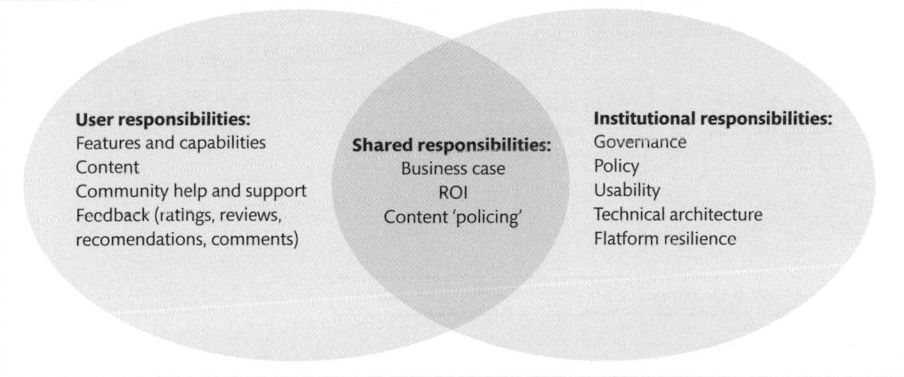

Fig 12.3
Responsibilities on a social media enabled intranet

Source: Courtesy of BT

say. However, BT employees have responded responsibly to being trusted with channels into which they can publish anything they like.

Lessons learned

A key lesson is to focus on the value social media tools can deliver rather than the risks. Many believe that trying to stop social media tools seeping onto intranets is a futile activity, so it is better to introduce them in a managed way.

Let users dictate the direction and speed of adoption. Allow users to dictate how they are going to derive value from new tools and don't be afraid to shut down unused applications. Let users play with new tools as soon as possible, warts and all. Engage the policy makers as early as possible. Emphasize that these tools represent an evolution rather than a revolution in the use of the web. After all, it's just another form of content management.

Finally, have realistic expectations about what can be achieved—the intranet and the internet are different beasts. Much of what makes social media successful on the internet does not directly translate to the corporate environment. For example, a cornerstone of social media on the internet is the concept of the 'wisdom of crowds'—ie if you have a large enough body of people collaborating on a single topic, you will distil the 'truth' from them. Does the wisdom of crowds work with a smaller population of people, or will the result be unbalanced opinion rather than 'truth'?

The demand for social media tools by employees to support their work is growing fast. The extent to which a company adopts user generated tools is bound to become a barometer of company culture for those looking for suitable employment in the future.

Figure 12.4 shows a map of BT's social media. Note all the platforms and the effort for transparency with ensuring the authorship of all posts.

Fig 12.4
**BT's social media
for internal
communications**

Source: Courtesy of BT

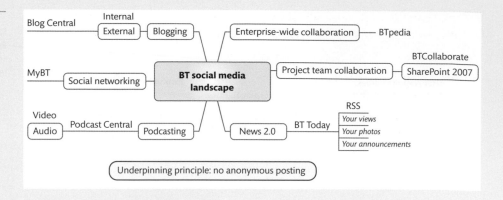

PR Tool

How to blog

- Have a character, be transparent about yourself, who you represent, what you want to achieve, and what your own views are to show that you are a real person and are not just recycling content.

- Make the blog a conversation so that people reading your blog feel as if they are talking to you. Even if you do try to promote or sell something be honest and not commercial.

- Keep content interesting, informative, and entertaining. It must fit the people you want to reach so know who they are and make sure the content engages them. Make it worthy of being retweeted and shared.

- Blog regularly, up to five times a week works well but it should be at least once a week.

- Show that you read and want comments. Respond personally if possible or if this is not possible make a mass response in a blog entry.

- Pay attention to grammar and punctuation. This shows respect for your readers and also makes the blog easier to read and navigate threads.

- Be courageous as blogging is opening yourself up to comment and criticism as well as positive feedback.

- Keep up with the technology in order to find new ways of keeping readers, getting listed in search directories, adding attachments, links and finding content and opinion leaders.

- Take responsibility for content. If there are errors be open about this—correct them as soon as possible.

- Don't copy and paste other blogs. Include them as links and cross links.

- Create good online relationships online. Promote and cross-promote and honour any commitments you have made.

- Use target keywords and pay attention to the header and title. Embed video, pdf, and images with keyword-rich filenames and content.

- Update your social media status such as Twitter and Facebook.

- Have a catchy headline and create a keyword list of your main terms and add content relevant to those terms.

- Link to other social media platforms. Post video to YouTube and images in photo sites such as Flickr and fill filenames, tags captions, and descriptions with keywords.

Summary

The internet now mediates all forms of communication and there are opportunities for the practitioner to influence communication and create conversations for organizations. From its embryonic beginnings in the 1950s to the social media functioning of today, the internet's rapid progress has pervaded our lives to create new relationships and interactions that affect lives. With its many platforms including laptops, gaming web, email, broadband, and social networks the internet allows people to create content and be used as an intermediary between diverse organizations and publics. The practitioner must consider the breadth and depth of these communications and their influence because they affect reputation.

Online communication means that the organization has increasing transparency. People can communicate freely with each other, often beyond the control of the organization. Everything is published in real time and news is no longer owned or controlled by a publisher; therefore the reputation of an organization can be influenced quickly. The organization's web pages are an asset as they have a value. People share their own values in websites and social media and people join online groups with those who have similar values. They then share their values through interaction and create relationships.

Publics can share their values with an organization and therefore have a relationship with it. These relationships create more values and increase the reputation of the organization. Grunig (2009) believes online monitoring helps to identify the different types of publics and their likely behaviour which can help to anticipate issues.

Social media means users interacting with each other, building networks, communities, and content. Social media is now being accessed and interacted with on mobile devices. The two-way symmetrical model cultivates relationships. The internet has empowered publics who are able to get information from wide sources, and makes it easier to form relations and create conversations. Grunig said online media focuses communications on the two-way symmetrical communications model and practitioners should take advantage of this—showing organizations how they also need to change their behaviour to negotiate with publics.

Social media is so widespread now that there are guidelines and it has a strategic purpose within an organization. It is very competitive and demands monitoring and assessing posts and publics to find out what other organizations are doing.

All online communications needs to consider branding and design and what it intends to achieve. It must be sure to integrate with other PR activities so that there is an integrated approach. As the internet is so visible anything that does not fit what the organization is doing will be highlighted. Everything has an online application, for example a press release can feed social media interactions. Therefore consider demographics of each social media platform—discussions must be compelling to this group and ideally interesting enough to spread virally, leveraging all media. Also consider working with legal teams, corporate communications, and marketing to ensure that everything is included and appropriate. Ethics are transparent and there should be a social media policy in place in which the whole organization participates.

Discussion points

A. Social media policy

1. Using your searching skills, find the IBM social media policy.

2. Based on this, create a Social Media Policy for University undergraduates using social media to implement a communications campaign.

3. Look at platform and channels, type and style, context, distribution and timing for release of content, and authorizations for users of the channels and platforms.

B. Create a strategy for promoting your public relations course to prospective students using social media

1. Include a comprehensive system for monitoring progress and effectiveness of the strategy.

2. Identify content you can use to implement your strategy as follows: video, images, sound files, texts.

3. Find a way to host this content and research the platforms and channels used by this target public.

4. Design a communication plan for alerting sixth formers to your social media campaign.

5. Publish your findings in a public wiki.

C. Identify a website of an organization

1. What are its business objectives?

2. What are the communications objectives of the website?

3. Can you identify the publics for this site?

4. Review the site content.

5. Does this fit its objectives?

6. Is it relevant to its publics?

7. What can be improved?

8. Are the design and graphics appropriate to the business objective?

Layout and design

1. Is there a site map and does it accurately reflect the site and its links?

2. Is there a table of contents on the home page?

3. Is it regularly updated?

Content

1. Are there links to pages within the site that guide the reader?

2. Are there appropriate links that function?

3. Is this a push or pull site?

4. How is it written—in chunks for easy reading, in diagrams, in hyperlinks?

5. What interactivity does it have—is this effective?

Search engines

1. Is the site listed with common search engines?

2. Where does the site come up when key terms are requested on common search engines?

3. What are the hyperlinks? Are they appropriate links?

4. What sites link to this site, and are they appropriate?

Access

1. Does the home page download easily?

2. Do the links download quickly?

3. Are there options such as text only, saving, sending, and printing?

4. Is the site compatible with major web page browsers?

References

Amaral, B. (2010) 'Concepts of Values for Public Relations'. Available at: http://www.euprera.org/?p=69

BBC (2009) 'Multitaskers bad at multitasking'. Available at: http://news.bbc.co.uk/1/hi/8219212.stm

Benkler, Y. (2006) *The Wealth of Networks: How Social Production Transforms Markets and Freedom*. New Haven, CT: Yale University Press

Berners-Lee, T. (1989) 'Information Management: A Proposal', March. Retrieved 2010 and available at: http://www.w3.org/History/1989/proposal.html

Brown, R. (2009) *Public Relations and the Social Web: How to Use Social Media and Web 2.0 In Communications*. London: Kogan Page

Greenpeace 'Ask Nestlé To Give Rainforests A Break'. Available at: http://www.greenpeace.org/international/campaigns/climate-change/kitkat/

Grunig, J. (2009) 'Paradigms of Global Public Relations in an Age of Digitalisation', Prism 6/2. Available at: http://praxis.massey.ac.nz/prism on-line journ.html

Kelly, K. (2009) 'Predicting the next 5,000 days of the web', Ted Talks. Available at: http://www.youtube.com/watch?v=yDYCf4ONh5M

Licklider, J.C.R. (1960) 'Man-Computer Symbiosis' in *IRE Transactions on Human Factors in Electronics*, vol HFE-1, pp 4–11

Macnamara, J. (2009) *The 21st Century Media (R)Evolution: Emergent Communication Practices*. New York: Peter Lang

Mayfield, A. (2009) 'What is Social Media'. Available at: http://www.icrossing.co.uk/fileadmin/uploads/eBooks/What_is_Social_Media_iCrossing_ebook.pdf

Perloff, S. (2003) The Dynamics of Persuasion: Communications and Attitudes in the 21st Century (2nd edn) Mahwah, NJ: Lawrence Erlbaum

Phillips, D. and Amaral, B. (2009) 'A Proof of Concept for Automated Discourse Analysis in Support of Identification of Relationship Building in Blogs'. Available at: http://www.bledcom.com/home/knowledge

Phillips, D. and Young, P. (2009) Online Public Relations: A Practical Guide to Developing an Online Strategy in the World of Social Media (PK in Practice) (2nd edn.) London: Kogan Page.

Porter, L., Sweetser Trammell, K., and Chung, D. (2009) 'The Blogosphere and Public Relations: Investigating Practitioners' Roles and Blog Use', Journal of Communications Management 13/3: 250–67

Protect the Human. Available at: http://blog.protectthehuman.com/1in10-a-case-study-in-social-media-campaigning/

Roussos, C. (2010) 'Social media marketing secrets and tools: Expert advice, tips and learning guide to SMO business plan success', 8 April. Available at: http://seo.tv/socialmedia/social-medial-marketing-secrets-tools-expert-advice-smo-business.html

Seoa, H., Kimb, J., and Yanga, S. (2009) 'Global Activism and New Media: A Study of Transnational NGOs' Online', Public Relations Review 35: 123–6

Shirky, C. (2008) 'Here Comes Everybody'. Available at: http://www.herecomeseverybody.org/

Warc (2010a) 'Retail, Grocery Brands Dominate on Social Media', Warc News, 10 June. Available at: http://www.warc.com

Warc (2010b) 'Web Usage Levels to Rise In Emerging Markets', Warc News, 10 June. Available at: http://www.warc.com

Public relations trends

Learning Objectives

1. Understand the changing communications environment influenced by technology, globalization, and developments in behavioural sciences that are influencing how public relations is defined.

2. Be able to identify how changes are manifesting in different areas of public relations such as consultancy and the charity sector.

3. Appreciate the value of critical thinking and research in public relations education which can build knowledge and help to improve and understand practice.

4. Be able to develop proposals through examining how to influence behaviour integrating the hierarchy of effects model with new psychological developments and marketing initiatives.

5. Explore how internet-based communications technology will affect the power of its end-users, the way information is managed, and the blurring of editorial and advertising.

6. Recognize the postmodern context of public relations and the need to find new ways of working with different cultures and nationalities often across different time zones and in virtual teams.

Practitioner Insight

Karen Campbell-White
Head of PR Content
Central Office of Information

Karen Campbell-White has over 15 years of experience in crafting strategic communications solutions for a variety of clients, both blue chip and public sector. Karen joined the COI from Talk Talk, where she was responsible for all external PR communications.

What do you think are the key changes taking place in public relations?

Public relations has become an essential part of the marketing/communications mix. Many organizations are recognizing the influence of PR and using this to support a wide range of innovative work, from co-creation with the third sector through to peer-to-peer engagement. Social media engagement by PR practitioners is helping to ensure content is influential.

Can you give an example of a campaign which demonstrated a whole new approach and explain why this happened?

Communities and Local Government Fire Kills tasked COI with raising awareness of a new TV advertising campaign. The creative compared the sensation of drowning to that of inhaling toxic smoke in the home. COI worked with a local Fire and Rescue Service to source an experiential training unit (laid out like a flat with bedroom, kitchen, and lounge). The unit was filled with fake smoke and a well-known opinion former (Jill Halfpenny), was asked to 'escape' from the unit in less than two minutes, the time it takes before individuals are rendered unconscious. Her experience was filmed, using both a crew and a headcam. Infra-red image technology was used to show her movement through the unit. The video film was then used to support a wide range of media coverage, from online news through to offline TV and print. This new approach brought alive an important issue, whilst also challenging the apathy that citizens often feel towards their own fire safety in the home.

How do you think the role of social media is changing your campaigns?

More and more government campaigns are using social media techniques to spread important messages to vulnerable audiences. All COI PR and news teams are able to map, monitor, and create a variety of content for social media platforms. Today a ministerial visit to a region is likely to result in a FlickR feed, Twitter posts, and YouTube video in addition to the offline media handling and engagement.

Which area of communications practice do you think needs more research in order to improve its practice?

All communications work needs to be measurable, from our perspective we are keen to encourage industry-wide behavioural change metrics.

What advice would you give someone studying public relations in the future?

Get plenty of experience (a mix of in-house, agency, and media) and try not to specialize too early in your career.

13.1 Definition

A trend is how an area is moving or changing. For example, market trends show how the market is growing or shrinking and assessing these helps to decide what to buy or sell and when. Public relations trends focus on the changes in how people and organizations are communicating. As publics are constantly developing and organizations are changing, a practitioner can be effective by monitoring the environment and identifying trends that are creating new communications challenges and opportunities. It is crucial that a practitioner is able to consider how these trends influence PR and how they should be considered within the changing communications arena.

Organizations are increasingly positioning themselves as corporate citizens and part of the community. It is the PR practitioner's role to monitor an organization's actions and their effects on its publics.

PR is not an isolated discipline. Although it is differentiating itself from other practices such as marketing, behavioural sciences, management consultancy, law, and media communications it is also drawing on them. For example, the Central Office of Information (COI) works with government departments and the public sector to produce information campaigns on issues that affect the lives of every citizen—from health and education to benefits, rights, and welfare. In 2009, it published guidelines advising government communication specialists to draw on aspects of behavioural sciences in order to influence behaviour. This approach was found to be very effective particularly with the government's No Tobacco and traffic safety programmes (COI 2009).

There are also real and emerging tensions between public relations and marketing (Tench and Willis 2009) as both areas look for a new way of engaging with audiences to grab their attention, get them talking about a brand, and move them to action.

Digital media is influencing change

Advances in technology are influencing how stakeholders are communicating and subsequently how public relations is practised. Digital media has the potential to make public relations much more global and strategic with improved dialogue between publics and organizations to encourage social responsibility (Grunig 2009). It means stakeholders can be more involved with organizations and technology but public relations needs to address the ramifications of this greater transparency. Practitioners need to work with the technology that gives more power to individuals, such as bloggers, who can use online media platforms to become immediate experts and influence publics.

For example, when xG Technology, a US-based company with a revolutionary wireless technology, wanted to generate awareness among large telecoms companies, technology bloggers were the first port of call. Influential bloggers needed to be convinced of the potential of xG's product as a truly 'disruptive' technology. The London consultancy, Threepipe, identified the most influential technology bloggers and gave them the opportunity to hear the xG story first, leading to debate and positive comments on their blogs. This in turn created more online buzz and generated interest among the top mainstream IT and business journalists, ultimately leading to positive coverage in the business media. This then led to over 90 telecommunications companies, including some of the largest and well known, picking up the phone to xG to discuss their technology.

As communications become faster, it is expected that everything will be known more quickly. However, Nick Davies, in his book, *Flat Earth News* (2009), reports on research that shows much of the news is recycled by global news websites which rely on the news coming from the big news agencies, AP and Reuters. Furthermore, very little is reported about the countries in which these agencies do not exist. For example, research on a day's coverage of Google News (Davies 2009: 108) found that there were 14,000 stories which could be accessed from the website's front page yet all of these accounted for only 24 news events. This means that a few world events are being turned into many reports by the main news agencies and appearing in a vast array of diverse media.

This increasing fragmentation of the media with more media outlets and smaller audiences means there can be information overload. In the UK, there are more than 3,000 consumer magazines, 2,800 regional newspapers, 600 radio and TV stations, plus websites, viral emails, and text messages. Media fragmentation means it is now difficult for a single communications channel to create and sustain a brand. Companies now have to allocate their budgets over dozens of media outlets when at one time they could reach a large piece of the public by advertising on one channel. Therefore, public relations has to develop new models to engage with the media and publics.

Grunig (2009: 6) argues that the internet means that information will be available to everyone and public relations practitioners need to use the internet to listen to what stakeholders are saying and build relationships with them. He believes that the internet has empowered publics as they are no longer limited to getting their information from traditional media or relying on what is given to them from organizations. Now publics can obtain information from a huge number of sources anywhere in the world. In addition, the internet allows publics to interact with each other and with their organizations, so practitioners need to join these conversations.

Ofcom is the UK regulator of UK TV and radio, fixed line telecoms, and mobiles, plus the airwaves over which wireless devices operate. The Ofcom 2009 consumer market report explains how young people use internet phones and MP3 players to create their own media channels where they can control and edit without outside interference therefore avoiding and ignoring channels traditionally employed such as television. Ofcom suggests that there is a trend towards media autonomy which is creating more opportunities for self-expression such as blogging, personal websites, and production of home-made reality shows such as YouTube which have maximum effects.

Guerilla techniques

As media relations becomes more focused on social media and the rise of the individual voice, turning to personal opinion leaders through **word of mouth (WOM)** is increasingly important. WOM means that someone who understands a product or service, shares their views, attitudes, and beliefs about it with others, creating awareness, but is not prompted to do (Ahuja cited Tench and Willis 2009).

WOM is considered a **guerilla technique** and is an unconventional and non-traditional form of marketing or public relations. Other guerilla techniques also get people talking and hide the involvement of brand owners who are struggling with how to market to audiences that are rejecting their messages. It may use activities that penetrate the daily lives of consumers or involve street-focused engagement, such as the online betting company, Betfair outlined in chapter 2. This campaign promoted its services through focusing on the London mayoral election and carried out street activities such as inflated helium balloons carrying caricatures of the mayoral candidates, and portable metres estimating the 'hot air' emitted during each candidate's speeches.

Other guerilla techniques include **grassroots marketing**, which is where power is with the individual; such as the US presidential campaign where voters could follow Barack Obama on Twitter and felt they were influencing the campaign; and **viral campaigns**, which is online peer-to-peer communication about a product issue or service; unconventional and memorable tactics such as projections of images onto buildings, creation of pirate radio stations, and anti-corporate irreverent activities.

Fan pages can also be a form of guerilla marketing. In the build up to the Beijing Olympic Games, the British Olympic Association (BOA) wanted to engage with fans to help develop the Team GB brand and drive traffic to http://www.teamgb.com, while also building up a fanbase for future official BOA events.

With a minimal budget, they harnessed the reach of Facebook, creating an official Team GB fan page several months ahead of the 2008 Games. The page was populated with exclusive content including athlete video diaries, imagery, and competitions to win tickets to BOA events. Crucially, the page was constantly updated with relevant and interesting content, avoiding the trap of being just another dormant Facebook group. In the build up to the Games, the page was promoted on other social network groups dedicated to supporting British athletes, and communicated regularly with fans. The fan page has attracted more than 10,000 fans and is now used to communicate the latest BOA news and events to a committed, engaged audience.

Go to the Online Resource Centre to access a link to the official team GB page

Ethics

Grunig (2009) states that practitioners need to be aware of ethical issues in online public relations as well as in traditional PR. He claims the most common online ethical issue is fake blogs where organizations create promotional blogs and pass them off as being developed by an unaffiliated individual. Grunig also mentions favourable blogs or comments on social media sites by practitioners who do not disclose their identity or their relationship with the organization they represent. Yet persuasion ethics means the communicator must disclose their interest in the topic.

Tench and Willis (2009) argue that transparency is seeing the origin of information sources. If ethical public relations is allowing people to make reasoned and informed decisions then covert practices do not do this. Is it ethical for consumers to act as advocates and promote marketing messages to their friends? Is concealing the purpose of WOM moral? WOM means that there is no editorial filter, no scrutiny, and no review of their party spokespeople. If an organization is funding and organizing a campaign should stakeholders know that they are?

There is a Word of Mouth Marketing Association (WOMMA) code which emphasizes honesty of relationships, where the communicator must declare who they are speaking for; honesty of opinion, where they say what they believe, and honesty of identity where they never obscure your identity. However, the difficulty for all practitioners is that guerilla campaigns are largely successful because of their anonymity and the appearance that no organization is involved.

⊕ **Go to the Online Resource Centre to access link to the WOMMA**

Changes in practice

In the UK, most public relations practitioners work in-house. However, consultancy is a thriving business. In 2007 research found that all consultancies now employ 8,000 staff compared to only 2,000 25 years ago and annual fees have grown from around £25 million in 1985 to £342 million in 2009 (Howard 2009).

Public relations in consultancies is growing, expanding what it offers, and has moved from being primarily media relations to offering strategic advice where it is involved in meeting the overall business objectives of an organization. Technology tools mean that specialist companies or freelancers can use them to carry out many traditional public relations activities such as evaluation of results, measuring media readership, and identifying meanings, which means that there are higher expectations of consultancies. For example, the media monitoring company, Cision, can provide information that can be used to develop and monitor PR programmes, these include:

- sending alerts as new content is posted
- quickly understanding what is being said about their organization, brands, and competitors on virtually any topic across the globe through online translation
- a dashboard that allows a search of the LexisNexis content database for articles written by specific journalists
- accessing outlet-related information market data and audience impressions

- evaluation
- ROI metrics
- social media analysis.

In a bid to get more business, Howard (2009) claims that consultancies are competing for media relations campaigns and lowering their fees for this work thus making media relations less profitable and less valued. She recommends that consultancies offer a premium service through analysing content across all media for all stakeholders. In this way, she believes that consultancies can compete by using new sets of analytical tools that can also be used to execute and manage stakeholder relationships and achieve strategic goals. Howard argues that providing a standardized media relations service is increasingly irrelevant, as organizations become more accessible and more accountable (see chapter 11) and therefore safeguarding brands and corporate reputation is crucial.

Grunig (2009) cites the Excellence Study that found that the most effective public relations departments participated in, or were consulted in, making overall decisions in the organization. He argues that when public relations is part of organizational decision making it is in a better position to identify the stakeholders who would be affected by organizational decisions or who, in turn, would affect them. This allows the development of programmes that identify the relevant public relations issues and objectives to communicate with stakeholders. Grunig argues that publicity about an organization is limited in its ability to create a positive relationship with an audience. He believes that digital media provides a practitioner with tools to communicate with publics and find out more about them and can therefore provide input in the strategic decision-making process of an organization before management decisions are made. Digital media can also be used for employee communication, media relations, customer relations, investor relations, and so on.

Grunig (2009) also observes that digital media can be used for developing two-way communication to interact with its publics in real time. When public relations participates in decision making, its contribution is to identify consequences, stakeholders, publics, and issues that result from decisions or require attention in decision making. In addition, Grunig points out that digital media is ideal for environmental scanning research and for developing public relations programmes.

Changes in the voluntary sector

An area that is seeing many changes is the voluntary sector. Charities now have many issues. They are in a crowded and competitive marketplace and have a problem with differentiating from each other, eg the housing and homelessness charity, Shelter, versus the charity for single homeless people, Crisis. Fundraising used to be the main aspect of external communications in the voluntary sector, now there is much more involvement in raising awareness about the charity and changing attitudes by demonstrating what charities do (Poynton 2009). Charities are starting to put fundraising and marketing together, rather than asking for money they are showing what an organization can do and how people can help.

Social media is driving many of these changes and is making organizations much more transparent, and publics are questioning how donations are used and what the charities do. For example, the World Wildlife Fund (WWF) wanted to send an urgent signal to political leaders to take action on climate change. In an effort to secure action at the Copenhagen UN climate summit in March 2009, they launched a campaign called 'Earth Hour', where an estimated 36 million people turned off non-essential lights in each participating country for an hour (http://www.earthour.org). This created a dramatic visual effect drawing attention to their campaign. Earth Hour is a now an annual global event organized by WWF and is held on the last Saturday of every March.

With ageing populations and medical advancements, public relations has a growing role in healthcare education. Already public relations has an expanding role in reducing heart disease in the UK where more than 2.6 million people are affected. For example, the high-profile charity, the British Heart Foundation (BHF), is successful in getting people to think differently about heart disease. Campaigns include an orchestrated grassroots lobbying campaign that encouraged members to tell their MPs that the government must be more active in dealing with obesity.

Another BHF communications campaign succeeded in getting children to think about physical activity and the food they ate. The campaign included school activities and influencing county councillors to ensure healthy options were available at centres which entertain children. Lobbying resulted in the government banning product media placement of food and drink high in fat, sugar, and salt. In addition, the BHF National Heart Month every February raises awareness of heart and circulatory issues as well as raising funds for research, prevention, and care services (BHF 2010).

Getting stakeholders engaged is a challenging aspect in an increasingly competitive environment for public relations practitioners and new online activities can be used to reach diverse publics. For example, the fundraising group of UK Cancer Research developed an alternative reality game to raise funds. It combined both online, traditional media, and text messaging and raised funds and awareness where teams were involved in accomplishing increasingly difficult missions.

Public relations is evolving and its university degrees—the first one in the UK started at Bournemouth University in 1989—are incorporating these changes into their curriculum. The changes focus largely on moving from teaching students technical skills and how to gain publicity to developing strategies which are research based.

Go to the Online Resource Centre to access a link to find out more about Earth Hour

Go to the Online Resource Centre to access the link to the BHF campaigns

13.2 Historical and theoretical overview

Education is the crucial plank in PR's quest for professional status.

(L'Etang 2002: 47)

The future of public relations means more education. Public relations without educa-tion can mean that there is too much focus on techniques such as media relations skills or how to run a campaign. Although learning these skills is essential to public relations practice it is also necessary to have self-reflection and a discerning approach in order to evaluate what is being done. Research and theory provide a deeper understanding of what public relations can actually do, how it can be part of strategic management, and how it can achieve its objectives ethically. The academic study of public relations involves research to produce new knowledge that can be used to improve decision making in the profession.

L'Etang (2002) notes that in the academic world public relations has to be accepted as a research discipline and demonstrate that it can transform public relations practice. She recommends that the theory of public relations needs to look at the concepts of propaganda, dialogue, and actual practice in order to define the mission of public relations and what it encompasses.

In addition, there is an ongoing argument about whether public relations is a profession. L'Etang (2002) argues that for public relations to be positioned as a profession there needs to be clear boundaries which separate public relations from advertising, marketing, and journalism. However, as these professions are themselves changing, largely owing to the burgeoning online media, it is becoming increasingly difficult to determine the finite role of each of these areas.

L'Etang (2002: 30) draws on sociological research that states the stages through which occupations must pass in order to gain professional status:

1. Full time occupation.
2. Training school.
3. Professional association.
4. Legal protection of association.
5. Formal code.

L'Etang argues that in our promotion-led society, people aspire to being professionals, and in turn being a professional is promoted within our culture. Therefore, public relations itself needs to be promoted as a discipline and as a practice.

In 2009, the COI promoted its own public relations practice as being research based. It launched a science-based publication, 'Communications and Behaviour Change' on behaviour change theory for use in supporting and sustaining the development of public sector campaigns. These government campaigns, which attempt to address society's problems, include global warming and its effects; poor diets which lead to obesity and disease; people driving too fast which leads to accidents; and smoking which has numerous ill effects.

The COI publication presents the argument that addressing society's problems usually requires people to change their behaviour. It argues that the hierarchy of effects model—awareness, interest, desire, and then action—which is used to develop public relations objectives, is not enough to encourage behavioural change. The COI (2009) developed a five-step process for behaviour change and communications planning which has drawn on behavioural theories which identify how behaviour can be changed. A brief outline of this process follows:

1. Identifying behaviours

This stage identifies the particular behaviour that the communications programme wants to influence, such as speeding when driving. Sometimes more complex issues such as obesity mean that there are many behaviours which need to be changed and these also need to be identified.

2. Understanding the influences by audience

This stage identifies what is influencing the particular behaviours and explores why people behave as they do. It reviews habits, knowledge, peer pressure, and social norms, as well as external factors such as access, legislation, price, and proximity. For example, the COI's No Tobacco campaign identified the role of attitudes and beliefs and how these can drive motivation to stop smoking. Previous no-smoking campaigns had focused only on motivating people to continue to stop smoking, however, a motivation theory identified that smokers also needed a trigger to help them to attempt to quit.

3. Developing a practical model of influences on behaviour

This stage focuses on behaviour and change theory and analyses the relationship between the influences and the behaviours to plan for successful behaviour change. For example, the No Tobacco campaign found that the motivation and triggers to quit could be drawn from:

- positive environmental pressure
- dissatisfaction with the present
- possible vision of the future
- confidence in ability to quit
- knowing how to quit successfully.

In addition, external factors such as legislation, price, peer influence, social and cultural norms, and access to tobacco played a part.

4. Building a marketing framework

This stage identifies the role of communications; what it is aiming to influence, the evaluation criteria, and the target publics and links to other initiatives. For example, in the No Tobacco campaign the behavioural goals were to decrease smoking prevalence among routine and manual workers to 26 per cent by 2010 by first increasing the number of quit attempts and then increasing the actual success of the quit attempts. Communications were also linked to the government's taxation and legislation initiatives to reduce tobacco use and their integration is shown in Table 13.1.

Table 13.1 **The role of marketing and communications with other tobacco control interventions**

Conditions for change	Positive environment for quitting	Confidence in ability to quit	Dissatisfaction with present	Positive vision of future	Triggers for action	Knowledge of how to quit
Primary change agent	Legislation	NHS services medication	Marketing and communication	Marketing and communications	Natural triggers, eg life stage illness	NHS services/ medication
Secondary change agent	Price		Legislation	Legislation	Marketing and communications	Marketing and communications

Source: COI (2009: 52)

5. Developing a communications model

Overall, this process looks at how communication influences behaviour and how it can be changed while recognizing that people start at different points, jump stages, and relapse.

Public relations and the brain

Finding out how people make decisions which influence their behaviour is crucial to public relations and there is growing research in psychology and behavioural science that may influence public relations practice. According to neuromarketing research, progress in neurological medicine research is purported to provide insights into how the subconscious affects decision making and how communication is interpreted (Admap 2010). An MRI scan can show someone's responses to images or information by recording which parts of the brain light up in response to stimuli. For example, a study showed that smoking had increased since the ban on advertising and the introduction of health warnings on packets. An MRI scan showed that when smokers saw cigarette packets, the addictive part of their brain was activated so that any message, even anti-smoking messages, associated with the product activated the addiction. This included images of cowboys, which represented Marlboro cigarettes. Therefore showing associated images or words was recognized as an effective marketing and advertising technique.

Lindstrom—described by the *Sunday Times* (Hattersley 2008: 6) as 'a Danish advertising guru' and author of *Buyology*, a book about neuromarketing—reports on neurological tests which can identify how people react to certain messages or images based on consumers' reaction times or accuracy in tasks rather than through direct questions which can filter out immediate responses. For example, Lindstrom claims that eye tests can observe eye tracking and visual attention, and show results that may be quite different from what people say they have focused on. They can reveal if colour creates any connection or whether company logos have any significance. A brainwave measurement (electroencephalogram), where the results are connected to other biological measurements such as pulse, temperature, and blinking show an individual's responses to comments, information, or images that happen too quickly to observe otherwise.

However, Bell (2008) in mindhacks.com claims that there has been no validation of neural activity predicting purchases or sales better than that of any other methods. Bell claims neuromarketing is popular because it is seen to be cutting edge, despite there being no evidence of its success. However, the *Guardian* (2007) reported on how a team of world-leading scientists, in a study led by the Max Planck Institute for Human Cognitive and Brain Sciences in Germany with University College London and Oxford University, have developed high-resolution brains scans that may be able to read people's intentions. The scans identify people's patterns of brain activity before translating them into meaningful thoughts revealing what they would do in the future. According to the report, scientists are now looking at ways to deduce what patterns are associated with different thoughts in order to read intentions.

Social media is changing public relations

Although there are still debates on the concept of mass communications based on how media reaches large audiences (Macnamara 2010: 125), public relations practitioners now engage with multiple publics through social media, either voluntarily or involuntarily. Furthermore, public relations is increasingly dependent on web-monitoring services to manage that two-way communication, as the speed of that dialogue accelerates and 'citizen journalism' explodes.

One of the most daunting tasks for organizations is to listen to the multiple voices on the internet, to enable them to take part in the many conversations that affect them. Web 2.0 watchers are likely to be familiar with Newswire's eWatch service, which began with monitoring internet content and is now sifting thousands of blogs through its filters. The service lists what Newswire believes are the most influential bloggers: it tracks client's keywords in the same way as print and broadcast monitors, and provides regular reports on where these keywords are being used.

Breakenridge (2008) notes in her book, *PR 2.0* that PR Newswire made a deal with Technorati to provide a more complete monitoring service. Technorati enables PR Newswire's clients to track online conversations triggered by a news release. So, if PR Newswire sends out a release, it can also report on who is talking about and writing about the news in the blogosphere, as well as in the mass media.

Internet-based monitoring services are responding to the demand from public relations consultancies and organizational communication managers for up-to-the-minute information on where and how opinion is changing in a Web 2.0 world.

Mersham et al (2009) refer to well-known examples, such as Google Groups (reference, social networking), Wikipedia (reference, knowledge sharing), MySpace (social networking), Last.fm (personal music), YouTube (video sharing), Second Life (virtual reality), Flickr (photo sharing), delicious (sharing of bookmarks), and Twitter (microblogging). They note that many of these social media services can be integrated via social network aggregation platforms like Mybloglog and Plaxo.

The authors argue that the small, niche conversations in social media can create a long-lasting impact and suggest content and communication are becoming tightly focused among small groups rather than large mass audiences. However, in the boundless blogosphere small readerships built with Mybloglog can expand exponentially, as bloggers sign up for free accounts and begin their own blog community for one or more blogs they author.

Now the instantaneous nature of the internet, and the aggregation of blogs, has shortened the adoption curve for ideas and opinions, so that good and bad news builds up to a crescendo in minutes, rather than days. This means that public relations practitioners not only need to monitor these blogs constantly for opinions and views, but also need to write their own/their clients' blogs and respond to other blogs extremely quickly. It is therefore not surprising that Euroblog's research showed that practitioners were concerned about having the knowledge and time to create blogs.

Also, extremely time-consuming is the monitoring of discussion or message boards that post messages which others can read and respond to when they have time. These are sometimes referred to as forums, but they are less immediate and slightly lower risk than 'chat' forums, which are live discussions in 'real time'.

Public relations can make use of these forums by participating and providing information, giving and getting feedback, and using them in times of change or a crisis to answer commonly asked questions, ensuring that everyone receives the same, consistent answer. Mersham et al (2009) note the frequently quoted instance of Barack Obama's presidential campaign, which used such bulletin boards and forums to identify and dispel false rumours.

Social networking sites, such as MySpace, Facebook, and Bebo, further challenge the capacity of monitoring agencies, and wikis or wikipages can be restricted access or public domain, allowing multiple editors and uncontrolled information. The positive value of wikis is that they use software which allows open dialogue and sharing of knowledge.

A further challenge for public relations media-monitoring agencies is the dozens of free tools that can help to measure the conversation. Many of these tools are accessible in the 'cloud' of applications available on the internet. However, most are not designed for in depth analysis or benchmarking, which has opened up opportunities for monitoring services which measure, track, and compare results of campaigns and communication initiatives.

Mersham et al (2009) ask 'Which attributes should be measured?' That includes not only the metrics of the number and size of posts, comments, messages, and articles, but also their subject (topic), sentiment (feelings), and influence (readership). The authors point out that computerized systems are ideal for metrics, but interpretation of meaning and emotion requires human judgement.

> **Thus, hybrid forms such as software-assisted human analysis and human-assisted software analysis are currently the most useful.**
>
> (Mersham et al 2009: 158)

If the profession plans to retain its pre-eminence in direct and mediated communication, practitioners need to be good listeners as well as authors in the conversations of social media. That is where opinion leaders and peer-group influencers will change what the world knows and believes.

13.3 Influences

A key trend in public relations is that information is becoming more easily available as internet-based technology means it can be searched far more efficiently and people can interact with it. According to Ofcom's sixth marketing report (2009), only ten years previously, mobiles, broadband, digital TV and radio, wireless networks, and WiFi hotspots were niche products or did not exist. Now these technologies are converging and merging over a variety of platforms.

Convergence means people are receiving different content types over the same distribution network, as well as receiving similar content over a full range of different networks (Ofcom 2009). They can also access a variety of different devices and there will be more emphasis on mobility; this means that practitioners need to ensure the information from communication programmes is appropriate and able to be used across all platforms.

The fast-changing communications sector that is converging, increasingly open, and competitive means that there will be difficulties distinguishing between broadcasting, entertainment, publishing, fixed or mobile, supplier or consumer. This will give rise to difficulties in differentiating between editorial and advertising. Information is becoming regulated and practitioners need to be alert to how it is managed and even controlled. This has ethical issues that requires engagement with consumers and industry to address issues of who is controlling the information and who can have access. Practitioners will need to be informed about, if not involved in, communications policy where the global environment has a regional impact on how information is managed.

For example, according to a report in the *Wall Street Journal* (Rhoads and Chao 2009) technology called **deep-packaging inspection**, allows authorities to block, monitor, and gather information about individuals. It also delays transmission of data and allows scanning of content and social media sites. The report suggested that this could be why the internet in Iran has been running at very slow speeds since the presidential election.

Globalization

These developments in communications technology are fuelling a globalization which is demanding more information more quickly and more often. Grunig (2009) argues that digital media have made most public relations global and force organizations to think globally about their public relations. In addition, Grunig notes that managing this new media is becoming a priority skill needed by communication practitioners. Wakefield states:

> **As the world careens into the 21st century, public relations people are being swept into a whole new global arena.**
>
> (2001: 639)

Globalization requires intercultural communication and the challenge in public relations campaigns is to be national and global, that is, address regional concerns and cultural issues while at the same time deliver global objectives. L'Etang (2008) suggests that practitioners must cultivate and promote global identities and at the same time take account of the local culture and build community relations.

Sriramesh (2009) notes that it was the last decade of the twentieth century which put globalization, and consequently the need for global public relations, on a different scale because of three principal factors.

1. The elimination of trade barriers among nations has created more culturally diverse organizations.

2. The onset and development of communication technology, such as social media, along with the global selling and delivery of goods and services.

3. The recognition that all countries need to address common problems such as environmental pollution, terrorism, nuclear proliferation, and overpopulation resulting in poverty and hunger.

Overall, the need for increased intercultural communication, global issues, and the greater amount of global products and their promotion has led to most public relations being global.

According to Sriramesh and White (1992) global public relations is best executed by a cross-cultural international team which reflects the cultural and societal norms of the host nation. These teams are usually virtual and rarely meet for face-to-face contact. **Virtual teams** are broadly defined by Powell et al (2004) as groups of geographically, organizationally, and time-dispersed workers relying on technology to communicate with each other and with the flexibility to traverse traditional organizational boundaries and time constraints.

Wakefield (2001) observes that these teams function laterally with everyone having a strategic role in executing the public relations objectives. Managing this process has its own challenges. Powell et al (2004: 10) argue that 'swift trust' among team members is found in virtual teams as they do not have sufficient time to build trust slowly, but this swift trust can often be lost risking demotivation of team members. These factors are important because Powell observed a positive link between the socio-emotional processes of the virtual team and its outcomes. Binder (2007) emphasizes the value of early social interaction in virtual teams to build relationships and recommends using an intranet and other technology which can quickly facilitate this early socialization.

Binder (2007) claims online projects need better team leaders than face-to-face projects and require skills that can obtain commitment and a team spirit. He recommends that the team leader must be able to communicate global perspectives and build camaraderie across different national sites and cultural borders rather than focusing on procedures. The development of motivation and relationship building without a shared time can be difficult and team members may ignore time zones (Binder 2007). A global collaboration project demands synchronous work through technology yet virtual teams are usually asynchronous. Better ways of working for online teams in public relations may be facilitated by developing online tools such as brainstorming templates, time zone plans, critical path analysis, and flow charts for the proposal, along with a time

Go to the Online Resource Centre to access a link to time zone chart

schedule, chatrooms, and file sharing to improve teamwork. In addition, virtual team guidelines, such as early socialization and notifying teams about a member's impending absence, may improve team cooperation.

Postmodernism

Practitioners may want to reflect on the critical thinking around communications, the media, and the role public relations has or is seen to have. Grunig (2009) has a **postmodern** perspective in that public relations gives organizations a way to empower publics in decision making and is moving away from controlling the environment to letting people have a voice in management. It is operating in a world where globalization and technology are changing the context in which information is communicated as well as how it is delivered. Information is being interpreted by different cultures who receive this information in different locations and from different perspectives. Consequently, it is increasingly hard to establish one understanding because the different information means people no longer know what is real or what is truth.

With more online activities and mini narratives open to interpretations by diverse publics, the trend is now for individuals to determine their own meaning. That is, people are becoming dependent upon their own way of making meaning, rather than accepting dominant viewpoints. Consequently, practitioners need to be aware that there can be infinite individual meanings made from the diverse output of ongoing mass media communications.

Habermas (1993) argues that the electronic media of mass communications developed in the twentieth century improves our own communication activity, offering us freedom by giving us more information.

In contrast, another French postmodernist Baudrillard (1994) believes we live in an unreal world, created by the media. For Baudrillard the spread of a mass technology of mass communications does not mean the freedom that Habermas describes. Baudrillard argues that the media brings a growing simulation of reality which makes us believe that these simulations—or, as he termed it simulacra—are real and this eventually undermines our own sense of reality.

Jameson (2000), who follows on from Baudrillard, believes that any meaning is determined by economic conditions and therefore we have lost our personal freedom. He argues that the economy has given rise to a media culture where the production and reception of media products is controlled. To Jameson, this means we have lost our personal freedom, any autonomy in our cultural development, or any sense of originality. In his view, everything has been absorbed into the global capitalist society and only reinforces consumer capitalism. Public relations has a role in creating an opportunity for more dialogue but this could mean simply reinforcing consumerism on the part of an organization.

13.4 Application to industry

Practitioners are aware of the new communications channels where everyone can publish, creating an open environment, a real example of an open system. The audience can talk back; there is strong interlinking and user-generated comment which means that practitioners have to give something of value, not simply promotional messages. The challenge is to rise above the ordinary communication and have the publics take notice.

Brown (2009) recommends making releases RSS-enabled; doing so means that people who receive them have chosen to do so by requesting content on a particular area. Brown also recommends combining RSS feeds with microblogging to create a way of disseminating information and links in an automated fashion which can reach large audiences and send them to the organization's blog posts.

Podcasting and vodcasting can be used to deliver information about events, conferences, and festivals. Social network sites can be used to list events and create a group based on a particular interest. For practitioners developing a new social network this might be a good way of communicating with stakeholders

Wikis are webpages designed to allow anyone with access to the site to add or modify content Wikipedia, the online collaborative encyclopedia, is the most well-known wiki. Many organizations appear on Wikipedia and the practitioner can influence content, but needs to present it objectively because anything promotional will be deleted. Brown (2009) recommends that a practitioner first declares their interest, being neutral but correcting any inaccuracies in content. It is important to know that attacks can be nominated for immediate deletion. If the information is incorrect, the corrections can first be discussed on the associated talk page which can be accessed via the discussion tab. In addition, files, audio, and video can be uploaded for the 'wikimedia commons' and may be used in articles and, in addition, the talk pages can alert others of their availability.

Blogging is now so prolific that many blogs will never be read. A practitioner needs to identify influential bloggers and engage them in offline conversations which can be generated simply by adding a post or comment to their blog. There is more likelihood of an organization boosting its online profile if it regularly updates its material; therefore an organization's blog is more valuable than its website as it is updated regularly. However, the need for an organization to approve the blog's content can mean it becomes uninteresting; but some filtering will be necessary to ensure nothing is communicated that could affect the company adversely. It is also important to be transparent about the authorship of blogs and fake blogs are an unfair commercial practice. (See chapter 12 on how to make corporate blogs effective.) Microblogging is text-only blogs that are restricted to a group. They can be uploaded anywhere at any time. The most well-known micro-blog is Twitter launched in 2006. Practitioners can use microblogs to promote an event or programme where the audience would be interested in short regular updates. Twitterfeed can push an organization's blogs directly to Twitter where they appear as breaking news. Twitter is also a great way to find people who are interested in a topic by doing a search and then posting information to them—although they may be small in number, they are interested.

Barack Obama used Twitter in 2007 and the leveraging of social media in the presidential election moved campaigning away from focusing on senior business leaders to grassroots political movements. According to Fraser and Dutta (2009) Obama's campaign used not only Facebook and YouTube (the BarackObama.com channel had about 115,000 subscribers), but also MySpace, Twitter, Flickr, Digg, BlackPlanet, LinkedIn, AsianAve, MiGente, and Glee which allowed user-generated content on the campaign and led to many viral campaign videos. Even an Obama mobile phone 'app' allowed supporters to message content to their contact list.

Below is a global case study on how a drinks company positioned itself as a responsible company using both digital and traditional media to develop its international reputation and address the increasingly important issue of alchol abuse.

Case Study

Champions Drink Responsibly

Source: Courtesy of Burson-Marsteller

Bacardi Limited (Bacardi), one of the largest spirits companies in the world, collaborated with the public relations agency Burson-Marsteller (B-M) to launch its first ever global corporate responsibility campaign, Champions Drink Responsibly, which ran from November 2008 to July 2009 (see Figure 13.1). The objective was to position Bacardi as a responsible company, prepared to address alcohol harm issues. This was in response to growing pressure from regulators and political stakeholders for the drinks industry to do more to tackle

Fig 13.1
Barcardi's Campaign: Champions Drink Responsibly

problems associated with excessive alcohol consumption, and it was Bacardi's belief that this was important.

The campaign specifically targeted the subject of drinking and driving using Formula 1™ World Champion Michael Schumacher. The campaign used a stakeholder mapping exercise to identify the key demographics of drivers most likely to drink and drive. The Champions Drink Responsibly campaign runs for three years, so B-M devised a phased strategy to build Bacardi's CR profile, and spread the message that 'Drinking and Driving Don't Mix' (see Table 13.2).

Table 13.2 **Building the global campaign over three years**

Date	Activity	Objective
November 2008	Digital campaign launch	Use online and offline PR to drive campaign website traffic
May 2009	Media hospitality event	Generated high-quality coverage with international lifestyle media
July 2009	Television stunt	Create stunt to attract large international audience

The programme involved strategic planning, event management, media outreach and internal communications, development of b-roll footage, photography, speech writing, viral creation, digital strategy, digital seeding, and the measurement and evaluation of these materials.

As an alcohol business, the campaign had to take account of local legislation around the marketing of alcohol.

Phase 1. Bringing the message online

Bacardi ran a consumer promotion offering winners the 'Driving Experience of a Lifetime' where winners would be driven round the infamous Ascari racetrack in Spain by Schumacher. The promotion was run online at the campaign website.

B-M devised a PR and digital strategy to drive traffic to this site and included two viral videos featuring Schumacher, translated into six languages for local market use. These videos, plus new photography, were seeded on key social networking sites such as Facebook, Flickr, and YouTube. B-M also used Google Adwords to drive further 'click-throughs' to the site. Press materials, photography, Q&A, and b-roll, together with feature and story ideas to support the online promotion were produced for 35 Bacardi markets around the world to adapt to their region. A social media news release announced a series of five exclusive videos with Schumacher on MSN in four countries plus an interview on Sky News.

Phase 2. Media trip of a lifetime

A media trip offered the opportunity to be driven by Schumacher around the Ascari race circuit. Attendees included a range of key lifestyle and sporting media, including; Hello, OK, GQ, and Esquire, and broadcast media such as ESPN Star Sports, Germany's RTL, Mexico's TV Azteca, and Times Now from India. The international media created coverage in over 48 countries delivering the message that 'Drinking and Driving Don't Mix'.

Go to the Online Resource Centre to access a link to this website

Schumacher held interviews with the media who also received media materials including B-roll footage of them driving with Schumacher. A Bacardi mixologist interacted with media, presenting non-alcoholic cocktails as a responsible, fun alternative to alcohol. Video messages from Schumacher were seeded to Facebook fan groups, resulting in growing support across the site.

Phase 3. *Top Gear* Champion

The BBC *Top Gear* programme was considered an excellent platform to reach the target demographic on a global scale and meant months negotiating with the *Top Gear* production team.

The result was one of the most watched *Top Gear* episodes, which was later viewed in a further 100 countries and was the second most viewed YouTube video that week. Schumacher's appearance on the show included an interview on his commitment to responsible drinking. *Top Gear* also showed a heavily branded Bacardi viral film shot in Ascari. The success and popularity of the show resulted in a surge of interest surrounding Bacardi's corporate responsibility campaign.

The extensive print, online, and broadcast coverage in 48 countries included a 30-minute programme on ESPN Star Sports dedicated to the campaign. Twenty journalists attended the Ascari event representing over 30 markets. The campaign reached at least 80 million people and the website received 250,000 competition hits with over 500,000 people watching the viral videos.

PR Tool

Virtual team guidelines

We need a certain amount of humility and a sense of humour to discover cultures other than our own; a readiness to enter a room in the dark and stumble over unfamiliar furniture until the pain in our shins reminds us where things are.

(Trompenaars)

This is a guide for a virtual team to develop to develop a global project. The purpose is to ensure that all team members work together in the same way.

First meeting

1. Identify your virtual team members. Write down the names of your team members and find something out about everyone. Attach a photograph. Keep this list online.
2. Carry out an online brainstorming process on how you intend to develop this campaign. This will set clear goals and directions at the project outset, with participation

from team members in different locations. Online brainstorming techniques can be very effective for collecting feedback and obtaining buy-in from people across locations. You can use this brainstorming process in all your meetings.

3. Use the brainstorming to set objectives and then document them.

4. Identify an overall identity of your team that reflects your vision and refer back to this at meetings.

5. Arrange a meeting schedule. Make sure you agree meeting dates where the group will discuss the progress of the project. Use the online meeting template shown in Table 13.3 at each meeting to record the meeting outcomes. Using the meeting template will make recording easy. Use a time zone converter to arrange meetings at mutually convenient times.

Go to the Online Resource Centre to access a link to the timezone converter

Table 13.3 Online meeting template

Insert dates	Meeting 1	Meeting 2	Meeting 3	Meeting 4
Attendees				
Actions				

6. Allocate roles. Decide how your group will carry out the work. Think about the division of research, writing, editing. It is better if everyone works laterally and everyone has a role in each aspect of the project. At each meeting allocate workloads within the group and record those on the meeting template.

7. Identify a global team leader. This must be someone who can lead a team and encourage networking and cultural integration. A dispute may arise as to the following matters:

- workload
- quality of work
- contribution.

Agree to joint responsibilities regarding a dispute, which means addressing issues early, and call a meeting with all group members to discuss a concern or a breach of agreement. Agree to notify the whole team regarding any absences and return times.

Second meeting

Analysis of issues. Read the brief together and brainstorm a way forward. Then carry out research to develop a situational analysis. You may find it helpful to divide it up under the following headings:

- Define the industry and the current market
- Identify the size of the market—sales volumes or revenues.
- Identify what segments there are within the market.
- Define who buys what within that market—use categories such as age, gender, occupation, social, and region

- What are the changes in the market?
- What is driving those changes?
- What is the significance of the main change?
- Evaluate the future direction of the market.
- Use the PEST and SWOT analysis.

Third meeting

Develop aim, objectives, and strategy and identify your target publics using your situational analysis. Ensure your objectives are SMART objectives.

Future meetings

Develop the following over the next few meetings:

- tactics and implementation
- budget and timeline
- evaluation.

Summary

Trends in other disciplines, trends in business, and trends in the media are all affecting public relations, which is not only differentiating itself from other disciplines but also drawing on them. As organizations see themselves as corporate citizens and as part of the community, public relations is starting to be responsible for monitoring an organization's actions. Corporate responsibility relies on public relations to identify and link an organization's values to shareholders' own needs and provide feedback which can be used to develop productive corporate responsibility programmes benefiting both parties.

Technology is more involved in communications and means greater transparency of messages. Individuals have more power and this is often demonstrated through blogging. The increasing media fragmentation with more media outlets and smaller audiences may be leading to information overload. Public relations needs new models to engage with publics who have more media autonomy and more self-expression. There is more communication using social media and guerilla techniques such as word of mouth and grassroots lobbying where power is with the public and from non-declared sources. This raises ethical issues regarding transparency about the source of information.

Changes are also in consultancies which although growing are also needing to move from media relations to offering strategic advice. The traditional media relations are seen to be of low value and now new technology tools can carry out low cost and standard public relations tasks such as media monitoring analysis. However, with improved education and interdisciplinary studies media monitoring could be taken further within a consultancy through more involved content analysis which focuses on semantics and discourse analysis.

Changes are also arising in specific sectors. The increasingly competitive not-for-profit areas are conscious that people want to have more understanding about a particular charity and how the money is spent. This means more effort is required to explain what the organization can do and how donations are used. Therefore, the charity has to offer large activities that promote its image, achieve its objectives as a charity, and raise funds.

Education in public relations is evolving since UK PR degrees first started in 1989 moving from training technicians to developing managers. PR education must be stimulated through research projects which can influence practice and help to promote the image of public relations as a profession. Public relations draws on disciplines such as psychology and sociology, which explore and indentify what influences people and how their behaviour can be changed. A communications programme needs to know how to integrate with other industries which are also changing, such as marketing, and how to involve new external influences, such as legislation and price.

It is important to assess when these interventions are likely to be successful and how much communications programmes should rely on them and work with them. For example, the COI report on behaviour looked at the influence of legislation and pricing in the No Tobacco campaign and showed when these particular influences were more important in influencing quit attempts and when communications needed to lead or support them.

Practitioners need to be constantly aware of developments and research in other disciplines, even in neuroscience for example, in order to draw on them to understand people's responses and decision making more clearly.

Social media means that there are many more ways of communicating with people, not simply en-masse but in small social media groups. There are multiple publics with an increasingly two-way communication. It is a challenge for public relations to be able to discern the different information, the different publics, and finding who is influential as a blogger. Monitoring the social media is vital and that small niche conversation can mean that news reaches a peak in a short time, therefore PR not only has to monitor them quickly but respond quickly, providing extra useful information and comment and also give feedback.

It seems that internet technology is changing how we live, creating a communications sector which is converging different technology, for example portable devices have broadcasting features. In addition, there is a need to consider who is controlling information and who is receiving it. End-users are becoming content providers and the original providers are not retaining their strength in controlling the information. Already, consumers are controlling their own media schedules and how they receive their information.

Technology and globalization means that PR is increasingly global and local, addressing regional concerns and global objectives. PR is taking place in virtual teams comprising geographically dispersed workers relying on IT with flexibility to traverse traditional organizational boundaries and time restraints. This team creates its own new issues compared to face-to-face teams and better ways of working need to be explored with virtual teams to ensure cooperation.

Overall, PR is a postmodern discipline, a pastiche of different disciplines working in a non-linear way trying to influence communication and open to interpretation by diverse publics. Largely owing to technology and globalization, organizations are an increasingly open system. The technology can be used to reach out to new and existing publics, drawing them to engage in discussions with organizations and form new ways of communicating.

Discussion points

A. Finding trends

Note down what you think most people are thinking about now. What trends do you think are occurring? Then go to Google Zeitgeist and see how these results match what you thought.

What do you think have been the influences?

Click on to other countries and check the trends there.

What differences and similarities can you see?

What do you think is influencing these?

B. Virtual teams

Virtual teams are the way of the future. This exercise allows you to notice the difference between face-to-face meetings and virtual meetings. With three or more people, arrange a ten-minute meeting and then meet at this set time to brainstorm how you would approach the case study. Then rate each team member on:

*   contribution

*   ideas

*   participation

*   work ethic.

Now set up a wiki and arrange an online meeting with pseudonyms. Discuss another case study (see the Online Resource Centre) and brainstorm online how you would approach it. Once again, rate each team member. At the end of the exercise, you can reveal your identities. Did the results differ from each rating? Aspects to discuss are why you assessed people in certain ways. Is it harder to tell if someone is participating online rather than face-to-face? If someone is quiet, does it seem as if they are shirking? If someone is late to arrive to the meeting how does that affect your impression of them online versus face-to-face? Note down what you think would make a good virtual team leader and discuss why.

C. New technology

New technology is changing our lives. Make a list of the communications technology you were using two years ago and what it did. Then make a list of the technology you use now and what it does. How has that changed the way you live? How do you think it changes the way organizations live? What regulations need to be reviewed based on this example? Think about pricing and access.

D. Publics

Think about how the internet is allowing publics to have a voice. What role do you think that public relations can play in the flow of information from organizations?

References

About Earth Hour http://earthhour.wwf.org.uk/about_earth_hour/global_lights/

Anderson, C. (2006) *The Long Tail: Why the Future of Business is Selling Less of More.* New York: Hyperion Books

Baudrillard, J. (2004) 'The Illusion of the End' in M. Drolet (ed) *The Postmodern Reader.* New York: Routledge, pp 272–8

Bell, V. (2008) 'Brain Scans and Buyer Beware', 31 October. Available at: http://www.mindhacks.com/blog/2008/10/brain_scans_and_buye.html

Binder, J. (2007) *Global Project Management.* Hampshire: Gower

Breakenridge, D. (2008) *PR 2.0: New Tools, New Media, New Audiences.* Upper Saddle River, NJ: FT Press

British Heart Foundation, 'National Heart Month'. Available at: http://www.bhf.org.uk/news_and_campaigning/our_campaigns/national_red_for_heart_month.aspx

Brown, R. (2009) *Public Relations and the Social Web.* London: Kogan Page

COI (2009) 'Communications and Behaviour Change', Government Communication Network, COI Publications. Available at: http://www.coi.gov.uk

COI (2010) http://www.coi.gov.uk/

Davies, N. (2009) *Flat Earth News.* London: Vintage

Dewhurst, M. and Wood, F. (2010) 'Steps to Achieve Social Benefits', Admap Magazine, March. Available at: http://www.Warc.com/Tracking/ArticleLink.asp?!D=91287&M=Asmap_Mar10

Fraser, M. and Dutta, S. (2008) 'Obama's Win Means Future Elections Must Be Fought Online', 7 November. Available at: http://www.guardian.co.uk/technology/2008/nov/07/barackobama-uselections

Grunig, J. (2009) 'Paradigms of Global Public Relations in an Age of Digitalisation', Prism 6/2. Available at: http://praxis.massey.ac.nz/prism on-line journ.html

Guardian (2007) 'Brain Laid Bare', Guardian Weekly, 23 February. Available at: http://www.guardian.co.uk/science/2007/feb/23/neuroscience.guardianweekly

Habermas, J. (1993) 'Modernity-An-Incomplete Project' in T. Docherty (ed) *Postmodernism Reader.* Cambridge: Cambridge University Press, pp 98–109

Hattersley, G. (2008) 'Now the Buyer Must Beware', Guardian, News Review, 2 November, p 6

Howard, J. (2009) 'The Future of the PR Industry—Communications: from Media Relations to Strategic Advice', 23 September, Mandate Communications

Jameson, F. (2000) 'Postmodernism or The Cultural Logic of Late Capitalism' in M. Hardt and K. Weeks (eds) *The Jameson Reader.* Oxford: Blackwell

L'Etang, J. (2002) 'Public Relations Education in Britain: A Review at the Outset of the Millennium and Thoughts for a Different Research Agenda', Journal of Communications Management 7/1: 43–53 at 47

Macnamara, J. (2010) *The 21st Century Media (R)evolution: Emergent Communication Practices.* New York: Peter Lang

Mersham, G., Theunissen, P., and Peart, J. (2009) *Public Relations and Communication Management: A New Zealand Perspective.* Wellington: Pearson

Ofcom (2009) '6th Annual Marketing Report'. Available at http://www.ofcom

Page (2010) 'How to Get the Best out of Neuromarketing', Admap magazine, January. Available at: http://www.warc.co

Powell, A., Piccili, G., and Ives, B. (2004) 'Virtual Teams: A Review of Current Literature and Directions for Further Research', Data Base for Advances in Information Systems 35/1: 6–23

Poynton, C. (2009) 'A Brave New World', Corporate Communications 42 (November): 14

Rhoads, C. and Chao, L. (2009) 'Iran's Web Spying Aided by Western Technology', Wall Street Journal, 22 June. Available at: http://online.wsj.com/article/SB124562668777335653.html

Sriramesh, K. (2009) 'Globalisation and Public Relations: The Past, Present, and the Future', PRism 6/2. Available at: http://praxis.massey.ac.nz/prism_on-line_journ.html 3

Sriramesh, K. and White, J. (1992) 'Societal Culture and Public Relations, in J.E. Grunig (ed) *Excellence in Public Relations and Communication Management.* Hillsdale, NJ: Lawrence Erlbaum, pp 597–614

Tench, R. and Willis, P. (2009) 'A Critique of the Trumanisation of Marketing Public Relations Through Guerrilla Campaigns: Ethical Space', International Journal of Communication Ethics 6/2

Wakefield, R. (2001) 'Effective Public Relations in the Multinational Organization' in R. Heath (ed) *Handbook of Public Relations.* Thousand Oaks, CA: Sage

WOMMA (Word of Mouth Marketing Association) http://womma.org/main/

Glossary

Above the line Payment is made for the actual costs of the activities, which is the space in the print media or the time on television.

Active publics Group of people communicating and doing something about an issue.

Activism Vigorous and sometimes aggressive action in pursuing a political or social end.

Activists Those who are carrying out activism.

Advertising Where media space or time is paid for in order for an organization to send its messages.

Advertising Standards Authority (ASA) The UK's independent regulator of advertising across all media, including TV, internet, sales promotions, and direct marketing which, in addition to consumer protection law, help to keep UK advertising responsible.

Advertising value equivalents (AVES) How much an advertisement in the same media would have cost.

Advertorials Paid for editorial.

Advocacy role Has the purpose of influencing people.

Affective Having a feeling about something.

Angle The hook that attracts media interest.

Annual Report Provides financial information as well as content about the organization's environmental and social impact. Available for anyone who is interested in the organization, that could be employees, consumers, competitors, educators, and investors.

ARPANET Acronym for Advanced Research Projects Agency Network. Precursor to the internet which began in 1969 as a way to communicate and exchange data between university computers.

Attitude An underlying predisposition towards something.

Audit Bureau of Circulation (ABC) Owned by the media industry and provides details of the detailed circulation, distribution, attendance, traffic, and related data across a broad range of media.

Avatars An icon or representation of a user in a shared virtual reality.

Aware publics Group of people who recognize that an issue affects them.

B-roll Quality footage which present a newsworthy angle and works as a type of broadcast release, and can help to encourage media interest.

B2B (business to business) Where a business sells its services or products to another business rather than an individual.

Balanced scorecards Are similar to dashboards but are more integrated with the organization's operations and strategy (Gregory and Watson 2008).

Behavioural change approach Helps people to identify risk factors, learn about a new way, and motivates them to change their behaviour.

Below-the-line expenditure Methods such as competitions, special offers, and media relations and consultancy advice that is charged on a time basis.

Benchmark A measurement that can be used to either set objectives or compare to other communication plans.

Blogging Gives a voice to anyone with an opinion and an internet connection.

Blogospheres The online universe of blogs.

Board members A group of people who make executive or managerial decisions for an organization.

Booklets Similar to leaflets but longer, usually with more content and images.

Brainstorming A common technique to get people generating ideas.

Broadcast quality footage Vidoe or film that can be used directly on television.

Broadcasters' Audience Research Board (BARB) Measures television ratings and collects the television viewing figures and audience sizes.

Broadcasting Authority Research Board (BARB) Measures television ratings in the UK and collects the television viewing figures and audience sizes.

Brochure Often called a leaflet and is a short document usually on one piece of paper that is folded once or in threes.

Budget How much a project costs and is based on fee and expenses.

Business goals The aims of the organization and can include increased sales, increased market share, increased profit, or reduced employee turnover.

Business plans Identifies the organization's goals, the issues surrounding them, and how to achieve them.

Business to business When organizations deal with other organizations, rather than individuals, to sell or buy services or products.

Business writing A style that makes a document recognizable as pertaining to business and includes reports and proposals.

Campaign A planned and organized series of actions intended to achieve a specific goal.

Capitalism An economic system characterized by a free competitive market and motivation by profit.

Carbon footprint The total set of greenhouse gases (GHG) emissions caused by an organization, event, or product expressed in terms of carbon dioxide.

Carbon-constrained world The nation will eventually have legislation constraining carbon emissions.

Case study An in-depth study or people, organizations, events, or even processes.

Central government The core government that is responsible for national issues such as taxation and trade.

Central Office of Information (COI) Formed mainly from the Ministry of Information.

CEO Chief Executive Officer, responsible for the organization and leads the board and reports to the Chairman.

Channel The medium which gives the information to the public.

Chat forum Online live discussions in 'real time' on one site.

Chatter Online interactive discussion.

Circular evaluation A full review which conducts research and gathers information from the beginning of a programme to its end.

Circulation The number of copies distributed by a publication.

Client The organization which is paying.

Code of ethics Provides an opportunity to ensure that the CR aspects of a business are monitored and evaluated, reviewing stakeholder concerns and issues.

Cognitive Thinking about something which creates an awareness of it.

Cognitive dissonance People do not like to have two opposing messages and try to change their attitude to fit the persuasive message.

Collective view A definition of public opinion, also known as the 'general will' or 'consensus' and assumes that people have come to an agreement on something.

Communication behaviour approach Requires a change in what publics know through gaining their attention, changing their attitudes, and then their behaviour.

Communications audit Analyses the nature and quality of communications between an organization and its publics.

Communications objectives Must take into account what is going on inside and outside the organization.

Communications plan A document that answers an organization's brief, that is where the organization outlines a problem or issue that requires a communications solution.

Community People around an organization and who are affected by what it does.

Conative Doing something and behaving in a certain way.

Connotation The non-literal meaning of a word suggested by its context and social and cultural influences.

Constraint recognition Identifies whether the public feels they can do anything about an issue.

Consultancy Another name for a public relations agency where experts provide advice or services.

Consultants Provide expert advice for a fee.

Consumers and users People who buy the products or services.

Consumer campaigns Promotional activities for consumer products.

Consumer sector Organizations that have products that can be consumed by eating, drinking, or using.

Content analysis Reviews texts, usually in the media, and analyses their meanings and value, as well as who read or viewed them.

Control mutuality The public does not feel dominated by the organization but has a say in the decision-making process.

Convergence Different content formats such as audio, video, text, and images reaching people through a range of digital networks such as the internet, mobile infrastructure, satellite, cable, digital, and terrestrial as well as consumer devices such as PC, TV, mobile, etc.

Copyright The right to control the copying of your work by others.

Corporate Relating to the whole organization.

Corporate citizens Organizations that perform financially and are environmentally and socially conscious.

Corporate communications Public relations relating to the overall organization and not just focused on one product or service.

Corporate responsibility Corporate self-regulation integrated into a business model.

Corporate responsibility report Annual document which provides information about the organization's values and its engagement with its stakeholders.

Corporate transparency Organizations are open about their activities.

Corporations A company recognized by law as a single body with its own powers and liabilities.

Crisis An issue affecting the organization and has not been resolved, or has had negative effects. It can also be a negative situation that has happened suddenly.

Crisis planning Requires a crisis management team and should include senior management and experts in public affairs, legal, operations and security, finance, and managers all trained in group decision making and media relations.

Critical thinking Required to develop clear and often persuasive messages, which can range from presenting an analysis of a situation, recommending a proposal, or presenting the progress of a campaign.

Cyber activists Online protestors.

Dagmar An acronym for Advertising Goals for Measured Advertising Results.

Dark site An empty place an organization has on the internet that is fully equipped and waiting to be used if a crisis occurs.

Dashboard Information about an organization in one visual document, combining sales and overhead costs, sales targets, marketing, and finance.

DDOS Acronym for 'distributed denial of service' attacks where cyberactivists bombard a website with requests for pages, often taking it offline.

Deadlines The time given by the media to deliver information to them.

Decode How a message is interpreted.

Deep-packaging inspection Blocks, monitors, and gathers online information about individuals.

Defamation Saying or writing something that lowers an organization's or individual's reputation.

Democracy Power is with the people who vote to form a government of elected representatives.

Demographics People can be divided into age, gender, geographical location, and income.

Denotation A literal meaning of a word and considered its standard meaning.

Diagrammatic models A representative drawing of an idea or a theory frozen in time and which shows interrelationships.

Diffused Publics who have no formalized relationship and may include people outside the organization where issues may arise but which are not immediately relevant.

Diffusion of innovations theory The process by which people accept or reject new information.

Digital networks Internet-based technologies.

Direct marketing Individuals are targeted with messages which encourages them to respond providing information which builds a relationship with them.

Disbursements The out-of-pockets or incidental costs of a campaign.

Dominant coalition The most influential decision makers within an organiziation.

Dormant The end of an issue which means it lies undetected.

Duty of confidence Assumed observation of confidentiality in business.

Early adopters The next group, after the innovators, to adopt an innovation.

Early majority The next group after the early adopters to adopt an innovation.

Elaboration likelihood model When attitudes change owing to relevant and rational arguments they are more lasting, more effective, and less likely to change than decisions made where less relevant information is considered.

Embargo A request for the media not to cover a topic until a certain time.

Emotional intelligence Recognizing one's own feelings and those of others.

Enabling Publics which give the authority or assistance to help an organization exist, e.g. government bodies and regulators.

Encode The meaning added to a message.

Environmental monitoring Research which is carried out to develop as well as observe the impact of a communications proposal.

Environmental scanning Also called intelligence gathering which is based on collecting and analysing research.

E-portal Online interactive gateway.

Ethical communications Where publics are given enough information to make voluntary, informed, rational, and reflective judgements.

Ethics What is considered morally right or wrong.

Ethos This is the communicator's personal character which establishes credibility.

European Economic Community Britain joined the European Economic Community in 1973.

Evaluation The measurement of an active communications programme.

Excellent communication A multinational study of public relations practice which found, among other things, that excellent communication was working towards symmetrical communications.

Executive summary A concise summary of an overall plan or report.

Facebook A social media networking site.

Fact sheets Media information sheets summarizing a particular area of an organization.

Features News that has a style which is longer and more in-depth and analytical than a news piece.

Fee The cost of people based on their time and skills.

Feedback The response about and reactions to something which may provide information for future decisions.

File sharing sites Where users can share online information simulataneously, file sharing sites include Flickr and YouTube.

Financial analysts Work with financial organizations and help people decide how to invest their money.

Focus group A research technique exploring people's ideas and attitudes through a series of group interviews carried out in an informal setting where everyone participates.

Formative evaluation Ongoing measurement checking that the programme is on track, and changing it as necessary.

Forums Discussion or message boards that post messages which others can read and respond to when they have time. They are less immediate and slightly lower risk than 'chat' forums, which are live discussions in 'real time'.

Four Ps Marketing focuses on ensuring these are right for the market, that is the type of product, its price, where it is sold (placed), and how it is promoted.

Fragmented Viewers can now flick between increasing numbers of channels meaning that viewing is more fragmented.

Functional Publics that give something to a company such as raw materials, and others take or buy something from a company such as consumers.

Gatekeeper Usually a journalist who performs the role of selecting the messages which are communicated to different publics.

Global Relating to or happening throughout the whole world.

Google Alert Regular email updates on the organization or product, a particular issue, or a competitor.

Google Analytics Generates statistics about visitors to websites and tracks a website or blog by identifying location of visitors.

Google Trends Monitors topics as to how often they have been searched on Google over a period of time.

Grassroots marketing Uses the power of personal relationships to promote a product, a service offering or a bran and creates a ripple effect of the marketing message.

Greenhouse gas emissions Chemical compounds that contribute to the greenhouse effect.

Guerilla techniques Includes unconventional and memorable tactics and includes social media campaigns where the source is difficult to identify. Includes grass roots marketing, word of mouth, and viral campaigns.

Handling charge Also called a 'mark up' is usually between 10–15 per cent and is added on to some costs to cover the time between the practitioner paying for something and it being reimbursed by the client.

Hierarchy of effects model Focuses on informing people first, followed by influencing their attitudes and finally their behaviour.

High-resonance photographs High-quality photographs that can be used for publishing without compromising their quality.

Homo narran How everyone's stories, narratives, or opinions overlap with the opinions of others.

House style An organization's standard formats for all their business writing.

Hypodermic needle model Suggested that the mass media had a direct and powerful impact on audiences who would react to the message content.

Implementation plan Outlines the tactics along with timing and budget.

Incorporated company Is registered at Companies House, a government branch which acts a registrar of companies.

Independent variables Variables that are not directly observed but affect a public's development.

Information transparency Not just keeping people informed about what is going on but the reasons behind the decisions and actions of the organization.

In-house Within an organization.

Innovation diffusion approach Uses early adopters of innovations to communicate benefits.

Innovators The first people to do something or buy something; these are a tiny percentage of the group and are usually people who dare to take risks.

Instant messaging Real-time chat.

Interactivity Involving the communication or collaboration of people or things which has greater feedback and the media has less of a gatekeeper role.

Internet Protocols A set of electronic rules on sending data and messages from any computer to any other computer.

Inverted pyramid An upside pyramid shape which shows that the most important information is at the beginning.

Investor relations Activities that enhance financial reputation.

Issue The difference between what a corporation does and says and what its stakeholders expect it should be doing and saying.

Issues management Identifies the threats around any business and develops relationships and communications in order to avert them.

Kantian philosophy of ethics Duty-based ethics which believe in doing good and people should not be used as a means to an end.

Key performance indicators (KPIs) Identify a measurable element of a goal. Used in public relations evaluation to see how it can generate revenue, reduce costs, and reduce risks in an attempt to ensure value for money or return on investment.

Keyword rich Popular search words included on copy to ensure it is found on search engines.

KPMG A global network of professional services firms providing audit, tax, and advisory services.

Laggards The last group to adopt an innovation.

Late majority The next group after the ealy majority to adopt an innovation.

Latent publics Group of people who are unaware of an issue.

Launch The start of an activity such as putting a product on sale.

Layout How a document looks—its headings, paragraphs, margins, spacing, and font sizes.

Leading question The answer is in the question.

Leaflet Short documents usually on one piece of paper folded once or in three.

Legislation Rules for an organization or sector that have been passed into law.

Level of involvement How much does a public feels an issue affects them.

Libel Defamation which is written or broadcast and also includes the internet. Slander is considered face-to-face words and gestures.

Liberal pluralists People who tolerate different groups within society.

Lifecycle of an issue Follows a lifecycle of potential, emerging, current, and resolution.

Likert scale Asks for the level of agreement or disagreement with a statement.

Limited company The liability is limited to the value of the shares issued.

Linear communication Communication which goes from one side to another when there is no other input or interaction.

Local authorities The part of government that has political and administrative powers to control a particular city or county.

Logos This is the use of facts and logic to create a reasoned argument, based on evidence that has been considered and evaluated.

Magic bullet Used in the same context as the hypodermic needle.

Majority view A definition of public opinion also known as an 'aggregate view', where more than half the public as measured by opinion polls, agree on something.

Maletzke model A model that showed that communication is an interactive process affected by the motivations, environment, and personal influences of the sender, message, and channel as well as feedback from all these sources.

Mark up See **Handling charge**.

Market research The gathering and analysis of information about what people want or like or what they actually buy.

Market research organization Provider of business intelligence, particularly market research.

Market segmentation Identifies the different ages, gender, and lifestyle of publics as this affects how they spend money.

Marketing A discipline that is involved in selling brands.

Marketing plan Outlines the marketing objectives for a service, a brand, or a product.

Maslow's hierarchy of needs Shows that people must answer their needs in order, starting from their basic needs to self actualization.

Mass communication Communication by means of broadcasting and newspapers, which reaches most people in society.

Mass perspective People who are constantly aware of what is going on in their country and community and this is what motivates them to act on most matters.

Materials Key purchases that are either made or bought such as slides, photographs, videos, exhibition centre space, conference hall hire, publication printing costs.

Measurable Capable of being measured.

Media audit Assesses the best channels for the organization's communications.

Media coverage The amount of media exposure given to an organization or product or person.

Media launch A launch of a product or service on which the media are encouraged to report.

Media monitoring agency An organization, often appointed during public relations campaigns, that tracks the media for specific coverage.

Media partner A media organization that joins with another organization for the purpose of a campaign.

Media release A written announcement to the media with the purpose of getting media coverage.

Media tours Taking journalists to a location to promote it.

Media writing A style that the media use and is also used in press releases and other media information.

Mergers The joining together of two or more companies.

Message boards Online posting of messages that others can read and respond to when they have time.

Microblogging Blogs that have restricted letters such as Twitter.

Ministry of Information Formed from the Home Office Information Bureau and various other Whitehall units.

Mission statement Most organizations have a mission statement which defines why the organization exists and what it hopes to achieve.

Model of intent Predicts what the online user is likely to do online and identifies areas in which they are most interested.

Mosaic A World Wide Web browser, developed in 1993, that improved storage.

Multiple choice The question provides a choice of answers.

Multi-step flow model Opinion leaders get information from other opinion leaders and not just the media and communicate to others in a socially mediated process.

Mutual understanding Communication where both sides interact and have equal involvement in the message development and the way they affect an organization and its reputation.

National Readership Survey (NRS) A type of large opinion poll which estimates the number of readers and their social grading.

National utilities Key services that can be used by households such as telephone, electricity, and gas.

Negotiated reading The reader juggles between the preferred and oppositional reading of the media messages to create their own meaning between the two readings.

Netizens Someone who uses the internet frequently.

New network media model Media model made up of individuals in groups, often referred to as nodes, and connected by communication flows.

News agenda The selection and construction of news topics.

News stories Editorial that has immediacy.

News values Identify what makes news.

Newsworthy An element that is worthwhile for the media to cover as it has values such as proximity or relevance to its audience.

Noise This additional input in communication can come from the receiver's own knowledge, attitudes, or beliefs as well as from transmission interference and can affect the message and its meaning.

Non-publics Group of people not likely to be affected by an issue.

Normative Peer organizations, that is, they share an industry interest and may belong to a joint association.

Not-for-profit sector Include charities, voluntary organizations, sports clubs, trade unions, and public arts organizations, such as museums and art galleries, as well as government and non-governmental agencies such as the World Health Organization and the Red Cross.

Objective aspects Elements which are measurable, such as time and money.

Objective variables Elements that change outcomes and can be measured.

Ofcom Created by the Office of Communications Act 2002 as the regulator for the UK communications industries, with responsibilities across television, radio, telecommunications, and wireless communications services.

Office of Communications (Ofcom 2010) see above.

Office of Fair Trading (OFT) An independent regulatory body that plays a leading role in promoting and protecting consumer interests while ensuring that businesses are fair and competitive.

Office overheads see Overheads.

One-way communication Communication which goes from sender to receiver without requiring or getting any feedback.

Online monitoring tools Help identify online content and how it is viewed.

Op cits (opposite editor) Editorial where journalists present their own opinion; these are persuasive pieces of writing about specific issues.

Open-ended Questions that allow a complete answer and do not encourage a yes or no answer.

Opinion How an attitude is communicated.

Opinion-formers People who influence others' opinion.

Opinion leaders People who are recognized as having specialized knowledge in a particular area such as teachers, doctors, parents, and certain friends.

Opinion polls A summary of a survey that identifies the views of a representative sample of the population.

Opinion surveys See **Opinion polls**

Organization A group of people identified by a shared interest or purpose, e.g. a business.

Organizational chart Information, usually in diagrammatic form presented vertically or horizontally, and showing the reporting structure of employees and their lines of responsibility.

Osgood and Schramm circular model This communication model shows how the sender and receiver encode and decode messages simultaneously.

Outcome Identifies a change in behaviour.

Outcomes What will be delivered at the end of the project.

Outputs What has been created, such as media information.

Outtakes Identifies the attitudes developing and is usually identified through opinion polls.

Overheads Also called fixed costs or house costs and include running costs such as office space, heating, electricity. Usually these are estimated as 10–15 per cent of the overall budget.

Packet-switching Small packets of online data with a web address.

Partnership Similar to a sole trader but with ownership between partners and has a legal partnership agreement.

Pathos The effect the communicator has on the audience's emotions.

Pay-per-view A television audience can purchase events to view via private telecast of that event to (say) their homes.

People, planet and profit Sums up the areas in which organizations are expected to achieve equally.

Persuasion Convincing people to make a choice and assumes people have free choice.

PEST Acronym for political, economic, social, and technological factors which gives a research framework for an overarching view of what is influencing the organization.

Photocall A newsworthy opportunity for the media to photograph someone or something.

Planning Decides the roles and mission, results, and effectiveness of a programme and how it can be measured.

Podcasting and vodcasting Used to deliver information about events, conferences, and festivals. Social network sites such as Facebook can be used to list events and create a group based on a particular interest.

Postmodern Moving away from controlling the environment with one view to realizing there are many different and equally important views.

Power and interest A public can be assessed as to how much control they have over an issue versus how much it affects them.

Practitioners A professional public relations consultant.

Preferred reading Agreeing with the media messages and their associated ideology, or rejected that and created their own meaning.

Press Complaints Commission Independent self-regulatory body which deals with complaints about the editorial content of newspapers and magazines and their websites.

Press rooms At events or conferences where the media can access information and have a place to interview people and write articles.

Primary research New, original research that is collected through observing people or doing a survey.

Private limited company A business with shareholders whose liability is limited by shares.

Problem recognition Identifying the issue.

Process objectives Statements setting out what people are to do such as to attend an event, or obtaining media coverage, or setting up a website, getting traffic to a website, and publishing a newsletter

Prodromal Time during warning signs.

Product's lifecycle A product's development, introduction, growth, maturity, and decline.

Professional and industry bodies Organizations which represent the interests of their members who belong to a particular industry sector or profession.

Promotional writing Appeals directly to a targeted public in order to persuade them.

Propaganda The unethical persuasion of publics where the truth is not considered important and communication is not transparent.

Proposal A public relations plan providing a communications solution to an organization's brief.

Psychographics The psychological profile of a public, its attitudes and opinions, beliefs and activities.

Public affairs Involves working with government regulations and legislation and often requires lobbying of government officials in order to change current rulings in order to help an organization progress.

Public information model The flow of factual information from the sender to the publics and is one-way as feedback is not considered important.

Public limited company (plc) Has shares which can be bought by the public.

Public opinion Attitudes communicated from a group of people.

Public sector Government departments such as health, education, and transport.

Publics Groups or individuals who have an interest in the organization, are affected by the organization or affect what the organization wants to achieve.

Publics who are active on all issues These are highly involved in the issue, have high recognition of the problem, and challenge organizations on most issues.

Publics who are active only on hot issues Groups who are interested in popular current issues, e.g. educational standards, reacting to the latest health scare, climate change.

Publics who are apathetic on all issues A group with low involvement in an issue.

Pyramid of evaluation The three levels of evaluation: output, outgrowth (outtakes), and output.

Pyramid structure of a press release Gives the who, what, where, when, and how in the first paragraph and then follows with more information and a quote.

Qualitative Research which measures what people think about something. It gives insight and understanding about a topic but not numerical data.

Quantitative Research that can be measured statistically.

RACE An acronym for research, action, communication, and evaluation.

Radio Joint Audience Research organization (RAJAR) An independent research body that collects the type and number of radio's listeners.

RAISE Acronym for research, adaptation, implementation strategy, and evaluation.

Rationale An outline of what the benefits are to the organization, individuals, or stakeholders in delivering the project.

Reactive Public opinion is caused by events and so is usually reactive, rather than proactive.

Readership Number of readers of a publication.

Reception theory Research that showed how people can make different meanings from the same media.

Regulations Rules for an organization or sector which have not been passed into law.

Regulatory body Organization which controls behaviour by rules or restrictions. Industries often have their own self-regulatory bodies.

Report Provides information, encourages understanding, answers questions, is accurate, is objective, and ranges from one page to many.

Resources Money, expertise, teams, and time which affects what can be planned.

Return on Investment (ROI) The profit made on a campaign versus the income generated from it.

Reuters The world's largest international multimedia news organization which has almost 200 news bureaux around the world and provides news content.

Risk analysis Must identify the lasting effects of an issue.

Risk benefit analysis Defining a a risk as there is never a zero risk rate, it is always balanced by a benefit, or a reward.

Risk management How and when to manage a risk is based on a risk versus benefit (reward) model.

ROPE An acronym for research, objective, programming, and evaluation.

ROSTE An acronym for research, objectives, strategy, tactics, and evaluation.

RSS An acronym for Really Simple Syndication. An online technology that pushes information to the user so they do not have to search for it.

Scenario planning Testing out different situations that may occur which highlight the weaknesses of the existing information.

Secondary research Information gained from sources other than primary or new research.

Semantic differential scale Ranks the attitudes towards different statements.

Semiotics The study of signs to explain how words and images are given meanings.

Sender What or who communicates the message to the receiver.

Shareholders and investors People who have bought into the organization and own parts of it.

Sidewiki technology A tool downloaded via a Google toolbar where anyone can write comments directly next to an organization's website and the organization cannot delete them.

Single-issue publics Groups interested in one issue and ignore others.

Situational analysis Identifies what is happening in an organization and defines the public relations problems.

Situational theory of publics How different groups of people respond to a situation.

Slander Derogatory face-to-face words and gestures.

Small or medium enterprises (SMEs) Enterprises employing fewer than 250 workers and have a turnover not exceeding €50 million.

SMART An acronym for Specific, Measurable, Achievable, Relevant, and Time-bound and objectives should meet these criteria.

Social grade classifications National Readership Survey ratings (A, B, C1, C2, D, and E) determined by the occupation of the household's chief earner.

Social media Online technologies which allow users to interact with each other in some way.

Sole trader The simplest type of business, it has no legal requirements but has unlimited liability.

Spiral of silence Society threatens to isolate people who are different and so most people fear to speak out if they think they are in a minority.

Sponsorship Funding of parts or all of an organization or event which, through association, can be used to provide benefits to the sponsor.

Stakeholder or public There is ongoing debate over whether there is a difference between these two. Generally they are the individuals or groups identified in a communications programme.

Strategic Uses strategy. A corporate communications strategy gives focus and direction for an organization's communication.

Strategic planning The planning of all the activities of a business to ensure competitive advantage and profitability which delivers the organization's goals.

Strategic thinking Predicting or establishing a desired future goal state, determining what forces will help and hinder movement towards the goal, and formulating a plan for achieving the desired state.

Strategy The overall game plan, concept, and approach and links to the organization's goals and mission.

Stunts A photo event where the story is really the picture.

Style book Gives guidelines to ensure acceptable clear and concise writing.

Subjective aspects Measuring people and their personal input and includes creativity, efficiency, and teamwork.

Subscription television Television that is paid for separately in packages and usually offers more diverse content.

Summative evaluation Analyses whether the programme's objectives have been achieved.

Suppliers Organizations that provide the raw product as well as anyone who consults to the company such as graphic artists.

Surveys A statistical study of a sample population.

SWOT Acronym for strengths, weaknesses, opportunities, and threats. It offers a closer view of the organization as well as identifying issues within the organization itself.

Symposium Formal meeting held to discuss a subject during which individual speakers may make presentations.

Systems theory Considers that the communication in an organization is full of interacting elements that may or may not interact with the outside environment.

Tabloid Smaller newspaper than the broadsheet and originally introduced at low cost.

Tactic An activity used to achieve objectives; can be a diverse range of activities such as a stunt, a launch, or an event.

Takeovers Control of a company gained through buying the majority of its shares.

Technology PR Public relations for a diverse range of technological products and services.

Telemarketing Selling or promoting goods and services by telephone.

Terms and conditions A set of rules that practitioners must advise clients on and work within.

Terrorist attacks 2005 Explosions by terrorists in the London Underground and bus systems.

Third parties Credible people who support the organization's views but are more influential as they are seen as independent and not part of the organization.

Trade and suppliers People the organization deals with in buying or selling its products or services.

Trade association An organization representing the interests of a number of businesses in the same sector.

Trading Standards Institute A not-for-profit professional body that helps safeguard consumers.

Traditional media Has limited feedback but publics could respond by writing letters to the media, phoning with comments, or completing research questionnaires.

Transparency of organizations Outsiders can look in and view documents and gain knowledge on the organization and insiders can transmit messages outside the organization.

Transparent communications The communication within an organization is clear and available for others to know about.

Triple bottom line People, planet, and profit are the areas in which organizations are expected to achieve equally.

Twin towers' terrorist attack A terrorist attack in New York City on 11 September 2001, where aeroplanes flew into the twin towers (World Trade Center) causing them to collapse.

Twitter search Identifying public opinion by following feeds on Twitter by using a key word such as a brand name.

Two-step flow model Where messages pass to the publics via opinion leaders who may change the message.

Two-way communication Where the sender and receiver communicate equally.

Two-way asymmetric model Communication which relies on persuasion and is used to influence behaviour such as buying or voting.

Two-way symmetric model Communication where there is a dialogue between both parties who adjust their attitudes to achieve mutual understanding and invite two-way symmetrical communication.

Unincorporated company A business that is not registered with Companies House.

Unmediated The internet allows for information to go directly to the public without being mediated by a third party such as a journalist.

User-generated content Where people using websites produce content, includes blogs, news, social media, video games, and messaging.

Uses and gratifications theory Research that suggests people have different psychological and social needs that lead to different expectations and use of the mass media that can affect how and why they use it.

Utilitarianism Judges circumstances by the amount of overall happiness or unhappiness created so that the moral value of an action is judged by its outcome.

Values A combination of personal beliefs and attitudes.

Viewers How many people see a TV programme or film.

Viral campaigns Online campaigns sent as peer-to-peer commmunication.

Viral film Video that travels through the internet.

Virtual communities Online users forming a particular group through a shared interest or shared values.

Virtual environments An online space or website.

Virtual press rooms Where the media can access online media information and communicate with an organization's public relations practitioners.

Virtual teams Groups of geographically, organizationally, and time-dispersed workers relying on technology to communicate with each other and traverse boundaries and time constraints.

Web 1.0 The first internet development where people put online what was already in traditional media with little change in its formatting.

Web 2.0 A second generation web development that encourages interactivity and information sharing and includes chatrooms, online forums, blogs, photosharing sites, and videosharing sites and collaborative sites such as wikis.

Web research tool Analyses online search queries, browsing history, and user interaction.

Westley and MacLean model Communication model which introduced the gatekeeper and the mass media.

Word of mouth (WOM) Someone who understands a product or service, shares their views attitudes and beliefs about it with others, creating awareness, but is not prompted to do so.

World Wide Web Started in 1991 and connected people to vast amounts of information.

Index